PowerPoint 2007 Feature	Ribbon Tab, Group	Button, Option	Keyboard Shortcut
Action buttons	Insert, Illustrations		
Built-in animations	Animations, Animations		
Bullets	Home, Paragraph		
Clip Art task pane	Insert, Illustrations		
Clipboard task pane	Home, Clipboard		
Close presentation		, Close	Ctrl + F4
Columns	Home, Paragraph	, More Columns	
Convert bulleted text to SmartArt	Home, Paragraph		
Copy text or slide	Home, Clipboard		Ctrl + C
Create New Theme Colors	Design, Themes	, Create New Theme Colors	
Create New Theme Fonts	Design, Themes	, Create New Theme Fonts	
Create photo album	Insert, Illustrations	, New Photo Album	
Custom Animation task pane	Animations, Animations	Custom Animation	
Cut text or slide	Home, Clipboard		Ctrl + X
Date and Time	Insert, Text		
Define Custom Show	Slide Show, Start Slide Show	Slide Show , Custom Shows	
Delete comment	Review, Comments		
Design theme	Design, Themes		
Digital signature		, Prepare, Add a Digital Signature	
Document information panel		, Prepare, Properties	
Document Inspector		, Prepare, Inspect Document	
Duplicate slide	Home, Slides	, Duplicate Selected Slides	
Edit comment	Review, Comments		
Edit photo album	Insert, Illustrations	, Edit Photo Album	
Encrypt Document		, Prepare, Encrypt Document	
Find	Home, Editing	Find	Ctrl + F
Font dialog box	Home, Font		Ctrl + Shift + F
Format Background	Design, Background	Background Styles , Format Background	
Format Painter	Home, Clipboard		
Format Text Effects	Home, Paragraph	, More Options	
Grid and Guides	Drawing Tools Format, Arrange	, Grid Settings	
Gridlines	View, Show/Hide	Gridlines	Shift + F9
Handout Master view	View, Presentation Views		
Header and Footer	Insert, Text		
Hide/unhide slide	Slide Show, Set Up		
Insert Chart	Insert, Illustrations		
Insert comment	Review, Comments		
Insert Hyperlink	Insert, Links		Ctrl + K
Insert Movie	Insert, Media Clips		
Insert Outline	Home, Slides	, Slides from Outline	
Insert Sound	Insert, Media Clips		
Insert Table	Insert, Tables	, Insert Table	
Microsoft Office PowerPoint Compatibility Checker		, Prepare, Run Compatibility Checker	

PowerPoint 2007 Feature	Ribbon Tab, Group	Button, Option	Keyboard Shortcut
New Presentation		, New	
New slide	Home, Slides		Ctrl + M
Next comment	Review, Comments		
Normal view	View, Presentation Views		
Notes Master view	View, Presentation Views		
Notes page	View, Presentation Views		
Numbering	Home, Paragraph		
Open			Ctrl + O
Package for CD		, Publish, Package for CD	
Page Setup	Design, Page Setup		
Paragraph dialog box	Home, Paragraph		
Paste Special	Home, Clipboard	, Paste Special	
Paste text or slide	Home, Clipboard		Ctrl + V
Picture	Insert, Illustrations		
PowerPoint Help			F1
Previous comment	Review, Comments		
Print		, Print	Ctrl + P
Print Preview		, Print, Print Preview	
Record Narration	Slide Show, Set Up	Record Narration	
Rehearsal toolbar	Slide Show, Set Up	Rehearse Timings	
Replace	Home, Editing	Replace	Ctrl + H
Reuse Slides task pane	Home, Slides	, Reuse Slides	
Rulers	View, Show/Hide	Ruler	
Run presentation	Slide Show, Start Slide Show		F5
Save As		, Save As	Ctrl + S
Save Current Theme	Design, Themes	, Save Current Theme	
Send To Microsoft Office Word		, Publish, Create Handouts in Microsoft Office Word	
Set Up Show	Slide Show, Set Up		
Shape	Insert, Illustrations or Home, Drawing		
Size and Position	Drawing Tools Format, Size or Picture Tools Format, Size		
Slide layout	Home, Slides	Layout	
Slide Master view	View, Presentation Views		
Slide number	Insert, Text		
Slide Sorter view	View, Presentation Views		
SmartArt	Insert, Illustrations		
Sound	Animation, Transition to This Slide	Transition Sound: [No Sound]	
Spelling check	Review, Proofing		F7
Symbol	Insert, Text		
Text box	Insert, Text		
Text pane	SmartArt Tools Design, Create Graphic	Text Pane	
Transition	Animation, Transition to This Slide		
WordArt	Insert, Text	WordArt	

Paradigm
PUBLISHING

Microsoft® PowerPoint® 2007

BENCHMARK SERIES

Nita Rutkosky
Pierce College at Puyallup
Puyallup, Washington

Audrey Rutkosky Roggenkamp
Pierce College at Puyallup
Puyallup, Washington

Managing Editor	Sonja Brown
Production Editor	Donna Mears
Cover and Text Designer	Leslie Anderson
Copy Editor	Susan Capecchi
Desktop Production	John Valo, Desktop Solutions
Proofreader	Laura Nelson
Indexer	Nancy Fulton

Acknowledgments: The authors and editors wish to thank Pamela J. Silvers, Chairperson, Business Computer Technologies, Asheville-Buncombe Technical Community College, Asheville, North Carolina, for testing the instruction and exercises for accuracy.

Care has been taken to verify the accuracy of information presented in this book. However, the authors, editors, and publisher cannot accept responsibility for Web, e-mail, newsgroup, or chat room subject matter or content, or for consequences from application of the information in this book, and make no warranty, expressed or implied, with respect to its content.

Photo Credits: Introduction page 1 (clockwise from top), Lexmark International, Inc., courtesy of Dell Inc., all rights Hewlett-Packard Company, Logitech, Micron Technology, Inc.; pages 1, 2, and 4, © Corbis; photos in Student Resources CD, courtesy of Kelly Rutkosky and Michael Rutkosky.

Trademarks: Microsoft is a trademark or registered trademark of Microsoft Corporation in the United States and/or other countries. Some of the product names and company names included in this book have been used for identification purposes only and may be trademarks or registered trade names of their respective manufacturers and sellers. The authors, editors, and publisher disclaim any affiliation, association, or connection with, or sponsorship or endorsement by, such owners.

We have made every effort to trace the ownership of all copyrighted material and to secure permission from copyright holders. In the event of any question arising as to the use of any material, we will be pleased to make the necessary corrections in future printings. Thanks are due to the aforementioned authors, publishers, and agents for permission to use the materials indicated.

Paradigm Publishing is independent from Microsoft Corporation, and not affiliated with Microsoft in any manner. While this publication may be used in assisting individuals to prepare for a Microsoft Business Certification exam, Microsoft, its designated program administrator, and Paradigm Publishing do not warrant that use of this publication will ensure passing a Microsoft Business Certification exam.

ISBN 978-0-76383-365-7 (Hardcover Text)
ISBN 978-0-76383-212-4 (Hardcover Text + CD)
ISBN 978-0-76382-993-3 (Softcover Text)
ISBN 978-0-76383-008-3 (Softcover Text + CD)

Printed in the United States of America

16 15 14 13 12 11 10 09 08 07   2 3 4 5 6 7 8 9 10

CONTENTS

powerpoint

Chapter 3 Formatting Slides 75

Chapter 4 Inserting Elements in Slides 119

Unit 1 Performance Assessment 165

Benchmark PowerPoint® 2007 teaches students how to build eye-catching presentations that communicate key information to audiences in business, academic, and organization settings. No prior knowledge of presentation software is required. After successfully completing a course using this textbook, students will be able to

- Plan, create, and revise presentations, including executing basic skills such as opening, editing, running, saving, and closing a file
- Format slides using design templates, slide and title masters, styles, bullets and numbering, headers and footers, and speaker notes
- Create visual appeal with images, SmartArt, charts, animation effects, and sound and video effects
- Share presentations for collaboration and review with others
- Given a workplace scenario requiring a presentation solution, assess the information requirements and then prepare the materials that achieve the goal efficiently and effectively

In addition to mastering PowerPoint skills, students will learn the essential features and functions of computer hardware, the Windows XP operating system, and Internet Explorer 7.0. Upon completing the text, they can expect to be proficient in using PowerPoint to organize, analyze, and present information.

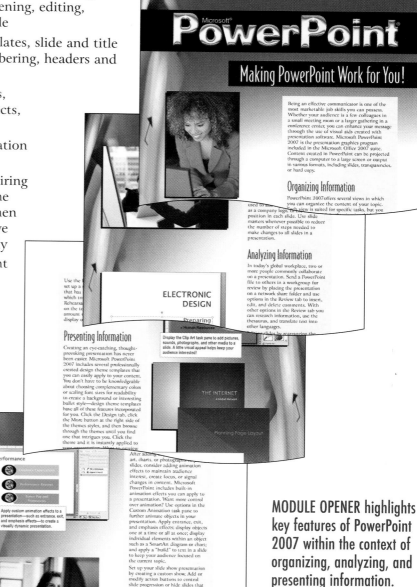

MODULE OPENER highlights key features of PowerPoint 2007 within the context of organizing, analyzing, and presenting information.

Achieving Proficiency in PowerPoint 2007

Since its inception several Office versions ago, the Benchmark Series has served as a standard of excellence in software instruction. Elements of the book function individually and collectively to create an inviting, comprehensive learning environment that produces successful computer users. On this and following pages, take a visual tour of the structure and features that comprise the highly popular Benchmark model.

Microsoft®
PowerPoint®

Unit 1: Creating and Formatting PowerPoint Presentations

➤ Preparing a PowerPoint Presentation

➤ Modifying a Presentation and Using Help

➤ Formatting Slides

➤ Inserting Elements in Slides

UNIT OPENERS display the unit's four chapter titles. Each unit concludes with a comprehensive unit performance assessment emphasizing the use of program features plus analytical, writing, and research skills.

CHAPTER

2

Modifying a Presentation and Using Help

CHAPTER OPENERS present the Performance Objectives and highlight the practical relevance of the skills students will learn.

PERFORMANCE OBJECTIVES

Upon successful completion of Chapter 2, you will be able to:

- Check spelling
- Insert and delete text in slides
- Find and replace text in slides
- Cut, copy, and paste text in slides
- Rearrange text in the Slides/Outline pane
- Size and rearrange placeholders
- Insert, delete, move, and copy slides
- Copy slides between presentations
- Duplicate slides
- Reuse slides
- Preview a presentation
- Use the Help feature

powerpoint Chapter 2

SNAP

Tutorial 2.1
Working with Text
Tutorial 2.2
Organizing Slides and Using Help

CD icon identifies a folder of data files to be copied to the student's storage medium.

The SNAP icon alerts students to corresponding SNAP tutorial titles.

When preparing a presentation, you may need to modify a presentation by inserting and deleting text in slides or finding and replacing specific text. Improve the quality of your presentation by completing a spelling check to ensure that the words in your presentation are spelled correctly. Additional modifications you may need to make to a presentation include sizing and rearranging placeholders and rearranging, inserting, deleting, or copying slides. In this chapter, you will learn how to make these modifications to a presentation as well as how to preview a presentation and use the Help feature.

Note: Before beginning computer projects, copy to your storage medium the PowerPoint2007C2 subfolder from the PowerPoint2007 folder on the CD that accompanies this textbook and then make PowerPoint2007C2 the active folder.

A prominent note reminds students to copy the appropriate data files folder and make it active.

powerpoint
Modifying a Presentation and Using Help   **41**

New! PROJECT APPROACH: Builds Skill Mastery within Realistic Context

Instruction and practice are organized into multipart projects that focus on related program features. A project overview identifies the tasks to accomplish and the key features to use in completing the work.

Complete a Spell Check
1. Click Review tab.
2. Click Spelling button.
3. Change or ignore errors.
4. Click OK.

Quick Steps provide feature summaries for reference and review.

Between project parts, the text presents instruction on the features and skills necessary to accomplish the next task.

P**roject** ① **Check Spelling and Manage Text in a Design Presentation**
You will open a presentation on steps for planning a design publication, complete a spelling check on the text in the presentation, and find and replace specific text in slides.

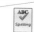

Checking Spelling

Complete a Spell Check
1. Click Review tab.
2. Click Spelling button.
3. Change or ignore errors.
4. Click OK.

ABC Spelling

When preparing a presentation, perform a spelling check on text in slides using PowerPoint's spelling feature. The spelling feature compares words in slides in a presentation with words in its dictionary. If a match is found, the word is passed over. If a match is not found, the spelling checker selects the word and offers replacement suggestions. To perform a spelling check on a PowerPoint presentation, click the Review tab and then click the Spelling button in the Proofing group. You can also start the spelling checker by pressing the F7 function key on the keyboard.

When you begin spell checking text in a presentation in Project 1a, the spelling checker will stop at the misspelled word *Layuot* and display the Spelling dialog box as shown in Figure 2.1. The options available in the Spelling dialog box are described in Table 2.1.

Figure 2.1 Spelling Dialog Box

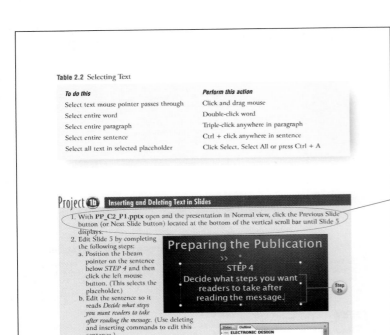

Table 2.2 Selecting Text

To do this	Perform this action
Select text mouse pointer passes through	Click and drag mouse
Select entire word	Double-click word
Select entire paragraph	Triple-click anywhere in paragraph
Select entire sentence	Ctrl + click anywhere in sentence
Select all text in selected placeholder	Click Select, Select All or press Ctrl + A

Project 1b   Inserting and Deleting Text in Slides

1. With **PP_C2_P1.pptx** open and the presentation in Normal view, click the Previous Slide button (or Next Slide button) located at the bottom of the vertical scroll bar until Slide 5 displays.
2. Edit Slide 5 by completing the following steps:
   a. Position the I-beam pointer on the sentence below *STEP 4* and then click the left mouse button. (This selects the placeholder.)
   b. Edit the sentence so it reads *Decide what steps you want readers to take after reading the message.* (Use deleting and inserting commands to edit this sentence.)
3. Click the Next Slide button to display Slide 6 and then edit Slide 6 in the Outline/Slides pane by completing the following steps:
   a. Click the Outline tab in the Slides/Outline pane.
   b. Click in the sentence below *STEP 5* and then edit the sentence so it reads *Collect and assess examples of effective designs.*
   c. Click the Slides tab.
4. Save **PP_C2_P1.pptx**.

Typically, a file remains open throughout a project. Students save their work incrementally.

Each project exercise guides students step by step to the desired outcome. Screen captures illustrate what the screen should look like at key points.

Text in magenta identifies material to type.

At the end of the project, students save, print, and close the file. Locked, watermarked model answers in PDF format on the Student Resources CD allow students to check their work. This option rewards careful effort and builds software mastery.

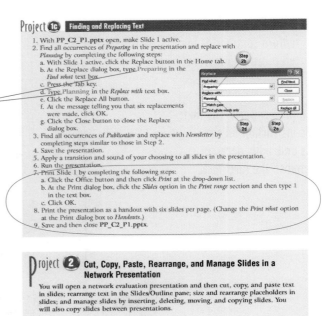

Project 1c   Finding and Replacing Text

1. With **PP_C2_P1.pptx** open, make Slide 1 active.
2. Find all occurrences of *Preparing* in the presentation and replace with *Planning* by completing the following steps:
   a. With Slide 1 active, click the Replace button in the Home tab.
   b. At the Replace dialog box, type Preparing in the *Find what* text box.
   c. Press the Tab key.
   d. Type Planning in the *Replace with* text box.
   e. Click the Replace All button.
   f. At the message telling you that six replacements were made, click OK.
   g. Click the Close button to close the Replace dialog box.
3. Find all occurrences of *Publication* and replace with *Newsletter* by completing steps similar to those in Step 2.
4. Save the presentation.
5. Apply a transition and sound of your choosing to all slides in the presentation.
6. Run the presentation.
7. Print Slide 1 by completing the following steps:
   a. Click the Office button and then click *Print* at the drop-down list.
   b. At the Print dialog box, click the *Slides* option in the *Print range* section and then type 1 in the text box.
   c. Click OK.
8. Print the presentation as a handout with six slides per page. (Change the *Print what* option at the Print dialog box to *Handouts*.)
9. Save and then close **PP_C2_P1.pptx**.

Project 2   Cut, Copy, Paste, Rearrange, and Manage Slides in a Network Presentation

You will open a network evaluation presentation and then cut, copy, and paste text in slides; rearrange text in the Slides/Outline pane; size and rearrange placeholders in slides; and manage slides by inserting, deleting, moving, and copying slides. You will also copy slides between presentations.

Cutting, Copying, and Pasting Text in Slides

With buttons in the Clipboard group in the Home tab and also with shortcut menu options, you can cut, copy, and/or paste text in slides. For example, to move text in a slide, click once in the placeholder containing the text to be moved, select the text, and then click the Cut button in the Clipboard group. Position the insertion point where you want the text inserted and then click the Paste button in the Clipboard group. To cut and paste with the shortcut menu, select the text you want to move, right-click the text, and then click *Cut* at the shortcut menu.

HINT
Ctrl + X is the keyboard shortcut to cut selected text, Ctrl + C is the keyboard shortcut to copy selected text, and Ctrl + V is the keyboard shortcut to paste cut or copied text.

CHAPTER REVIEW ACTIVITIES: A Hierarchy of Learning Assessments

CHAPTER summary

- Use the spelling feature to check spelling of slides in a presentation. Begin the spelling checker by clicking the Review tab and then clicking the Spelling button in the Proofing group.
- Refer to Table 2.1 for methods for selecting text in slides.
- Text in a placeholder is positioned inside of a placeholder. Click in a placeholder to select the placeholder and position the insertion point inside.
- Display the Find dialog box by clicking the Find button in the Editing group in the Home tab.
- Display the Replace dialog box by clicking the Replace button in the Editing group in the Home tab.
- With buttons in the Clipboard group or with options you can cut and paste or copy and paste text in slides
- You can use the mouse to move text in the Slides/O and then drag it to a new location or hold down th copy text to a new location.
- Use the sizing handles that display around a select decrease the size of the placeholder. You can use th placeholder to a new location in the slide.
- Use the New Slide button in the Home tab to inse
- Delete a selected slide by clicking the Delete butto Home tab or by pressing the Delete button.
- You can move or delete a selected slide in Normal pane or in Slide Sorter view.
- Copy a selected slide by holding down the Ctrl key the desired location.
- Use the Copy and Paste buttons in the Clipboard copy a slide between presentations.
- Select adjacent slides in the Slides/Outline pane o clicking the first slide, holding down the Shift key, slide. Select nonadjacent slides by holding down th each desired slide.
- Duplicate slides in a presentation by selecting th Slides/Outline pane, clicking the New Slide button the *Duplicate Selected Slides* option.
- You can copy slides from a presentation into the op at the Reuse Slides task pane. Display this task pa button arrow and then clicking *Reuse Slides* at the c
- Display a presentation in Print Preview by clicking to *Print*, and then clicking *Print Preview*.

CHAPTER SUMMARY captures the purpose and execution of key features.

- In Print Preview, display the Header and Footer dialog box by clicking the Options button and then clicking *Header and Footer* at the drop-down list. Use options in the dialog box to insert the date and time, a header, a footer, slide numbers, or page numbers. The options will vary depending on which tab is selected—*Slide* or *Notes and Handouts*.
- Click the Help button in a dialog box and the PowerPoint Help window displays with information specific to the dialog box.
- Click the Microsoft Office Word Help button or press F1 to display the PowerPoint Help window.

COMMANDS review

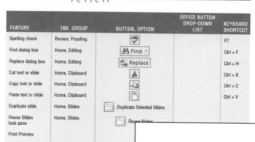

FEATURE	TAB, GROUP	BUTTON, OPTION	OFFICE BUTTON DROP-DOWN LIST	KEYBOARD SHORTCUT
Spelling check	Review, Proofing			F7
Find dialog box	Home, Editing	Find		Ctrl + F
Replace dialog box	Home, Editing	Replace		Ctrl + H
Cut text or slide	Home, Clipboard			Ctrl + X
Copy text or slide	Home, Clipboard			Ctrl + C
Paste text or slide	Home, Clipboard			Ctrl + V
Duplicate slide	Home, Slides	Duplicate Selected Slides		
Reuse Slides task pane	Home, Slides	Reuse Slides		
Print Preview				
PowerPoint Help window				

COMMANDS REVIEW summarizes visually the major features and alternative methods of access.

CONCEPTS CHECK questions assess knowledge recall.

CONCEPTS check

Test Your Knowledge

Completion: In the space provided at the right, indicate the correct term, symbol, or command.

1. The Spelling button is located in the Proofing group in this tab.

2. This is the keyboard shortcut to select all text in a placeholder.

3. The Find button is located in this group in the Home tab.

4. In the Slides/Outline pane with the Outline tab selected, hold down the left mouse button on this to select all text in the slide.

5. To copy text to a new location in the Slides/Outline pane with the Outline tab selected, hold down this key while dragging text.

6. The border of a selected placeholder displays these handles as well as a green rotation handle.

7. You can reorganize slides in a presentation in the Slides/Outline pane or in this view.

8. You can copy selected slides in a presentation using this option from the New Slide button drop-down list.

9. To select adjacent slides, click the first slide, hold down this key, and then click the last slide.

10. Click the New Slide button arrow and then click the *Reuse Slides* option at the drop-down list and this displays.

11. Display the presentation in Print Preview by clicking the Office button, pointing to this option, and then clicking *Print Preview*.

12. In Print Preview, display the Header and Footer dialog box by clicking this button in the Print Preview tab and then clicking *Header and Footer* at the drop-down list.

13. This is the keyboard shortcut to display the PowerPoint Help window.

SKILLS check
Demonstrate Your Proficiency

Assessment

1 CREATE AN ELECTRONIC DESIGN PRESENTATION

1. Create the presentation shown in Figure 2.7 using a design theme of your choosing. (When typing bulleted text, press the Tab key to move the insertion point to the desired tab level.)
2. After creating the slides, complete a spelling check on the text in the slides.
3. Save the presentation into the PowerPoint2007C2 folder on your storage medium and name the presentation **PP_C2_A1**.
4. Run the presentation.
5. Preview the presentation, change the *Print What* option to *Handouts (4 Slides Per Page)*, change the orientation to landscape, and then print the presentation.
6. Make the following changes to the presentation:
   a. Change to Slide Sorter view and then move Slide 3 between Slides 1 and 2.
   b. Move Slide 4 between Slides 2 and 3.
   c. Search for the word *document* and replace it with the word *brochure*. (Make Slide 1 active and then capitalize the "b" in "brochure.")
   d. Add a transition and sound of your choosing to each slide.
7. Save the presentation.
8. Display the Reuse Slides task pane, browse to the PowerPoint2007C2 folder on your storage medium, and then double-click *LayoutTips.pptx*.
9. Insert the *Layout Punctuation Tips* slide below Slide 4.
10. Insert the *Layout Tips* slide below Slide 5.
11. Close the Reuse Slides task pane.
12. Find all occurrences of *Layout* and replace with *Design*. (Insert a check mark in the *Match case* check box.)
13. Move Slide 5 between Slides 1 and 2.
14. Move Slide 6 between Slides 2 and 3.
15. Save the presentation.
16. Print the presentation as a handout with six slides per page.
17. Close **PP_C2_A1.pptx**.

SKILLS CHECK exercises ask students to design and develop presentations using newly acquired skills without how-to directions.

CASE study
Apply Your Skills

Part 1

You are the office manager at the Company Connections agency. One of your responsibilities is to conduct workshops for preparing individuals for the job search process. A coworker has given you a presentation for the workshop but the presentation needs some editing and modifying. Open **JobAnalysis.pptx** and then save the presentation and name it **PP_C2_CS_P1**. Check each slide in the presentation and then make modifications to maintain consistency in the size and location of placeholders (consider using the Reset button to reset the formatting and size of the placeholders), maintain consistency in heading text, move text from an overcrowded slide to a new slide, complete a spelling check, apply a design theme, and make any other modifications to improve the presentation. Save **PP_C2_CS_P1.pptx**.

Part 2

After reviewing the presentation, you realize that you need to include slides on resumes. Open the **ResumePresentation.pptx** presentation and then copy Slides 2 and 3 into the **PP_C2_CS_P1.pptx** presentation. You want to add additional information on resume writing tips and decide to use the Internet to find information. Locate information on the Internet with tips on writing a resume and then create a slide (or two) with the information you find. Add a transition and sound to all slides in the presentation. Save the **PP_C2_CS_P1.pptx** presentation.

Part 3

You know that Microsoft Word offers a number of resume templates you can download from the Microsoft Office Online site. You decide to include information in the presentation on how to download resumes. Open Microsoft Word, click the Office button, and then click *New* at the drop-down list. At the New Document dialog box, click the Help button that displays in the upper right corner of the dialog box. Read the information on downloading templates and then experiment with downloading a template. With the **PP_C2_CS_P1.pptx** presentation open, add an additional slide to the end of the presentation that provides steps on how to download a resume in Microsoft Word. Print the presentation as a handout with six slides per page. Save, run, and then close the **PP_C2_CS_P1.pptx** presentation.

The chapter CASE STUDY requires planning and executing multi-part workplace projects.

Students search the Web and/or use the Help feature to locate information.

UNIT PERFORMANCE ASSESSMENT: Cross-Disciplinary, Comprehensive Evaluation

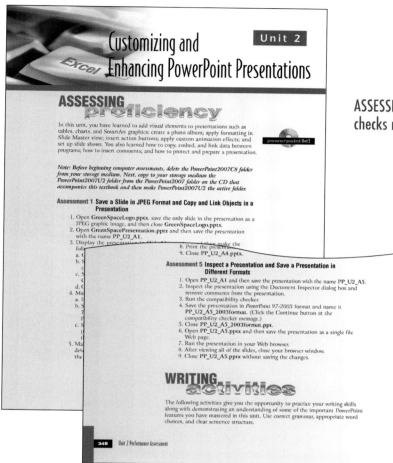

ASSESSING PROFICIENCY checks mastery of features.

WRITING ACTIVITIES involve applying program skills in a communication context.

INTERNET RESEARCH project reinforces research and presentation development skills.

JOB STUDY at the end of Unit 2 presents a capstone assessment requiring critical thinking and problem solving.

Presenting Office 2007

Make sure you are connected to the Internet and then explore the Microsoft Web site at www.microsoft.com. Browse the various categories and links on the Web site to familiarize yourself with how information is organized.

Create a PowerPoint presentation that could be delivered to someone who has just purchased Office 2007 and wants to know how to find more information about the software from the Microsoft Web site. Include points or tips on where to find product release information and technical support. Include hyperlinks to important pages at the Microsoft Web site. Add formatting and enhancements to make the presentation as dynamic as possible. Save the presentation and name it **PP_U2_Office2007**. Run the presentation and then print the presentation as a handout with six slides per page. Close **PP_U2_Office2007.pptx**.

Creating a Skills Presentation

You are preparing a presentation that you will use when presenting information on jobs at your local job fair. Open the Word document named **JobDescriptions.docx**, print the document, and then close the document and exit Word. Use the information in the document to prepare slides that describe each job (do not include the starting salary). Using the Internet, locate information on two other jobs that interest you and then create a slide for each job that provides information on job responsibilities. Determine the starting salary for the two jobs and then use that information along with the starting salary information for the jobs in the Word document to create a chart that displays the salary amounts. Locate at least two online job search Web sites and then include them in your presentation along with hyperlinks to the sites. Insert action buttons to move to the next page for the first slide through the second from the end. On your final slide, create an action button to return to the first slide.

Save the presentation and name it **PP_U2_JobStudy**. Run the presentation and then print the presentation as a handout with six slides per page. Close **PP_U2_JobStudy.pptx**.

Student Courseware

Student Resources CD Each Benchmark Series textbook is packaged with a Student Resources CD containing the data files required for completing the projects and assessments. A CD icon and folder name displayed on the opening page of chapters reminds students to copy a folder of files from the CD to the desired storage medium before beginning the project exercises. Directions for copying folders are printed on the inside back cover. The Student Resources CD also contains the model answers in PDF format for the project exercises within chapters. Files are locked and watermarked, but students can compare their completed documents with the PDF files, either on screen or in hard copy (printed) format.

Internet Resource Center Additional learning tools and reference materials are available at the book-specific Web site at www.emcp.net/BenchmarkPowerPoint07XP. Students can access the same resources that are on the Student Resources CD along with study aids, Web links, and tips for using computers effectively in academic and workplace settings.

SNAP Training and Assessment SNAP is a Web-based program that provides hands-on instruction, practice, and testing for learning Microsoft Office 2007 and Windows. SNAP course work simulates operations of Office 2007. The program is comprised of a Web-based learning management system, multimedia tutorials, performance skill items, a concept test bank, and online grade book and course planning tools. A CD-based set of tutorials teaching the basics of Office and Windows is also available for additional practice not requiring Internet access.

Class Connections Available for both WebCT and Blackboard e-learning platforms, Paradigm's Class Connection provides self-quizzes and study aids and facilitates communication among students and instructors via e-mail and e-discussion.

Instructor Resources

Curriculum Planner and Resources Instructor support for the Benchmark Series has been expanded to include a *Curriculum Planner and Resources* binder with CD. This all-in-one print resource includes planning resources such as Lesson Blueprints, teaching hints, and sample course syllabi; presentation resources such as PowerPoint presentations and handouts; and assessment resources including an overview of assessment venues, live program and PDF model answers for intrachapter projects, and live program and annotated PDF model answers for end-of-chapter and end-of-unit assessments. Contents of the *Curriculum Planner and Resources* binder are also available on the Instructor's CD and on the password-protected Instructor's section of the Internet Resource Center for this title at www.emcp.com.

Computerized Test Generator Instructors can use ExamView test generating software and the provided bank of multiple-choice items to create customized Web-based or print tests.

What is the Microsoft Business Certification Program?

The Microsoft Business Certification program enables candidates to show that they have something exceptional to offer—proven expertise in Microsoft Office programs. The two certification tracks allow candidates to choose how they want to exhibit their skills, either through validating skills within a specific Microsoft product or taking their knowledge to the next level and combining Microsoft programs to show that they can apply multiple skill sets to complete more complex office tasks. Recognized by businesses and schools around the world, over 3 million certifications have been obtained in over 100 different countries. The Microsoft Business Certification Program is the only Microsoft-approved certification program of its kind.

What is the Microsoft Certified Application Specialist Certification?

Microsoft
CERTIFIED

Application Specialist

The Microsoft Certified Application Specialist Certification exams focus on validating specific skill sets within each of the Microsoft® Office system programs. Candidates can choose which exam(s) they want to take according to which skills they want to validate. The available Application Specialist exams include:

- Using Microsoft® Windows Vista™
- Using Microsoft® Office Word 2007
- Using Microsoft® Office Excel® 2007
- Using Microsoft® Office PowerPoint® 2007
- Using Microsoft® Office Access 2007
- Using Microsoft® Office Outlook 2007

What is the Microsoft Certified Application Professional Certification?

Microsoft
CERTIFIED

Application Professional

The Microsoft Certified Application Professional Certification exams focus on a candidate's ability to use the 2007 Microsoft® Office system to accomplish industry-agnostic functions, for example, Budget Analysis and Forecasting, or Content Management and Collaboration. The available Application Professional exams currently include:

- Organizational Support
- Creating and Managing Presentations
- Content Management and Collaboration
- Budget Analysis and Forecasting

What do the Microsoft Business Certification Vendor of Approved Courseware logos represent?

Microsoft
CERTIFIED

Application Specialist

Approved Courseware

Microsoft
CERTIFIED

Application Professional

Approved Courseware

The logos validate that the courseware has been approved by the Microsoft® Business Certification Vendor program and that these courses cover objectives that will be included in the relevant exam. It also means that after utilizing this courseware, you may be prepared to pass the exams required to become a Microsoft Certified Application Specialist or Microsoft Certified Application Professional.

For more information:

To learn more about Microsoft Certified Application Specialist or Professional exams, visit www.microsoft.com/learning/msbc.

To learn about other Microsoft Certified Application Specialist or Professional approved courseware from Paradigm Publishing, visit www.emcp.com/microsoft-certified-courseware.

The availability of Microsoft Certified Application exams varies by Microsoft Office program, program version, and language. Visit www.microsoft.com/learning for exam availability.

Microsoft, the Office Logo, Outlook, and PowerPoint are either registered trademarks or trademarks of Microsoft Corporation in the United States and/or other countries. The Microsoft Certified Application Specialist and Microsoft Certified Application Professional Logos are used under license from Microsoft Corporation.

System Requirements

This text is designed for the student to complete projects and assessments on a computer running a standard installation of Microsoft Office 2007, Professional Edition, and the Microsoft Windows XP operating system with Service Pack 2 or later. To effectively run this suite and operating system, your computer should be outfitted with the following:

- 500 MHz processor or higher; 256 MB RAM or higher
- DVD drive
- 2 GB of available hard-disk space
- CD-ROM drive
- 800 by 600 minimum monitor resolution; 1024 by 768 recommended
  Note: Screen captures in this book were created using 1024 by 768 resolution; screens with higher resolution may look different.
- Computer mouse or compatible pointing device

About the Authors

Nita Rutkosky began teaching business education courses at Pierce College in Puyallup, Washington, in 1978. Since then she has taught a variety of software applications to students in postsecondary Information Technology certificate and degree programs. In addition to *Benchmark Office 2007* texts, she has authored *Marquee Office 2007, Using Computers in the Medical Office: Microsoft Word, Excel, and PowerPoint 2003* as well as textbooks on most earlier versions of Microsoft Office, keyboarding, WordPerfect, desktop publishing, and voice recognition for Paradigm Publishing, Inc.

Audrey Rutkosky Roggenkamp has been teaching courses in the Business Information Technology department at Pierce College in Puyallup including keyboarding, skill building, and Microsoft Office programs. In addition to titles in the *Benchmark Office 2007 Series*, she has co-authored *Marquee Office 2007, Using Computers in the Medical Office,* and *Signature Word 2007* for Paradigm Publishing, Inc.

Getting Started in Office 2007

In this textbook, you will learn to operate several computer application programs that combine to make an application "suite." This suite of programs is called Microsoft Office 2007. The programs you will learn to operate are the software, which includes instructions telling the computer what to do. Some of the application programs in the suite include a word processing program named Word, a spreadsheet program named Excel, a database program named Access, and a presentation program named PowerPoint.

Identifying Computer Hardware

The computer equipment you will use to operate the suite of programs is referred to as hardware. You will need access to a microcomputer system that should consist of the CPU, monitor, keyboard, printer, drives, and mouse. If you are not sure what equipment you will be operating, check with your instructor. The computer system shown in Figure G.1 consists of six components. Each component is discussed separately in the material that follows.

Figure G.1 Microcomputer System

Printer

CPU

Monitor

CD-ROM

DVD±RW

USB Drive

Keyboard

Mouse

CPU

CPU stands for Central Processing Unit and it is the intelligence of the computer. All the processing occurs in the CPU. Silicon chips, which contain miniaturized circuitry, are placed on boards that are plugged into slots within the CPU. Whenever an instruction is given to the computer, that instruction is processed through circuitry in the CPU.

Monitor

The monitor is a piece of equipment that looks like a television screen. It displays the information of a program and the text being input at the keyboard. The quality of display for monitors varies depending on the type of monitor and the level of resolution. Monitors can also vary in size—generally from 14-inch size up to 21-inch size or larger.

Keyboard

The keyboard is used to input information into the computer. Keyboards for microcomputers vary in the number and location of the keys. Microcomputers have the alphabetic and numeric keys in the same location as the keys on a typewriter. The symbol keys, however, may be placed in a variety of locations, depending on the manufacturer. In addition to letters, numbers, and symbols, most microcomputer keyboards contain function keys, arrow keys, and a numeric keypad. Figure G.2 shows an enhanced keyboard.

Figure G.2 Keyboard

The 12 keys at the top of the keyboard, labeled with the letter F followed by a number, are called *function keys*. Use these keys to perform functions within each of the suite programs. To the right of the regular keys is a group of *special* or *dedicated keys*. These keys are labeled with specific functions that will be performed when you press the key. Below the special keys are arrow keys. Use these keys to move the insertion point in the document screen.

A keyboard generally includes three mode indicator lights. When you select certain modes, a light appears on the keyboard. For example, if you press the Caps Lock key, which disables the lowercase alphabet, a light appears next to Caps Lock. Similarly, pressing the Num Lock key will disable the special functions on the numeric keypad, which is located at the right side of the keyboard.

Disk Drives

Depending on the computer system you are using, Microsoft Office 2007 is installed on a hard drive or as part of a network system. Whether you are using Office on a hard drive or network system, you will need to have available a DVD or CD drive and a USB drive or other storage medium. You will insert the CD (compact disc) that accompanies this textbook in the DVD or CD drive and then copy folders from the CD to your storage medium. You will also save documents you complete at the computer to folders on your storage medium.

Printer

A document you create in Word is considered soft copy. If you want a hard copy of a document, you need to print it. To print documents you will need to access a printer, which will probably be either a laser printer or an ink-jet printer. A laser printer uses a laser beam combined with heat and pressure to print documents, while an ink-jet printer prints a document by spraying a fine mist of ink on the page.

Mouse

Many functions in the suite of programs are designed to operate more efficiently with a mouse. A mouse is an input device that sits on a flat surface next to the computer. You can operate a mouse with the left or the right hand. Moving the mouse on the flat surface causes a corresponding mouse pointer to move on the screen. Figure G.1 shows an illustration of a mouse.

Using the Mouse

The programs in the Microsoft Office suite can be operated using a keyboard or they can be operated with the keyboard and a mouse. The mouse may have two or three buttons on top, which are tapped to execute specific functions and commands. To use the mouse, rest it on a flat surface or a mouse pad. Put your hand over it with your palm resting on top of the mouse and your wrist resting on the table surface. As you move the mouse on the flat surface, a corresponding pointer moves on the screen.

When using the mouse, you should understand four terms—point, click, double-click, and drag. When operating the mouse, you may need to point to a specific command, button, or icon. Point means to position the mouse pointer on the desired item. With the mouse pointer positioned on the desired item, you may need to click a button on the mouse. Click means quickly tapping a button on the mouse once. To complete two steps at one time, such as choosing and then executing a function, double-click a mouse button. Double-click means to tap the left mouse button twice in quick succession. The term drag means to press and hold the left mouse button, move the mouse pointer to a specific location, and then release the button.

Using the Mouse Pointer

The mouse pointer will change appearance depending on the function being performed or where the pointer is positioned. The mouse pointer may appear as one of the following images:

- The mouse pointer appears as an I-beam (called the I-beam pointer) in the document screen and can be used to move the insertion point or select text.

- The mouse pointer appears as an arrow pointing up and to the left (called the arrow pointer) when it is moved to the Title bar, Quick Access toolbar, ribbon, or an option in a dialog box. For example, to open a new document with the mouse, position the I-beam pointer on the Office button located in the upper left corner of the screen until the pointer turns into an arrow pointer and then click the left mouse button. At the drop-down list that displays, make a selection by positioning the arrow pointer on the desired option and then clicking the left mouse button.

- The mouse pointer becomes a double-headed arrow (either pointing left and right, pointing up and down, or pointing diagonally) when performing certain functions such as changing the size of an object.

- In certain situations, such as moving an object or image, the mouse pointer becomes a four-headed arrow. The four-headed arrow means that you can move the object left, right, up, or down.

- When a request is being processed or when a program is being loaded, the mouse pointer may appear with an hourglass beside it. The hourglass image means "please wait." When the process is completed, the hourglass image is removed.

- The mouse pointer displays as a hand with a pointing index finger in certain functions such as Help and indicates that more information is available about the item.

Choosing Commands

Once a program is open, you can use several methods in the program to choose commands. A command is an instruction that tells the program to do something. You can choose a command using the mouse or the keyboard. When a program such as Word or PowerPoint is open, the ribbon contains buttons for completing tasks and contains tabs you click to display additional buttons. To choose a button on the Quick Access toolbar or in the ribbon, position the tip of the mouse arrow pointer on a button and then click the left mouse button.

The Office suite provides access keys you can press to use a command in a program. Press the Alt key on the keyboard to display KeyTips that identify the access key you need to press to execute a command. For example, press the Alt key in a Word document and KeyTips display as shown in Figure G.3. Continue pressing access keys until you execute the desired command. For example, if you want to begin spell checking a document, you would press the Alt key, press the R key on the keyboard to display the Review tab, and then press the letter S on the keyboard.

Figure G.3 Word KeyTips

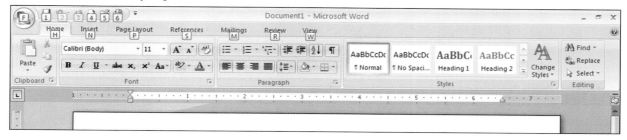

Choosing Commands from Drop-Down Lists

To choose a command from a drop-down list with the mouse, position the mouse pointer on the desired option and then click the left mouse button. To make a selection from a drop-down list with the keyboard, type the underlined letter in the desired option.

Some options at a drop-down list may be gray-shaded (dimmed), indicating that the option is currently unavailable. If an option at a drop-down list displays preceded by a check mark, that indicates that the option is currently active. If an option at a drop-down list displays followed by an ellipsis (…), a dialog box will display when that option is chosen.

Choosing Options from a Dialog Box

A dialog box contains options for applying formatting to a file or data within a file. Some dialog boxes display with tabs along the top providing additional options. For example, the Font dialog box shown in Figure G.4 contains two tabs—the Font tab and the Character Spacing tab. The tab that displays in the front is the

Figure G.4 Word Font Dialog Box

Dialog box tabs

Check boxes

active tab. To make a tab active using the mouse, position the arrow pointer on the desired tab and then click the left mouse button. If you are using the keyboard, press Ctrl + Tab or press Alt + the underlined letter on the desired tab.

To choose options from a dialog box with the mouse, position the arrow pointer on the desired option and then click the left mouse button. If you are using the keyboard, press the Tab key to move the insertion point forward from option to option. Press Shift + Tab to move the insertion point backward from option to option. You can also hold down the Alt key and then press the underlined letter of the desired option. When an option is selected, it displays with a blue background or surrounded by a dashed box called a marquee. A dialog box contains one or more of the following elements: text boxes, list boxes, check boxes, option buttons, spin boxes, and command buttons.

Text Boxes

Some options in a dialog box require you to enter text. For example, the boxes below the *Find what* and *Replace with* options at the Excel Find and Replace dialog box shown in Figure G.5 are text boxes. In a text box, you type text or edit existing text. Edit text in a text box in the same manner as normal text. Use the Left and Right Arrow keys on the keyboard to move the insertion point without deleting text and use the Delete key or Backspace key to delete text.

Figure G.5 Excel Find and Replace Dialog Box

List Boxes

Some dialog boxes such as the Word Open dialog box shown in Figure G.6 may contain a list box. The list of files below the *Look in* option is contained in a list box. To make a selection from a list box with the mouse, move the arrow pointer to the desired option and then click the left mouse button.

Figure G.6 Word Open Dialog Box

Some list boxes may contain a scroll bar. This scroll bar will display at the right side of the list box (a vertical scroll bar) or at the bottom of the list box (a horizontal scroll bar). You can use a vertical scroll bar or a horizontal scroll bar to move through the list if the list is longer than the box. To move down through a list on a vertical scroll bar, position the arrow pointer on the down-pointing arrow and hold down the left mouse button. To scroll up through the list in a vertical scroll bar, position the arrow pointer on the up-pointing arrow and hold down the left mouse button. You can also move the arrow pointer above the scroll box and click the left mouse button to scroll up the list or move the arrow pointer below the scroll box and click the left mouse button to move down the list. To move through a list with a horizontal scroll bar, click the left-pointing arrow to scroll to the left of the list or click the right-pointing arrow to scroll to the right of the list.

To make a selection from a list using the keyboard, move the insertion point into the box by holding down the Alt key and pressing the underlined letter of the desired option. Press the Up and/or Down Arrow keys on the keyboard to move through the list.

In some dialog boxes where enough room is not available for a list box, lists of options are inserted in a drop-down list box. Options that contain a drop-down list box display with a down-pointing arrow. For example, the *Underline style* option at the Word Font dialog box shown in Figure G.4 contains a drop-down list. To display the list, click the down-pointing arrow to the right of the *Underline style* option box. If you are using the keyboard, press Alt + U.

Check Boxes

Some dialog boxes contain options preceded by a box. A check mark may or may not appear in the box. The Word Font dialog box shown in Figure G.4 displays a variety of check boxes within the *Effects* section. If a check mark appears in the box, the option is active (turned on). If the check box does not contain a check mark, the option is inactive (turned off). Any number of check boxes can be active. For example, in the Word Font dialog box, you can insert a check mark in any or all of the boxes in the *Effects* section and these options will be active.

To make a check box active or inactive with the mouse, position the tip of the arrow pointer in the check box and then click the left mouse button. If you are using the keyboard, press Alt + the underlined letter of the desired option.

Option Buttons

The Word Print dialog box shown in Figure G.7 contains options in the *Print range* section preceded by option buttons. Only one option button can be selected at any time. When an option button is selected, a green circle displays in the button. To select an option button with the mouse, position the tip of the arrow pointer inside the option button and then click the left mouse button. To make a selection with the keyboard, hold down the Alt key and then press the underlined letter of the desired option.

Figure G.7 Word Print Dialog Box

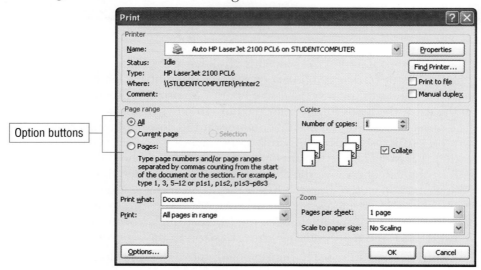

Spin Boxes

Some options in a dialog box contain measurements or numbers you can increase or decrease. These options are generally located in a spin box. For example, the Word Paragraph dialog box shown in Figure G.8 contains spin boxes located after the *Left, Right, Before*, and *After* options. To increase a number in a spin box, position the tip of the arrow pointer on the up-pointing arrow to the right of the desired option and then click the left mouse button. To decrease the number, click the down-pointing arrow. If you are using the keyboard, press Alt + the underlined letter of the desired option and then press the Up Arrow key to increase the number or the Down Arrow key to decrease the number.

Figure G.8 Word Paragraph Dialog Box

Command Buttons

In the Excel Find and Replace dialog box shown in Figure G.5, the boxes along the bottom of the dialog box are called command buttons. Use a command button to execute or cancel a command. Some command buttons display with an ellipsis (...). A command button that displays with an ellipsis will open another dialog box. To choose a command button with the mouse, position the arrow pointer on the desired button and then click the left mouse button. To choose a command button with the keyboard, press the Tab key until the desired command button contains the marquee and then press the Enter key.

Choosing Commands with Keyboard Shortcuts

Applications in the Office suite offer a variety of keyboard shortcuts you can use to executive specific commands. Keyboard shortcuts generally require two or more keys. For example, the keyboard shortcut to display the Open dialog box in an application is Ctrl + O. To use this keyboard shortcut, hold down the Ctrl key, type the letter O on the keyboard, and then release the Ctrl key. For a list of keyboard shortcuts, refer to the Help files.

Choosing Commands with Shortcut Menus

The software programs in the suite include menus that contain commands related to the item with which you are working. A shortcut menu appears in the file in the location where you are working. To display a shortcut menu, click the right mouse button or press Shift + F10. For example, if the insertion point is positioned in a paragraph of text in a Word document, clicking the right mouse button or pressing Shift + F10 will cause the shortcut menu shown in Figure G.9 to display in the document screen.

Figure G.9 Word Shortcut Menu

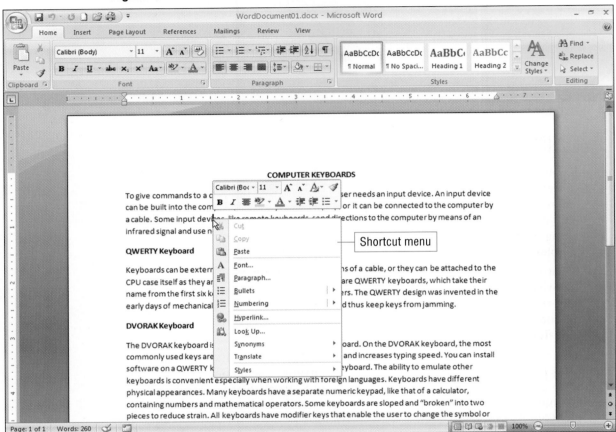

To select an option from a shortcut menu with the mouse, click the desired option. If you are using the keyboard, press the Up or Down Arrow key until the desired option is selected and then press the Enter key. To close a shortcut menu without choosing an option, click anywhere outside the shortcut menu or press the Esc key.

Working with Multiple Programs

As you learn the various programs in the Microsoft Office suite, you will notice how executing commands in each is very similar. For example, the steps to save, close, and print are virtually the same whether you are working in Word, Excel, or PowerPoint. This consistency between programs greatly enhances a user's ability to transfer knowledge learned in one program to another within the suite. Another appeal of Microsoft Office is the ability to have more than one program open at the same time. For example, you can open Word, create a document, and then open Excel, create a spreadsheet, and copy the spreadsheet into Word.

When you open a program, the name of the program displays in the Taskbar. If you open a file within the program, the file name follows the program name on the button on the Taskbar. If you open another program, the program name displays on a button positioned to the right of the first program button. Figure G.10 shows the Taskbar with Word, Excel, and PowerPoint open. To move from one program to another, click the button on the Taskbar representing the desired program file.

Figure G.10 Taskbar with Word, Excel, and PowerPoint Open

Completing Computer Projects

Some computer projects in this textbook require that you open an existing file. Project files are saved on the Student CD that accompanies this textbook. The files you need for each chapter are saved in individual folders. Before beginning a chapter, copy the necessary folder from the CD to your storage medium. After completing projects in a chapter, delete the chapter folder before copying the next chapter folder. (Check with your instructor before deleting a folder.)

The Student CD also contains model answers in PDF format for the project exercises within (but not at the end of) each chapter so you can check your work. To access the PDF files, you will need to have Adobe Acrobat Reader installed on your computer's hard drive. A free download of Adobe Reader is available at Adobe Systems' Web site at www.adobe.com.

Copying a Folder

As you begin working in a chapter, copy the chapter folder from the CD to your storage medium using the My Computer window by completing the following steps:

1. Insert the CD that accompanies this textbook in the CD drive.
2. Insert your storage medium in the appropriate drive.
3. At the Windows XP desktop, open the My Computer window by clicking the Start button and then clicking *My Computer* at the Start menu.
4. Double-click the CD drive in the contents pane (probably displays as *Office2007_Bench* or *Word2007, Excel 2007*, etc. followed by the drive letter).
5. Double-click the *StudentDataFiles* folder in the contents pane.
6. Double-click the desired folder name in the contents pane. (For example, if you are copying a folder for a Word Level 1 chapter, double-click the *Word2007L1* folder.)
7. Click once on the desired chapter subfolder name to select it.
8. Click the <u>Copy this folder</u> hyperlink in the *File and Folder Tasks* section of the task pane.
9. At the Copy Items dialog box, click the drive where your storage medium is located and then click the Copy button.
10. After the folder is copied to your storage medium, close the My Computer window by clicking the Close button (white X on red background) that displays in the upper right corner of the window.

Deleting a Folder

Before copying a chapter folder onto your storage medium, you may need to delete any previous chapter folders. Do this in the My Computer window by completing the following steps:

1. Insert your storage medium in the appropriate drive.
2. At the Windows XP desktop, open the My Computer window by clicking the Start button and then clicking *My Computer* at the Start menu.
3. Double-click the drive where you storage medium is located in the contents pane.
4. Click the chapter folder in the list box.
5. Click the <u>Delete this folder</u> hyperlink in the *File and Folder Tasks* section of the task pane.
6. At the message asking if you want to remove the folder and all its contents, click the Yes button.
7. If a message displays asking if you want to delete a read-only file, click the Yes to All button.
8. Close the My Computer window by clicking the Close button (white X on red background) that displays in the upper right corner of the window.

Viewing or Printing the Project Model Answers

If you want to access the PDF model answer files, first make sure that Adobe Acrobat Reader is installed on your hard drive. Double-click the folder, double-click the desired chapter subfolder name, and double-click the appropriate file name to open the file. You can view and/or print the file to compare it with your own completed exercise file.

Customizing the Quick Access Toolbar

The four applications in the Office 2007 suite—Word, Excel, PowerPoint, and Access—each contain a Quick Access toolbar that displays at the top of the screen. By default, this toolbar contains three buttons: Save, Undo, and Redo. Before beginning chapters in this textbook, customize the Quick Access toolbar by adding three additional buttons: New, Open, and Quick Print. To add these three buttons to the Word Quick Access toolbar, complete the following steps:

1. Open Word.
2. Click the Customize Quick Access Toolbar button that displays at the right side of the toolbar.
3. At the drop-down list, click *New*. (This adds the New button to the toolbar.)
4. Click the Customize Quick Access Toolbar button and then click *Open* at the drop-down list. (This adds the Open button to the toolbar.)
5. Click the Customize Quick Access Toolbar button and then click *Quick Print* at the drop-down list. (This adds the Quick Print button to the toolbar.)

Complete the same steps for Excel, Access, and PowerPoint. You will only need to add the buttons once to the Quick Access toolbar. These buttons will remain on the toolbar even when you exit and then reopen the application.

Using Windows XP

A computer requires an operating system to provide necessary instructions on a multitude of processes including loading programs, managing data, directing the flow of information to peripheral equipment, and displaying information. Windows XP Professional is an operating system that provides functions of this type (along with much more) in a graphical environment. Windows is referred to as a ***graphical user interface*** (GUI— pronounced *gooey*) that provides a visual display of information with features such as icons (pictures) and buttons. In this introduction, you will learn the basic features of Windows XP:

Tutorial WXP1
Exploring Windows XP
Tutorial WXP2
Working with Files and Folders
Tutorial WXP3
Customizing Windows
Tutorial WXP4
Using Applications

- Use desktop icons and the Taskbar to launch programs and open files or folders
- Organize and manage data, including copying, moving, creating, and deleting files and folders
- Customize the desktop by changing the theme, background, colors, and settings, and adding a screen saver
- Use the Help and Support Center features
- Customize monitor settings

Historically, Microsoft has produced two editions of Windows—one edition for individual users (on desktop and laptop computers) and another edition for servers (on computers that provide service over networks). Windows XP is an upgrade and a merging of these two Windows editions and is available in two versions. The Windows XP Home Edition is designed for home use and Windows XP Professional is designed for small office and workstation use. Whether you are using Windows XP Home Edition or Windows XP Professional, you will be able to complete the steps in the projects in this introduction.

Before using one of the software programs in the Microsoft Office suite, you will need to start the Windows XP operating system. To do this, turn on the computer. Depending on your computer equipment configuration, you may also need to turn on the monitor and printer. If you are using a computer that is part of a network system or if your computer is set up for multiple users, a screen will display showing the user accounts defined for your computer system. At this screen, click your user account name and, if necessary, type your password and then press the Enter key. The Windows XP operating system will start and, after a few moments, the desktop will display as shown in Figure W.1. (Your desktop may vary from what you see in Figure W.1.)

Figure W.1 Windows XP Desktop

Exploring the Desktop

When Windows XP is loaded, the main portion of the screen is called the ***desktop***. Think of the desktop in Windows as the top of a desk in an office. A business person places necessary tools—such as pencils, pens, paper, files, calculator—on the desktop to perform functions. Like the tools that are located on a desk, the desktop contains tools for operating the computer. These tools are logically grouped and placed in dialog boxes or panels that you can display using icons on the desktop. The desktop contains a variety of features for using your computer and software programs installed on the computer. The features available on the desktop are represented by icons and buttons.

Using Icons

Icons are visual symbols that represent programs, files, or folders. Figure W.1 identifies the *Recycle Bin* icon located on the Windows XP desktop. The Windows XP desktop on your computer may contain additional icons. Programs that have been installed on your computer may be represented by an icon on the desktop. Also, icons may display on your desktop representing files or folders. Double-click an icon and the program, file, or folder it represents opens on the desktop.

Using the Taskbar

The bar that displays at the bottom of the desktop (see Figure W.1) is called the Taskbar. The Taskbar, shown in Figure W.2, contains the Start button, a section that displays task buttons representing open programs, and the notification area.

Figure W.2 Windows XP Taskbar

Start button   Task button area   Notification area

Click the Start button, located at the left side of the Taskbar, and the Start menu displays as shown in Figure W.3 (your Start menu may vary). You can also display the Start menu by pressing the Windows key on your keyboard or by pressing Ctrl + Esc. The left column of the Start menu contains *pinned programs*, which are programs that always appear in that particular location on the Start menu, and links to the most recently and frequently used programs. The right column contains links to folders, the Control Panel, online help, and the search feature.

Figure W.3 Start Menu

Pinned programs

Frequently used programs

Folders

To choose an option from the Start menu, drag the arrow pointer to the desired option (referred to as *pointing*) and then click the left mouse button. Pointing to options at the Start menu that are followed by a right-pointing arrow will cause a side menu to display with additional options. When a program is open, a task button representing the program appears on the Taskbar. If multiple programs are open, each program will appear as a task button on the Taskbar (a few specialized tools may not).

Project ① Opening Programs and Switching between Programs

1. Open Windows XP. (To do this, turn on the computer and, if necessary, turn on the monitor and/or printer. If you are using a computer that is part of a network system or if your computer is set up for multiple users, you may need to click your user account name and, if necessary, type your password and then press the Enter key. Check with your instructor to determine if you need to complete any additional steps.)
2. When the Windows XP desktop displays, open Microsoft Word by completing the following steps:
   a. Position the arrow pointer on the Start button on the Taskbar and then click the left mouse button.
   b. At the Start menu, point to *All Programs* (a side menu displays) and then point to *Microsoft Office* (another side menu displays).
   c. Drag the arrow pointer to *Microsoft Office Word 2007* in the side menu and then click the left mouse button.
   d. When the Microsoft Word program is open, notice that a task button representing Word displays on the Taskbar.

Step
2d

3. Open Microsoft Excel by completing the following steps:
   a. Position the arrow pointer on the Start button on the Taskbar and then click the left mouse button.
   b. At the Start menu, point to *All Programs* and then point to *Microsoft Office*.
   c. Drag the arrow pointer to *Microsoft Office Excel 2007* in the side menu and then click the left mouse button.
   d. When the Microsoft Excel program is open, notice that a task button representing Excel displays on the Taskbar to the right of the task button representing Word.
4. Switch to the Word program by clicking the task button on the Taskbar representing Word.

Step
4

Step
6

5. Switch to the Excel program by clicking the task button on the Taskbar representing Excel.
6. Exit Excel by clicking the Close button that displays in the upper right corner of the Excel window.
7. Exit Word by clicking the Close button that displays in the upper right corner of the Word window.

Exploring the Notification Area

The notification area is located at the right side of the Taskbar and contains the system clock along with small icons representing specialized programs that run in the background. Position the arrow pointer over the current time in the notification area of the Taskbar and today's date displays in a small yellow box above the time. Double-click the current time displayed on the Taskbar and the Date and Time Properties dialog box displays as shown in Figure W.4.

Figure W.4 Date and Time Properties Box

Change the date with options in the *Date* section of the dialog box. For example, to change the month, click the down-pointing arrow at the right side of the option box containing the current month and then click the desired month at the drop-down list. Change the year by clicking the up- or down-pointing arrow at the right side of the option box containing the current year until the desired year displays. To change the day, click the desired day in the monthly calendar that displays in the dialog box. To change the time, double-click either the hour, minute, or seconds and then type the appropriate time or use the up- and down-pointing arrows to adjust the time.

Some programs, when installed, will add an icon to the notification area of the Taskbar. Display the name of the icon by positioning the mouse pointer on the icon and, after approximately one second, the icon label displays in a small yellow box. Some icons may display information in the yellow box rather than the icon label. If more icons have been inserted in the notification area than can be viewed at one time, a left-pointing arrow button displays at the left side of the notification area. Click this left-pointing arrow button and the remaining icons display.

Setting Taskbar Properties

By default, the Taskbar is locked in its current position and size. You can change this default setting, along with other default settings, with options at the Taskbar and Start Menu Properties dialog box, shown in Figure W.5. To display this dialog box, position the arrow pointer on any empty spot on the Taskbar and then click the right mouse button. At the shortcut menu that displays, click *Properties*.

Figure W.5 Taskbar and Start Menu Properties Box

Each property is controlled by a check box. Property options containing a check mark are active. Click the option to remove the check mark and make the option inactive. If an option is inactive, clicking the option will insert a check mark in the check box and turn on the option (make it active).

Project ② Changing Taskbar Properties

1. Make sure Windows XP is open and the desktop displays.
2. Hide the Taskbar and remove the display of the clock by completing the following steps:
   a. Position the arrow pointer on any empty area on the Taskbar and then click the right mouse button.
   b. At the shortcut menu that displays, click *Properties*.
   c. At the Taskbar and Start Menu Properties dialog box, click *Auto-hide the taskbar*. (This inserts a check mark in the check box.)
   d. Click *Show the clock*. (This removes the check mark from the check box.)
   e. Click the Apply button.
   f. Click OK to close the dialog box.

3. Display the Taskbar by positioning the mouse pointer at the bottom of the screen. When the Taskbar displays, notice that the time no longer displays at the right side of the Taskbar.
4. Return to the default settings for the Taskbar by completing the following steps:
   a. With the Taskbar displayed (if it does not display, position the mouse pointer at the bottom of the desktop), position the arrow pointer on any empty area on the Taskbar and then click the right mouse button.
   b. At the shortcut menu that displays, click *Properties*.
   c. At the Taskbar and Start Menu Properties dialog box, click *Auto-hide the taskbar*. (This removes the check mark from the check box.)
   d. Click *Show the clock*. (This inserts a check mark in the check box.)
   e. Click the Apply button.
   f. Click OK to close the dialog box.

Turning Off the Computer

When you are finished working with your computer, you can choose to shut down the computer completely, shut down and then restart the computer, put the computer on standby, or tell the computer to hibernate. Do not turn off your computer until your screen goes blank. Important data is stored in memory while Windows XP is running and this data needs to be written to the hard drive before turning off the computer.

To shut down your computer, click the Start button on the Taskbar and then click *Turn Off Computer* at the Start menu. At the Turn off computer window, shown in Figure W.6, click the *Stand By* option and the computer switches to a low power state causing some devices such as the monitor and hard drives to turn off. With these devices off, the computer uses less power. Stand By is particularly useful for saving battery power for portable computers. Tell the computer to "hibernate" by holding down the Shift key while clicking the *Stand By* option. In hibernate mode, the computer saves everything in memory, turns off the monitor and hard drive, and then turns off the computer. Click the *Turn Off* option if you want to shut down Windows XP and turn off all power to the computer. Click the *Restart* option if you want to restart the computer and restore the desktop exactly as you left it. You can generally restore your desktop from either standby or hibernate by pressing once on the computer's power button. Usually, bringing a computer out of hibernation takes a little longer than bringing a computer out of standby.

Figure W.6 Turn Off Computer Window

Managing Files and Folders

As you begin working with programs in Windows XP, you will create files in which data (information) is saved. A file might contain a Word document, an Excel workbook, or a PowerPoint presentation. As you begin creating files, consider creating folders into which those files will be stored. You can complete file management tasks such as creating a folder and copying and moving files and folders at the My Computer window. To display the My Computer window shown in Figure W.7, click the Start button on the Taskbar and then click My Computer. The various components of the My Computer window are identified in Figure W.7.

Figure W.7 My Computer Window

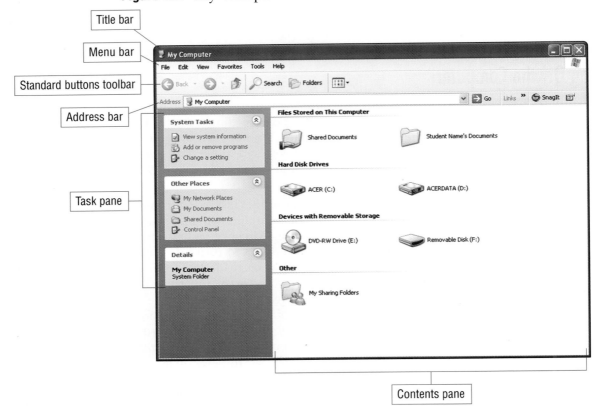

Copying, Moving, and Deleting Files/Folders

File and folder management activities might include copying and moving files or folders from one folder or drive to another, or deleting files or folders. The My Computer window offers a variety of methods for copying, moving, and deleting files/folders. You can use options in the task pane, drop-down menu options, or shortcut menu options. This section will provide you with the steps for copying, moving, and deleting files/folders using options in the task pane.

To copy a file/folder to another folder or drive, first display the file in the contents pane by identifying the location of the file. If the file is located in the My Documents folder, click the <u>My Documents</u> hyperlink in the *Other Places* section of the task pane. If the file is located on the hard drive, double-click the desired drive in the contents pane; if the file is located on a USB drive, DVD, or CD, double-click the desired drive letter. Next, click the folder or file name in the contents pane that you want to copy. This changes the options in the task pane to include management options such as renaming, moving, copying, and deleting folders or files. Click the Copy this folder (or Copy this file) hyperlink in the task pane and the Copy Items dialog box displays as shown in Figure W.8. At the Copy Items dialog box, click the desired folder or drive and then click the Copy button.

Figure W.8 Copy Items Dialog Box

To move adjacent files/folders, click the first file or folder, hold down the Shift key, and then click the last file or folder. This selects and highlights all files/folders from the first file/folder you clicked to the last file/folder you clicked. With the adjacent files/folders selected, click the Move the selected items hyperlink in the File and Folder Tasks section of the task pane and then specify the desired location at the Move Items dialog box. To select nonadjacent files/folders, click the first file/folder to select it, hold down the Ctrl key, and then click any other files/folders you want to move or copy.

You can easily remove (delete) a file or folder from the My Computer window. To delete a file or folder, click the file or folder in the contents pane, and then click the Delete this folder (or Delete this file) hyperlink in the task pane. At the dialog box asking you to confirm the deletion, click Yes. A deleted file or folder is sent to the Recycle Bin. You will learn more about the Recycle Bin in the next section.

In Project 3, you will insert the CD that accompanies this book into the DVD or CD drive. When the CD is inserted, the drive may automatically activate and a dialog box may display on the screen telling you that the disk or device contains more than one type of content and asking what you want Windows to do. If this dialog box displays, click Cancel to remove the dialog box.

Project ③ Copying a File and Folder and Deleting a File

1. At the Windows XP desktop, insert the CD that accompanies this textbook into the appropriate drive. If a dialog box displays telling you that the disk or device contains more than one type of content and asking what you want Windows to do, click Cancel.
2. At the Windows XP desktop, open the My Computer window by clicking the Start button on the Taskbar and then clicking *My Computer* at the Start menu.
3. Copy a file from the CD that accompanies this textbook to the drive containing your storage medium by completing the following steps:
   a. Insert your storage medium in the appropriate drive.
   b. In the contents pane, double-click the drive containing the CD (probably displays as *Office2007_Bench* followed by a drive letter). (Make sure you double-click the mouse button because you want the contents of the CD to display in the contents pane.)
   c. Double-click the *StudentDataFiles* folder.
   d. Double-click the *WindowsXP* folder in the contents pane.
   e. Click **WordDocument01.docx** in the contents pane to select it.
   f. Click the <u>Copy this file</u> hyperlink located in the *File and Folder Tasks* section of the task pane.

g. At the Copy Items dialog box, click in the list box the drive containing your storage medium.
h. Click the Copy button.

4. Delete **WordDocument01.docx** from your storage medium by completing the following steps:

   a. Click the <u>My Computer</u> hyperlink located in the *Other Places* section of the task pane.

   b. Double-click in the contents pane the drive containing your storage medium.

   c. Click ***WordDocument01.docx***.

   d. Click the <u>Delete this file</u> hyperlink in the *File and Folder Tasks* section of the task pane.

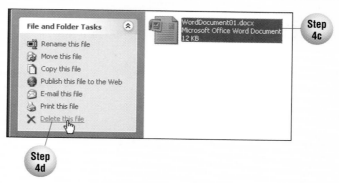

   e. At the message asking you to confirm the deletion, click Yes.

5. Copy the WindowsXP folder from the CD drive to the drive containing your storage medium by completing the following steps:

   a. Click the My Computer hyperlink in the *Other Places* section of the task pane.

   b. In the contents pane, double-click the drive containing the CD (probably displays as *Office2007_Bench* followed by a drive letter).

   c. Double-click the *StudentDataFiles* folder.

   d. Click the *WindowsXP* folder in the contents pane to select it.

   e. Click the <u>Copy this folder</u> hyperlink in the *File and Folder Tasks* section of the task pane.

   f. At the Copy Items dialog box, click the drive containing your storage medium.

   g. Click the Copy button.

6. Close the window by clicking the Close button (contains a white *X* on a red background) located in the upper right corner of the window. (You can also close the window by clicking File on the Menu bar and then clicking *Close* at the drop-down list.)

Selecting Files/Folders

You can move, copy, or delete more than one file or folder at the same time. Before moving, copying, or deleting files/folders, select the desired files or folders. Selecting files/folders is easier when you change the display in the contents pane to List or Details. To change the display, open the My Computer window and then click the Views button on the Standard Buttons toolbar. At the drop-down list that displays, click the *List* option or the *Details* option.

    To move adjacent files/folders, click the first file or folder, hold down the Shift key, and click the last file or folder. This selects and highlights all files/folders from the first file/folder you clicked to the last file/folder you clicked. With the adjacent files/folders selected, click the <u>Move the selected items</u> hyperlink in the *File and Folder Tasks* section of the task pane and then specify the desired location at the Move Items dialog box. To select nonadjacent files/folders, click the first file/folder to select it, hold down the Ctrl key, and then click any other files/folders you want to move or copy.

Project ④ Copying and Deleting Files

1. At the Windows XP desktop, open the My Computer window by clicking the Start button and then clicking *My Computer* at the Start menu.

2. Copy files from the CD that accompanies this textbook to the drive containing your storage medium by completing the following steps:

   a. Make sure the CD that accompanies this textbook and your storage medium are inserted in the appropriate drives.

   b. Double-click the CD drive in the contents pane (probably displays as *Office2007_Bench* followed by the drive letter).

   c. Double-click the *StudentDataFiles* folder in the contents pane.

   d. Double-click the *WindowsXP* folder in the contents pane.

   e. Change the display to Details by clicking the Views button on the Standard Buttons toolbar and then clicking *Details* at the drop-down list.

   f. Position the arrow pointer on **WordDocument01.docx** in the contents pane and then click the left mouse button.

   g. Hold down the Shift key, click **WordDocument05.docx**, and then release the Shift key. (This selects **WordDocument01.docx, WordDocument02.docx, WordDocument03.docx, WordDocument04.docx,** and **WordDocument05.docx.**)

   h. Click the <u>Copy the selected items</u> hyperlink in the *File and Folder Tasks* section of the task pane.

   i. At the Copy Items dialog box, click the drive containing your storage medium and then click the Copy button.

3. Display the files and folder saved on your storage medium by completing the following steps:

   a. Click the <u>My Computer</u> hyperlink in the *Other Places* section of the task pane.

   b. Double-click the drive containing your storage medium.

4. Delete the files from your storage medium that you just copied by completing the following steps:

   a. Change the view by clicking the Views button on the Standard Buttons toolbar and then clicking *List* at the drop-down list.

   b. Click **WordDocument01.docx** in the contents pane.

   c. Hold down the Shift key, click **WordDocument05.docx**, and then release the Shift key. (This selects **WordDocument01.docx, WordDocument02.docx, WordDocument03.docx, WordDocument04.docx,** and **WordDocument05.docx.**)

   d. Click the <u>Delete the selected items</u> hyperlink in the *File and Folder Tasks* section of the task pane.

   e. At the message asking you to confirm the deletion, click Yes.

5. Close the window by clicking the Close button (white *X* on red background) that displays in the upper right corner of the window.

Manipulating and Creating Folders

As you begin working with and creating a number of files, consider creating folders in which you can logically group the files. To create a folder, display the My Computer window and then display in the contents pane the drive where you want to create the folder. Click File on the Menu bar, point to *New*, and then click *Folder* at the side menu. This inserts a folder icon in the contents pane and names the folder *New Folder*. Type the desired name for the new folder and then press Enter.

Project ⑤ Creating a New Folder

1. At the Windows XP desktop, open the My Computer window.
2. Create a new folder by completing the following steps:
   a. Double-click in the contents pane the drive that contains your storage medium.
   b. Double-click the *WindowsXP* folder in the contents pane. (This opens the folder.)
   c. Click File on the Menu bar, point to *New*, and then click *Folder*.

Step 2c

   d. Type **SpellCheckFiles** and then press Enter. (This changes the name from *New Folder* to *SpellCheckFiles*.)
3. Copy **WordSpellCheck01.docx**, **WordSpellCheck02.docx**, and **WordSpellCheck03.docx** into the SpellCheckFiles folder you just created by completing the following steps:
   a. Click the Views button on the Standard Buttons toolbar and then click *List* at the drop-down list.
   b. Click once on the file named **WordSpellCheck01.docx** located in the contents pane.

Step 2d

   c. Hold down the Shift key, click once on the file named ***WordSpellCheck03.docx***, and then release the Shift key. (This selects **WordSpellCheck01.docx**, **WordSpellCheck02.docx**, and **WordSpellCheck03.docx**.)
   d. Click the <u>Copy the selected items</u> hyperlink in the *File and Folder Tasks* section of the task pane.
   e. At the Copy Items dialog box, click in the list box the drive containing your storage medium.
   f. Click *WindowsXP* in the list box.
   g. Click *SpellCheckFiles* in the list box.
   h. Click the Copy button.
4. Display the files you just copied by double-clicking the *SpellCheckFiles* folder in the contents pane.

Step 3e

Step 3f

Step 3g

Step 3h

5. Delete the SpellCheckFiles folder and its contents by completing the following steps:
   a. Click the Up button on the Standard Buttons toolbar. (This displays the contents of the WindowsXP folder which is up one folder from the SpellCheckFiles folders.)
   b. Click the *SpellCheckFiles* folder in the contents pane to select it.
   c. Click the <u>Delete this folder</u> hyperlink in the *File and Folder Tasks* section of the task pane.
   d. At the message asking you to confirm the deletion, click Yes.
6. Close the window by clicking the Close button located in the upper right corner of the window.

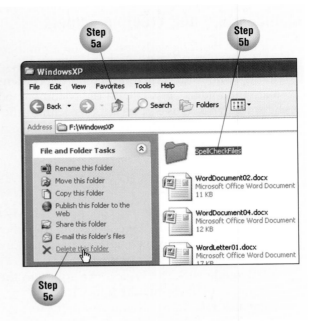

Using the Recycle Bin

Deleting the wrong file can be a disaster but Windows XP helps protect your work with the Recycle Bin. The Recycle Bin acts just like an office wastepaper basket; you can "throw away" (delete) unwanted files, but you can "reach in" to the Recycle Bin and take out (restore) a file if you threw it away by accident.

Deleting Files to the Recycle Bin

A file/folder or selected files/folders deleted from the hard drive are sent automatically to the Recycle Bin. Files/folders deleted from a disk are deleted permanently. (Recovery programs are available, however, that will help you recover deleted text. If you accidentally delete a file/folder from a disk, do not do anything more with the disk until you can run a recovery program.)

One method for deleting files is to display the My Computer window and then display in the contents pane the file(s) and/or folder(s) you want deleted. Click the file or folder or select multiple files or folders and then click the appropriate delete option in the task pane. At the message asking you to confirm the deletion, click Yes. Another method for deleting a file is to drag the file to the *Recycle Bin* icon on the desktop. Drag a file icon to the Recycle Bin until the *Recycle Bin* icon is selected (displays with a blue background) and then release the mouse button. This drops the file you are dragging into the Recycle Bin.

Recovering Files from the Recycle Bin

You can easily restore a deleted file from the Recycle Bin. To restore a file, double-click the *Recycle Bin* icon on the desktop. This opens the Recycle Bin window shown in Figure W.9. (The contents of the Recycle Bin will vary.) To restore a file, click the file you want restored, and then click the <u>Restore this item</u> hyperlink in the *Recycle Bin Tasks* section of the task pane. This removes the file from the Recycle Bin and returns it to its original location. You can also restore a file by positioning the arrow pointer on the file, clicking the right mouse button, and then clicking *Restore* at the shortcut menu.

Figure W.9 Recycle Bin Window

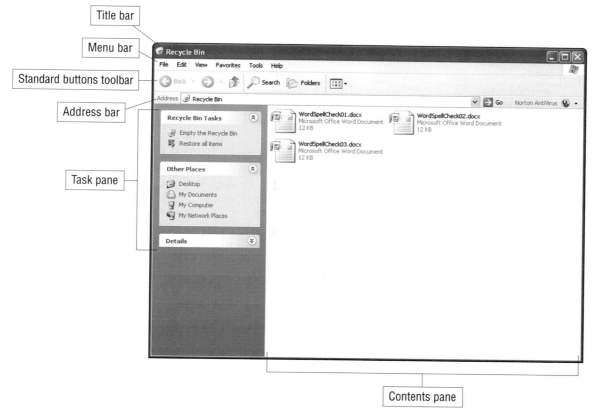

Project ⑥ Deleting Files to and Recovering Files from the Recycle Bin

Before beginning this project, check with your instructor to determine if you can copy files to the hard drive.

1. At the Windows XP desktop, open the My Computer window.
2. Copy files from your storage medium to the My Documents folder on your hard drive by completing the following steps:
    a. Double-click in the contents pane the drive containing your storage medium.
    b. Double-click the *WindowsXP* folder in the contents pane.
    c. Click the Views button on the Standard Buttons toolbar and then click *List* at the drop-down list.
    d. Position the arrow pointer on **WordSpellCheck01.docx** and then click the left mouse button.
    e. Hold down the Shift key, click **WordSpellCheck03.docx**, and then release the Shift key.

f. Click the Copy the selected items hyperlink in the *File and Folder Tasks* section of the task pane.

g. At the Copy Items dialog box, click *My Documents* in the list box.

h. Click the Copy button.

3. Click the <u>My Documents</u> hyperlink in the *Other Places* section of the task pane. (The files you copied, **WordSpellCheck01.docx** through **WordSpellCheck03.docx,** will display in the contents pane in alphabetical order.)

Step 2g

4. Delete **WordSpellCheck01.docx** through **WordSpellCheck03.docx** from the My Documents folder and send them to the Recycle Bin by completing the following steps:

a. Select **WordSpellCheck01.docx** through **WordSpellCheck03.docx** in the contents pane. (If these files are not visible, you will need to scroll down the list of files.)

b. Click the <u>Delete the selected items</u> hyperlink in the *File and Folder Tasks* section of the task pane.

c. At the message asking you to confirm the deletion to the Recycle Bin, click Yes.

5. Click the Close button to close the window.

6. At the desktop, display the contents of the Recycle Bin by double-clicking the *Recycle Bin* icon.

7. At the Recycle Bin window, restore **WordSpellCheck01.docx** through **WordSpellCheck03.docx** to the My Documents folder by completing the following steps:

a. Select **WordSpellCheck01.docx** through **WordSpellCheck03.docx** in the contents pane of the Recycle Bin window. (If these files are not visible, you will need to scroll down the list of files.)

b. With the files selected, click the <u>Restore the selected items</u> hyperlink in the *Recycle Bin Tasks* section of the task pane.

Step 7a

Step 7b

8. Close the Recycle Bin window by clicking the Close button located in the upper right corner of the window.

9. Display the My Computer window.

10. Click the <u>My Documents</u> hyperlink in the *Other Places* section of the task pane.

11. Delete the files you restored by completing the following steps:

a. Select **WordSpellCheck01.docx** through **WordSpellCheck03.docx** in the contents pane. (If these files are not visible, you will need to scroll down the list of files. These are the files you recovered from the Recycle Bin.)

b. Click the <u>Delete the selected items</u> hyperlink in the *File and Folder Tasks* section of the task pane.

c. At the message asking you to confirm the deletion, click Yes.

12. Close the window.

Emptying the Recycle Bin

Just like a wastepaper basket, the Recycle Bin can get full. To empty the Recycle Bin, position the arrow pointer on the *Recycle Bin* icon on the desktop and then click the right mouse button. At the shortcut menu that displays, click *Empty Recycle Bin*. At the message asking you to confirm the deletion, click Yes. You can also empty the Recycle Bin by double-clicking the *Recycle Bin* icon. At the Recycle Bin window, click the <u>Empty the Recycle Bin</u> hyperlink in the *Recycle Bin Tasks* section of the task pane. At the message asking you to confirm the deletion, click Yes. (You can also empty the Recycle Bin by clicking File on the Menu bar and then clicking *Empty Recycle Bin* at the drop-down menu.)

Emptying the Recycle Bin deletes all files/folders. You can delete a specific file/folder from the Recycle Bin (rather than all files/folders). To do this, double-click the *Recycle Bin* icon on the desktop. At the Recycle Bin window, select the file/folder or files/folders you want to delete. Click File on the Menu bar and then click *Delete* at the drop-down menu. (You can also right-click a selected file/folder and then click *Delete* at the shortcut menu.) At the message asking you to confirm the deletion, click Yes.

Project ⑦   Emptying the Recycle Bin

Before beginning this project, check with your instructor to determine if you can delete files/folders from the Recycle Bin.

1. At the Windows XP desktop, double-click the *Recycle Bin* icon.
2. At the Recycle Bin window, empty the contents of the Recycle Bin by completing the following steps:
   a. Click the <u>Empty the Recycle Bin</u> hyperlink in the *Recycle Bin Tasks* section of the task pane.

Step
2a

   b. At the message asking you to confirm the deletion, click Yes.
3. Close the Recycle Bin window by clicking the Close button located in the upper right corner of the window.

When you empty the Recycle Bin, the files cannot be recovered by the Recycle Bin or by Windows XP. If you have to recover a file, you will need to use a file recovery program such as Norton Utilities. These utilities are separate programs, but might be worth their cost if you ever need them.

Creating a Shortcut

If you use a file or program on a consistent basis, consider creating a shortcut to the file or program. A shortcut is a specialized icon that represents very small files that point the operating system to the actual item, whether it is a file, a folder, or an application. If you create a shortcut to a Word document, the shortcut icon is not the actual document but a path to the document. Double-click the shortcut icon and Windows XP opens the document in Word.

One method for creating a shortcut is to display the My Computer window and then display the drive or folder where the file is located. Right-click the desired file, point to *Send To*, and then click *Desktop (create shortcut)*. You can easily delete a shortcut icon from the desktop by dragging the shortcut icon to the Recycle Bin icon. This deletes the shortcut icon but does not delete the file to which the shortcut pointed.

Project ⑧ Creating a Shortcut

1. At the Windows XP desktop, display the My Computer window.
2. Double-click the drive containing your storage medium.
3. Double-click the *WindowsXP* folder in the contents pane.
4. Change the display of files to a list by clicking the Views button on the Standard Buttons toolbar and then clicking *List* at the drop-down list.
5. Create a shortcut to the file named **WordLetter01.docx** by right-clicking on **WordLetter01.docx**, pointing to *Send To*, and then clicking *Desktop (create shortcut)*.

Step 5

Step 7

6. Close the My Computer window by clicking the Close button located in the upper right corner of the window.
7. Open Word and the file named **WordLetter01.docx** by double-clicking the *WordLetter01.docx* shortcut icon on the desktop.
8. After viewing the file in Word, exit Word by clicking the Close button that displays in the upper right corner of the window.
9. Delete the *WordLetter01.docx* shortcut icon by completing the following steps:
   a. At the desktop, position the mouse pointer on the *WordLetter01.docx* shortcut icon.
   b. Hold down the left mouse button, drag the icon on top of the *Recycle Bin* icon, and then release the mouse button.

Customizing the Desktop

You can customize the Windows XP desktop to fit your particular needs and preferences. For example, you can choose a different theme, change the desktop background, add a screen saver, and apply a different appearance to windows, dialog boxes, and menus. To customize the desktop, position the arrow pointer on any empty location on the desktop and then click the right mouse button. At the shortcut menu that displays, click *Properties*. This displays the Display Properties dialog box with the Themes tab selected as shown in Figure W.10.

Figure W.10 Display Properties Dialog Box

Changing the Theme

A Windows XP theme specifies a variety of formatting such as fonts, sounds, icons, colors, mouse pointers, background, and screen saver. Windows XP contains two themes—Windows XP (the default) and Windows Classic (which appears like earlier versions of Windows). Other themes are available as downloads from the Microsoft Web site. Change the theme with the *Theme* option at the Display Properties dialog box with the Themes tab selected.

Changing the Desktop

With options at the Display Properties dialog box with the Desktop tab selected, as shown in Figure W.11, you can choose a different desktop background and customize the desktop. Click any option in the *Background* list box and preview the results in the preview screen. With the *Position* option, you can specify that the background image is centered, tiled, or stretched on the desktop. Use the *Color* option to change the background color and click the Browse button to choose a background image from another location or Web site.

Figure W.11 Display Properties Dialog Box with Desktop Tab Selected

Adding a Screen Saver

If your computer sits idle for periods of time, consider adding a screen saver. A screen saver is a pattern that changes constantly, thus eliminating the problem of an image staying on the screen too long. To add a screen saver, display the Display Properties dialog box and then click the Screen Saver tab. This displays the dialog box as shown in Figure W.12.

Figure W.12 Display Properties Dialog Box with Screen Saver Tab Selected

Click the down-pointing arrow at the right side of the *Screen saver* option box to display a list of installed screen savers. Click a screen saver and a preview displays in the monitor located toward the top of the dialog box. Click the Preview button and the dialog box is hidden and the screen saver displays on your monitor. Move the mouse or click a button on the mouse and the dialog box will reappear. Click the Power button in the *Monitor power* section and a dialog box displays with options for choosing a power scheme appropriate to the way you use your computer. The dialog box also includes options for specifying how long the computer can be left unused before the monitor and hard disk are turned off and the system goes to standby or hibernate mode.

Changing Colors

Click the Appearance tab at the Display Properties dialog box and the dialog box displays as shown in Figure W.13. At this dialog box, you can change the desktop scheme. Schemes are predefined collections of colors used in windows, menus, title bars, and system fonts. Windows XP loads with the Windows XP style color scheme. Choose a different scheme with the Windows and buttons option and choose a specific color with the Color scheme option.

Figure W.13 Display Properties Dialog Box with Appearance Tab Selected

Changing Settings

Click the Settings tab at the Display Properties dialog box and the dialog box displays as shown in Figure W.14. At this dialog box, you can set color and screen resolution. The *Color quality* option determines how many colors your monitor displays. The more colors that are shown, the more realistic the images will appear. However, a lot of computer memory is required to show thousands of colors. Your exact choice is determined by the specific hardware you are using. The *Screen resolution* slide bar sets the screen's resolution. The higher the number, the more you can fit onto your screen. Again, your actual values depend on your particular hardware.

Figure W.14 Display Properties Dialog Box with Settings Tab Selected

Project ⑨   Customizing the Desktop

Before beginning this project, check with your instructor to determine if you can customize the desktop.

1. At the Windows XP desktop, display the Display Properties dialog box by positioning the arrow pointer on an empty location on the desktop, clicking the right mouse button, and then clicking *Properties* at the shortcut menu.
2. At the Display Properties dialog box, change the desktop background by completing the following steps:
   a. Click the Desktop tab.
   b. If a background is selected in the *Background* list box (other than the *(None)* option), make a note of this background name.
   c. Click *Blue Lace 16* in the *Background* list box. (If this option is not available, choose another background.)
   d. Make sure *Tile* is selected in the *Position* list box.
   e. Click OK to close the dialog box.

3. After viewing the desktop with the Blue Lace 16 background, remove the background image and change the background color by completing the following steps:
   a. Display the Display Properties dialog box.
   b. At the Display Properties dialog box, click the Desktop tab.
   c. Click *(None)* in the *Background* list box.
   d. Click the down-pointing arrow at the right side of the *Color* option and then click the dark red option at the color palette.
   e. Click OK to close the Display Properties dialog box.

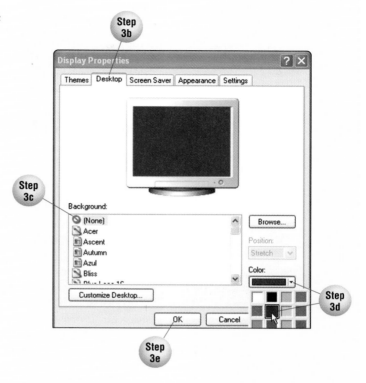

4. After viewing the desktop with the dark red background color, add a screen saver and change the wait time by completing the following steps:
   a. Display the Display Properties dialog box.
   b. At the Display Properties dialog box, click the Screen Saver tab. (If a screen saver is already selected in the *Screen saver* option box, make a note of this screen saver name.)
   c. Click the down-pointing arrow at the right side of the *Screen saver* option box.
   d. At the drop-down list that displays, click a screen saver that interests you. (A preview of the screen saver displays in the screen located toward the top of the dialog box.)
   e. Click a few other screen savers to see how they will display on the monitor.
   f. Click OK to close the Display Properties dialog box.
5. Return all settings back to the default by completing the following steps:
   a. Display the Display Properties dialog box.
   b. Click the Desktop tab.
   c. If a background and color were selected when you began this project, click that background name in the *Background* list box and change the color back to the original color.
   d. Click the Screen Saver tab.
   e. At the Display Properties dialog box with the Screen Saver tab selected, click the down-pointing arrow at the right side of the *Screen saver* option box, and then click *(None)*. (If a screen saver was selected before completing this project, return to that screen saver.)
   f. Click OK to close the Display Properties dialog box.

Exploring Windows XP Help and Support

Windows XP includes an on-screen reference guide providing information, explanations, and interactive help on learning Windows features. The on-screen reference guide contains complex files with hypertext used to access additional information by clicking a word or phrase.

Using the Help and Support Center Window

Display the Help and Support Center window shown in Figure W.15 by clicking the Start button on the Taskbar and then clicking *Help and Support* at the Start menu. The appearance of your Help and Support Center window may vary slightly from what you see in Figure W.15.

If you want to learn about a topic listed in the *Pick a Help topic* section of the window, click the desired topic and information about the topic displays in the window. Use the other options in the Help and Support Center window to get assistance or support from a remote computer or Windows XP newsgroups, pick a specific task, or learn about the additional help features. If you want help on a specific topic and do not see that topic listed in the *Pick a Help topic* section of the window, click inside the *Search* text box (generally located toward the top of the window), type the desired topic, and then press Enter or click the Start searching button (white arrow on a green background).

Figure W.15 Help and Support Center Window

1. At the Windows XP desktop, use the Help and Support feature to learn about new Windows XP features by completing the following steps:
   a. Click the Start button on the Taskbar and then click *Help and Support* at the Start menu.
   b. At the Help and Support Center window, click the <u>What's new in Windows XP</u> hyperlink located in the *Pick a Help topic* section of the window.

   c. Click the <u>What's new</u> hyperlink located in the *What's new in Windows XP* section of the window. (This displays a list of Help options at the right side of the window.)
   d. Click the <u>What's new in Windows XP</u> hyperlink located at the right side of the window below the subheading *Overviews, Articles, and Tutorials*.
   e. Read the information about Windows XP that displays at the right side of the window.
   f. Print the information by completing the following steps:
      1) Click the Print button located on the toolbar that displays above the information titled *What's new in Windows XP Professional*.

      2) At the Print dialog box, make sure the correct printer is selected and then click the Print button.
2. Return to the opening Help and Support Center window by clicking the Home button located on the Help and Support Center toolbar.
3. Use the *Search* text box to search for information on deleting files by completing the following steps:
   a. Click in the *Search* text box located toward the top of the Help and Support Center window.
   b. Type deleting files and then press Enter.
   c. Click the <u>Delete a file or folder</u> hyperlink that displays in the *Search Results* section of the window (below the *Pick a task* subheading).

d. Read the information about deleting a file or folder that displays at the right side of the window and then print the information by clicking the Print button on the toolbar and then clicking the Print button at the Print dialog box.

e. Click the <u>Delete or restore files in the Recycle Bin</u> hyperlink that displays in the *Search Results* section of the window.

f. Read the information that displays at the right side of the window about deleting and restoring files in the Recycle Bin and then print the information.

4. Close the Help and Support Center window by clicking the Close button located in the upper right corner of the window.

Displaying an Index of Help and Support Topics

Display a list of help topics available by clicking the Index button on the Help and Support Center window toolbar. This displays an index of help topics at the left side of the window as shown in Figure W.16. Scroll through this list until the desired topic displays and then double-click the topic. Information about the selected topic displays at the right side of the window. If you are looking for a specific topic or keyword, click in the *Type in the keyword to find* text box, type the desired topic or keyword, and then press Enter.

Figure W.16 Help and Support Center Window with Index Displayed

Project (11) Using the Index to Search for Information

1. At the Windows XP desktop, use the Index to display information on accessing programs by completing the following steps:
   a. Click the Start button on the Taskbar and then click *Help and Support* at the Start menu.
   b. Click the Index button on the Help and Support Center window toolbar.
   c. Scroll down the list of Index topics until *accessing programs* is visible and then double-click the subheading *overview* that displays below *accessing programs*.

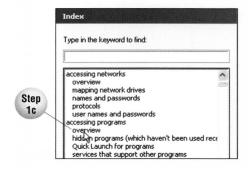

Step 1c

   d. Read the information that displays at the right side of the window and then print the information.
2. Find information on adding a shortcut to the desktop by completing the following steps:
   a. Select and delete the text *overview* that displays in the *Type in the keyword to find* text box and then type **shortcuts**.
   b. Double-click the subheading *for specific programs* that displays below the *shortcuts* heading.

Step 2a

Step 2b

   c. Read the information that displays at the right side of the window and then print the information.
3. Close the Help and Support Center window by clicking the Close button located in the upper right corner of the window.

Customizing Settings

Before beginning computer projects in this textbook, you may need to customize the monitor settings and turn on the display of file extensions. Projects in the chapters in this textbook assume that the monitor display is set to 1024 by 768 pixels and that the display of file extensions is turned on. To change the monitor display to 1024 by 768, complete the following steps:

1. At the Windows XP desktop, right-click on any empty location on the desktop and then click *Properties* at the shortcut menu.
2. At the Display Properties dialog box, click the Settings tab.
3. Using the mouse, drag the slide bar button in the *Screen resolution* section to the left or right until *1024 by 768* displays below the slider bar.
4. Click the Apply button.
5. Click the OK button.

To turn on the display of file extensions, complete the following steps:

1. At the Windows XP desktop, click the Start button and then click *My Computer*.
2. At the My Computer window, click Tools on the Menu bar and then click *Folder Options* at the drop-down list.

3. At the Folder Options dialog box, click the View tab.
4. Click the *Hide extentions for known file types* check box to remove the check mark.
5. Click the Apply button.
6. Click the OK button.

Browsing the Internet
Using Internet Explorer 7.0

Microsoft Internet Explorer 7.0 is a Web browser program with options and features for displaying sites as well as navigating and searching for information on the Internet. The *Internet* is a network of computers connected around the world. Users access the Internet for several purposes: to communicate using instant messaging and/or e-mail, to subscribe to newsgroups, to transfer files, to socialize with other users around the globe in "chat" rooms, and also to access virtually any kind of information imaginable.

Tutorial IE1
Browsing the Internet with Internet Explorer 7.0
Tutorial IE2
Gathering and Downloading Information and Files

Using the Internet, people can find a phenomenal amount of information for private or public use. To use the Internet, three things are generally required: an Internet Service Provider (ISP), a program to browse the Web (called a *Web browser*), and a *search engine*. In this section, you will learn how to:

- Navigate the Internet using URLs and hyperlinks
- Use search engines to locate information
- Download Web pages and images

Browsing the Internet

You will use the Microsoft Internet Explorer Web browser to locate information on the Internet. Uniform Resource Locators, referred to as URLs, are the method used to identify locations on the Internet. The steps for browsing the Internet vary but generally include: opening Internet Explorer, typing the URL for the desired site, navigating the various pages of the site, navigating to other sites using links, and then closing Internet Explorer.

To launch Internet Explorer 7.0, double-click the *Internet Explorer* icon on the Windows desktop. Figure IE.1 identifies the elements of the Internet Explorer, version 7.0, window. The Web page that displays in your Internet Explorer window may vary from what you see in Figure IE.1.

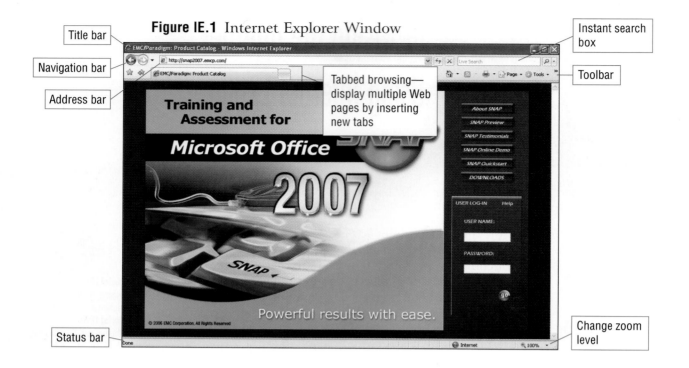

Figure IE.1 Internet Explorer Window

Title bar

Navigation bar

Address bar

Instant search box

Tabbed browsing—display multiple Web pages by inserting new tabs

Toolbar

Status bar

Change zoom level

If you know the URL for the desired Web site, click in the Address bar, type the URL, and then press Enter. The Web site's home page displays in a tab within the Internet Explorer window. URLs (Uniform Resource Locators) are the method used to identify locations on the Internet. The format of a URL is *http://server-name.path*. The first part of the URL, *http*, stands for HyperText Transfer Protocol, which is the protocol or language used to transfer data within the World Wide Web. The colon and slashes separate the protocol from the server name. The server name is the second component of the URL. For example, in the URL http://www.microsoft.com, the server name is *microsoft*. The last part of the URL specifies the domain to which the server belongs. For example, *.com* refers to "commercial" and establishes that the URL is a commercial company. Other examples of domains include *.edu* for "educational," *.gov* for "government," and *.mil* for "military."

Project ① Browsing the Internet Using URLs

1. Make sure you are connected to the Internet through an Internet Service Provider and that the Windows desktop displays. (Check with your instructor to determine if you need to complete steps for accessing the Internet such as typing a user name and password to log on.)
2. Launch Microsoft Internet Explorer by double-clicking the *Internet Explorer* icon located on the Windows desktop.
3. At the Internet Explorer window, explore the Web site for Yosemite National Park by completing the following steps:
   a. Click in the Address bar, type **www.nps.gov/yose**, and then press Enter.

Step 3a

b. Scroll down the home page for Yosemite National Park by clicking the down-pointing arrow on the vertical scroll bar located at the right side of the Internet Explorer window.

c. Print the home page by clicking the Print button located on the Internet Explorer toolbar.

4. Explore the Web site for Glacier National Park by completing the following steps:

a. Click in the Address bar, type **www.nps.gov/glac**, and then press Enter.

b. Print the home page by clicking the Print button located on the Internet Explorer toolbar.

5. Close Internet Explorer by clicking the Close button (contains an X) located in the upper right corner of the Internet Explorer window.

Navigating Using Hyperlinks

Most Web pages contain "hyperlinks" that you click to connect to another page within the Web site or to another site on the Internet. Hyperlinks may display in a Web page as underlined text in a specific color or as images or icons. To use a hyperlink, position the mouse pointer on the desired hyperlink until the mouse pointer turns into a hand, and then click the left mouse button. Use hyperlinks to navigate within and between sites on the Internet. The navigation bar in the Internet Explorer window contains a Back button that, when clicked, takes you to the previous Web page viewed. If you click the Back button and then want to return to the previous page, click the Forward button. You can continue clicking the Back button to back your way out of several linked pages in reverse order since Internet Explorer maintains a history of the Web sites you visit.

Project ② Navigating Using Hyperlinks

1. Make sure you are connected to the Internet and then double-click the *Internet Explorer* icon on the Windows desktop.

2. At the Internet Explorer window, display the White House Web page and navigate in the page by completing the following steps:

a. Click in the Address bar, type **whitehouse.gov**, and then press Enter.

b. At the White House home page, position the mouse pointer on a hyperlink that interests you until the pointer turns into a hand, and then click the left mouse button.

c. At the linked Web page, click the Back button. (This returns you to the White House home page.)

d. At the White House home page, click the Forward button to return to the previous Web page viewed.

e. Print the Web page by clicking the Print button on the Internet Explorer toolbar.

3. Display the Web site for Amazon.com and navigate in the site by completing the following steps:

a. Click in the Address bar, type www.amazon.com, and then press Enter.

b. At the Amazon.com home page, click a hyperlink related to books.

c. When a book Web page displays, click the Print button on the Internet Explorer toolbar.

4. Close Internet Explorer by clicking the Close button (contains an X) located in the upper right corner of the Internet Explorer window.

Searching for Specific Sites

If you do not know the URL for a specific site or you want to find information on the Internet but do not know what site to visit, complete a search with a search engine. A search engine is a software program created to search quickly and easily for desired information. A variety of search engines are available on the Internet, each offering the opportunity to search for specific information. One method for searching for information is to click in the *Instant Search* box (displays the text *Live Search*) located at the right end of the navigation bar, type a keyword or phrase related to your search, and then click the Search button or press Enter. Another method for completing a search is to visit the Web site for a search engine and use options at the site.

Project ③ Searching for Information by Topic

1. Start Internet Explorer.

2. At the Internet Explorer window, search for sites on bluegrass music by completing the following steps:

a. Click in the *Instant Search* box (may display with *Live Search*) located at the right end of the of the navigation bar.

b. Type bluegrass music and then press Enter.

c. When a list of sites displays in the Live Search tab, click a site that interests you.

d. When the page displays, click the Print button.

3. Use the Yahoo! search engine to find sites on bluegrass music by completing the following steps:
   a. Click in the Address bar, type www.yahoo.com, and then press Enter.
   b. At the Yahoo! Web site, with the insertion point positioned in the *Search* text box, type bluegrass music and then press Enter. (Notice that the sites displayed vary from sites displayed in the earlier search.)

   c. Click hyperlinks until a Web site displays that interests you.
   d. Print the page.

Step 3b

4. Use the Google search engine to find sites on jazz music by completing the following steps:
   a. Click in the Address bar, type www.google.com, and then press Enter.
   b. At the Google Web site, with the insertion point positioned in the search text box, type jazz music and then press Enter.

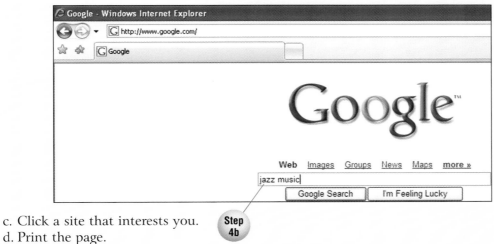

   c. Click a site that interests you.
   d. Print the page.

Step 4b

5. Close Internet Explorer.

Completing Advanced Searches for Specific Sites

The Internet contains an enormous amount of information. Depending on what you are searching for on the Internet and the search engine you use, some searches can result in several thousand "hits" (sites). Wading through a large number of sites can be very time-consuming and counterproductive. Narrowing a search to very specific criteria can greatly reduce the number of hits for a search. To narrow a search, use the advanced search options offered by the search engine.

Web Search

Project ④ Narrowing a Search

1. Start Internet Explorer.
2. Search for sites on skydiving in Oregon by completing the following steps:
   a. Click in the Address bar and then type www.yahoo.com.
   b. At the Yahoo! Web site, click the Web Search button next to the Search text box and then click the Advanced Search hyperlink.

   c. At the Advanced Web Search page, click in the search text box next to *all of these words*.
   d. Type **skydiving Oregon tandem static line**. (This limits the search to Web pages containing all of the words typed in the search text box.)

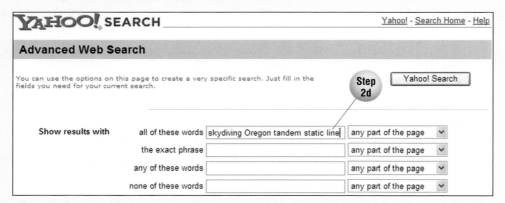

   e. Choose any other options at the Advanced Web Search page that will narrow your search.
   f. Click the Yahoo! Search button.
   g. When the list of Web sites displays, click a hyperlink that interests you.
   h. Print the page.
3. Close Internet Explorer.

Downloading Images, Text, and Web Pages from the Internet

The image(s) and/or text that display when you open a Web page as well as the Web page itself can be saved as a separate file. This separate file can be viewed, printed, or inserted in another file. The information you want to save in a separate file is downloaded from the Internet by Internet Explorer and saved in a folder of your choosing with the name you specify. Copyright laws protect much of the information on the Internet. Before using information downloaded from the Internet, check the site for restrictions. If you do use information, make sure you properly cite the source.

Project ⑤ Downloading Images and Web Pages

1. Start Internet Explorer.
2. Download a Web page and image from Banff National Park by completing the following steps:
   a. Search for sites on the Internet for Banff National Park.
   b. From the list of sites that displays, choose a site that contains information about Banff National Park and at least one image of the park.
   c. Save the Web page as a separate file by clicking the Page button on the Internet Explorer toolbar, and then clicking *Save As* at the drop-down list.
   d. At the Save Webpage dialog box, click the down-pointing arrow at the right side of the *Save in* option and then click the drive you are using as your storage medium at the drop-down list.
   e. Select the text in the *File name* text box, type BanffWebPage, and then press Enter.

Step 2c

Step 2d

Step 2e

3. Save an image file by completing the following steps:
   a. Right-click an image that displays on the Web site. (The image that displays may vary from what you see below.)
   b. At the shortcut menu that displays, click *Save Picture As*.

Step 3b

c. At the Save Picture dialog box, change the *Save in* option to your storage medium.

d. Select the text in the *File name* text box, type **BanffImage**, and then press Enter.

4. Close Internet Explorer.

Step 3c

Step 3d

Project Opening the Saved Web Page and Image in a Word Document

1. Open Microsoft Word by clicking the Start button on the Taskbar, pointing to *All Programs*, pointing to *Microsoft Office*, and then clicking *Microsoft Office Word 2007*.

2. With Microsoft Word open, insert the image in a document by completing the following steps:

   a. Click the Insert tab and then click the Picture button in the Illustrations group.

   b. At the Insert Picture dialog box, change the *Look in* option to the location where you saved the Banff image and then double-click *BanffImage.jpg*.

   Step 2b

   c. When the image displays in the Word document, print the document by clicking the Print button on the Quick Access toolbar.

   d. Close the document by clicking the Office button and then clicking *Close* at the drop-down menu. At the message asking if you want to save the changes, click No.

3. Open the **BanffWebPage.mht** file by completing the following steps:

   a. Click the Office button and then click *Open* at the drop-down menu.

   b. At the Open dialog box, change the *Look in* option to the location where you saved the Banff Web page and then double-click *BanffWebPage.mht*.

   Step 3b

   c. Print the Web page by clicking the Print button on the Quick Access toolbar.

   d. Close the **BanffWebPage.mht** file by clicking the Office button and then *Close*.

4. Close Word by clicking the Close button (contains an X) that displays in the upper right corner of the screen.

Microsoft® PowerPoint®

Course Performance Objectives

After successfully completing *Benchmark Series Microsoft PowerPoint 2007*, students will be able to

➤ Analyze and evaluate school, work, and home situations requiring the preparation of information visually and use PowerPoint to communicate with intended audiences efficiently and effectively.

➤ Use and customize interface and computer operations using the operating system utilities.

➤ Access the Internet and use the browse, search, hyperlink, and download capabilities of Web browsers.

➤ Design, format, and edit presentations starting with a blank presentation and by using templates and design themes. Topics include inserting and deleting text, adding transitions and sounds, rearranging slides, inserting images and objects, and creating WordArt text.

➤ Customize and enhance presentations using tables, charts, SmartArt graphics, slide masters, action buttons, and hyperlinks.

➤ Plan and set up slide shows with built-in animation effects, animated shapes and images, builds, motion paths, recorded narration, downloaded designs, and movie clips.

➤ Use strategies for merging and integrating source data from different Office applications using the commands for copying and pasting, importing and exporting, and linking and embedding.

➤ Protect and share presentations using encryption, digital signatures, permission restrictions, comments, and PDF formats.

Microsoft® PowerPoint®

Making PowerPoint Work for You!

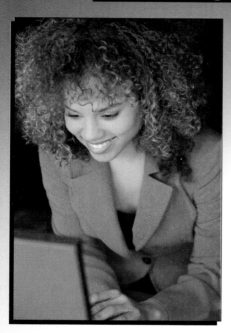

Being an effective communicator is one of the most marketable job skills you can possess. Whether your audience is a few colleagues in a small meeting room or a larger gathering in a conference center, you can enhance your message through the use of visual aids created with presentation software. Microsoft PowerPoint 2007 is the presentation graphics program included in the Microsoft Office 2007 suite. Content created in PowerPoint can be projected through a computer to a large screen or output in various formats, including slides, transparencies, or hard copy.

Organizing Information

PowerPoint 2007 offers several views in which you can organize the content of your topic. Each view is suited for specific tasks, but you can choose to work in the view in which you are most comfortable. For example, if you have a lot of typing to do, use Normal view with the Outline tab selected in the Slides/Outline pane. Switch to Slide Sorter view to rearrange several slides by dragging slide miniatures to new positions in the presentation. Use Notes Page view to add speaker notes to your slides. Insert and position graphics in Normal view with the Slides tab selected in the Slides/Outline pane. Preview the presentation in Slide Show view.

Organize your content and slides in the various views available in Microsoft PowerPoint.

Changing slide formatting such as the font, font size, and color is made easier with the use of *slide masters*. Open a presentation in Slide Master view to make global changes—changes you want applied to all slides. Changes can be made before or after content has been added. A slide master can also be used to add a graphic object, such as a company logo, to the same position in each slide. Use slide masters whenever possible to reduce the number of steps needed to make changes to all slides in a presentation.

Analyzing Information

In today's global workplace, two or more people commonly collaborate on a presentation. Send a PowerPoint file to others in a workgroup for review by placing the presentation on a network share folder and use options in the Review tab to insert, edit, and delete comments. With other options in the Review tab you can research information, use the thesaurus, and translate text into other languages.

Editing slides by rearranging the progression of content is easily accomplished using a drag and drop technique in either Slide Sorter view or Outline view. Use the Spelling feature to help find common misspellings. Everyone remembers the speaker with the slides that had typos. Make sure your audience remembers you for the brilliant insight you gave about your topic and not for the typing errors!

Rearrange the order of slides using a drag and drop technique.

Use the Rehearse Timings feature to set up a self-running presentation that has to synchronize times in which to advance slides. Display the Rehearsal toolbar and use buttons on the toolbar to set the appropriate amount of time each slide should display on the screen.

Presenting Information

Creating an eye-catching, thought-provoking presentation has never been easier. Microsoft PowerPoint 2007 includes several professionally created design theme templates that you can easily apply to your content. You don't have to be knowledgeable about choosing complementary colors or scaling font sizes for readability to create a background or interesting bullet style—design theme templates have all of these features incorporated for you. Click the Design tab, click the More button at the right side of the themes styles, and then browse through the themes until you find one that intrigues you. Click the theme and it is instantly applied to your presentation. Want to preview more design themes? Click the option *More Themes on Microsoft Office Online* to browse the Web site where you can download additional design theme templates. This site is constantly updated, so check back often for creative new offerings.

No one wants to sit and watch a presentation that is text, text, and more text! Add interest to your presentation by inserting objects such as clip art, pictures, SmartArt diagrams, charts, photographs, movies, sounds, and more. Display the Clip Art task pane and search both your computer's media Gallery and the Microsoft Office Online Gallery for the right media clip to spruce up that text-only slide.

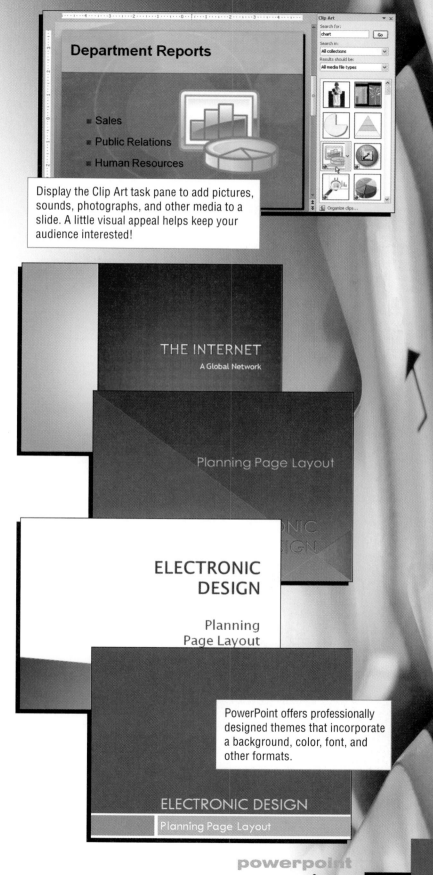

Display the Clip Art task pane to add pictures, sounds, photographs, and other media to a slide. A little visual appeal helps keep your audience interested!

PowerPoint offers professionally designed themes that incorporate a background, color, font, and other formats.

Apply custom animation effects to a presentation—such as entrance, exit, and emphasis effects—to create a visually dynamic presentation.

After adding objects such as clip art, charts, or photographs to your slides, consider adding animation effects to maintain audience interest, create focus, or signal changes in content. Microsoft PowerPoint includes built-in animation effects you can apply to a presentation. Want more control over animation? Use options in the Custom Animation task pane to further animate objects in your presentation. Apply entrance, exit, and emphasis effects; display objects one at a time or all at once; display individual elements within an object such as a SmartArt diagram or chart; and apply a "build" to text in a slide to keep your audience focused on the current topic.

Set up your slide show presentation by creating a custom show. Add or modify action buttons to control slide progression or hide slides that you do not want the audience to view. On the day you are to deliver your presentation, use the slide show features to advance slides and use the pointer options to focus attention on a slide element by drawing with a ballpoint pen, felt tip pen, or highlighter.

Get started and have fun learning to use Microsoft PowerPoint. You will soon be amazing audiences with your ability to produce effective and visually appealing presentations that help make your point!

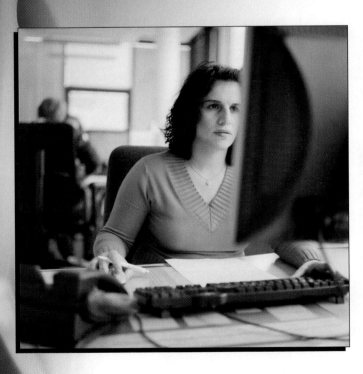

Microsoft®
PowerPoint®

Unit 1: Creating and Formatting PowerPoint Presentations

- ➤ Preparing a PowerPoint Presentation
- ➤ Modifying a Presentation and Using Help
- ➤ Formatting Slides
- ➤ Inserting Elements in Slides

Benchmark Microsoft® PowerPoint 2007

Microsoft Certified Application Specialist Skills—Unit 1

Reference No.	Skill	Pages
1	**Creating and Formatting Presentations**	
1.1	Create new presentations	
1.1.1	Create presentations from blank presentations	27-29
1.1.2	Create presentations from templates	10-11, 14-16
1.1.3	Create presentations from existing presentations	22-24
1.4	Create and change presentation elements	
1.4.1	Change presentation orientation	54-56
1.4.2	Add, change, and remove transitions between slides at the presentation level	29-32
1.4.3	Set slide size	95-97
1.5	Arrange slides	48-50
2	**Creating and Formatting Slide Content**	
2.1	Insert and format text boxes	
2.1.1	Insert and remove text boxes	120-124
2.1.2	Size text boxes	120, 122-123
2.1.3	Format text boxes	120-126
2.1.4	Select text orientation and alignment	122, 124, 128
2.1.5	Set margins	123
2.1.6	Create columns in text boxes	123-126
2.2	Manipulate text	
2.2.1	Cut, copy, and paste text	41-45
2.2.2	Apply Quick Styles from the Style Gallery	88-92
2.2.3	Format font attributes	70-74
2.2.4	Use the Format Painter to format text	74-75
2.2.5	Create and format bulleted and numbered lists	76-79, 84-88
2.2.6	Format paragraphs	76-88
2.2.7	Insert and modify WordArt	145-148
2.3	Add and link existing content to presentations	
2.3.1	Reuse slides from an existing presentation	52-53
2.3.2	Copy elements from one slide to another	41-44, 50, 129-133
3	**Working With Visual Content**	
3.3	Insert illustrations and shapes	
3.3.1	Insert pictures from file	137
3.3.2	Insert shapes	126-135
3.3.3	Insert clip art	140-144
3.3.4	Add text to shapes	127, 132
3.4	Modify illustrations	
3.4.1	Apply Quick Styles to shapes and pictures	127, 131, 135, 138
3.4.2	Add change and remove illustration effects	138, 139
3.5	Arrange illustrations and other content	
3.5.1	Size, scale, and rotate illustrations and other content	136-138, 142-144
3.5.2	Order illustrations and other content	136-138
3.5.3	Group and align illustrations and other content	134-135
3.5.4	Use gridlines and guides to arrange illustrations and other content	129-135
4	**Collaborating on and Delivering Presentations**	
4.3	Secure and share presentations	
4.3.5	Compress images	135-138
4.4	Prepare printed materials	
4.4.2	Print a presentation in various formats	19-20, 32
4.5	Prepare for and rehearse presentation delivery	
4.5.3	Use presentation tools	17-18, 21-24

Preparing a PowerPoint Presentation

PERFORMANCE OBJECTIVES

Upon successful completion of Chapter 1, you will be able to:

- Create a PowerPoint presentation with an installed template
- Open, save, run, print, close, and delete a presentation
- Plan a presentation
- Create a presentation using a theme template
- Insert slides, insert text in slides, and choose slide layouts
- Change presentation views
- Navigate and edit slides
- Create a presentation from an existing presentation
- Apply a design theme to slides in a presentation
- Prepare a presentation from a blank presentation
- Prepare a presentation in Slides/Outline pane
- Add transitions and sounds to a presentation

Tutorial 1.1
Creating, Saving, and Printing a
    Presentation
Tutorial 1.2
Organizing and Enhancing
    Presentations

During a presentation, the person doing the presenting may use visual aids to strengthen the impact of the message as well as help organize the presentation. Visual aids may include transparencies, slides, photographs, or an on-screen presentation. With Microsoft's PowerPoint program, you can easily create visual aids for a presentation and then print copies of the aids as well as run the presentation. PowerPoint is a presentation graphics program that you can use to organize and present information.

Note: Before beginning computer projects, copy to your storage medium the PowerPoint2007C1 subfolder from the PowerPoint2007 folder on the CD that accompanies this textbook. Steps on how to copy a folder are presented on the inside of the back cover of this textbook. Do this every time you start a chapter's projects.

roject **1** **Open and Run a Template Presentation**

You will open an installed template presentation, run the presentation, and then close the presentation.

Creating a PowerPoint Presentation

PowerPoint provides several methods for creating a presentation. You can create a presentation using an installed template or using a theme template and prepare a presentation from a blank presentation or from an existing presentation. The steps you follow to create a presentation will vary depending on the method you choose, but will probably follow these basic steps:

1. Open PowerPoint.
2. Choose the desired installed template or theme or open an existing presentation or start with a blank presentation.
3. Type the text for each slide, adding additional elements as needed such as graphic images.
4. If necessary, apply a design theme.
5. Save the presentation.
6. Print the presentation as slides, handouts, notes pages, or an outline.
7. Run the presentation.
8. Close the presentation.
9. Exit PowerPoint.

Understanding the PowerPoint Window

When you choose the specific type of presentation you want to create, you are presented with the PowerPoint window in the Normal view. What displays in the window will vary depending on the type of presentation you are creating. However, the PowerPoint window contains some consistent elements as shown in Figure 1.1.

Figure 1.1 PowerPoint Window

The PowerPoint window contains many elements that are similar to other Microsoft Office programs such as Word and Excel. For example, the PowerPoint window, like the Word window, contains an Office button, Quick Access toolbar, tabs, ribbon, vertical and horizontal scroll bars, and a Status bar. The PowerPoint window elements are described in Table 1.1.

Table 1.1 PowerPoint Window Elements

Feature	*Description*
Office button	Displays as a Microsoft Office logo and, when clicked, displays a list of options along with the most recently opened presentations.
Quick Access toolbar	Contains buttons for commonly used commands.
Title bar	Displays presentation name followed by the program name.
Tabs	Contains commands and features organized into groups.
Ribbon	Area containing the tabs and commands divided into groups.
Slides/Outline pane	Displays at the left side of the window with two tabs—Slides and Outline. With the Slides tab selected, slide miniatures (thumbnails) display in the pane; with the Outline tab selected, presentation contents display in the pane.
Slide pane	Displays the slide and slide contents.
Notes pane	Add notes to a presentation in this pane.
Vertical scroll bar	Display specific slides using this scroll bar.
I-beam pointer	Used to move the insertion point or to select text.
Insertion point	Indicates the location of the next character entered at the keyboard.
View area	Located toward the right side of the Status bar and contains buttons for changing the presentation view.
Status bar	Displays the slide number and number of slides, name of the applied design theme, view buttons, and the Zoom slider bar.

PowerPoint, like other Microsoft Office programs, provides enhanced ScreenTips for buttons and options. Hover the mouse pointer on a button or option and, after approximately one second, an enhanced ScreenTip displays near the button or option. The enhanced ScreenTip displays the name of the button or option, any shortcut command if one is available, and a description of the button or option.

Open a Presentation
1. Click Open button.
2. Navigate to desired folder or drive.
3. Double-click presentation.

Open an Installed Template
1. Click Office button, *New*.
2. Click *Installed Templates* option.
3. Double-click desired presentation.

Opening a Presentation

When you create and then save a presentation, you can open the presentation at the Open dialog box. Display this dialog box by clicking the Open button on the Quick Access toolbar or click the Office button and then click *Open* at the drop-down list. (If the Open button does not display on the Quick Access toolbar, click the Customize Quick Access Toolbar button located at the right side of the toolbar and then click *Open* at the drop-down list.) At the Open dialog box, navigate to the desired folder and then double-click the desired presentation in the list box. By default, PowerPoint displays the nine most recently opened presentations in the Office button drop-down list. To open one of these presentations, click the Office button and then click the desired presentation in the *Recent Documents* section. If you want a presentation to remain in the drop-down list, "pin" the presentation to the drop-down list by clicking the pin button that displays at the right side of the presentation name. This changes the dimmed gray stick pin to a green stick pin. To "unpin" the presentation, click the pin button to change it from a green pin to a gray pin.

Opening an Installed Template

Office button

Open

Microsoft provides a number of predesigned presentation templates you can view and also use as a basis for preparing your own presentation. To display the installed templates, click the Office button and then click *New* at the drop-down list. At the New Presentation dialog box, click the *Installed Templates* option in the *Templates* section. To open a template presentation, double-click the desired presentation in the *Installed Templates* list box.

Starting a Presentation

Run a Presentation
1. Click Slide Show button in view area on Status bar.
2. Click left mouse button to advance slides.

Close a Presentation
1. Click Office button.
2. Click *Close*.
OR
Press Ctrl + F4.

When you open a presentation, the presentation displays in Normal view. In this view, you can edit and customize the presentation. To run the presentation, click the Slide Show button in the view area on the Status bar or click the Slide Show tab and then click the From Beginning button in the Start Slide Show group. Navigate through slides in the presentation by clicking the left mouse button.

Closing a Presentation

To remove a presentation from the screen, close the presentation. You can close a presentation by clicking the Office button and then clicking *Close* at the drop-down list. You can also close a presentation with the keyboard shortcut Ctrl + F4. To use this shortcut, hold down the Ctrl key on the keyboard, press the F4 function key located toward the top of the keyboard, and then release the Ctrl key. If you made any changes to the presentation, you will be asked if you want to save the presentation.

Project ❶ Opening, Running, and Closing a Template Presentation

1. Open PowerPoint.
2. Click the Office button and then click *New* at the drop-down list.
3. At the New Presentation dialog box, click the *Installed Templates* option in the *Templates* section.
4. Double-click *Introducing PowerPoint 2007* in the *Installed Templates* list box.
5. Run the presentation by completing the following steps:
   a. Click the Slide Show button in the view area on the Status bar.
   b. Read the information in the first slide in the presentation and then click the left mouse button.
   c. Continue reading information in slides and clicking the left mouse button to advance slides.
   d. At the black screen with the message "End of slide show, click to exit." click the left mouse button. (This returns the presentation to Normal view.)
6. Close the presentation by clicking the Office button and then clicking *Close* at the drop-down list.

Step 3

Step 4

Step 5a

Project ❷ Create an Internet Presentation Using a Theme Template

You will use a theme template to create a presentation, insert text in slides in the presentation, choose a slide layout, insert new slides, change views, navigate through the presentation, edit text in slides, and then print the presentation.

Planning a Presentation

With PowerPoint, you can create slides for an on-screen presentation and you can print handouts of the presentation, print an outline, or print the entire presentation. When planning a presentation, first define the purpose of the presentation. Is the intent to inform? educate? sell? motivate? and/or entertain? Additionally, consider the audience who will be listening to and watching the presentation. Determine the content of the presentation and also the medium that will be used to convey the message. Will a computer be used to display the slides of a presentation or will overhead transparencies be created from the slides? Some basic guidelines to consider when preparing the content of the presentation include:

- **Determine the main purpose of the presentation.** Do not try to cover too many topics—this may strain the audience's attention or cause confusion. Identifying the main point of the presentation will help you stay focused and convey a clear message to the audience.

- **Determine the output.** Is the presentation going to be presented in PowerPoint? Will slides be used? Or will black and white or color transparencies be made for an overhead? To help decide the type of output needed, consider the availability of equipment, the size of the room where the presentation will be made, and the number of people who will be attending the presentation.

- **Show one idea per slide.** Each slide in a presentation should convey only one main idea. Too many thoughts or ideas on a slide may confuse the audience and cause you to stray from the purpose of the slide. Determine the specific message you want to convey to the audience and then outline the message to organize ideas.

- **Maintain a consistent layout.** A consistent layout and color scheme for slides in a presentation will create continuity and cohesiveness. Do not get carried away by using too many colors and too many pictures or other graphic elements.

- **Keep slides easy to read and uncluttered.** Keep slides simple and easy for the audience to read. Keep words and other items such as bullets to a minimum.

- **Determine the output needed.** Will you be providing audience members with handouts? If so, will these handouts consist of a printing of each slide? an outline of the presentation? a printing of each slide with space for taking notes?

Create a Presentation Using a Theme Template
1. Click Office button, *New*.
2. Click *Installed Themes* option.
3. Double-click desired theme.

Creating a Presentation Using a Theme Template

PowerPoint provides a variety of predesigned theme templates you can use when creating slides for a presentation. These theme templates include formatting such as color, background, fonts, and so on. You can choose a theme template at the New Presentation dialog box. To do this, click the Office button and then click *New* at the drop-down list. At the New Presentation dialog box, click *Installed Themes* in the *Templates* section and then double-click the desired theme template in the list box.

Inserting Text in Slides

When you choose a theme template at the New Presentation dialog box or start with a blank presentation, click the Design tab and then click the desired theme in the Themes group, a slide displays in the Slide pane in Normal view. The slide displays with a Title default slide layout. This layout contains placeholders for entering the slide title and the slide subtitle. To insert text in a placeholder, click the placeholder text. This moves the insertion point inside the placeholder, removes the default placeholder text, and selects the placeholder. A selected placeholder displays surrounded by a dashed border with sizing handles and a green rotation handle. Figure 1.2 displays a selected placeholder.

Figure 1.2 Selected Placeholder

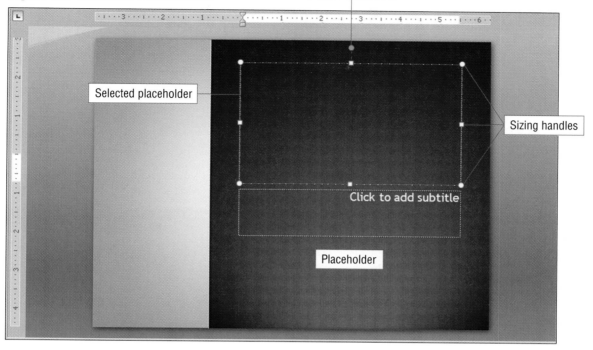

With the insertion point positioned in a placeholder, type the desired text. Edit text in a placeholder in the same manner as editing text in a Word document. Press the Backspace key to delete the character immediately left of the insertion point and press the Delete key to delete the character immediately right of the insertion point. Use the arrow keys on the keyboard to move the insertion point in the desired direction.

Choosing a Slide Layout

When you choose a theme template or a theme in a blank presentation, the slide displays in the Title Slide layout. This layout provides two placeholders for text— title text and subtitle text. You can change the slide layout with the Layout button in the Slides group in the Home tab. Click the Layout button and a drop-down list of layouts displays. Click the desired layout at the drop-down list and the layout is applied to the current slide.

Inserting a New Slide

Create a new slide in a presentation by clicking the New Slide button in the Slides group in the Home tab. By default, PowerPoint inserts a new slide with the Title and Content layout. You can choose a different slide layout for a new slide by clicking the New Slide button arrow and then clicking the desired layout at the drop-down list. You can also change the slide layout by clicking the Layout button in the Slides group in the Home tab and then clicking the desired layout at the drop-down list.

QUICK STEPS

Choose a Slide Layout
1. Click Layout button.
2. Click desired layout option in drop-down list.

Insert a New Slide
Click New Slide button.

HINT
PowerPoint includes nine built-in standard layouts.

Saving a Presentation

After creating a presentation, save it by clicking the Save button on the Quick Access toolbar or by clicking the Office button and then *Save As*. This displays the Save As dialog box. At the Save As dialog box, type a name for the presentation in the *File name* text box. Click the down-pointing arrow at the right side of the *Save in* option, click the drive containing your storage medium, and then click the Save button.

Save

Project 2a   Creating a Presentation Using a Theme Template

1. With PowerPoint open, click the Office button and then click *New* at the drop-down list.
2. At the New Presentation dialog box, click *Installed Themes* in the *Templates* section of the dialog box.
3. Scroll down the *Installed Themes* list box and then double-click *Opulent*.

4. Click in the placeholder text *CLICK TO ADD TITLE* and then type the internet (the design theme changes the text to uppercase letters).
5. Click in the placeholder text *Click to add subtitle* and then type A Global Network.
6. Click the New Slide button in the Slides group in the Home tab (this inserts a slide with the Title and Contents layout).

7. Click the placeholder text *CLICK TO ADD TITLE* and then type communications (the design theme changes the text to uppercase letters).
8. Click the placeholder text *Click to add text* and then type E-mail.
9. Press the Enter key (this moves the insertion point to the next line and inserts a bullet) and then type Chat Rooms.
10. Press the Enter key and then type Instant Messaging.
11. Press the Enter key and then type Blogs.
12. Press the Enter key and then type Electronic Bulletin Boards.

13. Click the New Slide button in the Slides group in the Home tab.
14. Click the placeholder text *CLICK TO ADD TITLE* and then type entertainment.
15. Click the placeholder text *Click to add text* and then type Online Games.
16. Press the Enter key and then type Online Gambling.
17. Press the Enter key and then type Music.
18. Press the Enter key and then type Video.
19. Click the New Slide button arrow and then click the Title Slide layout.

20. Click the placeholder text *CLICK TO ADD TITLE* and then type internet issues.
21. Click the placeholder text *Click to add subtitle* and then type Community and Policy Issues.
22. Click the New Slide button.
23. Click the placeholder text *CLICK TO ADD TITLE* and then type community issues.
24. Click the placeholder text *Click to add text* and then type Flaming.
25. Press the Enter key and then type Netiquette.
26. Press the Enter key and then type Moderated Environments.
27. Click the New Slide button in the Slides group in the Home tab.
28. Click the placeholder text *CLICK TO ADD TITLE* and then type policy issues.
29. Click the placeholder text *Click to add text* and then type Privacy Issues.
30. Press the Enter key and then type Security Protection.
31. Press the Enter key and then type Viruses.
32. Press the Enter key and then type Copyright Infringement.
33. Click in the Slide pane but outside the slide. (This deselects the placeholder.)
34. Save the presentation by completing the following steps:
    a. Click the Save button on the Quick Access toolbar.
    b. At the Save As dialog box type PP_C1_P2 (for PowerPoint, Chapter 1, Project 2).
    c. Click the down-pointing arrow at the right side of the *Save in* option and then click the drive containing your storage medium.
    d. Click the Save button.

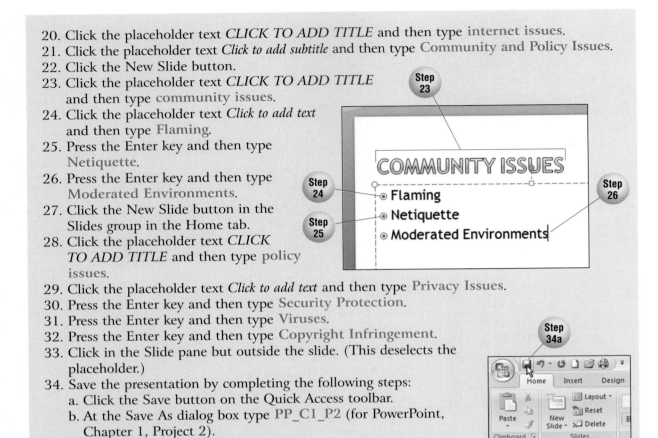

HINT

In Normal view, you can increase or decrease the size of the Slides/Outline pane and the Notes pane.

Changing Views

PowerPoint provides a variety of viewing options for a presentation. You can change the view with buttons in the view area on the Status bar or with options in the Presentation Views group in the View tab. The viewing choices include:

- **Normal view:** This is the default view and displays three panes—Slides/Outline, Slide, and Notes. With these three panes, you can work with all features in one place. This view is also referred to as tri-pane view.
- **Slide Sorter view:** Choosing the Slide Sorter view displays all slides in the presentation in slide miniatures. In this view, you can easily add, move, rearrange, and delete slides.
- **Notes Page view:** Change to the Notes Page view and an individual slide displays on a page with any added notes displayed below the slide.
- **Slide Show view:** Use the Slide Show view to run a presentation. When you choose this view, the slide fills the entire screen.

The view area on the Status bar contains three buttons for changing the view—Normal, Slide Sorter, and Slide Show with the active button displaying with a light orange background. You can also change views with buttons in the View tab. The Presentation Views group in the View tab contains a number of buttons for changing views. Four buttons in the group include the Normal, Slide Sorter, Notes Page, and Slide Show button. Click the Notes Page button and the active slide displays along with a space below the slide for inserting text. Click the text *Click to add text* that displays in the box below the slide and then type the desired note. When running the presentation, you can display any note attached to the slide.

Normal

Slide Sorter

Slide Show

Navigating in a Presentation

In the Normal view, change slides by clicking the Previous Slide or Next Slide buttons located at the bottom of the vertical scroll bar. You can also change to a different slide using the mouse pointer on the vertical scroll bar. To do this, position the mouse pointer on the scroll box on the vertical scroll bar, hold down the left mouse button, drag up or down until a box displays with the desired slide number, and then release the button.

Previous   Next
Slide   Slide

You can also use the keyboard to display slides in a presentation. In Normal view, press the Down Arrow or Page Down key to display the next slide or press the Up Arrow or Page Up key to display the previous slide in the presentation. Press the Home key to display the first slide in the presentation and press End to display the last slide in the presentation. Navigate in the Slides/Outline pane by clicking the desired slide thumbnail. Navigate in the Slide Sorter view by clicking the desired slide or using the arrow keys on the keyboard.

Project **2b** **Navigating and Editing Slides in a Presentation**

1. With **PP_C1_P2.pptx** open, navigate in the presentation by completing the following steps:
   a. Make sure that a placeholder in the slide is not selected.
   b. Press the Home key to display Slide 1 in the Slide pane.
   c. Click the Next Slide button located toward the bottom of the vertical scroll bar.
   d. Press the End key to display the last slide in the Slide pane.
   e. Click the Slide Sorter button in the view area on the Status bar.

Step 1c

Step 1e

   f. Click Slide 1. (Notice that the active slide displays with a dark orange border.)
   g. Double-click Slide 5. (This closes Slide Sorter view and displays the presentation in Normal view with Slide 5 active.)
2. Insert text in slides by completing the following steps:
   a. Click on any character in the bulleted text. (This selects the placeholder.)
   b. Move the insertion point so it is positioned immediately right of *Flaming*.

c. Press the Enter key and then type E-mail Pointers.

Step 2c

Step 2d

  d. Click Slide 3 in the Slides/Outline pane. (This displays Slide 3 in the Slide pane.)
  e. Click on any character in the bulleted text.
  f. Move the insertion point so it is positioned immediately right of *Video*.
  g. Press the Enter key and then type Travel.
3. Type a note in the Notes pane by completing the following steps:
  a. Click Slide 6 in the Slides/Outline pane.
  b. Click the text *Click to add notes* that displays in the Notes pane.
  c. Type Discuss the Digital Millennium Copyright Act of 1998.

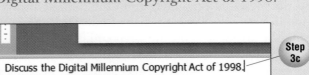

Step 3c

  d. Display the slide in Notes Page view by clicking the View tab and then clicking the Notes Page button in the Presentation Views group. (Notice the note you typed displays below the slide in this view.)

Step 3d

  e. Return to Normal view by clicking the Normal button in the view area on the Status bar.
  f. Press the Home key to make Slide 1 the active slide.
4. Save the presentation by clicking the Save button on the Quick Access toolbar.

Printing a Presentation

You can print a PowerPoint presentation in a variety of formats. You can print each slide on a separate piece of paper; print each slide at the top of the page, leaving the bottom of the page for notes; print up to nine slides or a specific number of slides on a single piece of paper; or print the slide titles and topics in outline form. Use the *Print what* option at the Print dialog box, shown in Figure 1.3, to specify what you want printed. To display the Print dialog box, click the Office button and then click *Print* at the drop-down list. At the Print dialog box, click the down-pointing arrow at the right side of the *Print what* option box and then click the desired printing format.

To print specific slides in a presentation, click the *Slides* option in the *Print range* section and then type the slide number in the *Slides* text box. Print a range of slides using the hyphen and print specific slides using a comma. For example, to print Slides 2 through 6, you would type *2-6* in the *Slides* text box. To print Slides 1, 3 and 7, you would type *1,3,7*. You can combine a hyphen and comma. For example, to print Slides 1 through 4 and Slide 8, you would type *1-4,8*.

If you want to send the presentation directly to the printer, click the Quick Print button on the Quick Access toolbar. (If this button does not display on the toolbar, click the Customize Quick Access Toolbar button located at the right side of the toolbar and then click *Quick Print* at the drop-down list.)

Print a Presentation
1. Click Office button, *Print*.
2. Click down-pointing arrow at right of *Print what* option.
3. Click desired printing option.
4. Click OK.

HINT
Printing a hard copy of your presentation and distributing it to your audience helps reinforce your message.

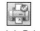
Quick Print

Figure 1.3 Print Dialog Box

Click the *Slides* option and then type the specific slide numbers in the *Slides* text box.

Click this down-pointing arrow to display a list of printing options.

Project 2c Printing a Presentation

1. With **PP_C1_P2.pptx** open, print the presentation as a handout with six slides per page by completing the following steps:
   a. Click the Office button and then click *Print* at the drop-down list.
   b. At the Print dialog box, click the down-pointing arrow at the right side of the *Print what* option and then click *Handouts* at the drop-down list.
   c. Make sure the number *6* displays in the *Slides per page* text box in the *Handouts* section of the dialog box.
   d. Click OK.

Step 1b

Step 1c

Step 1d

2. Print Slide 6 as a notes page by completing the following steps:
   a. Click the Office button and then click *Print* at the drop-down list.
   b. At the Print dialog box, click *Slides* in the *Print range* section.
   c. Type *6* in the *Slides* text box.
   d. Click the down-pointing arrow at the right side of the *Print what* option and then click *Notes Pages* at the drop-down list.
   e. Click OK.

Step 2c

Step 2b

Step 2d

3. Print Slides 1 through 3 and Slide 5 by completing the following steps:
   a. Click the Office button and then click *Print* at the drop-down list.
   b. At the Print dialog box, click *Slides* in the *Print range* section.
   c. Type *1-3,5* in the *Slides* text box.
   d. Change the *Print what* option to *Slides*.
   e. Click OK.

Step 3b

Step 3c

4. Close the presentation by clicking the Office button and then clicking *Close* at the drop-down list.

Project 3 Create a Planning Presentation from an Existing Presentation

You will create a presentation from an existing presentation, apply a design theme to the presentation, run the presentation, and then delete the presentation.

Running a Slide Show

As you learned earlier in this chapter, run a presentation by clicking the Slide Show button in the view area on the Status bar or by clicking the Slide Show tab and then clicking the From Beginning button in the Start Slide Show group. This group also contains a From Current Slide button. Use this button to begin running the slide show with the currently active slide rather than the first slide in the presentation.

PowerPoint offers a wide variety of options for navigating through slides in a presentation. Figure 1.4 displays the Slide Show Help window that contains keyboard commands for running a presentation.

Figure 1.4 Slide Show Help Menu

In addition to the methods described in the Slide Show Help window, you can also navigate in a presentation using buttons on the Slide Show toolbar shown in Figure 1.5. To display this toolbar, run the presentation, and then move the mouse pointer. Click the right arrow button on the toolbar to display the next slide and click the left arrow button to display the previous slide. Click the slide icon button and a pop-up list displays with the following options: *Next, Previous, Last Viewed, Go to Slide, Custom Show, Screen, Help, Pause,* and *End Show*. Use these options to navigate to a particular slide in the presentation, display the Slide Show Help window, and pause or end the show. Click the pen button and a pop-up list displays with the following options: *Arrow, Ballpoint Pen, Felt Tip Pen, Highlighter, Ink Color, Eraser, Erase All Ink on Slide,* and *Arrow Options*.

QUICK STEPS

Use Pen/Highlighter during Presentation
1. Run presentation.
2. Display desired slide.
3. Click pen button on Slide Show toolbar.
4. Click pen or highlighter option.
5. Drag to draw line or highlight text.

HINT

If you use the pen or highlighter on a slide when running a presentation, choose an ink color that the audience can see easily.

Figure 1.5 Slide Show Toolbar

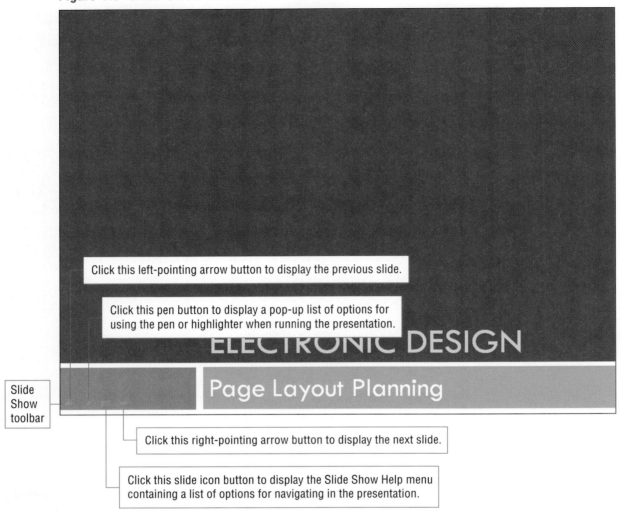

Click this left-pointing arrow button to display the previous slide.

Click this pen button to display a pop-up list of options for using the pen or highlighter when running the presentation.

ELECTRONIC DESIGN

Page Layout Planning

Slide
Show
toolbar

Click this right-pointing arrow button to display the next slide.

Click this slide icon button to display the Slide Show Help menu containing a list of options for navigating in the presentation.

When running a presentation, the mouse pointer is set, by default, to be hidden automatically after three seconds of inactivity. The mouse pointer will appear again when you move the mouse. You can change this default setting by clicking the pen button on the Slide Show toolbar, pointing to *Arrow Options*, and then clicking *Visible* if you want the mouse pointer always visible or *Hidden* if you do not want the mouse to display at all as you run the presentation. The *Automatic* option is the default setting.

Create a Presentation from an Existing Presentation
1. Click Office button, *New.*
2. Click *New from existing* option.
3. Double-click desired presentation.
4. Edit presentation.
5. Save presentation with new name.

Creating a Presentation from an Existing Presentation

You can create a presentation from an installed template, an installed theme, a blank presentation, or from an existing presentation. To create a presentation from an existing presentation, click the Office button and then click *New* at the drop-down list. At the New Presentation dialog box, click the *New from existing* option in the *Templates* section. This displays the New from Existing Presentation dialog box with options similar to the Open dialog box. Double-click the desired presentation in the dialog box list box. This opens a new presentation based on the existing presentation and the Title bar displays *Presentation* followed by a number. Edit the presentation and then save the presentation with a new name.

Project 3a   Creating and Running a Presentation from an Existing Presentation

1. Click the Office button and then click *New* at the drop-down list.
2. At the New Presentation dialog box, click the *New from existing* option in the *Templates* section.
3. At the New from Existing Presentation dialog box, navigate to the PowerPoint2007C1 folder on your storage medium and then double-click ***PlanningPresentation.pptx***.
4. Save the presentation by completing the following steps:
   a. Click the Save button on the Quick Access toolbar.
   b. At the Save As dialog box, make sure the PowerPoint2007C1 folder on your storage medium is active and then type PP_C1_P3 in the *File name* text box.
   c. Press Enter or click the Save button.
5. Run the presentation by completing the following steps:
   a. Click the Slide Show button in the view area on the Status bar.
   b. When Slide 1 fills the screen, move the mouse to display the Slide Show toolbar. (This toolbar displays in a dimmed manner in the lower left corner of the slide.)
   c. Click the button containing the right arrow. (This displays the next slide.)
   d. Continue clicking the button containing the right arrow until a black screen displays.
   e. Click the left mouse button. (This displays the presentation in Normal view.)

Step 5c

6. Run the presentation from the current slide and use the pen and highlighter to emphasize specific words by completing the following steps:
   a. Click Slide 2 in the Slides/Outline pane. (This makes Slide 2 active.)
   b. Click the Slide Show tab.
   c. Click the From Current Slide button in the Start Slide Show group.

Step 6b

Step 6c

   d. With Slide 2 active, use the felt tip pen to underline a word by completing the following steps:
      1) Move the mouse to display the Slide Show toolbar.
      2) Click the pen button on the Slide Show toolbar and then click *Felt Tip Pen* at the pop-up list. (This changes the mouse pointer to a small circle.)

Step 6d2

3) Using the mouse, draw a circle around the text *STEP 1*.
4) Draw a line below the word *identify*.
5) Click the pen button on the Slide Show toolbar and then click *Arrow* at the pop-up list. (This returns the mouse pointer to an arrow.)

e. Erase the pen markings by clicking the pen button on the Slide Show toolbar and then clicking *Erase All Ink on Slide* at the pop-up list.

f. Click the pen button on the Slide Show toolbar and then click *Ballpoint Pen* at the pop-up list.

g. Change the color of the ink by clicking the pen button, pointing to *Ink Color*, and then clicking the purple color (first option from the right in the bottom row).

h. Draw a circle around *STEP 1*.

i. Click the pen button on the Slide Show toolbar and then click *Arrow* at the pop-up list.

j. Click the left mouse button to display the next slide (Slide 3).

k. Click the pen button in the Slide Show toolbar and then click *Highlighter* at the pop-up list.

l. Drag through the word *target* to highlight it.

m. Click the button in the Slide Show toolbar containing the right arrow. (This displays Slide 4.)

n. Drag through the words *best format* to highlight them.

o. Click the pen button on the Slide Show toolbar and then click *Arrow* at the pop-up list.

7. Continue clicking the left mouse button to run the presentation.

8. At the black screen, click the left mouse button.

9. At the message asking if you want to keep your ink annotations, click the Discard button.

10. Save **PP_C1_P3.pptx**.

Applying a Design Theme

As you learned, PowerPoint provides a variety of predesigned theme templates you can use when creating slides for a presentation. You can choose a theme template at the New Presentation dialog box or with options in the Themes group in the Design tab. Click the Design tab and theme thumbnails display in the Themes group. Click one of these themes to apply it to the current presentation. To display additional themes, click the More button that displays at the right side of the visible themes. You can also click the up-pointing or down-pointing arrow at the right side of the visible themes to scroll through the list. Hover your mouse pointer over a theme and the active slide in the presentation displays with the theme formatting applied. This is an example of the *live preview* feature, which allows you to see how theme formatting affects your presentation.

Themes similar to the ones available in PowerPoint are also available in Word, Excel, and Outlook. When you hover the mouse pointer over a theme thumbnail, a ScreenTip displays (after approximately a second) containing the theme name. Theme names in PowerPoint are similar in Word, Excel, and Outlook and apply similar formatting. With the availability of the themes across these applications, you can "brand" your business files such as documents, workbooks, and presentations with a consistent and uniform appearance.

QUICK STEPS

Apply a Design Theme
1. Click Design tab.
2. Click desired theme in Themes group.

HINT
Design themes were designed by professional graphic artists who understand the use of color, space, and design.

Project 3b Applying Design Themes

1. With **PP_C1_P3.pptx** open, make Slide 1 active, and make sure the presentation displays in Normal view.
2. Apply a different design theme to the presentation by completing the following steps:
   a. Click the Design tab.
   b. Hover the mouse pointer over the third theme thumbnail in the Themes group and notice the theme formatting applied to the slide in the Slide pane.
   c. Hover the mouse pointer over the remaining visible theme thumbnails and notice the formatting applied to the active slide.
   d. Click the *Civic* theme.

3. Run the presentation and notice the formatting applied by the theme.
4. After running the presentation, you decide you do not like the formatting applied by the theme. Click the *Flow* theme in the Themes group.
5. Run the presentation and notice the formatting applied by the theme.

6. With the presentation in Normal view, apply a different design theme by completing the following steps:
   a. Click the More button that displays at the right side of the theme thumbnails.
   b. Click *Verve* at the drop-down gallery.

Step 6a

7. Run the presentation.
8. Print the presentation as a handout by completing the following steps:
   a. Click the Office button and then click *Print* at the drop-down list.
   b. At the Print dialog box, click the down-pointing arrow at the right side of the *Print what* option and then click *Handouts* at the drop-down list.
   c. Make sure the number *6* displays in the *Slides per page* text box in the *Handouts* section of the dialog box.
   d. Click OK.
9. Save and then close **PP_C1_P3.pptx**.

QUICK STEPS

Delete a Presentation
1. Click Office button, *Open*.
2. Navigate to desired folder or drive.
3. Click the presentation.
4. Click Delete button.
5. Click Yes.

Deleting a Presentation

File management tasks in PowerPoint can be performed at the Open or Save As dialog box. To delete a PowerPoint presentation (presentation must be closed), display the Open dialog box, click the presentation you want deleted, and then click the Delete button on the dialog box toolbar. At the message asking if you are sure you want to delete the presentation, click the Yes button.

Project 3c Deleting PowerPoint Presentation

1. Click the Open button on the Quick Access toolbar to display the Open dialog box. (If the Open button does not display on the Quick Access toolbar, click the Customize Quick Access Toolbar button located at the right side of the toolbar and then click *Open* at the drop-down list.)
2. At the Open dialog box, make sure the PowerPoint2007C1 folder on your storage medium is the active folder, and then click ***PlanningPresentation.pptx*** in the list box.
3. Click the Delete button on the dialog box toolbar.

Step 2   Step 3

4. At the message asking if you are sure you want to delete the presentation, click Yes.
5. Click the Cancel button to close the Open dialog box.

Project ④ Create a Technology Presentation in the Slides/Outline Pane

You will create a computer technology presentation in the Slides/Outline pane with the Outline tab selected, add and remove transitions and sounds to the presentation, and set up the presentation to advance slides automatically after a specified amount of time.

Preparing a Presentation from a Blank Presentation

When you first open PowerPoint, a blank presentation displays in which you can enter text in slides. You can also display a blank presentation by clicking the Office button and pointing to *New*. At the New Presentation dialog box, click the *Blank Presentation* option in the *Blank and recent* section and then click the Create button that displays in the lower right corner of the dialog box. You can also double-click *Blank Presentation*.

Prepare a Presentation from a Blank Presentation
1. Click Office button, *New*.
2. Click *Blank Presentation* option.
3. Click Create button.

Preparing a Presentation in the Slides/Outline Pane

In Normal view, you can enter text in a slide in the Slide pane and you can also enter text in a presentation in the Slides/Outline pane with the Outline tab selected. To create a slide in the Outline/Slides pane, click the Outline tab, click in the pane, and then type the text. Press the Tab key to move the insertion point to the next tab stop. This moves the insertion point and also changes the formatting. The formatting will vary depending on the theme you chose. Press Shift + Tab to move the insertion point to the previous tab stop and change the formatting. Moving the insertion point back to the left margin will begin another slide. Slides are numbered at the left side of the screen and are followed by a slide icon.

Project ④a   Preparing a Presentation in the Slides/Outline Pane

1. At a blank screen, click the Office button and then click *New* at the drop-down list.
2. At the New Presentation dialog box, double-click the *Blank Presentation* option in the *Blank and recent* section.
3. At the blank presentation, click the Outline tab in the Slides/Outline pane.

Step 3

4. Click immediately right of the Slide 1 icon in the Slides/Outline pane, type the first slide title shown in Figure 1.6 *(Computer Technology)*, and then press Enter.
5. Type the second slide title shown in Figure 1.6 *(The Motherboard)* and then press Enter.
6. Press the Tab key, type the text after the first bullet in Figure 1.6 *(Buses)*, and then press Enter.
7. Continue typing the text as it displays in Figure 1.6. Press the Tab key to move the insertion point to the next tab stop or press Shift + Tab to move the insertion point back to a previous tab stop.

8. After typing all of the information as shown in Figure 1.6, click the Slides tab in the Slides/Outline tab.
9. Click Slide 1 in the Slides/Outline pane. (This displays Slide 1 in the Slide pane.)
10. Apply a design theme by completing the following steps:
    a. Click the Design tab.
    b. Click the More button that displays at the right side of the design theme thumbnails.
    c. Click *Module* at the drop-down gallery.
11. Save the presentation with Save As and name it **PP_C1_P4**.
12. Run the presentation.

Figure 1.6 Project 4a

1 Computer Technology
2 The Motherboard
   - Buses
   - System clock
   - Microprocessor
   - ROM and RAM
   - Power supply
   - Ports
   - Expansion slots
3 Input Devices
   - Keyboard
   - Mouse
   - Trackball
   - Touch pad and touch screen
   - Pen and tablet
   - Joystick
   - Scanner
4 Output Devices
   - Monitor
   - Printer
     - Dot matrix
     - Laser
     - Ink jet
   - Speakers

Adding Transition and Sound Effects

You can apply interesting transitions and sounds to a presentation. A transition is how one slide is removed from the screen during a presentation and the next slide is displayed. You can apply transitions such as fades, wipes, push, cover, stripes, and bar. To add transitions and sounds, open a presentation, and then click the Animations tab. This displays transition buttons and options as shown in Figure 1.7.

Figure 1.7 Animations Tab

Transitions and sounds apply by default to the active slide. If you want transitions and sound to affect all slides, click the Apply To All button in the Transition to This Slide group. In Slide Sorter view, you can select all slides by pressing Ctrl + A (or by clicking the Home tab, clicking the Select button, and then clicking *Select All* at the drop-down list) and then applying the desired transition and/or sound.

QUICK STEPS

Apply Transition to Slides
1. Click Animations tab.
2. Click desired transition in Transition to This Slide group.
3. Click Apply To All button.

Apply Sound to Slides
1. Click Animations tab.
2. Click down-pointing arrow at right of *Transition Sound* option.
3. Click desired sound.
4. Click Apply To All button.

HINT

Make a presentation more appealing by adding effects such as transitions and sounds.

Adding Transitions

To add a transition, click a transition thumbnail in the Transition to This Slide group in the Animations tab. Hover the mouse pointer over a transition thumbnail and the transition displays in the slide in the Slide pane. Use the down-pointing and up-pointing arrows at the right side of the transition thumbnails to display additional transitions. Click the More button that displays at the right side of the visible transitions and a drop-down gallery displays with additional transition options. Use the Transition Speed option to specify the speed slides transition when running the presentation. Click the down-pointing arrow at the right side of the Transition Speed option box and you can choose *Slow*, *Medium*, or *Fast*.

When you apply a transition to slides in a presentation, animation icons display below the slides in the Slides/Outline pane and in Slide Sorter view. Click an animation icon for a particular slide and the slide will display the transition effect.

Adding Sounds

As a slide is removed from the screen and another slide is displayed, you can add a sound. To add a sound, click the down-pointing arrow at the right side of the *Transition Sound* option box and then click the desired sound at the drop-down gallery. Hover your mouse pointer over a sound in the list box and you can hear the sound.

Removing Transitions and Sounds

You can remove a transition and sound from specific slides or from all slides in a presentation. To remove a transition, click the More button that displays at the right side of the transition thumbnails and then click the *No Transition* option at the drop-down gallery. To remove transitions from all slides, click the Apply To All button in the Apply to This Slide group. To remove sound from a slide, click the down-pointing arrow at the right side of the *Transition Sound* option and then click *[No Sound]* at the drop-down gallery. To remove sound from all slides, click the Apply To All button.

1. With **PP_C1_P4.pptx** open, click the Animations tab.
2. Hover the mouse pointer over each of the transition thumbnails (except the first one) and notice how the transition displays in the slide in the Slide pane.
3. Apply transitions and sound to all slides in the presentation by completing the following steps:

   a. Click the More button at the right side of the transition thumbnails and then click the second option from the left in the fourth row in the *Wipes* section *(Wheel Clockwise, 8 Spokes).*

   b. Click the down-pointing arrow at the right side of the *Transition Speed* option box and then click *Slow* at the drop-down list.

   c. Click the down-pointing arrow at the right side of the *Transition Sound* option box in the Transition to This Slide group and then click *Chime* at the drop-down gallery.

   d. Click the Apply To All button in the Transition to This Slide group.
4. Run the presentation. (Notice the transitions and sounds as you move from slide to slide.)
5. With the presentation in Normal view and the Animations tab active, remove the transitions and sound by completing the following steps:

   a. Click the More button at the right side of the transition thumbnails and then click *No Transition* at the drop-down gallery.

   b. Click the down-pointing arrow at the right side of the *Transition Sound* option box and then click *[No Sound]* at the drop-down gallery.

   c. Click the Apply To All button.
6. Apply transitions and sounds to specific slides by completing the following steps:

   a. Make sure the presentation displays in Normal view.

   b. Click Slide 1 in the Slides/Outline pane.

   c. Hold down the Shift key and then click Slide 2. (Slides 1 and 2 will display with orange backgrounds).

d. Click the More button at the right side of the transition thumbnails and then click a transition of your choosing.

e. Click the down-pointing arrow at the right side of the *Transition Sound* option box and then click a sound of your choosing.

f. Click Slide 3 in the Slides/Outline pane.

g. Hold down the Shift key and then click Slide 4.

h. Click the More button at the right side of the transition thumbnails and then click a transition of your choosing.

i. Click the down-pointing arrow at the right side of the *Transition Sound* option box and then click a sound of your choosing.

7. Run the presentation from the beginning.

8. Remove the transitions and sounds from all slides. (Refer to Step 5.)

9. Save **PP_C1_P4.pptx**.

QUICK STEPS

Advance Slides Automatically

1. Click Animations tab.
2. Click *Automatically after* check box.
3. Insert desired number of seconds in text box.
4. Click Apply To All button.

Advancing Slides Automatically

You can advance slides in a slide show after a specific number of seconds with options in the Transition to This Slide group in the Animations tab. To advance slides automatically, click in the *Automatically after* check box and then insert the desired number of seconds in the text box. You can select the current time in the text box and then type the desired time or click the up- or down-pointing arrow to increase or decrease the time. If you want the transition time to affect all slides in the presentation, click the Apply To All button. In Slide Sorter view, the transition time displays below each affected slide.

Project 4c Advancing Slides Automatically

1. With **PP_C1_P4.pptx** open, make sure the Animations tab is active.

2. Click in the *Automatically After* check box in the Apply to This Slide group to insert a check mark.

3. Click in the *On Mouse Click* check box to remove the check mark.

4. Click the up-pointing arrow at the right side of the *Automatically After* option box until *00:04* displays in the box.

5. Click the Apply To All button.

6. Run the presentation. (Each slide will advance automatically after four seconds.)

7. At the black screen, click the left mouse button.

8. Print the presentation as an outline by completing the following steps:

a. Click the Office button and then click *Print* at the drop-down list.

b. At the Print dialog box, click the down-pointing arrow at the right side of the *Print what* option and then click *Outline View* at the drop-down list.

c. Click OK.

9. Print the presentation as a handout with six slides per page.

10. Save and then close **PP_C1_P4.pptx**.

CHAPTER summary

- PowerPoint is a software program you can use to create slides for an on-screen presentation.

- Open a presentation at the Open dialog box. Display this dialog box by clicking the Open button on the Quick Access toolbar or by clicking the Office button and then clicking *Open*. The Office button drop-down list displays the nine recently opened presentations.

- Predesigned presentation templates are available at the New Presentation dialog box. Display this dialog box by clicking the Office button and then clicking *New*.

- Start running a presentation by clicking the Slide Show button in the view area on the Status bar or by clicking the View tab and then clicking the From Beginning button.

- Close a presentation by clicking the Office button and then clicking *Close* or with the keyboard shortcut, Ctrl + F4.

- Before creating a presentation in PowerPoint, plan the presentation by defining the purpose and determining the content and medium.

- You can use a predesigned theme template to create a presentation. A theme template provides slides with formatting such as color, background elements, and fonts.

- To insert text in a slide, click the desired placeholder and then type text.

- A slide layout provides placeholders for specific data in a slide. Choose a slide layout by clicking the Layout button in the Slides group in the Home tab.

- Insert a new slide in a presentation with the Title and Content layout by clicking the New Slide button in the Slides group in the Home tab. Insert a new slide with a specific layout by clicking the New Slide button arrow and then clicking the desired layout at the drop-down list.

- Save a presentation by clicking the Save button on the Quick Access toolbar or clicking the Office button and then clicking *Save As*. At the Save As dialog box, type a name for the presentation.

- View a presentation in one of the following four views: Normal view, which is the default and displays three panes—Slides/Outline, Slide, and Notes; Slide Sorter view, which displays all slides in the presentation in slide miniatures; Notes Page view, which displays an individual slide with any added notes displayed below the slide; and Slide Show view, which runs the presentation.

- Navigate to various slides in a presentation using the mouse and/or keyboard. You can use the Previous Slide and Next Slide buttons located at the bottom of the vertical scroll bar, the scroll box on the vertical scroll bar, arrow keys on the keyboard, and the Page Up and Page Down buttons on the keyboard.

- With options at the Print dialog box, you can print presentations with each slide on a separate piece of paper; each slide at the top of the page, leaving room for notes; all or a specific number of slides on a single piece of paper; or slide titles and topics in outline form.

- The Slide Show toolbar contains buttons and options for running a presentation. You can navigate to slides, make ink notations on slides, and display a Help menu. Click the slide show icon on the toolbar and then click *Help* and the Slide Show Help menu displays with options for using the keyboard to navigate in a presentation.
- Apply a design theme to a presentation by clicking the Design tab and then clicking the desired theme in the Themes group. Click the More button to display additional themes.
- Delete a presentation at the Open dialog box by clicking the presentation file name and then clicking the Delete button on the dialog box toolbar.
- At the New Presentation dialog box you can choose to prepare a presentation from an existing presentation or a blank presentation.
- You can type text in a slide in the Slide pane or in the Slides/Outline pane with the Outline tab selected.
- Enhance a presentation by adding transitions (how one slide is removed from the screen and replaced with the next slide) and sound. Add transitions and sound to a presentation with options in the Transition to This Slide group in the Animations tab.
- Advance slides automatically in a slide show by removing the check mark from the *On Mouse Click* check box in the Animations tab, inserting a check mark in the *Automatically After* check box, and then specifying the desired time in the time option box.
- Click the Apply To All button to apply transitions, sounds, and/or time settings to all slides in a presentation.

COMMANDS review

FEATURE	RIBBON TAB, GROUP	BUTTON	QUICK ACCESS TOOLBAR	OFFICE BUTTON DROP-DOWN LIST	KEYBOARD SHORTCUT
Open dialog box				Open	Ctrl + O
New Presentation dialog box				New	
Run presentation	Slide Show, Start Slide Show				F5
Close presentation				Close	Ctrl + F4
Slide layout	Home, Slides	Layout			
New slide	Home, Slides				Ctrl + M
Save As dialog box				Save As	Ctrl + S
Normal view	View, Presentation Views				
Slide Sorter view	View, Presentation Views				
Notes page	View, Presentation Views				
Print dialog box				Print	Ctrl + P
Design theme	Design, Themes				
Transition	Animation, Transition to This Slide				
Sound	Animation, Transition to This Slide	Transition Sound: [No Sound]			
Transition speed	Animation, Transition to this Slide	Transition Speed: Fast			

CONCEPTS check

Test Your Knowledge

Completion: In the space provided at the right, indicate the correct term, command, or number.

1. Click this button to display a list of options along with the most recently opened presentations. _____

2. This toolbar contains buttons for commonly used commands. _____

3. This area contains the tabs and commands divided into groups. _____

4. Display installed templates in this dialog box. _____

5. This is the keyboard shortcut to close a presentation. _____

6. Apply a theme to a presentation by clicking this tab and then clicking the desired theme in the Themes group. _____

7. Insert a new slide by clicking the New Slide button in this group in the Home tab. _____

8. Change to this view to view displays of all slides in the presentation in slide miniatures. _____

9. This is the default view and displays three panes. _____

10. The Previous Slide or Next Slide buttons display in this location. _____

11. To print six slides on a page, change the *Print what* option to this. _____

12. To run a presentation beginning with Slide 1, click this button in the Slide Show tab. _____

13. In Normal view, you can enter text in a slide in this pane or in the Slides/Outline pane with the Outline tab selected. _____

14. To add a transition, click a transition in the Transition to This Slide group in this tab. _____

15. When you apply a transition to slides in a presentation, these display below the slides in the Slides/Outline pane. _____

16. To advance slides automatically, insert a check mark in this option and then insert the desired number of seconds. _____

SKILLS check

Demonstrate Your Proficiency

1 CREATE A DEDUCTIBLE INCOME EXCEPTIONS PRESENTATION

1. Create a presentation with the text shown in Figure 1.8 by completing the following steps:
   a. With PowerPoint open, click the Office button and then click *New*.
   b. At the New Presentation dialog box, click the *Installed Themes* option, and then double-click *Paper* in the list box. (You may need to scroll down the list to display this theme.)
   c. Create slides with the text shown in Figure 1.8. Choose the *Title Slide* layout when inserting new slides.
2. Save the completed presentation in the PowerPoint2007C1 folder on your storage medium and name the presentation **PP_C1_A1**.
3. Apply the *Blinds Vertical* transition (second option from left in the *Stripes and Bars* row) to all slides in the presentation.
4. Change the transition speed to *Medium*.
5. Apply the *Laser* sound to all slides in the presentation.
6. Run the presentation.
7. Print the presentation as a handout with six slides per page.
8. Save and then close **PP_C1_A1.pptx**.

Figure 1.8 Assessment 1

Slide 1	Title	=	DEDUCTIBLE INCOME
	Subtitle	=	Exceptions to Deductible Income
Slide 2	Title	=	EXCEPTION 1
	Subtitle	=	Any cost of living increase if increase becomes effective while disabled
Slide 3	Title	=	EXCEPTION 2
	Subtitle	=	Reimbursement for hospital, medical, or surgical expense
Slide 4	Title	=	EXCEPTION 3
	Subtitle	=	Reasonable attorney's fees incurred in connection with a claim for deductible income
Slide 5	Title	=	EXCEPTION 4
	Subtitle	=	Benefits from any individual disability insurance policy
Slide 6	Title	=	EXCEPTION 5
	Subtitle	=	Group credit or mortgage disability insurance benefits

2 CREATE A PRESENTATION ON PREPARING A COMPANY NEWSLETTER PRESENTATION

1. At the blank screen, click the Office button and then click *New*.
2. At the New Presentation dialog box, double-click the *Blank Presentation* option in the *Blank and recent* section.
3. Create slides with the text shown in Figure 1.9.
4. Apply a design theme of your choosing.
5. Run the presentation.
6. Print the presentation as a handout with six slides per page.
7. Make the following changes to the presentation:
   a. Apply a different design theme.
   b. Add a transition of your choosing to all slides.
   c. Add a sound of your choosing to all slides.
   d. Specify that all slides advance automatically after five seconds.
8. Run the presentation.
9. Save the presentation and name it **PP_C1_A2**.
10. Close **PP_C1_A2.pptx**.

Figure 1.9 Assessment 2

Slide 1   Title   =   PREPARING A COMPANY NEWSLETTER
             Subtitle =   Planning and Designing the Layout

Slide 2   Title   =   Planning a Newsletter
             Bullets =
- If a scanner is available, use pictures of different people from your organization in each issue.
- Distribute contributor sheets soliciting information from employees.
- Keep the focus of the newsletter on issues of interest to employees.

Slide 3   Title   =   Planning a Newsletter
             Bullets =
- Make sure the focus is on various levels of employment; do not focus on top management only.
- Conduct regular surveys to see if your newsletter provides a needed source of information.

Slide 4   Title   =   Designing a Newsletter
             Bullets =
- Maintain consistent elements from issue to issue such as:
  - Column layout
  - Nameplate formatting and location
  - Formatting of headlines
  - Use of color

Slide 5   Title   =   Designing a Newsletter
             Bullets =
- Consider the following elements when designing a newsletter:
  - Focus
  - Balance
  - White space
  - Directional flow

Slide 6   Title   =   Creating a Newsletter Layout
             Bullets =
- Choose paper size
- Choose paper weight
- Determine margins
- Specify column layout

CASE study

Apply Your Skills

Part 1

You work for Citizens for Consumer Safety, a non-profit organization providing information on household safety. Your supervisor, Melinda Johansson, will be presenting information on smoke detectors at a community meeting and has asked you to prepare a PowerPoint presentation. Open the Word document named **PPSmokeDetectors.docx**. Read over the information and then use the information to prepare a presentation. Consider the information in the *Planning a Presentation* section of this chapter and then prepare at least five slides. Apply an appropriate design theme and add a transition and sound to all slides. Save the presentation and name it **PP_C1_CS_P1**. Run the presentation and then print the presentation as a handout with all slides on one page.

Part 2

Ms. Johansson has looked at the printout of the presentation and has asked you to print the presentation with two slides per page and a frame around each slide. Display the Print dialog box, click the Help button that displays in the upper right corner of the dialog box (white question mark on a blue background), and then navigate through hyperlinks to read information about printing in Microsoft Office PowerPoint. After reading the information, print the presentation with two slides per page and the slides framed.

Part 3

Ms. Johansson would like to provide information to participants at the presentation on online companies that sell smoke detectors. Using the Internet, locate at least three online stores that sell smoke detectors. Insert a new slide in the presentation that includes the names of the stores, Web addresses, and any additional information you feel is important. Save the presentation and then print the presentation in Outline view. Close the presentation.

Modifying a Presentation and Using Help

PERFORMANCE OBJECTIVES

Upon successful completion of Chapter 2, you will be able to:

- Check spelling
- Insert and delete text in slides
- Find and replace text in slides
- Cut, copy, and paste text in slides
- Rearrange text in the Slides/Outline pane
- Size and rearrange placeholders
- Insert, delete, move, and copy slides
- Copy slides between presentations
- Duplicate slides
- Reuse slides
- Preview a presentation
- Use the Help feature

Tutorial 2.1
Working with Text
Tutorial 2.2
Organizing Slides and Using Help

When preparing a presentation, you may need to modify a presentation by inserting and deleting text in slides or finding and replacing specific text. Improve the quality of your presentation by completing a spelling check to ensure that the words in your presentation are spelled correctly. Additional modifications you may need to make to a presentation include sizing and rearranging placeholders and rearranging, inserting, deleting, or copying slides. In this chapter, you will learn how to make these modifications to a presentation as well as how to preview a presentation and use the Help feature.

Note: Before beginning computer projects, copy to your storage medium the PowerPoint2007C2 subfolder from the PowerPoint2007 folder on the CD that accompanies this textbook and then make PowerPoint2007C2 the active folder.

Project ① Check Spelling and Manage Text in a Design Presentation

You will open a presentation on steps for planning a design publication, complete a spelling check on the text in the presentation, and find and replace specific text in slides.

QUICK STEPS

Complete a Spell Check
1. Click Review tab.
2. Click Spelling button.
3. Change or ignore errors.
4. Click OK.

ABC
Spelling

Checking Spelling

When preparing a presentation, perform a spelling check on text in slides using PowerPoint's spelling feature. The spelling feature compares words in slides in a presentation with words in its dictionary. If a match is found, the word is passed over. If a match is not found, the spelling checker selects the word and offers replacement suggestions. To perform a spelling check on a PowerPoint presentation, click the Review tab and then click the Spelling button in the Proofing group. You can also start the spelling checker by pressing the F7 function key on the keyboard.

When you begin spell checking text in a presentation in Project 1a, the spelling checker will stop at the misspelled word *Layuot* and display the Spelling dialog box as shown in Figure 2.1. The options available in the Spelling dialog box are described in Table 2.1.

Figure 2.1 Spelling Dialog Box

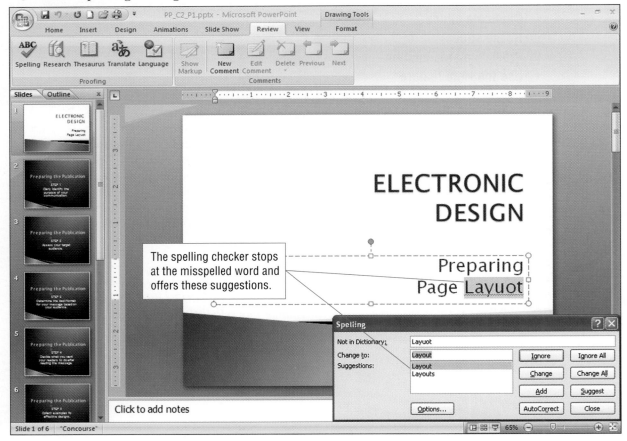

Table 2.1 Spelling Dialog Box Options

Button	Function
Ignore	Skips that occurrence of the word.
Ignore All	Skips that occurrence of the word and all other occurrences of the word in slides.
Change	Replaces selected word in slide with selected word in *Suggestions* list box.
Change All	Replaces selected word in slide with selected word in *Suggestions* list box and all other occurrences of the word.
Add	Adds selected word to the main spelling check dictionary.
Suggest	Makes active the first suggestion in the *Suggestions* list box.
AutoCorrect	Inserts selected word and correct spelling of word in AutoCorrect dialog box.
Close	Closes the Spelling dialog box.
Options	Displays PowerPoint Options dialog box with *Proofing* selected that contains options for customizing a spelling check.

Project 1a — Checking the Spelling in a Presentation

1. Open **ElectronicDesign.pptx** (located in the PowerPoint2007C2 folder on your storage medium) and then save the presentation and name it **PP_C2_P1**.
2. With the presentation in Normal view, complete a spelling check by completing the following steps:
   a. Click the Review tab.
   b. Click the Spelling button in the Proofing group.
   c. When the spelling checker selects the misspelled word *Layuot* and displays the correct spelling (*Layout*) in the *Change to* text box, click the Change button (or Change All button).
   d. When the spelling checker selects the misspelled word *Clerly* and displays the correct spelling (*Clearly*) in the *Change to* text box, click the Change button (or Change All button).

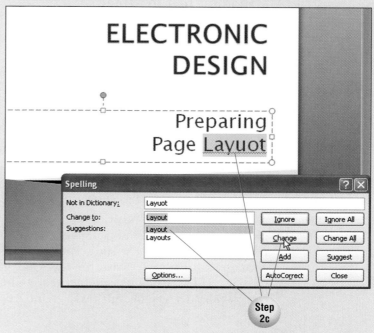

e. When the spelling checker selects the misspelled word *massege*, click *message* in the *Suggestions* list box and then click the Change button (or Change All button).

f. When the spelling checker selects the misspelled word *fo* and displays the correct spelling (*of*) in the *Change to* text box, click the Change button.
g. At the message telling you that the spelling check is complete, click the OK button.
3. Save **PP_C2_P1.pptx**.

Managing Text in Slides

As you enter text in slides or as you manage existing slides, you may need to edit, move, copy, or delete text from slides. You may also want to find specific text in slides and replace with other text. Text is generally inserted in a slide placeholder and this placeholder can be moved, sized, and/or deleted.

Inserting and Deleting Text in Slides

To insert or delete text in an individual slide, open the presentation, edit the text as needed, and then save the presentation again. If you want to delete more than an individual character, consider selecting the text first. Several methods can be used for selecting text as shown in Table 2.2.

Text in a slide is positioned inside of a placeholder. Slide layouts provide placeholders for text and generally display with a message suggesting the type of text to be entered in the slide. For example, the Title and Content slide layout contains a placeholder with the text *Click to add title* and another with the text *Click to add text*. Click placeholder text and the insertion point is positioned inside the placeholder, the default text is removed, and the placeholder is selected.

Table 2.2 Selecting Text

To do this	Perform this action
Select text mouse pointer passes through	Click and drag mouse
Select entire word	Double-click word
Select entire paragraph	Triple-click anywhere in paragraph
Select entire sentence	Ctrl + click anywhere in sentence
Select all text in selected placeholder	Click Select, Select All or press Ctrl + A

Project 1b Inserting and Deleting Text in Slides

1. With **PP_C2_P1.pptx** open and the presentation in Normal view, click the Previous Slide button (or Next Slide button) located at the bottom of the vertical scroll bar until Slide 5 displays.
2. Edit Slide 5 by completing the following steps:
   a. Position the I-beam pointer on the sentence below *STEP 4* and then click the left mouse button. (This selects the placeholder.)
   b. Edit the sentence so it reads *Decide what steps you want readers to take after reading the message.* (Use deleting and inserting commands to edit this sentence.)
3. Click the Next Slide button to display Slide 6 and then edit Slide 6 in the Outline/Slides pane by completing the following steps:
   a. Click the Outline tab in the Slides/Outline pane.
   b. Click in the sentence below *STEP 5* and then edit the sentence so it reads *Collect and assess examples of effective designs.*
   c. Click the Slides tab.
4. Save **PP_C2_P1.pptx**.

Step 2b

Step 3b

QUICK STEPS

Find Text
1. Click Find button.
2. Type text for which you are searching.
3. Click Find Next button.

Replace Text
1. Click Replace button.
2. Type text for which you are searching.
3. Press Tab key.
4. Type replacement text.
5. Click Replace All button.

Finding and Replacing Text in Slides

Use the find feature to look for specific text in slides in a presentation and use the find and replace feature to look for specific text in slides in a presentation and replace with other text. Begin a find by clicking the Find button in the Editing group in the Home tab. This displays the Find dialog box shown in Figure 2.2. In the *Find what* text box, type the text you want to find and then click the Find Next button. Continue clicking this button until a message displays telling you that the search is complete. At this message, click OK.

Figure 2.2 Find Dialog Box

In this text box, type the text for which you are searching.

Use options at the Replace dialog box shown in Figure 2.3 to search for text and replace it with other text. Display this dialog box by clicking the Replace button in the Home tab. Type the text you want to find in the *Find what* text box, press the Tab key, and then type the replacement text in the *Replace with* text box. Click the Find Next button to find the next occurrence of the text or click the Replace All button to replace all occurrences in the presentation.

Figure 2.3 Replace Dialog Box

In this text box, type the text for which you are searching.

In this text box, type the replacement text.

Both the Find and Replace dialog boxes contain two additional options for conducting a find and a find and replace. Insert a check mark in the *Match case* check box to specify that the text should exactly match the case of the text entered in the *Find what* text box. For example, if you search for *Planning*, PowerPoint will stop at *Planning* but not *planning* or *PLANNING*. Insert a check mark in the *Find whole words only* check box to specify that the text is a whole word and not part of a word. For example, if you search for *plan*, and did not check the *Find whole words only* option, PowerPoint would stop at ex*plan*ation, *plan*ned, *plan*et, and so on.

Project 1c   **Finding and Replacing Text**

1. With **PP_C2_P1.pptx** open, make Slide 1 active.
2. Find all occurrences of *Preparing* in the presentation and replace with *Planning* by completing the following steps:
   a. With Slide 1 active, click the Replace button in the Home tab.
   b. At the Replace dialog box, type Preparing in the *Find what* text box.
   c. Press the Tab key.
   d. Type Planning in the *Replace with* text box.
   e. Click the Replace All button.
   f. At the message telling you that six replacements were made, click OK.
   g. Click the Close button to close the Replace dialog box.
3. Find all occurrences of *Publication* and replace with *Newsletter* by completing steps similar to those in Step 2.
4. Save the presentation.
5. Apply a transition and sound of your choosing to all slides in the presentation.
6. Run the presentation.
7. Print Slide 1 by completing the following steps:
   a. Click the Office button and then click *Print* at the drop-down list.
   b. At the Print dialog box, click the *Slides* option in the *Print range* section and then type 1 in the text box.
   c. Click OK.
8. Print the presentation as a handout with six slides per page. (Change the *Print what* option at the Print dialog box to *Handouts*.)
9. Save and then close **PP_C2_P1.pptx**.

Project 2   **Cut, Copy, Paste, Rearrange, and Manage Slides in a Network Presentation**

You will open a network evaluation presentation and then cut, copy, and paste text in slides; rearrange text in the Slides/Outline pane; size and rearrange placeholders in slides; and manage slides by inserting, deleting, moving, and copying slides. You will also copy slides between presentations.

Cutting, Copying, and Pasting Text in Slides

With buttons in the Clipboard group in the Home tab and also with shortcut menu options, you can cut, copy, and/or paste text in slides. For example, to move text in a slide, click once in the placeholder containing the text to be moved, select the text, and then click the Cut button in the Clipboard group. Position the insertion point where you want the text inserted and then click the Paste button in the Clipboard group. To cut and paste with the shortcut menu, select the text you want to move, right-click the text, and then click *Cut* at the shortcut menu.

HINT
Ctrl + X is the keyboard shortcut to cut selected text, Ctrl + C is the keyboard shortcut to copy selected text, and Ctrl + V is the keyboard shortcut to paste cut or copied text.

Cut   Copy

Paste

Position the insertion point where you want the text inserted, right-click the location, and then click *Paste* at the shortcut menu. Complete similar steps to copy and paste text except click the Copy button instead of the Cut button or click the *Copy* option at the shortcut menu instead of the *Cut* option.

Project 2a   Cutting, Copying, and Pasting Text in Slides

1. Open **NetworkSystem.pptx** located in the PowerPoint2007C2 folder on your storage medium and then save the presentation and name it **PP_C2_P2**.
2. Insert a new slide by completing the following steps:
   a. Make Slide 4 active.
   b. Click the New Slide button in the Slides group in the Home tab.
   c. Click the *Click to add title* placeholder and then type TIME.
3. Cut text from Slide 3 and paste it into Slide 5 by completing the following steps:
   a. Make Slide 3 active.
   b. Click on any character in the bulleted text (in the Slide pane).
   c. Using the mouse, select the text following the bottom three bullets. (The bullets will not be selected.)
   d. With the text selected, click the Cut button in the Clipboard group in the Home tab.

   e. Make Slide 5 the active slide (contains the title *TIME*).
   f. Click the *Click to add text* placeholder.

g. Click the Paste button in the Clipboard group.

h. If the insertion point is positioned below the third bulleted item following a bullet, press the Backspace key twice. (This removes the bullet and deletes the blank line below the bullet.)

4. Insert a new slide by completing the following steps:

   a. With Slide 5 the active slide, click the New Slide button in the Slides group in the Home tab.

   b. Click the *Click to add title* placeholder and then type EASE OF USE.

5. Cut text from Slide 4 and paste it into Slide 6 by completing the following steps:

   a. Make Slide 4 active.

   b. Click on any character in the bulleted text.

   c. Select the text following the bottom three bullets.

   d. Click the Cut button in the Clipboard group.

   e. Make Slide 6 active (contains the title *EASE OF USE*).

   f. Click the *Click to add text* placeholder.

   g. Click the Paste button in the Clipboard group.

   h. If the insertion point is positioned below the third bulleted item following a bullet, press the Backspace key twice.

6. Copy text from Slide 3 to Slide 5 by completing the following steps:

   a. Make Slide 3 active.

   b. Click on any character in the bulleted text.

   c. Position the mouse pointer on the last bullet until the pointer turns into a four-headed arrow and then click the left mouse button. (This selects the text following the bullet.)

   d. Click the Copy button in the Clipboard group.

   e. Make Slide 5 active.

   f. Click in the bulleted text and then move the insertion point so it is positioned immediately right of the question mark in the second bulleted item.

g. Press the Enter key. (This moves the insertion point down to the next line and inserts another bullet.)

h. Click the Paste button in the Clipboard group.

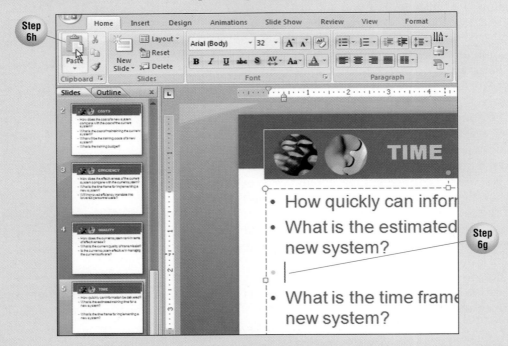

i. If a blank line is inserted between the third and fourth bullets, press the Backspace key twice.

7. Save **PP_C2_P2.pptx**.

Rearranging Text in the Slides/Outline Pane

HINT

Press Ctrl + Shift + Tab to switch between the Slides and Outline tabs in the Slides/Outline pane.

You can use the mouse to move text in the Slides/Outline pane with the Outline tab selected. To do this, position the mouse pointer on the slide icon or bullet at the left side of the text until the arrow pointer turns into a four-headed arrow. Hold down the left mouse button, drag the arrow pointer (a thin horizontal line displays) to the desired location, and then release the mouse button.

If you position the arrow pointer on the slide icon and then hold down the left mouse button, all of the text in the slide is selected. If you position the arrow pointer on the bullet and then hold down the left mouse button, all text following that bullet is selected.

Dragging selected text with the mouse moves the selected text to a new location in the presentation. You can also copy selected text. To do this, click the slide icon or click the bullet to select the desired text. Position the arrow pointer in the selected text, hold down the Ctrl key, and then the left mouse button. Drag the arrow pointer (displays with a light gray box and a plus sign attached) to the desired location, release the mouse button, and then release the Ctrl key.

1. With **PP_C2_P2.pptx** open, make Slide 1 active.
2. Click the Outline tab in the Slides/Outline pane.
3. Move the first bulleted item in Slide 4 to the end of the list by completing the following steps:
   a. Position the mouse pointer on the first bullet below *QUALITY* until it turns into a four-headed arrow.
   b. Hold down the left mouse button, drag the arrow pointer down until a thin horizontal line displays below the last bulleted item, and then release the mouse button.

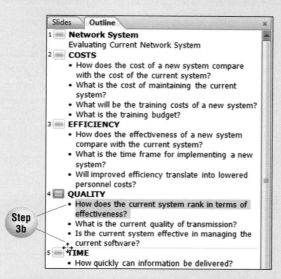

Step 3b

4. Copy and paste text by completing the following steps:
   a. In the Slides/Outline pane, move the insertion point to the end of the text in Slide 6 and then press the Enter key. (This inserts a new bullet in the slide.)
   b. Scroll up the Slides/Outline pane until the last bulleted item in Slide 2 is visible in the Slides/Outline pane as well as the last bullet in Slide 6.
   c. Position the mouse pointer on the fourth bullet below *COSTS* until it turns into a four-headed arrow and then click the left mouse button. (This selects the text.)
   d. Position the mouse pointer in the selected text, hold down the left mouse button, hold down the Ctrl key, and then drag down until the arrow pointer and light blue vertical line display on the blank line below the text in Slide 6.
   e. Release the mouse button and then release the Ctrl key.
5. Click the Slides tab in the Slides/Outline pane.
6. Save **PP_C2_P2.pptx**.

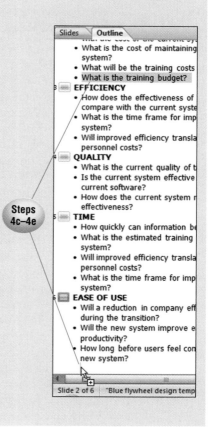

Steps 4c–4e

Sizing and Rearranging Placeholders in a Slide

Click inside a placeholder to select it and white sizing handles and a green rotation handle display around the placeholder border. With the sizing handles, you can increase or decrease the size of the placeholder. You can also move a placeholder by dragging it with the mouse. Increase or decrease the size of a placeholder by positioning the arrow pointer on a sizing handle until the pointer turns into a double-headed arrow and then dragging the placeholder border to the desired size. To move a placeholder, position the arrow pointer on the placeholder border until the arrow pointer displays with a four-headed arrow attached. Hold down the left mouse button, drag the outline of the placeholder to the desired position, and then release the mouse button.

Dragging a selected placeholder with the mouse moves the placeholder. If you want to copy a placeholder, hold down the Ctrl key while dragging the placeholder. When the outline of the placeholder is in the desired position, release the mouse button, and then release the Ctrl key. If you make a change to the size and/or location of a placeholder, click the Reset button in the Slides group in the Home tab to return the formatting of the placeholder back to the default.

Project 2c   Sizing and Rearranging Placeholders

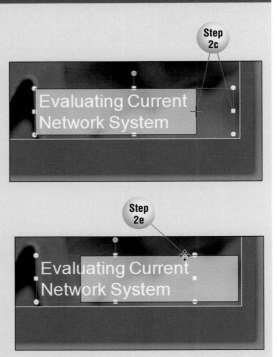

1. With **PP_C2_P2.pptx** open, make Slide 1 active.
2. Size and move a placeholder by completing the following steps:
   a. Click on any character in the subtitle *Evaluating Current Network System*.
   b. Position the arrow pointer on the sizing handle that displays in the middle of the right border until the pointer turns into a left- and right-pointing arrow.
   c. Hold down the left mouse button, drag to the left until the right border displays just to the right of the text in the placeholder, and then release the mouse button (see image at right).
   d. Position the arrow pointer on the border of the placeholder until the pointer turns into a four-headed arrow.
   e. Hold down the left mouse button, drag the placeholder to the right so the placeholder is positioned as shown at the right, and then release the mouse button.
3. Make Slide 4 active.
4. Size and move a placeholder by completing the following steps:
   a. Click on any character in the bulleted text.
   b. Position the arrow pointer on the sizing handle that displays in the middle of the right border until the pointer turns into a left- and right-pointing arrow.

c. Hold down the left mouse button and then drag to the left until the right border displays just to the right of the word *in* in the third bulleted text (see image below).

Step 4c

d. Drag the middle sizing handle on the bottom border up until the bottom border of the placeholder displays just below the last bulleted text.

e. Position the arrow pointer on the border of the placeholder until the pointer turns into a four-headed arrow.

f. Hold down the left mouse button and then drag the placeholder to the right so the placeholder is positioned approximately in the middle of the white portion of the slide.

Step 4f

5. Print the presentation as a handout with six slides per page.
6. Save **PP_C2_P2.pptx**.

Managing Slides

As you edit a presentation, you may need to reorganize slides and insert a new slide or delete an existing slide. You can manage slides in the Slides/Outline pane or in Slide Sorter view. Switch to Slide Sorter view by clicking the Slide Sorter button in the view area on the Status bar or by clicking the View tab and then clicking Slide Sorter in the Presentation Views group.

Inserting and Deleting Slides

As you learned in Chapter 1, click the New Slide button in the Slides group in the Home tab to insert a new slide in the presentation immediately following the currently active slide. You can also insert a new slide in Slide Sorter view. To do this, click the slide that will immediately precede the new slide and then click the New Slide button in the Slides group. Delete a slide in Normal view by clicking the slide miniature in the Slides/Outline pane and then clicking the Delete button in the Slides group in the Home tab or by pressing the Delete key. You can also delete a slide by switching to Slide Sorter view, clicking the slide miniature, and then clicking the Delete button or pressing the Delete key.

Moving Slides

Move slides in a presentation in Normal view or Slide Sorter view. In Normal view, click the desired slide in the Slides/Outline pane (with the Slides tab selected) and then position the mouse pointer on the selected slide. Hold down the left mouse button, drag up or down until a thin horizontal line displays in the desired location, and then release the mouse button. In Slide Sorter view, click the desired slide and then position the mouse pointer on the selected slide. Hold down the left mouse button, drag with the mouse until a thin vertical line displays in the desired location, and then release the mouse button.

HINT
Press Ctrl + M to insert a new slide.

HINT
Press Ctrl + X to cut the selected slide and then press Ctrl + V to insert the cut slide.

HINT
Press Ctrl + C to copy the selected slide and then press Ctrl + V to insert the copied slide.

Copying a Slide

Slides in some presentations may contain similar text, objects, and formatting. Rather than create a new slide, consider copying a slide. To do this, display the presentation in either Slide Sorter view or in Normal view with the Slides tab selected in the Slides/Outline pane. Position the arrow pointer in the slide, hold down the Ctrl key and then the left mouse button. Drag to the location where you want the slide copied, then release the mouse button and then the Ctrl key.

1. With **PP_C2_P2.pptx** open in Normal view, move slides by completing the following steps:
   a. Make sure the Slides tab is selected in the Slides/Outline pane.
   b. Click Slide 3 (*EFFICIENCY*) in the Slides/Outline pane.
   c. Position the mouse pointer on Slide 3, hold down the left mouse button, drag up until a thin horizontal line displays between Slides 1 and 2, and then release the mouse button.
   d. Click Slide 4 (*QUALITY*) in the Slides/Outline pane.
   e. Position the mouse pointer on Slide 4, hold down the left mouse button, drag down until a thin horizontal line displays below Slide 6, and then release the mouse button.
2. Move and copy slides in Slide Sorter view by completing the following steps:
   a. Click the Slide Sorter button in the view area on the Status bar.
   b. Click Slide 4 to make it the active slide (slide displays with orange border).
   c. Position the mouse pointer on Slide 4, hold down the left mouse button, drag to the left until the thin vertical line displays between Slides 1 and 2, and then release the mouse button.

   d. Click Slide 1 to make it the active slide.
   e. Position the mouse pointer on Slide 1, hold down the left mouse button, and then hold down the Ctrl key.
   f. Drag down and to the right until the thin vertical line displays immediately right of Slide 6.
   g. Release the mouse button and then the Ctrl key.
3. Click the Normal button in the view area on the Status bar.
4. Save **PP_C2_P2.pptx**.

Copying a Slide between Presentations

You can copy slides within a presentation as well as between presentations. To copy a slide, click the slide you want to copy (either in Slide Sorter view or in Normal view with the Slides tab selected in the Slides/Outline pane) and then click the Copy button in the Clipboard group in the Home tab. Open the presentation into which the slide is to be copied (in either Slide Sorter view or Normal view with the Slides tab selected in the Slides/Outline pane). Click in the location where you want the slide positioned and then click the Paste button. The copied slide will take on the design theme of the presentation into which it is copied.

Project 2e Copying Slides between Presentations

1. With **PP_C2_P2.pptx** open, open the presentation named **EvaluatingNetwork.pptx** located in the PowerPoint2007C2 folder on your storage medium.
2. Copy Slide 2 to the **PP_C2_P2.pptx** presentation by completing the following steps:
   a. Click Slide 2 in the Slides/Outline pane to make it the active slide.
   b. Click the Copy button in the Clipboard group in the Home tab.
   c. Click the button on the Taskbar representing the **PP_C2_P2.pptx** presentation.
   d. Click Slide 4 (*COSTS*) in the Slides/Outline pane.
   e. Click the Paste button in the Clipboard group.
   f. Click the button on the Taskbar representing the **EvaluatingNetwork.pptx** presentation.
3. Copy Slide 3 to the **PP_C2_P2.pptx** by completing the following steps:
   a. Click Slide 3 in the Slides/Outline pane.
   b. Position the mouse pointer on Slide 3 and then click the right mouse button. (This displays a shortcut menu.)
   c. Click *Copy* at the shortcut menu.
   d. Click the button on the Taskbar representing the **PP_C2_P2.pptx** presentation.
   e. Right-click Slide 3 in the Slides/Outline pane.
   f. Click *Paste* at the shortcut menu.
4. Click the button on the Taskbar representing the **EvaluatingNetwork.pptx** presentation.
5. Close the presentation.
6. With **PP_C2_P2.pptx** open, delete Slide 9 by completing the following steps:
   a. If necessary, scroll down the Slides/Outline pane until Slide 9 is visible.
   b. Click Slide 9 to select it.
   c. Press the Delete key.
7. Save the presentation.
8. Print the presentation as a handout with nine slides per page.
9. Close **PP_C2_P2.pptx**.

Step 3c

Project ③ Insert and Manage Slides in an Adventure Tours Presentation

You will open a presentation on Adventure Tours and then insert additional slides in the presentation by duplicating existing slides in the presentation and reusing slides from another presentation. You will also preview the presentation, make changes to the presentation in Print Preview, and then print the presentation.

Duplicating Slides

In Project 2, you used the Copy and Paste buttons in the Clipboard group and also options from a shortcut menu to copy slides in a presentation. You can also copy slides in a presentation using the *Duplicate Selected Slides* option from the New Slide button drop-down list. This option is useful if you are copying more than one slide. To use the option, select the desired slides in the Slides/Outline pane with the Slides tab selected, click the New Slide button arrow, and then click *Duplicate Selected Slides* at the drop-down list.

To select adjacent (sequential) slides, click the first slide in the Slides/Outline pane, hold down the Shift key, and then click the last in the sequence. For example, if you want to duplicate Slides 3 through 6, you would click Slide 3, hold down the Shift key, and then click Slide 6. To select nonadjacent (nonsequential) slides, hold down the Ctrl key while clicking each desired slide.

QUICK STEPS

Duplicate Slides
1. Select desired slides in Slides/Outline pane.
2. Click New Slide button arrow.
3. Click *Duplicate Selected Slides* at drop-down list.

Project ③a Duplicating Selected Slides

1. Open **AdventureTours.pptx** and then save the presentation and name it **PP_C2_P3**.
2. Make sure the presentation displays in Normal view and that the Slides tab is active in the Slides/Outline pane.
3. Select and then duplicate slides by completing the following steps:
   a. Click Slide 1 in the Slides/Outline pane.
   b. Hold down the Ctrl key.
   c. Click Slide 3, Slide 4, and Slide 5.
   d. Release the Ctrl key.
   e. Click the New Slide button arrow and then click *Duplicate Selected Slides* at the drop-down list.
4. With Slide 6 active in the Slide pane, change *Fiji Tour* to *Costa Rica Tour*.
5. Make Slide 7 active, select and delete the bulleted text, and then type the following bulleted text:
   - Round-trip airfare from Los Angeles to San Jose, Costa Rica
   - 8 days and 7 nights in Costa Rica
   - Monthly tours
   - Prices from $1099 to $1599

Step 3e

6. Make Slide 8 active, select and delete the bulleted text, and then type the following bulleted text:
   - San Jose, Emerald Suites
   - Tortuguero, Plantation Spa and Resort
   - Fortuna, Pacific Resort
   - Jaco, Monteverde Cabanas
7. Make Slide 9 active, select and delete the bulleted text, and then type the following bulleted text:
   - San Jose city tour
   - Rainforest tram
   - Canal cruise
   - Forest hike
8. Save **PP_C2_P3.pptx**.

Reuse Slides
1. Click New Slide button arrow.
2. Click *Reuse Slides*.
3. Click Browse button, *Browse File*.
4. Navigate to desired folder.
5. Double-click desired presentation.
6. Click desired slide in Reuse Slides task pane.

Reusing Slides

PowerPoint provides another method for copying slides from one presentation to another. Click the New Slide button arrow and then click the *Reuse Slides* option at the drop-down list and the Reuse Slides task pane displays at the right side of the screen as shown in Figure 2.4. At this task pane, click the Browse button, click *Browse File* at the drop-down list, and the Browse dialog box displays. At this dialog box, navigate to the desired folder and then double-click the desired presentation. This inserts the presentation slides in the Reuse Slides task pane. Click a slide in the Reuse Slides task pane to insert it in the currently open presentation.

Figure 2.4 Reuse Slides Task Pane

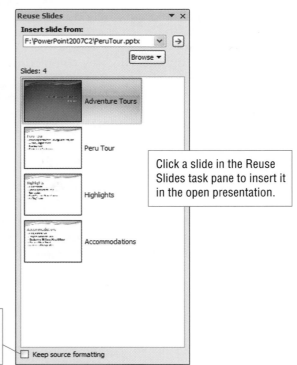

Click a slide in the Reuse Slides task pane to insert it in the open presentation.

Insert a check mark in this check box if you want the inserted slide to maintain source formatting.

By default, the slides you insert from the Reuse Slides task pane into the currently open presentation take on the formatting of the current presentation. If you want the slides to retain their original formatting when inserted in the presentation, insert a check mark in the *Keep source formatting* check box located toward the bottom of the Reuse Slides task pane.

Project ③b   Reusing Slides

1. With **PP_C2_P3.pptx** open, click the New Slide button arrow and then click *Reuse Slides* at the drop-down list. (This displays the Reuse Slides task pane at the right side of the screen.)
2. Click the Browse button in the Reuse Slides task pane and then click *Browse File* at the drop-down list.
3. At the Browse dialog box, navigate to the PowerPoint2007C2 folder on your storage medium and then double-click *PeruTour.pptx*.
4. In the Slides/Outline pane, scroll down the slide thumbnails until Slide 9 displays and then click below Slide 9. (This inserts a thin, horizontal line below the Slide 9 thumbnail in the Slides/Outline pane.)
5. Click the first slide thumbnail (*Adventure Tours*) in the Reuse Slides task pane. (This inserts the slide in the open presentation immediately below Slide 9.)
6. Click the second slide thumbnail (*Peru Tour*) in the Reuse Slides task pane.
7. Click the fourth slide thumbnail (*Accommodations*) in the Reuse Slides task pane.
8. Click the third slide thumbnail (*Highlights*) in the Reuse Slides task pane.
9. Close the Reuse Slides task pane by clicking the Close button (contains an X) located in the upper right corner of the task pane.
10. Save **PP_C2_P3.pptx**.

Step 2

Step 5

Previewing a Presentation

Before printing a presentation, consider previewing the presentation. In Print Preview you can specify printing options, change the zoom display, and display specific slides. To display a presentation in Print Preview, click the Office button, point to *Print*, and then click *Print Preview*. The Print Preview tab, shown in Figure 2.5, displays toward the top of the screen. Click the Print button to send the presentation to the printer. Click the Options button and a drop-down list displays with options for inserting a header or footer, changing from color to grayscale, scaling the presentation to fit on a page, framing the slides, and specifying a print order. Use the Print What button to specify whether you want to print slides, handouts, notes pages, or an outline.

Print Preview
1. Click Office button.
2. Point to *Print*.
3. Click *Print Preview*.

With the Orientation button you can choose to print the presentation on paper in portrait or landscape orientation. At the portrait orientation, data is printed on a page that is 11 inches tall and 8.5 inches wide. At the landscape orientation, the page is 8.5 inches tall and 11 inches wide. Click the Zoom button and the Zoom dialog box displays with options for changing the zoom by percentage. Click the Fit to Window button to return the display to the default. Use the Next Page or Previous Page buttons to navigate through the presentation and click the Close Print Preview button to close the preview window.

Figure 2.5 Print Preview Window

Print Preview tab

Inserting Headers and Footers

Insert Header/Footer
1. Display presentation in Print Preview.
2. Click Options button, *Header and Footer*.
3. Make desired changes at dialog box.
4. Click Apply to All button.

You can choose to print a presentation as individual slides, handouts, notes pages, or an outline. If you print a presentation as handouts or an outline, PowerPoint will automatically print the current date in the upper right corner of the page and the page number in the lower right corner. If you print the presentation as notes pages, PowerPoint will automatically print the page number in the lower right corner. PowerPoint does not insert the date or page number when you print individual slides.

You can modify existing header and footer elements or insert additional elements with options in the Header and Footer dialog box. If *Slides* is selected in the *Print What* option box, the Header and Footer dialog box displays with the Slide tab selected. If *Handouts*, *Notes Pages*, or *Outline* is selected in the *Print What* option, the Header and Footer dialog box displays with the Notes and Handouts tab selected as shown in Figure 2.6. The options in the dialog box are similar with either tab selected.

With options at the Header and Footer dialog box, you can insert the date and time, a header, a footer, and page numbers. If you insert the date and time in a presentation, you can choose the *Update automatically* option if you want the date and time updated each time the presentation is opened. Choose the date and time formatting by clicking the down-pointing arrow at the right side of the *Update automatically* option box and then choose the desired formatting at the drop-down list. If you choose the *Fixed* option, type the desired date and/or time in the *Fixed* text box. Type header text in the *Header* text box and type footer text in the *Footer* text box. If you want to print the slide number on slides, insert a check mark in the *Slide number* check box in the Header and Footer dialog box with the Slide tab selected. If you want to include page numbers on handouts, notes pages, or outline pages, insert a check mark in the *Page number* check box in the Header and Footer dialog box with the Notes and Handouts tab selected. If you want all changes you make to the Header and Footer dialog box to apply to all slides or all handouts, notes pages, and outline pages, click the Apply to All button located in the upper right corner of the dialog box.

Figure 2.6 Header and Footer Dialog Box with the Notes and Handouts Tab Selected

Insert a check mark in this check box to insert the date and/or time.

If you want the date and/or time updated each time you open the presentation, click *Update automatically* and then choose the desired formatting at the drop-down list.

Text you type in the *Header* text box or *Footer* text box will print when you print the presentation as notes pages, handouts, or an outline.

Project 3C   Previewing a Presentation

1. With **PP_C2_P3.pptx** open, display the presentation in Print Preview by clicking the Office button, pointing to *Print*, and then clicking *Print Preview*.
2. At the Print Preview window, click the down-pointing arrow at the right side of the *Print What* option box in the Page Setup group and then click *Handouts (9 Slides Per Page)* at the drop-down list.

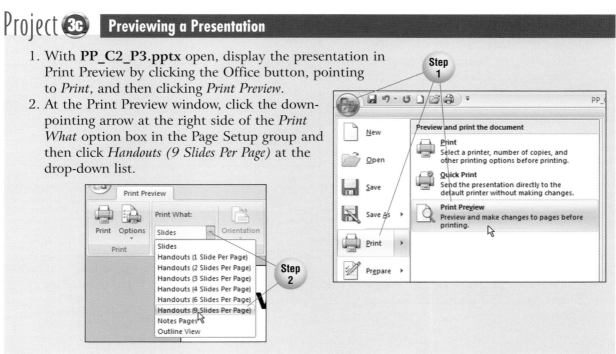

3. Click the Options button in the Print group, point to *Color/Grayscale*, and then click *Color (On Black and White Printer)*.

4. Click the Options button in the Print group, point to *Printing Order*, and then click *Vertical*.

5. Click the Orientation button in the Page Setup group and then click *Landscape* at the drop-down list.

6. Change the Zoom by completing the following steps:
   a. Click the Zoom button in the Zoom group.
   b. At the Zoom dialog box, click *100%* in the *Zoom to* group.
   c. Click OK.

7. Click the Fit to Window button in the Zoom group.

8. Click the Options button in the Print group, point to *Color/Grayscale*, and then click *Grayscale*.

9. Make changes at the Header and Footer dialog box by completing the following steps:

   a. Click the Options button in the Print group and then click *Header and Footer* at the drop-down list.

   b. At the Header and Footer dialog box with the Notes and Handouts tab selected, click the *Date and time* option.

   c. Click the down-pointing arrow at the right side of the *Update automatically* option box and then click the eighth option from the top.

   d. Click the *Header* check box to insert a check mark and then type Adventure Tours in the *Header* text box.

   e. Click the *Footer* check box to insert a check mark and then type your first and last names in the *Footer* text box.

   f. Click the Apply to All button located in the upper right corner of the dialog box.

10. Click the Print button in the Print group and then click OK at the Print dialog box.

11. Click the down-pointing arrow at the right side of the *Print What* option box in the Page Setup group and then click *Slides* at the drop-down list.

12. Make changes at the Header and Footer dialog box by completing the following steps:
   a. Click the Options button in the Print group and then click *Header and Footer* at the drop-down list.
   b. At the Header and Footer dialog box with the Slide tab selected, click the *Date and time* check box to insert a check mark.
   c. Click the *Update automatically* option.
   d. Click the *Slide number* check box to insert a check mark.
   e. Click the *Footer* check box to insert a check mark and then type your first and last names in the *Footer* text box.
   f. Click the *Don't show on title slide* check box to insert a check mark.
   g. Click the Apply to All button located in the upper right corner of the dialog box.
   h. Click the Next Page button in the Preview group to display the next slide. (Notice the date, your name, and the slide number that displays along the bottom of the slide.)
   i. Click the Next Page button a couple of more times to view other slides.
13. Click the Print button in the Print group and then click OK at the Print dialog box.
14. Click the Close Print Preview button.
15. Add a transition and sound of your choosing to all slides in the presentation.
16. Run the presentation.
17. Save and then close **PP_C2_P3.pptx**.

P roject **4** **Use the PowerPoint Help Feature and Create a Presentation**

You will use the Help feature to learn more about the options in the Save As dialog box. You will also use the PowerPoint Help window to find information on keyboard shortcuts and then use the information to create a presentation.

Using Help

PowerPoint provides a Help feature you can use to find information on specific options in a dialog box or on PowerPoint features and commands. You can use the Help button to find information about specific features in a dialog box and you can use the Microsoft Office PowerPoint Help button to find information on PowerPoint features.

HINT
Press F1 to display the PowerPoint Help window.

Getting Help in a Dialog Box

Dialog Box Help

Some dialog boxes contain a Help button you can click to display information in the PowerPoint Help window that is specific to the dialog box. This button is located in the upper right corner of the dialog box and displays as a question mark inside a square. Click this button and the PowerPoint Help window displays with topics related to the dialog box.

Project 4a — Using a ScreenTip to Access Help

1. At a blank presentation, click the Office button and then click *Save As* at the drop-down list.
2. At the Save As dialog box, click the Help button located in the upper right corner of the dialog box.
3. At the PowerPoint Help window, click the *Save As* hyperlink.

Step 2

Step 3

4. In the Save As list box, click *Microsoft Office PowerPoint*.
5. Read the information that displays about saving in PowerPoint and then click the Close button to close the PowerPoint Help window.
6. Close the Save As dialog box.

Using the Microsoft Office PowerPoint Help Button

Get Help in a Dialog Box
1. Click Microsoft Office PowerPoint Help button.
2. Type help topic.
3. Press Enter.

Help

PowerPoint's Help feature is an on-screen reference manual containing information about all PowerPoint features and commands. PowerPoint's Help feature is similar to the Windows Help and the Help features in Word, Excel, and Access. Get help by clicking the Microsoft Office PowerPoint Help button located in the upper right corner of the screen (a question mark in a circle) or by pressing the keyboard shortcut, F1. This displays the PowerPoint Help window. In this window, type a topic, feature, or question in the *Search* text box and then press Enter. Topics related to the search text display in the Help window. Click a topic that interests you. If the topic window contains a <u>Show All</u> hyperlink in the upper right corner, click this hyperlink and the information expands to show all help information related to the topic. When you click the <u>Show All</u> hyperlink, it becomes the <u>Hide All</u> hyperlink.

1. At a blank presentation screen, click the Microsoft Office PowerPoint Help button located in the upper right corner of the screen.

2. At the PowerPoint Help window, type keyboard shortcuts in the *Search* text box.
3. Press the Enter key.
4. When the list of topics displays, click the *Keyboard shortcuts for PowerPoint 2007* hyperlink. (The location of this hyperlink may vary.)

5. Click the Show All hyperlink that displays in the upper right corner of the window.

6. Scroll through the PowerPoint Help window and notice the information that displays about keyboard shortcuts.
7. Scroll back to the beginning of the Help text and then click the Hide All hyperlink.

8. Scroll down toward the bottom of the list and then click the <u>Delete and copy text</u> <u>and objects</u> hyperlink. (This option is located in the *Common tasks in Microsoft Office PowerPoint* section.)
9. Click the Print button that displays on the PowerPoint Help window toolbar.

10. At the Print dialog box, click the Print button.
11. Click the Close button to close the PowerPoint Help window.
12. At the blank presentation, create a presentation with the information you printed that contains the following information:
    a. Slide 1: Insert the text **PowerPoint Help** as the title and **Keyboard Shortcuts** as the subtitle.
    b. Slide 2: Insert the text **Delete Text** as the title and then insert the four delete keyboard shortcuts as bulleted text.
    c. Slide 3: Insert the text **Cut, Copy, Paste Text** as the title and then insert the three cut, copy, and paste keyboard shortcuts as bulleted text.
    d. Slide 4: Insert the text **Undo and Redo** as the title and then insert the two undo and redo keyboard shortcuts as bulleted text.
    e. Slide 5: Insert the text **Copy and Paste Formatting** as the title and then insert the three copy and paste formatting keyboard shortcuts as bulleted text.
13. Apply a design theme of your choosing. Check each slide to make sure the text displays appropriately on each slide.
14. Apply a transition and sound to all slides in the presentation.
15. Save the presentation and name it **PP_C2_P4**.
16. Run the presentation.
17. Print the presentation as a handout with six slides per page.
18. Close **PP_C2_P4.pptx**.

CHAPTER summary

- Use the spelling feature to check spelling of slides in a presentation. Begin the spelling checker by clicking the Review tab and then clicking the Spelling button in the Proofing group.

- Refer to Table 2.1 for methods for selecting text in slides.

- Text in a placeholder is positioned inside of a placeholder. Click in a placeholder to select the placeholder and position the insertion point inside.

- Display the Find dialog box by clicking the Find button in the Editing group in the Home tab.

- Display the Replace dialog box by clicking the Replace button in the Editing group in the Home tab.

- With buttons in the Clipboard group or with options from a shortcut menu, you can cut and paste or copy and paste text in slides.

- You can use the mouse to move text in the Slides/Outline pane. You can select and then drag it to a new location or hold down the Ctrl key while dragging to copy text to a new location.

- Use the sizing handles that display around a selected placeholder to increase or decrease the size of the placeholder. You can use the mouse to drag a selected placeholder to a new location in the slide.

- Use the New Slide button in the Home tab to insert a slide in a presentation.

- Delete a selected slide by clicking the Delete button in the Slides group in the Home tab or by pressing the Delete button.

- You can move or delete a selected slide in Normal view in the Slides/Outline pane or in Slide Sorter view.

- Copy a selected slide by holding down the Ctrl key while dragging the slide to the desired location.

- Use the Copy and Paste buttons in the Clipboard group in the Home tab to copy a slide between presentations.

- Select adjacent slides in the Slides/Outline pane or in Slide Sorter view by clicking the first slide, holding down the Shift key, and then clicking the last slide. Select nonadjacent slides by holding down the Ctrl key while clicking each desired slide.

- Duplicate slides in a presentation by selecting the desired slides in the Slides/Outline pane, clicking the New Slide button arrow, and then clicking the *Duplicate Selected Slides* option.

- You can copy slides from a presentation into the open presentation with options at the Reuse Slides task pane. Display this task pane by clicking the New Slide button arrow and then clicking *Reuse Slides* at the drop-down list.

- Display a presentation in Print Preview by clicking the Office button, pointing to *Print*, and then clicking *Print Preview*.

- In Print Preview, display the Header and Footer dialog box by clicking the Options button and then clicking *Header and Footer* at the drop-down list. Use options in the dialog box to insert the date and time, a header, a footer, slide numbers, or page numbers. The options will vary depending on which tab is selected—*Slide* or *Notes and Handouts*.
- Click the Help button in a dialog box and the PowerPoint Help window displays with information specific to the dialog box.
- Click the Microsoft Office Word Help button or press F1 to display the PowerPoint Help window.

COMMANDS review

FEATURE	TAB, GROUP	BUTTON, OPTION	OFFICE BUTTON DROP-DOWN LIST	KEYBOARD SHORTCUT
Spelling check	Review, Proofing	ABC✓		F7
Find dialog box	Home, Editing	Find		Ctrl + F
Replace dialog box	Home, Editing	Replace		Ctrl + H
Cut text or slide	Home, Clipboard	✂		Ctrl + X
Copy text or slide	Home, Clipboard	📋		Ctrl + C
Paste text or slide	Home, Clipboard	📋		Ctrl + V
Duplicate slide	Home, Slides	, Duplicate Selected Slides		
Reuse Slides task pane	Home, Slides	, Reuse Slides		
Print Preview			Print, Print Preview	
PowerPoint Help window		?		F1

CONCEPTS check

Test Your Knowledge

Completion: In the space provided at the right, indicate the correct term, symbol, or command.

1. The Spelling button is located in the Proofing group in this tab. _____

2. This is the keyboard shortcut to select all text in a placeholder. _____

3. The Find button is located in this group in the Home tab. _____

4. In the Slides/Outline pane with the Outline tab selected, hold down the left mouse button on this to select all text in the slide. _____

5. To copy text to a new location in the Slides/Outline pane with the Outline tab selected, hold down this key while dragging text. _____

6. The border of a selected placeholder displays these handles as well as a green rotation handle. _____

7. You can reorganize slides in a presentation in the Slides/Outline pane or in this view. _____

8. You can copy selected slides in a presentation using this option from the New Slide button drop-down list. _____

9. To select adjacent slides, click the first slide, hold down this key, and then click the last slide. _____

10. Click the New Slide button arrow and then click the *Reuse Slides* option at the drop-down list and this displays. _____

11. Display the presentation in Print Preview by clicking the Office button, pointing to this option, and then clicking *Print Preview*. _____

12. In Print Preview, display the Header and Footer dialog box by clicking this button in the Print Preview tab and then clicking *Header and Footer* at the drop-down list. _____

13. This is the keyboard shortcut to display the PowerPoint Help window. _____

SKILLS check
Demonstrate Your Proficiency

Assessment

1 CREATE AN ELECTRONIC DESIGN PRESENTATION

1. Create the presentation shown in Figure 2.7 using a design theme of your choosing. (When typing bulleted text, press the Tab key to move the insertion point to the desired tab level.)
2. After creating the slides, complete a spelling check on the text in the slides.
3. Save the presentation into the PowerPoint2007C2 folder on your storage medium and name the presentation **PP_C2_A1**.
4. Run the presentation.
5. Preview the presentation, change the *Print What* option to *Handouts (4 Slides Per Page)*, change the orientation to landscape, and then print the presentation.
6. Make the following changes to the presentation:
   a. Change to Slide Sorter view and then move Slide 3 between Slides 1 and 2.
   b. Move Slide 4 between Slides 2 and 3.
   c. Search for the word *document* and replace it with the word *brochure*. (Make Slide 1 active and then capitalize the "b" in "brochure.")
   d. Add a transition and sound of your choosing to each slide.
7. Save the presentation.
8. Display the Reuse Slides task pane, browse to the PowerPoint2007C2 folder on your storage medium, and then double-click **LayoutTips.pptx**.
9. Insert the *Layout Punctuation Tips* slide below Slide 4.
10. Insert the *Layout Tips* slide below Slide 5.
11. Close the Reuse Slides task pane.
12. Find all occurrences of *Layout* and replace with *Design*. (Insert a check mark in the *Match case* check box.)
13. Move Slide 5 between Slides 1 and 2.
14. Move Slide 6 between Slides 2 and 3.
15. Save the presentation.
16. Print the presentation as a handout with six slides per page.
17. Close **PP_C2_A1.pptx**.

Figure 2.7 **Assessment 1**

Slide 1   Title   =   Electronic Design and Production
                   Subtitle =   Designing a Document

Slide 2   Title   =   Creating Balance
                   Bullets =

- Symmetrical balance: Balancing similar elements equally on a page (centered alignment) of the document
- Asymmetrical balance: Balancing contrasting elements on a page of the document

Slide 3   Title   =   Creating Focus
                   Bullets =

- Creating focus with titles, headings, and subheads in a document
- Creating focus with graphic elements in a document
  - Clip art
  - Watermarks
  - Illustrations
  - Photographs
  - Charts
  - Graphs

Slide 4   Title   =   Providing Proportion
                   Bullets =

- Evaluating proportions in a document
- Sizing graphic elements in a document
- Using white space in a document

Assessment

2   CREATE A NETIQUETTE PRESENTATION

1. Create a presentation with the text shown in Figure 2.8. You determine the design template and the slide layout.
2. If necessary, size and move placeholders so the text is positioned attractively on the slide.
3. Select Slides 4 through 6 and then duplicate the slides.
4. Type the following text in place of the existing text in the identified slides:
   a. Slide 7: Select the placeholder netiquette rule text and then type Do not plagiarize.
   b. Slide 8: Select the netiquette rule text in the placeholder and then type Respect and accept people's differences.
   c. Slide 9: Select the netiquette rule text in the placeholder and then type Share expert knowledge.
5. Complete a spelling check on text in the presentation.
6. Save the presentation and name it **PP_C2_A2**.
7. Print the presentation as a handout with nine slides per page.

8. Make the following edits to the presentation:
   a. Display the presentation in Slide Sorter view.
   b. Move Slide 3 between Slide 5 and Slide 6.
   c. Move Slide 7 between Slide 3 and Slide 4.
9. Add a transition and sound of your choosing to all slides in the presentation.
10. Save the presentation.
11. Run the presentation.
12. Print the presentation as a handout with nine slides per page.
13. Close **PP_C2_A2.pptx**.

Figure 2.8 Assessment 2

Slide 1	Title	=	INTERNET APPLICATIONS
	Subtitle	=	Internet Community
Slide 2	Title	=	Community Issues
	Bullets	=	• Flaming
			• E-mail
			• Moderated environments
			• Netiquette
Slide 3	Title	=	Netiquette Rule
	Subtitle	=	Remember you are dealing with people.
Slide 4	Title	=	Netiquette Rule
	Subtitle	=	Adhere to the same standards of behavior online that you follow in real life.
Slide 5	Title	=	Netiquette Rule
	Subtitle	=	Know where you are in cyberspace.
Slide 6	Title	=	Netiquette Rule
	Subtitle	=	Respect others' time and bandwidth.

Assessment

3 DOWNLOAD A DESIGN THEME

1. If your computer is connected to the Internet, Microsoft Office Online provides a number of design themes you can download to your computer.
2. Display the New Presentation dialog box and then click *Design slides* in the *Microsoft Office Online* section. Browse through the design themes and then download a design theme that interests you.
3. Open **PP_C2_A2.pptx** and then save the presentation and name it **PP_C2_A3**.
4. Apply the design theme you downloaded to the presentation.
5. Check each slide to make sure the text displays in an attractive manner on the slide.
6. Run the presentation.
7. Print Slide 1 and Slide 5 of the presentation.
8. Save and then close **PP_C2_A3.pptx**.

CASE study

Apply Your Skills

You are the office manager at the Company Connections agency. One of your responsibilities is to conduct workshops for preparing individuals for the job search process. A coworker has given you a presentation for the workshop but the presentation needs some editing and modifying. Open **JobAnalysis.pptx** and then save the presentation and name it **PP_C2_CS_P1**. Check each slide in the presentation and then make modifications to maintain consistency in the size and location of placeholders (consider using the Reset button to reset the formatting and size of the placeholders), maintain consistency in heading text, move text from an overcrowded slide to a new slide, complete a spelling check, apply a design theme, and make any other modifications to improve the presentation. Save **PP_C2_CS_P1.pptx**.

After reviewing the presentation, you realize that you need to include slides on resumes. Open the **ResumePresentation.pptx** presentation and then copy Slides 2 and 3 into the **PP_C2_CS_P1.pptx** presentation. You want to add additional information on resume writing tips and decide to use the Internet to find information. Locate information on the Internet with tips on writing a resume and then create a slide (or two) with the information you find. Add a transition and sound to all slides in the presentation. Save the **PP_C2_CS_P1.pptx** presentation.

You know that Microsoft Word offers a number of resume templates you can download from the Microsoft Office Online site. You decide to include information in the presentation on how to download resumes. Open Microsoft Word, click the Office button, and then click *New* at the drop-down list. At the New Document dialog box, click the Help button that displays in the upper right corner of the dialog box. Read the information on downloading templates and then experiment with downloading a template. With the **PP_C2_CS_P1.pptx** presentation open, add an additional slide to the end of the presentation that provides steps on how to download a resume in Microsoft Word. Print the presentation as a handout with six slides per page. Save, run, and then close the **PP_C2_CS_P1.pptx** presentation.

CHAPTER

Formatting Slides

PERFORMANCE OBJECTIVES

Upon successful completion of Chapter 3, you will be able to:

- Apply font and paragraph formatting to text in slides
- Apply formatting with the Mini toolbar and Format Painter
- Customize bullets and numbers
- Modify theme colors and fonts
- Change slide background
- Change page setup
- Create custom themes including custom theme colors and theme fonts
- Delete custom themes

powerpoint Chapter 3

Tutorial 3.1
Formatting Slide Content
Tutorial 3.2
Formatting Slide Appearance

The Font and Paragraph groups in the Home tab contain a number of buttons and options you can use to format text in slides. PowerPoint also provides a Mini toolbar and the Format Painter feature to help you format text. You can modify the design theme colors and fonts provided by PowerPoint and you can create your own custom themes. You will learn to use these features in this chapter along with how to change page setup options.

Note: Before beginning computer projects, copy to your storage medium the PowerPoint2007C3 subfolder from the PowerPoint2007 folder on the CD that accompanies this textbook and then make PowerPoint2007C3 the active folder.

Project ① Format an E-commerce Presentation

You will open an e-commerce presentation, apply font and paragraph formatting, apply formatting with Format Painter, apply column formatting to text in placeholders, and rotate and vertically align text in placeholders.

Formatting a Presentation

PowerPoint provides a variety of design themes you can apply to a presentation. These themes contain formatting such as font, color, and graphics. In some situations, the formatting provided by the theme is appropriate; in other situations, you may want to change or enhance the formatting of a slide.

Applying Font Formatting

The Font group in the Home tab contains a number of buttons for applying font formatting to text in a slide such as changing the font, font size, color, and applying font effects. Table 3.1 describes the buttons in the Font group along with any keyboard shortcuts to apply font formatting.

Changing Fonts

Design themes apply a font to text in slides. You may want to change this default to some other font for such reasons as changing the mood of a presentation, enhancing the visual appeal of slides, and increasing the readability of the text in slides. Change the font with the Font and Font Size buttons in the Font group in the Home tab.

When you select text and then click the Font button arrow, a drop-down gallery displays with font options. Hover your mouse pointer over a font option and the selected text in the slide displays with the font applied. You can continue hovering your mouse pointer over different font options to see how the selected text displays in the specified font. The Font button drop-down gallery is an example of the ***live preview*** feature, which allows you to see how the font formatting affects your text without having to return to the presentation. The live preview feature is also available when you click the Font Size button arrow.

HINT
Consider using a sans serif typeface for titles and headings and a serif typeface for body text.

Fonts may be decorative or plain and generally fall into one of two categories: ***serif*** or ***sans serif***. A serif is a small line at the end of a character stroke. A serif font is easier to read and is generally used for large amounts of text. A sans serif font does not have serifs (*sans* is French for *without*) and is generally used for titles and headings.

HINT
Use options at the Font dialog box with the Character Spacing tab selected to increase or decrease spacing between characters and to apply kerning to text.

In addition to buttons in the Font group in the Home tab, you can use options at the Font dialog box shown in Figure 3.1 to apply character formatting to text. Display the Font dialog box by clicking the Font group dialog box launcher or with the keyboard shortcut Ctrl + Shift + F. (The dialog box launcher is the small button containing a diagonal arrow that displays in the lower right corner of the group.) Use options at the Font dialog box to choose a font, font style, font size, and to apply special effects to text in slides such as Superscript, Subscript, and Double Strikethrough.

Table 3.1 PowerPoint Home Tab Font Group Buttons

Button	Name	Function	Keyboard Shortcut
Calibri (Body)	Font	Changes selected text to a different font	
32	Font Size	Changes selected text to a different font size	
A▲	Increase Font Size	Increases font size of selected text to next available larger size	Ctrl + Shift + >
A▼	Decrease Font Size	Decreases font size of selected text to next available smaller size	Ctrl + Shift + <
✐	Clear All Formatting	Clears all character formatting from selected text	Ctrl + Spacebar
B	Bold	Adds or removes bold formatting to or from selected text	Ctrl + B
I	Italic	Adds or removes italic formatting to or from selected text	Ctrl + I
U	Underline	Adds or removes underline formatting to or from selected text	Ctrl + U
abc	Strikethrough	Inserts or removes a line through the middle of selected text	
S	Text Shadow	Adds or removes shadow formatting to or from selected text	
AV↔	Character Spacing	Adjusts spacing between characters	
Aa	Change Case	Changes the case of selected text	Shift + F3
A	Font Color	Changes the font color for selected text	

Figure 3.1 Font Dialog Box

Click this down-pointing arrow and then choose a font at the drop-down list.

Click this down-pointing arrow and then choose a font style at the drop-down list.

Click the Font color button and then choose a color at the color palette.

Use these arrows to increase or decrease the font size.

Insert a check mark in those effects you want applied to text.

Formatting with the Mini Toolbar

When you select text, the Mini toolbar displays in a dimmed fashion above the selected text. Hover the mouse pointer over the Mini toolbar and it becomes active. Click a button on the Mini toolbar to apply formatting to selected text. If you do not want the Mini toolbar to display when you select text, you can turn it off. To do this, click the Office button and then click the PowerPoint Options button that displays in the lower right corner of the drop-down list. At the PowerPoint Options dialog box with the *Popular* option selected in the left panel, click the *Show Mini Toolbar on selection* check box to remove the check mark.

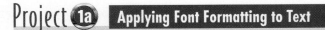

Project 1a Applying Font Formatting to Text

1. Open **E-Commerce.pptx** and then save the presentation and name it **PP_C3_P1**.
2. Apply the Urban design theme to the presentation.
3. Change the font formatting of the Slide 1 subtitle by completing the following steps:
   a. With Slide 1 active, click any character in the subtitle *Online Services*.
   b. Select *Online Services*.
   c. Click the Home tab.
   d. Click the Font button arrow, scroll down the drop-down gallery, and then click *Trebuchet MS*.

e. Click the Font Size button arrow and then click *40* at the drop-down gallery.

f. Click the Bold button.

g. Click the Text Shadow button in the Font group.

h. Click the Font Color button arrow and then click the *Blue-Gray, Accent 6, Darker 25%* option as shown below.

4. Change the size of the title text by completing the following steps:
   a. Click any character in the title *ELECTRONIC COMMERCE* and then select the title.
   b. Click the Increase Font Size button in the Font group.

5. Change the case of text by completing the following steps:
   a. Make Slide 2 active.
   b. Click in the title *ELECTRONIC COMMERCE* and then select the title.
   c. Click the Change Case button in the Font group and then click *Capitalize Each Word* at the drop-down list.

6. Apply and clear formatting to text by completing the following steps:
   a. Make Slide 3 active.
   b. Click in the bulleted text placeholder.
   c. Select *m-commerce* located in the parentheses.
   d. Click the Underline button in the Font group in the Home tab.
   e. Click the Bold button in the Font group.
   f. After looking at the text set with underlining and bold formatting, you decide to remove the formatting by clicking the Clear All Formatting button in the Font group.
   g. With the text still selected, click the Italic button in the Font group in the Home tab.

7. Apply italic formatting with the Mini toolbar by completing the following steps:
   a. Select *B2C*, hover the mouse pointer over the Mini toolbar to make it active, and then click the Italic button.
   b. Select *B2B*, hover the mouse pointer over the Mini toolbar to make it active, and then click the Italic button.
8. Save **PP_C3_P1.pptx**.

Electronic Commerce Terminology

* Mobile commerce (*m-comm*
* Business-to-consumer (B2C) electronic commerce

Step 7a

Formatting with Format Painter

If you apply character and/or paragraph formatting to text in a slide and want to apply the same formatting to text in the slide or other slides, use the Format Painter. With Format Painter, you can apply the same formatting in more than one location in a slide or slides. To use the Format Painter, apply the desired formatting to text, position the insertion point anywhere in the formatted text, and then double-click the Format Painter button in the Clipboard group in the Home tab. Using the mouse, select the additional text to which you want the formatting applied. After applying the formatting in the desired locations, click the Format Painter button to deactivate it. If you need to apply formatting in only one other location, click the Format Painter button once. The first time you select text, the formatting is applied and the Format Painter is deactivated.

Project 1b | **Applying Formatting with Format Painter**

1. With **PP_C3_P1.pptx** open, make sure Slide 3 is active.
2. Apply formatting to the title by completing the following steps:
   a. Click in the title text and then select the title *Electronic Commerce Technology*.
   b. Click the Font group dialog box launcher.

Step 2b

c. At the Font dialog box, click the down-pointing arrow at the right side of the *Font style* option box and then click *Bold Italic* at the drop-down list.

d. Select the current number in the *Size* text box and then type **36**.

e. Click the Font color button and then click the *Blue-Gray, Accent 6, Darker 25%* option.

f. Click OK to close the dialog box.

3. Click on any character in the title.

4. Double-click the Format Painter button in the Clipboard group.

5. Make Slide 8 active.

6. Using the mouse, select the title *Advantages of Online Shopping*. (The mouse pointer displays as an I-beam with a paintbrush attached. You can also click each word in the title to apply the formatting.)

7. Make Slide 9 active and then select the title (or click each word in the title).

8. Make Slide 10 active and then select the title (or click each word in the title).

9. Click the Format Painter button to deactivate it.

10. If necessary, deselect the text.

Formatting Paragraphs

The Paragraph group in the Home tab contains a number of buttons for applying paragraph formatting to text in a slide such as applying bullets and numbers, increasing and decreasing list levels, changing the horizontal and vertical alignment of text, changing line spacing, and rotating text in a placeholder. Table 3.2 describes the buttons in the Paragraph group along with any keyboard shortcuts.

Table 3.2 PowerPoint Home Tab Paragraph Group Buttons

Button	Name	Function	Keyboard Shortcut
	Bullets	Adds or removes bullets to or from selected text	
	Numbering	Adds or removes numbers to or from selected text	
	Decrease List Level	Moves text to the previous tab stop (level)	Shift + Tab
	Increase List Level	Moves text to the next tab stop (level)	Tab
	Line Spacing		
	Align Text Left	Left-aligns text	Ctrl + L
	Center	Center-aligns text	Ctrl + E
	Align Text Right	Right-aligns text	Ctrl + R
	Justify	Justifies text	
	Columns	Splits text into two or more columns	
	Text Direction	Rotates or stacks text	
	Align Text	Changes the alignment of text within a text box	
	Convert to SmartArt Graphic	Converts selected text to a SmartArt graphic	

1. With **PP_C3_P1.pptx** open, change bullets by completing the following steps:
   a. Make Slide 3 active.
   b. Click on any character in the bulleted text.
   c. Select the bulleted text.
   d. Click the Bullets button arrow and then click the *Filled Square Bullets* option at the drop-down gallery.

2. Change bullets to numbers by completing the following steps:
   a. Make Slide 8 active.
   b. Click on any character in the bulleted text.
   c. Select the bulleted text.
   d. Click the Numbering button arrow in the Paragraph group in the Home tab and then click the *A. B. C.* option at the drop-down gallery.

   e. After looking at the numbering, you decide to change to numbers by clicking the Numbering button arrow and then clicking the *1. 2. 3.* option at the drop-down gallery.
3. Decrease and increase list levels by completing the following steps:
   a. With Slide 8 active and the numbered text selected, click the Increase List Level button in the Paragraph group in the Home tab.
   b. With the text still selected, click the Font Color button arrow and then click the Dark Blue color (second color from the right in the bottom row).

c. Make Slide 10 active.

d. Click on any character in the bulleted text.

e. Move the insertion point so it is positioned immediately left of the *J.* in *J.C. Penney*.

f. Click the Decrease List Level button in the Paragraph group in the Home tab.

g. Move the insertion point so it is positioned immediately left of the *M* in *Macy's*.

h. Press Shift + Tab.

i. Move the insertion point so it is positioned immediately left of the first *L.* in *L.L. Bean*.

j. Click the Increase List Level button in the Paragraph group.

k. Move the insertion point so it is positioned immediately left of the *T* in *The Gap*.

l. Press the Tab key.

m. Complete similar steps to those in 3h or 3i to indent the following text to the next level: *Bloomingdale's*, *Expedia*, *Travelocity*, and *Orbitz*.

Steps
3e–3m

4. Change text line spacing by completing the following steps:

a. Make Slide 3 active.

b. Click in the bulleted text and then select the bulleted text.

c. Click the Line Spacing button in the Paragraph group in the Home tab and then click *1.5* at the drop-down list.

d. Make Slide 8 active.

e. Click in the bulleted text and then select the bulleted text.

f. Click the Line Spacing button and then click *2.0* at the drop-down list.

Step
4c

5. Change paragraph alignment by completing the following steps:

a. Make Slide 3 active, click on any character in the title, and then click the Center button in the Paragraph group.

Step
5a

b. Make Slide 8 active, click on any character in the title, and then click the Center button.

c. Make Slide 9 active, click on any character in the title, and then click the Center button.

d. Make Slide 10 active, click on any character in the title, and then click the Center button.

6. Split text into two columns by completing the following steps:
   a. Make Slide 9 active.
   b. Click in the bulleted text and then select the bulleted text.
   c. Click the Columns button in the Paragraph group and then click *Two Columns* at the drop-down list.

   d. Select the first sentence in the first bulleted paragraph (the sentence *Clear selling terms.*) and then click the Bold button.
   e. Select and then bold the first sentence in the remaining bulleted paragraphs of text in Slide 9.
7. Save **PP_C3_P1.pptx**.

Customizing Paragraphs

If you want more control over paragraph alignment, indenting, and spacing, click the Paragraph group dialog box launcher. This displays the Paragraph dialog box with the Indents and Spacing tab selected as shown in Figure 3.2. You can also display this dialog box by clicking the Line Spacing button in the Paragraph group and then clicking *Line Spacing Options* at the drop-down list. Use options at this dialog box to specify text alignment, paragraph indention, spacing before and after paragraphs, and line spacing.

Line Spacing

Figure 3.2 Paragraph Dialog Box with Indents and Spacing Tab Selected

Click this arrow to display a list of alignment options.

Use options in this section to indent text.

Use options in this section to specify spacing before and after text and to choose text line spacing.

HINT

Format text into columns to make the text attractive and easy to read.

Columns

Customizing Columns

Click the Columns button in the Paragraph group and you can choose one, two, or three columns. If you want to choose a number for columns other than the three choices or if you want to control spacing between columns, click the *More Columns* option at the drop-down list. This displays the Columns dialog box shown in Figure 3.3. With options in this dialog box, you can specify the number of columns and the spacing measurement between columns.

Figure 3.3 Columns Dialog Box

Specify the number of columns and spacing between columns in this dialog box.

Project **1d** **Customizing Paragraph and Column Formatting**

1. With **PP_C3_P1.pptx** open, change line and paragraph spacing by completing the following steps:
   a. Make Slide 3 active.
   b. Click in the bulleted text and then select the bulleted text.
   c. Click the Paragraph group dialog box launcher.
   d. At the Paragraph dialog box, click twice on the up-pointing arrow at the right side of the *Before text* measurement box. (This inserts *0.6"* in the measurement box.)
   e. Click twice on the up-pointing arrow at the right side of the *After* measurement box in the *Spacing* section. (This inserts *12 pt* in the box.)
   f. Click the down-pointing arrow at the right side of the *Line Spacing* option box and then click *Multiple* at the drop-down list.
   g. Select the current measurement in the *At* text box and then type 1.8.
   h. Click OK.

2. Format text in columns by completing the following steps:
   a. Make Slide 10 active.
   b. Click in the bulleted text and then select the text.
   c. Click the Columns button in the Paragraph group and then click *More Columns*.
   d. At the Columns dialog box, click once on the up-pointing arrow at the right side of the *Number* option. (This inserts a *2* in the text box.)
   e. Click the up-pointing arrow at the right side of the *Spacing* measurement box until *0.5"* displays in the box.
   f. Click OK.
   g. With the text still selected, click the Paragraph group dialog box launcher.
   h. At the Paragraph dialog box, click once on the up-pointing arrow at the right side of the *After* measurement box in the *Spacing* section. (This inserts *6 pt* in the box.)
   i. Click OK.
3. Save **PP_C3_P1.pptx**.

Rotating and Vertically Aligning Text

If you click the Text Direction button in the Paragraph group, a drop-down list displays with options for rotating and stacking text. Click *More Options* at the drop-down list and the Format Text Effects dialog box with *Text Box* selected in the left panel displays as shown in Figure 3.4. Use options in this dialog box to specify vertical alignment and text direction, autofit contents, and change internal margins. Click the Align Text button in the Paragraph group and a drop-down list displays with options for changing the alignment to top, middle, or bottom of the placeholder. Click *More Options* that displays at the bottom of the drop-down list and the Format Text Effects dialog box shown in Figure 3.4 displays.

Text Direction

Align Text

Figure 3.4 Format Text Effects Dialog Box with Text Box Selected

Use options in this section to specify internal margins for text in a placeholder.

1. With **PP_C3_P1.pptx** open, change vertical alignment by completing the following steps:
   a. Make Slide 9 active.
   b. Click on any character in the bulleted text.
   c. Click the Align Text button in the Paragraph group and then click *Middle* at the drop-down list.

2. Modify Slide 8 so it displays as shown in Figure 3.5 by completing the following steps:
   a. Click in the numbered text and then select the numbered text.
   b. Click the Bullets button arrow and then click the *Filled Square Bullets* option.
   c. Decrease the size of the bulleted text placeholder so the placeholder borders display just outside the text.
   d. Drag the placeholder so the bulleted text is positioned as shown in Figure 3.5.
   e. Click on any character in the title *Advantages of Online Shopping*.
   f. Delete *of Online Shopping*.
   g. Select *Advantages* and then change the font size to 60.
   h. Drag in the right border of the placeholder to the left so it is positioned just outside the text.
   i. Click the Text Direction button in the Paragraph group and then click *Rotate all text 270°*.

   j. Using the sizing handles that display around the title placeholder, increase the height and decrease the width of the placeholder and then drag the placeholder so the title displays as shown in Figure 3.5.
3. Apply a transition and sound to all slides in the presentation.
4. Display the presentation in Print Preview and insert the date, header, and footer in handouts pages by completing the following steps:
   a. Click the Office button, point to *Print*, and then click *Print Preview*.
   b. At the Print Preview window, click the down-pointing arrow at the right of the *Print What* option box in the Page Setup group and then click *Handouts (6 Slides Per Page)* at the drop-down list.

c. Click the Options button in the Print group in the Print Preview tab and then click *Header and Footer* at the drop-down list.

d. At the Header and Footer dialog box with the Notes and Handouts tab selected, click the *Date and time* check box to insert a check mark.

e. Click the *Header* check box to insert a check mark and then type Electronic Commerce in the *Header* text box.

f. Click the *Footer* check box to insert a check mark and then type your first and last names in the *Footer* text box.

g. Click the Apply to All button located in the upper right corner of the dialog box.

h. Click the Print button in the Print group and then click OK at the Print dialog box.

5. Save and then close **PP_C3_P1.pptx**.

Figure 3.5 **Project 1e, Slide 8**

Project ② **Customize Bullets and Numbers in a Color Presentation**
You will open a presentation on using colors in publications and then create and
apply custom bullets and numbering.

Customizing Bullets

Each design theme contains a Title and Content slide layout containing bullets.
The appearance and formatting of the bullets varies with each design theme. You
can choose to use the bullet provided by the design theme or create custom bullets.
Customize bullets with options at the Bullets and Numbering dialog box with the
Bulleted tab selected as shown in Figure 3.6. Display this dialog box by clicking in
a bulleted list placeholder, clicking the Bullets button arrow and then clicking
Bullets and Numbering at the drop-down gallery.

Bullets

Figure 3.6 Bullets and Numbering Dialog Box with Bulleted Tab Selected

Use this option to
increase or decrease
the size of the bullet.

Use this option to change
the bullet color.

Click this button to display
the Picture Bullet dialog box
containing picture bullets.

Click this button to display the
Symbol dialog box containing
bullet symbol options.

At the Bullets and Numbering dialog box, choose one of the predesigned
bullets from the list box, change the size of the bullets by percentage in relation
to the text size, change the bullet color, and display bullet pictures and characters.
Click the Picture button located toward the bottom of the dialog box and the
Picture Bullet dialog box displays. Click the desired bullet in the list box and then
click OK. Click the Customize button located toward the bottom of the Bullets
and Numbering dialog box and the Symbol dialog box displays. Choose a symbol
bullet option at the Symbol dialog box and then click OK. Picture or symbol bullets
are particularly effective in adding visual interest.

If you want to move the insertion point down to the next line without inserting
a bullet, press Shift + Enter. This inserts a line break without inserting a bullet. If
you press the Enter key, bulleting is turned back on.

Project **2a** Customizing Bullets and Numbers

1. Open **ColorPresentation.pptx** and then save the presentation and name it **PP_C3_P2**.
2. Increase list level and create custom bullets by completing the following steps:
   a. Make Slide 2 active.
   b. Select the second, third, and fourth bulleted paragraphs.
   c. Click the Increase List Level button in the Paragraph group.
   d. With the three bulleted paragraphs still selected, click the Bullets button arrow and then click *Bullets and Numbering* at the drop-down list.
   e. At the Bullets and Numbering dialog box with the Bulleted tab selected, click the up-pointing arrow at the right side of the *Size* option until *75* displays in the text box.
   f. Click the Picture button located toward the bottom right corner of the dialog box.
   g. At the Picture Bullet dialog box, click the first bullet option from the left in the third row (gold, square bullet).
   h. Click OK to close the Picture Bullet dialog box and the Bullets and Numbering dialog box.

3. Insert symbol bullets by completing the following steps:
   a. Make Slide 3 active.
   b. Select all of the bulleted text.
   c. Click the Bullets button arrow and then click *Bullets and Numbering* at the drop-down list.
   d. At the Bullets and Numbering dialog box with the Bulleted tab selected, click the up-pointing arrow at the right side of the *Size* option until *80* displays in the text box.
   e. Click the Customize button located toward the bottom right corner of the dialog box.

f. At the Symbol dialog box, click the down-pointing arrow at the right side of the *Font* option box, scroll down the drop-down list, and then click *Wingdings*. (This option is located toward the bottom of the list.)

g. Scroll to the bottom of the Symbol dialog box list box until the last row of symbols displays and then click the second symbol from the right in the bottom row (check mark inside of a square).

h. Click OK.

i. At the Bullets and Numbering dialog box, click the Font Color button and then click the Red color (second color from the left in the *Standard Colors* section).

j. Click OK to close the Bullets and Numbering dialog box. (This applies the red check mark symbol bullets to the selected text.)

4. Save **PP_C3_P2.pptx**.

Customizing Numbering

QUICK STEPS

Customize Numbering
1. Click in numbered text.
2. Click Numbering button arrow.
3. Click *Bullets and Numbering* at drop-down gallery.
4. Make desired changes.
5. Click OK.

Click the Numbering button arrow in the Paragraph group and several numbering options display in a drop-down gallery. You can customize numbering with options at the Bullets and Numbering dialog box with the Numbered tab selected as shown in Figure 3.7. Display this dialog box by clicking the Numbering button arrow and then clicking *Bullets and Numbering* at the drop-down gallery. Use options at this dialog box to change the size and color of numbers as well as the starting number.

If you want to move the insertion point down to the next line without inserting a number, press Shift + Enter. If you press Enter, numbering is turned back on.

Numbering

Figure 3.7 Bullets and Numbering Dialog Box with Numbered Tab Selected

Use this option to increase or decrease the size of the number.

Use this option to change the number color.

Change the starting number with this option.

Project 2b Customizing Numbers

1. With **PP_C3_P2.pptx** open, make sure the presentation displays in Normal view.
2. Customize and insert numbers by completing the following steps:
   a. Make Slide 4 active.
   b. Select the bulleted text in the slide.
   c. Click the Numbering button arrow in the Home tab and then click the *Bullets and Numbering* option at the drop-down list.
   d. At the Bullets and Numbering dialog box with the Numbered tab selected, click the *1. 2. 3.* option (second option from the left in the top row).
   e. Click the up-pointing arrow at the right side of the *Size* option until *80* displays in the text box.
   f. Click the Font Color button and then the Dark Red color (first color option from the left in the *Standard Colors* row).
   g. Click OK.

Step 2d

Step 2e

Step 2f

Step 2g

h. Make Slide 5 active.
i. Select the bulleted text in the slide.
j. Click the Numbering button arrow and then click the *Bullets and Numbering* option at the drop-down list.
k. At the Bullets and Numbering dialog box with the Numbered tab selected, click the *1. 2. 3.* option (second option from the left in the top row).
l. Click the up-pointing arrow at the right side of the *Size* option until *80* displays in the text box.
m. Click the Font Color button and then click the Dark Red color (first color option from the left in the *Standard Colors* row).
n. Click the up-pointing arrow at the right of the *Start at* option until *6* displays in the text box.
o. Click OK.
3. Add a transition and sound of your choosing to all slides in the presentation.
4. Run the presentation.
5. Display the presentation in Print Preview and insert the date, header, and footer in handouts pages by completing the following steps:
a. Click the Office button, point to *Print*, and then click *Print Preview*.
b. At the Print Preview window, click the down-pointing arrow at the right side of the *Print What* option box in the Page Setup group and then click *Handouts (6 Slides Per Page)* at the drop-down list.
c. Click the Options button in the Print group in the Print Preview tab and then click *Header and Footer* at the drop-down list.
d. At the Header and Footer dialog box with the Notes and Handouts tab selected, click the *Date and time* check box to insert a check mark.
e. Click the *Header* check box to insert a check mark and then type Company Publications in the *Header* text box.
f. Click the *Footer* check box to insert a check mark and then type your first and last names in the *Footer* text box.
g. Click the Apply to All button located in the upper right corner of the dialog box.
h. Click the Print button in the Print group and then click OK at the Print dialog box.
6. Save **PP_C3_P2.pptx**.

HINT

Customizing Placeholders

You can customize a placeholder in a slide with buttons in the Drawing group in the Home tab. For example, you can apply a fill color, an outline, and an effect to a placeholder. You can also customize a placeholder by applying a Quick Style. To customize a placeholder, click in the placeholder to select it and then click the desired button in the Drawing group. Apply a Quick Style to the selected placeholder by clicking the Quick Styles button and then clicking the desired style at the drop-down gallery. Click the *Other Theme Fills* option that displays at the bottom of the drop-down gallery and a side menu displays with additional fills.

In addition to the Quick Styles button, you can use the Shape Fill, Shape Outline, and Shape Effects buttons in the Drawing group in the Home tab to customize a placeholder. Click the Shape Fill button arrow and a drop-down gallery displays with options for applying a color, picture, gradient, or texture to the placeholder. Use the Shape Outline button to apply an outline to a placeholder and specify the outline color, weight, and style. With the Shape Effects button, you can choose from a variety of effects such as shadow, reflection, glow, and soft edges.

Changing Internal Margins

When you apply formatting to a placeholder, you may need to move text within the placeholder. You can do this with the internal margins measurements in the Format Text Effects dialog box with the *Text Box* option selected in the left panel (shown in Figure 3.4). Use the *Left*, *Right*, *Top*, and *Bottom* measurements boxes to specify internal margins for text inside the placeholder.

Project 2c Customizing Placeholders

1. With **PP_C3_P2.pptx** open, customize the title placeholder in Slide 1 by completing the following steps:
   a. If necessary, make Slide 1 active.
   b. Click in the title to select the placeholder.
   c. If necessary, click the Home tab.
   d. Click the Quick Styles button in the Drawing group.
   e. Click the *Moderate Effect - Accent 1* option at the drop-down gallery (second option from the left in the fifth row).

   f. Click the Shape Outline button arrow in the Drawing group and then click *Blue* in the *Standard Colors* section.

g. Click the Shape Outline button arrow, point to *Weight*, and then click *3 pt* at the side menu.

h. Click the Shape Effects button, point to *Bevel*, and then click *Cool Slant* at the side menu (last option in the top row in the *Bevel* section).

i. After looking at the fill color, you decide to change it by clicking the Quick Styles button in the Drawing group, pointing to *Other Theme Fills* that displays at the bottom of the drop-down gallery, and then clicking *Style 11* at the side menu (third option from the left in the bottom row).

2. Change the internal margins for the text in the title placeholder by completing the following steps:

a. With the title placeholder selected, click the Text Direction button in the Paragraph group in the Home tab and then click *More Options* at the drop-down list.

b. At the Format Text Effects dialog box with *Text Box* selected in the left panel, click the up-pointing arrow at the right side of the *Left* measurement box until *0.3"* displays in the measurement box.

c. Click the up-pointing arrow at the right side of the *Right* measurement box until *0.3"* displays in the measurement box.

d. Complete similar steps to change the measurement in the *Top* box and the *Bottom* box to *0.2".*

e. Click the Close button to close the dialog box.

f. Decrease the size of the placeholder border so the border displays an equal distance from text along the top, bottom, left, and right sides.

3. Customize the subtitle placeholder by completing the following steps:
   a. Click in the subtitle text to select the placeholder.
   b. Click the Shape Fill button arrow in the Drawing group, point to *Texture*, and then click *Water droplets* at the drop-down gallery (first option from the left in the second row).
   c. Click the Shape Effects button, point to *Bevel*, and then click *Cool Slant* at the side menu (last option in the top row in the *Bevel* section).

4. Change the internal margins for the text in the subtitle placeholder by completing the following steps:
   a. With the subtitle placeholder selected, click the Text Direction button in the Paragraph group in the Home tab and then click *More Options* at the drop-down list.
   b. At the Format Text Effects dialog box with *Text Box* selected in the left panel, click the up-pointing arrow at the right side of the *Left* measurement box until *0.5″* displays in the measurement box.
   c. Click the up-pointing arrow at the right side of the *Right* measurement box until *0.5″* displays in the measurement box.
   d. Complete similar steps to change the measurement in the *Top* box and the *Bottom* box to *0.2″*.
   e. Click the Close button to close the dialog box.
   f. Decrease the size of the placeholder border so the border displays an equal distance from text along the top, bottom, left, and right sides.
   g. Position the placeholders attractively in the slide.
5. Make Slide 3 active and then change the spacing after paragraphs by completing the following steps:
   a. Select the bulleted text.
   b. Click the Paragraph group dialog box launcher.
   c. At the Paragraph dialog box, click the up-pointing arrow at the right side of the *After* option in the *Spacing* section to display *6 pt* in the option box.
   d. Click OK to close the dialog box.
6. Customize the placeholder by completing the following steps:
   a. With the bulleted text placeholder selected, click the Quick Styles button in the Drawing group and then click *Subtle Effect - Accent 6* at the drop-down gallery (last option in the fourth row).
   b. Click the Shape Effects button, point to *Soft Edges*, and then click *2.5 Point* at the side menu.

c. Click the Text Direction button and then click *More Options* at the drop-down list.
d. At the Format Text Effects dialog box, change the left, right, top, and bottom measurements to *0.4"*.
e. Click the Close button to close the dialog box.
f. Move the placeholder so it is positioned attractively in the slide.
7. Run the presentation.
8. Print the presentation as a handout with six slides per page.
9. You decide that you do not like the appearance of the formatting of the subtitle placeholder in Slide 1 so you decide to remove the formatting by completing the following steps:
a. Make Slide 1 active.
b. Click on any character in the subtitle placeholder text.
c. Make sure the Home tab is selected.
d. Click the Quick Styles button in the Drawing group and then click the *Colored Outline - Accent 3* option (fourth option from the left in the top row).
10. Print Slide 1.
11. Save and then close **PP_C3_P2.pptx**.

Project ③ Modify the Theme and Slide Background of a Job Search Presentation

You will open a job search presentation, apply a design theme, and then change the theme colors and fonts. You will also apply and customize a background style.

HINT
Themes are shared across Office programs such as PowerPoint, Word, and Excel.

Modifying Theme Colors and Fonts

A design theme is a set of formatting choices that includes a color theme (a set of colors), a font theme (heading and text fonts), and an effects theme (a set of lines and fill effects). Use buttons at the right side of the Themes group to change design theme colors, fonts, and effects.

A theme contains specific color formatting, which you can change with options from the Colors button in the Themes group. Click this button and a drop-down gallery displays with named color schemes. The names of the color schemes correspond to the names of the themes. Each theme applies specific fonts, which you can change with options from the Fonts button in the Themes group. Click this button and a drop-down gallery displays with font choices. Each font group in the drop-down gallery contains two choices. The first choice in the group is the font that is applied to slide titles and the second choice is the font that is applied to slide subtitles and text. If you are formatting a presentation that contains graphic elements such as illustrations, pictures, clip art, or text boxes, you can specify theme effects with options at the Effects drop-down gallery.

Changing Slide Background

The Background group in the Design tab contains a button and an option for customizing the background of slides in a presentation. Click the Background Styles button and a drop-down gallery of background styles displays. Click the desired style at this drop-down gallery or click the *Format Background* option to display the Format Background dialog box shown in Figure 3.8. You can also display the dialog box by clicking the Background group dialog box launcher. Use options in this dialog box to customize background fill, gradient, direction, and color. If you make changes to the slide background, you can reset the background to the default by clicking the Reset Background button in the Format Background dialog box. You can also reset the background to the default by clicking the Background Styles button and then clicking *Reset Slide Background* at the drop-down gallery.

Figure 3.8 Format Background Dialog Box

Some of the design themes provided by PowerPoint contain a background graphic. You can remove this graphic from a slide by clicking the *Hide Background Graphics* check box in the Background group. This removes the background from the currently active slide. If you want to remove the background from more than one slide, select the slides. You can also remove background graphics from all slides by inserting a check mark in the Hide background graphics check box in the Format Background dialog box and then clicking the Apply to All button.

Project 3a Customizing Theme Colors and Fonts

1. Open **JobSearch.pptx** and then save the presentation and name it **PP_C3_P3**.
2. Apply a design theme by completing the following steps:
   a. Click the Design tab.
   b. Click the More button at the right side of the design themes and then click *Metro* at the drop-down gallery.

3. Change the theme colors by clicking the Colors button in the Themes group and then clicking *Paper* at the drop-down gallery.

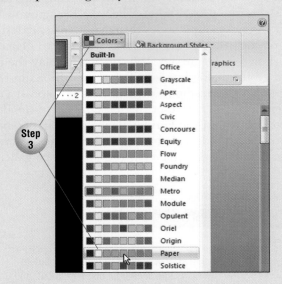

4. Change the theme fonts by clicking the Fonts button in the Themes group, scrolling down the drop-down gallery, and then clicking *Solstice*.

5. Change the background style by clicking the Background Styles button in the Background group and then clicking *Style 10* at the drop-down gallery.
6. With Slide 1 active, run the presentation and notice the formatting applied by the theme, theme colors, theme fonts, and background style.
7. With the presentation in Normal view, change the background style by clicking the Background Styles button in the Background group in the Design tab and then clicking *Style 7* at the drop-down gallery.

8. Apply and customize a background style by completing the following steps:

a. Click the Background group dialog box launcher.

b. At the Format Background dialog box, click the *Hide background graphics* check box to insert a check mark.

c. Click the down-pointing arrow to the right of the *Type* option box and then click *Path* at the drop-down list.

d. Drag the button on the *Stop position* slider bar until *85%* displays in the percentage box at the right.

e. Click the Color button and then click *Black, Background 1, Lighter 35%* at the drop-down list (first color option from the left in the third row).

f. Drag the button on the *Transparency* slider bar until *15%* displays in the percentage box at the right. (You can also click the up-pointing arrow at the right side of the percentage box until *15%* displays.)

g. Click the Apply to All button.

h. Click the Close button.

9. Run the presentation and notice the background formatting.

10. Save **PP_C3_P3.pptx**.

Changing Page Setup

As you learned in Chapter 2, the Print Preview tab contains buttons for changing orientation and page setup options. You can also control page setup and the orientation of slides with buttons in the Page Setup group in the Design tab. The default slide orientation is *Landscape*. You can change this to *Portrait* with the Slide Orientation button. Click the Page Setup button and the Page Setup dialog box displays as shown in Figure 3.9. With options at this dialog box, you can specify how you want the slides sized. By default, slides are sized for an on-screen show with a 4:3 ratio. Click the down-pointing arrow at the right side of the *Slides sized for* option and a drop-down list displays with options for changing the slide size ratio and choosing other paper sizes. With other options in the dialog box, you can specify slide width and height and change the starting slide number. You can also change the orientation of slides and the orientation of notes, handouts, and outline pages.

Slide Orientation

Page Setup

Figure 3.9 Page Setup Dialog Box

Click this down-pointing arrow and choose a slide size at the drop-down list.

Use these options to specify the slide width and height measurements.

Project **3b** | **Changing Orientation and Page Setup**

1. With **PP_C3_P3.pptx** open, change slide orientation by clicking the Design tab, clicking the Slide Orientation button, and then clicking *Portrait* at the drop-down list.

Step 1

2. Run the presentation and notice how the slides appear in portrait orientation.
3. After running the presentation, click the Slide Orientation button and then click *Landscape* at the drop-down list.
4. Suppose you are going to run the presentation on a wide screen monitor. To do this, you decide to change the slide size ratio by completing the following steps:
   a. Click the Page Setup button in the Page Setup group in the Design tab.
   b. At the Page Setup dialog box, click the down-pointing arrow at the right side of the *Slides sized for* option and then click *On-screen Show (16:10)*. (Notice that the slide height changed from *7.5* to *6.25*.)
   c. Click OK.

Step 4b   Step 4c

5. Run the presentation.
6. Specify slide width and height by completing the following steps:
   a. Click the Page Setup button.
   b. At the Page Setup dialog box, click the down-pointing arrow at the right side of the *Width* measurement box until *9* displays in the box.
   c. Click the down-pointing arrow at the right side of the *Height* measurement box until *6* displays in the box.
   d. Click OK.
7. Run the presentation.
8. Return the slide size to the default by completing the following steps:
   a. Click the Page Setup button.
   b. At the Page Setup dialog box, click the down-pointing arrow at the right side of the *Slides sized for* option and then click *On-screen Show (4:3)*.
   c. Click OK.
9. Save and then close **PP_C3_P3.pptx**.

Project ④ Create and Apply Custom Themes to Presentations

You will create custom theme colors and custom theme fonts and then save the changes as a custom theme. You will then apply the custom theme to a job search presentation and a resume writing presentation.

Creating Custom Themes

If the default themes, theme colors, and theme fonts do not provide the formatting you desire for your presentation, you can create your own custom theme colors, custom theme fonts, and a custom theme. A theme you create will display in the Themes drop-down gallery under the *Custom* section. To create a custom theme, change the theme colors, theme fonts, and/or theme effects.

The buttons at the right side of the Themes group in the Design tab display a visual representation of the current theme. If you change the theme colors, the colors are reflected in the small color squares on the Colors button. If you change the theme fonts, the A on the Fonts button reflects the change.

Creating Custom Theme Colors

To create custom theme colors, click the Design tab, click the Colors button in the Themes group, and then click *Create New Theme Colors* at the drop-down gallery. This displays the Create New Theme Colors dialog box similar to the one shown in Figure 3.10. Theme colors contain four text and background colors, six accent colors, and two hyperlink colors as shown in the *Themes color* section of the dialog box. Change a color in the list box by clicking the color button at the right side of the color option and then clicking the desired color at the color palette.

QUICK STEPS

Create Custom Theme Colors
1. Click Design tab.
2. Click Theme Colors button.
3. Click *Create New Theme Colors*.
4. Change to desired background, accent, and hyperlink colors.
5. Type name for custom theme colors.
6. Click Save button.

Figure 3.10 Create New Theme Colors Dialog Box

Click the Reset button to reset color back to the default.

Change a theme color by clicking the color button and then clicking the desired color at the drop-down palette.

After you have made all desired changes to colors, click in the *Name* text box, type a name for the custom theme colors, and then click the Save button. This saves the custom theme colors and applies the color changes to the currently open presentation. Display the custom theme colors by clicking the Colors button in the Themes group in the Design tab. Your custom theme colors will display toward the top of the drop-down gallery in the *Custom* section. If you make changes to colors at the Create New Theme Colors dialog box and then decide you do not like the color changes, click the Reset button located in the lower left corner of the dialog box.

When you create custom theme colors, you can apply the theme to your presentation by clicking the Colors button in the Themes group in the Design tab and then clicking the custom theme colors that display toward the top of the drop-down gallery in the *Custom* section.

Note: If you are running PowerPoint 2007 on a computer connected to a network in a public environment such as a school, you may need to complete all of Project 4 during the same session. Network system software may delete your custom themes when you exit PowerPoint. Check with your instructor.

Project 4a Creating Custom Theme Colors

1. At a blank presentation, click the Design tab, click the More button at the right side of the Themes group, and then click *Technic* at the drop-down gallery.
2. Create custom theme colors by completing the following steps:
   a. Click the Colors button in the Themes group and then click the *Create New Theme Colors* option at the drop-down gallery.

b. At the Create New Theme Colors dialog box, click the color button that displays at the right side of the *Text/Background - Dark 1* option and then click the *Olive Green, Accent 4, Lighter 60%* option.

c. Click the color button that displays at the right side of the *Text/Background - Light 1* option and then click the *Gold, Accent 2, Lighter 80%* option.
d. Click the color button that displays at the right side of the *Text/Background - Dark 2* option and then click the *Lavender, Accent 3, Darker 25%* option.
3. Save the custom colors by completing the following steps:
   a. Select the current text in the *Name* text box.
   b. Type your first and last names.
   c. Click the Save button.

4. Save the presentation and name it **CustomTheme**.

Creating Custom Theme Fonts

To create custom theme fonts, click the Design tab, click the Fonts button, and then click *Create New Theme Fonts* at the drop-down gallery. This displays the Create New Theme Fonts dialog box similar to the one shown in Figure 3.11. At this dialog box, choose a heading font and a font for body text. Type a name for the custom theme fonts in the *Name* box and then click the Save button.

Create Custom Fonts
1. Click Design tab.
2. Click Theme Fonts button.
3. Click *Create New Theme Fonts*.
4. Choose desired fonts.
5. Type name for custom theme fonts.
6. Click Save button.

Figure 3.11 Create New Theme Fonts Dialog Box

Choose a heading font and body font, type a new name for the theme in the *Name* text box, and then click Save.

Project 4h Creating Custom Theme Fonts

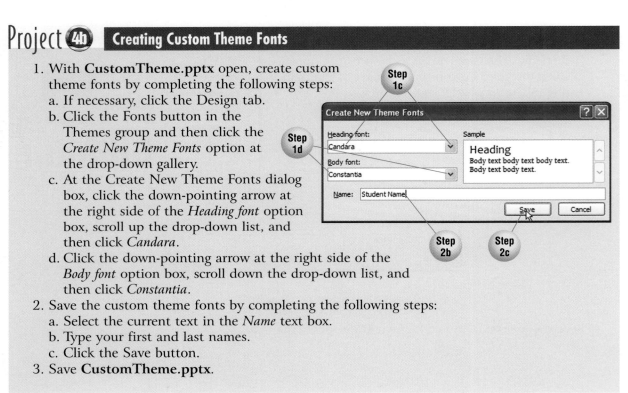

1. With **CustomTheme.pptx** open, create custom theme fonts by completing the following steps:
   a. If necessary, click the Design tab.
   b. Click the Fonts button in the Themes group and then click the *Create New Theme Fonts* option at the drop-down gallery.
   c. At the Create New Theme Fonts dialog box, click the down-pointing arrow at the right side of the *Heading font* option box, scroll up the drop-down list, and then click *Candara*.
   d. Click the down-pointing arrow at the right side of the *Body font* option box, scroll down the drop-down list, and then click *Constantia*.
2. Save the custom theme fonts by completing the following steps:
   a. Select the current text in the *Name* text box.
   b. Type your first and last names.
   c. Click the Save button.
3. Save **CustomTheme.pptx**.

Step 1c
Step 1d
Step 2b
Step 2c

QUICK STEPS

Save a Custom Theme
1. Click Design tab.
2. Click More button in Themes group.
3. Click *Save Current Theme.*
4. Type name for custom theme.
5. Click Save button.

Saving a Custom Theme

When you have customized theme colors and fonts, you can save these as a custom theme. To do this, click the More button at the right side of the Themes group in the Design tab and then click *Save Current Theme*. This displays the Save Current Theme dialog box with many of the same options as the Save As dialog box. Type a name for your custom theme in the *File name* text box and then click the Save button. To apply a custom theme, click the More button and then click the desired theme in the *Custom* section of the drop-down gallery.

1. With **CustomTheme.pptx** open, save the custom theme colors and fonts as a custom theme by completing the following steps:
   a. If necessary, click the Design tab.
   b. Click the More button at the right side of the themes thumbnails in the Themes group.
   c. Click the *Save Current Theme* option that displays at the bottom of the drop-down gallery.
   d. At the Save Current Theme dialog box, type C3 and then type your last name in the *File name* text box.
   e. Click the Save button.

2. Save and then close **CustomTheme.pptx**.
3. Open **JobSearch.pptx** and then save the presentation and name it **PP_C3_P4a**.
4. Apply your custom theme by completing the following steps:
   a. Click the Design tab.
   b. Click the More button that displays at the right side of the themes thumbnails.
   c. Click the custom theme that begins with *C3* followed by your last name. (The theme will display in the *Custom* section of the drop-down gallery.)

5. Run the presentation and notice how the slides display with the custom theme applied.
6. Print Slide 1 of the presentation.
7. Save and then close **PP_C3_P4a.pptx**.
8. Open **ResumePresentation.pptx** and then save the presentation and name it **PP_C3_P4b**.
9. Apply your custom theme (the theme that displays beginning with *C3* followed by your last name).
10. Make Slide 2 active and then adjust the placeholder containing the bulleted text so it is positioned attractively on the slide.
11. Make Slide 1 active and then run the presentation.
12. Print Slide 1 of the presentation.
13. Save and then close **PP_C3_P4b.pptx**.

Editing Custom Themes

You can edit the custom theme colors and custom theme fonts. To edit the custom theme colors, click the Colors button in the Themes group in the Design tab. At the drop-down gallery of custom and built-in themes, right-click your custom theme and then click *Edit* at the shortcut menu. This displays the Edit Theme Colors dialog box that contains the same options as the Create New Theme Colors dialog box shown in Figure 3.10. Make the desired changes to theme colors and then click the Save button.

To edit custom theme fonts, click the Fonts button in the Themes group in the Design tab, right-click your custom theme fonts, and then click *Edit* at the shortcut menu. This displays the Edit Theme Fonts dialog box that contains the same options as the Create New Theme Fonts dialog box shown in Figure 3.11. Make the desired changes and then click the Save button.

Edit Custom Theme Colors
1. Click Design tab.
2. Click Theme Colors button.
3. Right-click desired custom theme.
4. Click *Edit*.
5. Make desired changes.
6. Click Save button.

Edit Custom Theme Fonts
1. Click Page Layout tab.
2. Click Theme Fonts button.
3. Right-click desired custom theme.
4. Click *Edit*.
5. Make desired changes.
6. Click Save button.

Deleting Custom Themes

You can delete custom theme colors from the Colors button drop-down gallery, delete custom theme fonts from the Fonts drop-down gallery, and delete custom themes from the Save Current Theme dialog box. To delete custom theme colors, click the Colors button, right-click the theme you want to delete, and then click *Delete* at the shortcut menu. At the message asking if you want to delete the theme colors, click Yes. Complete similar steps to delete custom theme fonts.

Delete a custom theme at the Save Current Theme dialog box. To display this dialog box, click the More button at the right side of the Themes group in the Design tab and then click *Save Current Theme* at the drop-down gallery. At the dialog box, click the custom theme file name and then click the Delete button on the dialog box toolbar. At the message asking if you are sure you want to send the theme to the Recycle Bin, click Yes.

Delete Custom Theme Colors
1. Click Design tab.
2. Click Theme Colors button.
3. Right-click desired custom theme.
4. Click *Delete*.
5. Click Yes.

Delete Custom Theme Fonts
1. Click Design tab.
2. Click Theme Fonts button.
3. Right-click desired custom theme.
4. Click *Delete*.
5. Click Yes.

Delete Custom Theme
1. Click Design tab.
2. Click More button in Themes group.
3. Click *Save Current Theme*.
4. Click custom theme.
5. Click Delete button.
6. Click Yes.

1. At a blank presentation, delete the custom theme colors by completing the following steps:
   a. Click the Design tab.
   b. Click the Colors button in the Themes group.
   c. Right-click the custom theme colors named with your first and last names.
   d. Click *Delete* at the shortcut menu.

   e. At the question asking if you want to delete the theme colors, click Yes.
2. Complete steps similar to those in Step 1 to delete the custom theme fonts you created named with your first and last names.
3. Delete the custom theme by completing the following steps:
   a. Click the More button that displays at the right side of the themes thumbnails.
   b. Click *Save Current Theme* located toward the bottom of the drop-down gallery.
   c. At the Save Current Theme dialog box, click the custom theme that begins with *C3* followed by your last name.
   d. Click the Delete button on the dialog box toolbar.

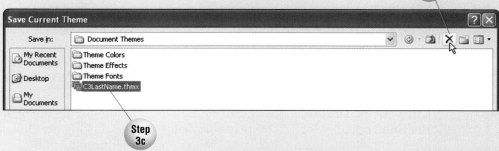

   e. At the message asking if you are sure you want to send the theme to the Recycle Bin, click Yes.
   f. Click the Cancel button to close the dialog box.
4. Close the presentation without saving it.

CHAPTER summary

- The Font group in the Home tab contains buttons for applying character formatting to text in slides. Refer to Table 3.1 for a listing of the Font group buttons, a description of the button function, and keyboard shortcuts.

- Design themes apply a font to text in slides. You can change this default font with the Font and Font Size buttons in the Font group.

- Some buttons, such as the Font and Font Size buttons, contain the *live preview* feature, which allows you to see how the formatting affects your text without having to return to the presentation.

- You can also apply character formatting with options at the Font dialog box. Display this dialog box by clicking the Font group dialog box launcher.

- Select text in a slide and the Mini toolbar displays above the selected text in dimmed fashion. Move the mouse pointer to the toolbar and it becomes active.

- Use the Format Painter feature to apply formatting to more than one location in a slide or slides.

- The Paragraph group in the Home tab contains a number of buttons for applying paragraph formatting to text in slides. Refer to Table 3.2 for a listing of the Paragraph group buttons, a description of the button function, and keyboard shortcuts.

- Customize paragraph formatting with options at the Paragraph dialog box with the Indents and Spacing tab selected. Display this dialog box by clicking the Paragraph group dialog box launcher or by clicking the Line Spacing button in the Paragraph group and then clicking *Line Spacing Options* at the drop-down list.

- Use the Columns button in the Paragraph group or options at the Columns dialog box to format selected text into columns. Display the Columns dialog box by clicking the Columns button and then clicking *More Columns* at the drop-down list.

- Use the Text Direction button or options at the Format Text Effects dialog box to rotate or stack text in a slide. Display the Format Text Effects dialog box by clicking the Text Direction button and then clicking *More Options* at the drop-down list.

- Use the Align Text button or options at the Format Text Effects dialog box to vertically align text in a slide.

- Customize bullets with options at the Bullets and Numbering dialog box with the Bulleted tab selected. Display this dialog box by clicking the Bullets button arrow and then clicking *Bullets and Numbering* at the drop-down list.

- Customize numbering with options at the Bullets and Numbering dialog box with the Numbered tab selected. Display this dialog box by clicking the Numbering button arrow and then clicking *Bullets and Numbering* at the drop-down list.

- Click the Quick Styles button in the Drawing group in the Home tab to apply formatting to a placeholder. The Drawing group also contains the Shape Fill, Shape Outline, and Shape Effects buttons you can use to customize a placeholder.

- Use the Colors button in the Themes group in the Design tab to change the theme colors and use the Fonts button to change the theme fonts.

- Use the Background Styles button in the Background group in the Design tab to customize the background of slides and insert a check mark in the *Hide Background Graphics* check box to remove the slide background graphic.

- Click the Page Setup button in the Design tab and the Page Setup dialog box displays containing options for changing the slide size and ratio, starting slide number, and the orientation of slides and notes, handouts, and outline pages.

- Create custom theme colors with options at the Create New Theme Colors dialog box. Display this dialog box by clicking the Colors button in the Themes group in the Design tab and then clicking *Create New Theme Colors* at the drop-down gallery.

- Create custom theme fonts with options at the Create New Theme Fonts dialog box. Display this dialog box by clicking the Fonts button in the Themes group in the Design tab and then clicking *Create New Theme Fonts* at the drop-down gallery.

- Save a custom theme at the Save Current Theme dialog box. Display this dialog box by clicking the Themes button in the Themes group in the Design tab and then clicking *Save Current Theme* at the drop-down gallery.

- Edit custom theme colors with options at the Edit Theme Colors dialog box and edit custom theme fonts with options at the Edit Theme Fonts dialog box.

- Delete custom theme colors by clicking the Theme Colors button, right-clicking the custom theme, and then clicking the *Delete* option.

- Delete custom theme fonts by clicking the Theme Fonts button, right-clicking the custom theme, and then clicking the *Delete* option.

- Delete a custom theme at the Save Current Theme dialog box. Display this dialog box by clicking the Themes button and then clicking *Save Current Theme* at the drop-down gallery.

COMMANDS review

FEATURE	RIBBON TAB, GROUP	BUTTON, OPTION	KEYBOARD SHORTCUT
Font dialog box	Home, Font		Ctrl + Shift + F
Format Painter	Home, Clipboard		
Paragraph dialog box	Home, Paragraph		
Columns dialog box	Home, Paragraph	, More Columns	
Format Text Effects dialog box	Home, Paragraph	, More Options	
Bullets and Numbering dialog box with Bulleted tab selected	Home, Paragraph	, Bullets and Numbering	
Bullets and Numbering dialog box with Numbered tab selected	Home, Paragraph	, Bullets and Numbering	
Format Background dialog box	Design, Background		
Page Setup dialog box	Design, Page Setup		
Create New Theme Colors dialog box	Design, Themes	Colors , Create New Theme Colors	
Create New Theme Fonts dialog box	Design, Themes	A Fonts , Create New Theme Fonts	
Save Current Theme dialog box	Design, Themes	, Save Current Theme	

CONCEPTS check

Test Your Knowledge

Completion: In the space provided at the right, indicate the correct term, symbol, or command.

1. The Font button drop-down gallery is an example of this feature, which allows you to see how the font formatting affects your text without having to return to the presentation. _____

2. Click this button to clear character formatting from selected text. _____

3. Click this to display the Font dialog box. _____

4. Select text in a slide and this displays in a dimmed fashion above the selected text. _____

5. The Format Painter button is located in this group in the Home tab. _____

6. Press this key to move text to the next tab stop (level). _____

7. Use options at this dialog box to change text alignment, indention, and spacing. _____

8. Click this button in the Paragraph group and a drop-down list displays with options for rotating and stacking text. _____

9. Customize numbering with options at the Bullets and Numbering dialog box with this tab selected. _____

10. Use the Align Text button or options at this dialog box to vertically align text in a slide. _____

11. The Quick Styles button is located in this group in the Home tab. _____

12. Click this button to apply fill to a placeholder. _____

13. Create custom theme colors with options at this dialog box. _____

14. Save a custom theme at this dialog box. _____

SKILLS check
Demonstrate Your Proficiency

Assessment

1 CREATE, FORMAT, AND MODIFY A BENEFITS PRESENTATION

1. At a blank presentation, create the slides shown in Figure 3.12.
2. Apply the Oriel design theme.
3. Make Slide 1 active and then make the following changes:
   a. Select the title *BENEFITS PROGRAM*, change the font to Candara, the font size to 48, the font color to Ice Blue, Accent 5, Darker 50%, and apply italic formatting.
   b. Select the subtitle *Change to Plans*, change the font to Candara, the font size to 32, the font color to Orange, Accent 1, Darker 50%, and apply shadow formatting.
   c. Click the title placeholder and then drag the placeholder up until the title is vertically centered on the slide.
   d. Click the subtitle placeholder and then drag the placeholder up so the subtitle is positioned just below the title.
4. Make Slide 2 active and then make the following changes:
   a. Select the title *INTRODUCTION*, change the font to Candara, the font size to 48 points, and apply shadow formatting.
   b. Using Format Painter, apply the title formatting to the titles in the remaining slides.
5. Center-align the titles in Slides 2 through 5.
6. Make Slide 2 active, select the bulleted text, and then change the line spacing to *2.0*.
7. Make Slide 3 active, select the bulleted text, and then change the line spacing to *2.0*.
8. Make Slide 4 active, select the bulleted text, and then change the line spacing to *1.5*.
9. Make Slide 5 active, select the bulleted text, and then change the spacing after paragraphs to *18 pt*. **Hint: Do this at the Paragraph dialog box.**
10. Make Slide 2 active and then select the bulleted text. Display the Bullets and Numbering dialog box with the Numbered tab selected, choose the *1. 2. 3.* option, change the size to *85%*, and then close the dialog box.
11. Make Slide 3 active and then select the bulleted text. Display the Bullets and Numbering dialog box with the Numbered tab selected, choose the *1. 2. 3.* option, change the size to *85%*, change the starting number to *5*, and then close the dialog box.
12. Make Slide 4 active, select the bulleted text, and then change the bullets to *Hollow Square Bullets*.
13. Make Slide 5 active, select the bulleted text, and then change the bullets to *Hollow Square Bullets*.
14. Apply the *Style 5* background style to slides.
15. Save the presentation and name it **PP_C3_A1**.
16. Run the presentation.
17. Print the presentation as a handout with six slides per page.
18. Change the theme colors to *Solstice*.

19. Apply the *Style 2* background style to slides.
20. Apply a transition and sound of your choosing to each slide.
21. Run the presentation.
22. Print the presentation as a handout with six slides per page.
23. Save and then close **PP_C3_A1.pptx**.

Figure 3.12 Assessment 1

Slide 1	Title	=	BENEFITS PROGRAM
	Subtitle	=	Changes to Plans

Slide 2   Title   =   INTRODUCTION
           Bullets =   • Changes made for 2010
                         • Description of eligibility
                         • Instructions for enrolling new members
                         • Overview of medical and dental coverage

Slide 3   Title   =   INTRODUCTION
           Bullets =   • Expanded enrollment forms
                         • Glossary defining terms
                         • Telephone directory
                         • Pamphlet with commonly asked questions

Slide 4   Title   =   WHAT'S NEW
           Bullets =   • New medical plans
                           - Plan 2010
                           - Premiere Plan
                         • Changes in monthly contributions
                         • Paying with pretax dollars
                         • Contributions toward spouse's coverage

Slide 5   Title   =   COST SHARING
           Bullets =   • Increased deductible
                         • New coinsurance amount
                         • Higher coinsurance amount for retail prescription drugs
                         • Co-payment for mail-order medicines
                         • New stop loss limit

Assessment

2   FORMAT AND MODIFY A PERENNIALS PRESENTATION

1. Open **PerennialsPresentation.pptx** and then save the presentation and name it **PP_C3_A2**.
2. Change the theme fonts to *Opulent*.
3. Make Slide 3 active, select the bulleted text, and then create and apply a custom bullet using a flower symbol in a complementary color. (You can find a flower symbol in the *Wingdings* font in the Symbol dialog box.)

4. With Slide 3 active, format the bulleted text into two columns and change the line spacing to *2*. Make sure each column contains four bulleted items. If not, make any spacing or other corrections to make the columns even.

5. Make Slide 4 active and then arrange the bulleted text more attractively on the slide. (You determine the formatting and position.)

6. Make Slide 5 active and then format the bulleted text into two columns with three bulleted items in each column. Make any spacing or formatting changes to improve the visual appeal of the slide.

7. Make Slide 6 active and then format the bulleted text into two columns with three bulleted items in each column. Make any spacing or formatting change to improve the visual appeal of the slide.

8. Make any other changes to slides to improve the visual appeal of each slide.

9. Display the presentation in Print Preview, change the *Print What* option to *Handouts (4 Slides Per Page)*, add a header that prints *Perennial Presentation* on all pages and a footer that prints your first and last names on all pages.

10. Print the presentation.

11. Add a transition and sound of your choosing to all slides in the presentation.

12. Run the presentation.

13. Save and then close **PP_C3_A2.pptx**.

Assessment

3 CREATE AND APPLY A CUSTOM THEME TO A TRAVEL PRESENTATION

1. At a blank presentation, apply the *Opulent* design.

2. Create custom theme colors named with your first and last names that changes the following colors:
   a. At the Create New Theme Colors dialog box, change the *Text/Background - Light 1* option to *Gold, Accent 4, Lighter 80%*.
   b. Change the *Text/Background - Dark 2* option to *Green* (sixth color from the left in the *Standard Colors* row).

3. Create custom theme fonts named with your first and last names that applies the following fonts:
   a. At the Create New Theme Fonts dialog box, change the *Heading font* to *Copperplate Gothic Bold*.
   b. Change the *Body font* to *Rockwell*.

4. Save the current theme as a custom theme named with your first and last names. **Hint: Do this at the Save Current Theme dialog box.**

5. Close the presentation without saving it.

6. Open **TravelEngland.pptx** and then save the presentation and name it **PP_C3_A3**.

7. Apply the custom theme named with your first and last names.

8. Improve the visual display of the bulleted text in Slides 2 and 3 by increasing the spacing between items and positioning the bulleted item placeholders attractively in the slides.

9. Make Slide 4 active, increase the spacing between bulleted items and then format the text into two columns. Make sure that each column contains three bulleted items. Consider decreasing the size of the placeholder.

10. Format the bulleted text in Slides 5 and 6 into two columns with four bulleted items in each column. Consider decreasing the size of the placeholder.

11. Display the presentation in Print Preview, change the *Print What* option to *Handouts (3 Slides Per Page)*, add a header that prints *Traveling in England* on all pages and a footer that prints your first and last names on all pages.
12. Print the presentation.
13. Add a transition and sound of your choosing to all slides in the presentation.
14. Run the presentation.
15. Save and then close **PP_C3_A3.pptx**.
16. Display a blank presentation and then delete the custom theme colors, custom theme fonts, and custom theme you created for this assessment.
17. Close the presentation without saving it.

Assessment

4   PREPARE AND FORMAT A PRESENTATION AT THE FONT DIALOG BOX

1. At a blank presentation, click in a placeholder in the blank slide and then click the Font group dialog box launcher.
2. At the Font dialog box, click the Help button that displays in the upper right corner of the dialog box.
3. Click the <u>Microsoft Office PowerPoint</u> hyperlink, click the <u>Font tab</u> hyperlink, click the <u>Character Spacing tab</u> hyperlink, and then print the Help information.
4. Using the information you printed, create a PowerPoint presentation with the following specifications:
   a. Create a slide with the title of your presentation. Type your name as the subtitle of the presentation.
   b. Create slides (you determine the number of slides) that summarize the information you printed. (Make sure that the slides are not crowded with too much information.) Include a definition for *kerning* on one of the slides.
   c. Apply a design theme of your choosing.
   d. Change the design theme colors.
   e. Change the design theme fonts.
   f. Apply a transition and sound of your choosing to all slides.
5. Save the presentation and name it **PP_C3_A4**.
6. Run the presentation.
7. Print the presentation as an outline.
8. Close **PP_C3_A4.pptx**.

CASE study
Apply Your Skills

Part 1

You are the assistant to Gina Coletti, manager of La Dolce Vita, an Italian restaurant. She has been working on a new lunch menu and wants to present the new menu at the upcoming staff meeting. She has asked you to prepare a presentation she can use at the meeting. Open the Word document named **LunchMenu.docx** and then print the document. Close the document and then exit Word. Using the information you printed, create a presentation and apply the Civic design theme to the presentation. Make any formatting changes to improve the visual appeal of the presentation. Save the presentation and name it **PP_C3_CS_P1**.

Part 2

Ms. Coletti has looked over the presentation and has asked you to apply color and font formatting consistent with other restaurant publications. With **PP_C3_CS_P1.pptx** open, create custom theme colors that change the *Text/Background - Light 2* color to a light yellow and the *Accent 3* color to a green of your choosing. Make sure the colors are complementary. Create custom theme fonts that apply Monotype Corsiva as the heading font and Garamond as the body font. Save the custom theme and name it *LaDolceVita* followed by your initials. Add a transition and sound to all slides in the presentation. Display the presentation in Print Preview, specify that you want the presentation printed as a handout (you determine the number of slides) insert a header and footer of your choosing, and then print the presentation. Save and then close **PP_C3_CS_P1.pptx**.

Part 3

Ms. Coletti needs further information for the meeting. She wants you to use the Internet and search for two companies that print restaurant menus, two companies that design restaurant menus, and the names of two restaurant menu design software programs. Prepare a presentation with the information you find on the Internet and then apply your custom theme to the presentation. Make any formatting changes to improve the visual appeal of each slide. Add a transition and sound to each slide in the presentation. Save the information and name it **PP_C3_CS_P3.pptx**. Print the presentation in the same manner as you printed **PP_C3_CS_P1.pptx**. Close **PP_C3_CS_P3.pptx**.

Part 4

When running **PP_C3_CS_P3.pptx**, Ms. Coletti would like to link to a couple of the sites you list in the presentation. Use PowerPoint's Help feature to learn how to insert a hyperlink in a slide to a Web page or Web site. Create at least two hyperlinks between sites you list in the presentation and the Web page or Web site. Print the slide(s) containing the hyperlinks. Save and then close **PP_C3_CS_P3.pptx**.

CHAPTER 4

Inserting Elements in Slides

PERFORMANCE OBJECTIVES

Upon successful completion of Chapter 4, you will be able to:

- **Insert, format, select, and align a text box**
- **Set tabs in a text box**
- **Insert, format, and copy shapes**
- **Display rulers, gridlines, and guides**
- **Group and ungroup objects**
- **Insert, crop, size, move, and format a picture**
- **Insert a picture as a slide background**
- **Insert, size, scale, rotate, and position a clip art image**
- **Create and format WordArt text**
- **Insert objects such as a header, footer, date, slide number, and symbol**

Tutorial 4.1
Working with Shapes
Tutorial 4.2
Working with Images and
Animation Schemes

A presentation consisting only of text slides may have important information in it that will be overlooked by the audience because a slide contains too much text. Adding visual elements, where appropriate, can help deliver the message to your audience by adding interest and impact to the information. In this chapter, you will learn how to create visual elements on slides such as text boxes, shapes, pictures, clip art images, and WordArt text. These elements will make the delivery of your presentation a dynamic experience for your audience.

Note: Before beginning computer projects, copy to your storage medium the PowerPoint2007C4 subfolder from the PowerPoint2007 folder on the CD that accompanies this textbook and then make PowerPoint2007C4 the active folder.

Project 1 — Create a Company Presentation Containing Text Boxes, Shapes, and Images

You will create a company presentation that includes slides with text boxes, a slide with tabbed text in a text box, slides with shapes and text, slides with pictures, and slides with clip art images. You will also insert elements in slides such as slide numbers, headers, footers, date, and symbols.

Inserting and Formatting Text Boxes

Draw a Text Box
1. Click Insert tab.
2. Click Text Box button.
3. Drag in slide to create box.
OR
1. Click Insert tab.
2. Click Text Box button.
3. Click in slide.

HINT
Use a text box to place text anywhere in a slide.

Many of the slide layouts contain placeholders for entering text and other elements in a document. Along with placeholders, you can insert and format a text box. To insert a text box in a slide, click the Insert tab, click the Text Box button in the Text group, and the mouse pointer displays as a thin, down-pointing arrow. Using the mouse, drag in the slide to create the text box. You can also click in the desired location and a small text box is inserted in the slide.

Formatting a Text Box

When you insert a text box in the document, the Home tab displays. Use options in the Drawing group to format the text box by applying a Quick Style or adding a shape fill, outline, or effect. Format a text box in a manner similar to formatting a placeholder. In addition to the options in the Drawing group, you can also apply formatting to a text box with options in the Drawing Tools Format tab. Click this tab and the ribbon displays as shown in Figure 4.1. The Shape Styles group contains the same options as the Drawing group in the Home tab. With other options in the tab, you can apply WordArt formatting to text and arrange and size the text box.

Figure 4.1 Drawing Tools Format Tab

Move a text box in the same manner as you move a placeholder. Click the text box to select it, position the mouse pointer on the text box border until the pointer displays with a four-headed arrow attached, and then drag the text box to the desired position. Change the size of a selected text box using the sizing handles that display around the box. You can also use the *Shape Height* and *Shape Width* measurement boxes in the Size group in the Drawing Tools Format tab to specify the text box height and width.

You can apply the same formatting to text in a text box that you apply to text in a placeholder. For example, you can use the buttons in the Paragraph group in the Home tab to align text horizontally and vertically in a text box, change text direction, set text in columns, and set internal margins for the text in the text box.

Selecting Multiple Objects

You can select multiple text boxes and other objects in a slide and then apply formatting or align and arrange the objects in the slide. To select all objects in a slide, click the Select button in the Editing group in the Home tab and then click *Select All* at the drop-down list. You can also select all objects in a slide with the keyboard shortcut, Ctrl + A. To select specific text boxes or objects in a slide, click the first object, hold down the Shift key, and then click each of the other desired objects.

Aligning Text Boxes

With the Align button in the Arrange group in the Drawing Tools Format tab, you can align the edge of multiple objects in a slide. Click the Align button and a drop-down list of alignment options displays including options for aligning objects vertically and horizontally and distributing objects.

Project 1a Inserting and Formatting Text Boxes

1. At a blank presentation, apply a design and change colors by completing the following steps:
   a. Click the Design tab.
   b. Click the More button that displays at the right side of the themes thumbnails and then click *Technic* at the drop-down gallery.
   c. Click the Colors button in the Themes group and then click *Trek* at the drop-down gallery.
2. Click in the title placeholder, type Addison, press the Enter key, and then type Industries.
3. Click in the subtitle placeholder and then type Annual Report.
4. Insert a text box in the slide by completing the following steps:
   a. Click the Insert tab.
   b. Click the Text Box button in the Text group.
   c. Click in the lower right corner of the slide. (This inserts a small, selected text box in the slide.)
   d. Type January, 2010.
   e. Click outside the text box to deselect it.
5. After looking at the slide, you decide to delete the text box by completing the following steps:
   a. Click in the text box to select it.
   b. Position the mouse pointer on the text box border until the mouse pointer displays with a four-headed arrow attached and then click the left mouse button (this changes the text box border from a dashed border line to a solid border line).
   c. Press the Delete key.

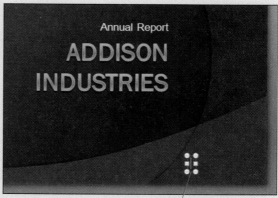

Step 4c

6. Insert a new slide with the *Blank* layout by completing the following steps:
   a. Click the Home tab.
   b. Click the New Slide button arrow.
   c. Click the *Blank* layout at the drop-down list.
7. Insert and format the *Safety* text box shown in Figure 4.2 by completing the following steps:
   a. Click the Insert tab.
   b. Click the Text Box button in the Text group.
   c. Click in the slide. (This inserts a small, selected text box in the slide.)
   d. Type **Safety**.
   e. Select the text and then change the font to Copperplate Gothic Bold, the font size to 36, and the font color to Orange (third color option from the left in the *Standard Colors* row).
   f. Click the Text Direction button in the Paragraph group in the Home tab and then click *Stacked* at the drop-down list.
   g. Click the Drawing Tools Format tab.
   h. Click the down-pointing arrow at the right side of the *Shape Height* measurement box in the Size group until *4″* displays in the box. (Make sure the measurement in the *Shape Width* box is *0.86″.*)
   i. Click the More button that displays at the right side of the styles thumbnails in the Shape Styles group and then click the *Moderate Effect - Accent 6* option (last option in the fifth row).
   j. Drag the text box so it is positioned as shown in Figure 4.2.
8. Insert and format the other text box shown in Figure 4.2 by completing the following steps:
   a. Click the Insert tab.
   b. Click the Text Box button in the Text group.
   c. Drag in the slide to create a text box. (Drag to the approximate width of the text box in Figure 4.2.)
   d. Type the text shown in the text box as shown in Figure 4.2 in a single column. Type the text in the first column and then type the text in the second column. (Your text will display as shown at the right in one column, in a smaller font, and in a different line spacing than you see in the figure.)
   e. Select the text and then change the font size to 32.

Step 7f

Step 7i

Step 8d

f. Click the Line Spacing button in the Paragraph group and then click *2.0* at the drop-down list. (The text may flow off the slide.)

g. Click the Columns button in the Paragraph group and then click *Two Columns* at the drop-down list.

h. Click the Drawing Tools Format tab.

i. Click the down-pointing arrow at the right side of the *Shape Height* measurement box until *4″* displays in the box.

j. Click the up- or down-pointing arrow at the right side of the *Shape Width* measurement box until *7″* displays in the box.

k. Click the Shape Fill button arrow in the Shape Styles group and then click *Orange, Accent 6, Lighter 40%* at the drop-down gallery.

l. Click the Shape Fill button arrow, point to *Gradient*, and then click *Linear Up* in the *Dark Variations* section at the side menu.

m. Click the Shape Outline button arrow in the Shape Styles group and then click *Dark Red* at the drop-down gallery (first color from the left in the *Standard Colors* row).

n. Click the Shape Effects button in the Shape Styles group, point to *Shadow*, and then click *Inside Diagonal Top Right* at the side menu (last option in the top row of the *Inner* section).

o. Change the internal margins by completing the following steps:

1) Click the Home tab.

2) Click the Text Direction button and then click *More Options* at the drop-down list.

3) In the *Internal margin* section of the Format Text Effects dialog box, change the *Left* measurement to *0.6″* and the *Top* and *Bottom* measurements to *0.4″*.

4) Click the Close button to close the dialog box.

5) Click in the slide outside the text boxes.

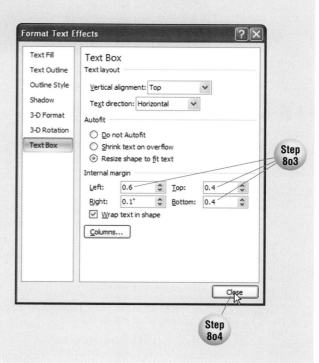

9. Arrange the text boxes by completing the following steps:
   a. Press Ctrl + A to select both text boxes.
   b. Click the Drawing Tools Format tab.
   c. Click the Align button in the Arrange group and then click *Align Middle* at the drop-down list.
   d. Drag both boxes to the approximate location in the slide as shown in Figure 4.2.
10. Save the presentation and name it **PP_C4_P1**.

Step 9c

Figure 4.2 Project 1a, Slide 2

Left Tab

Center Tab

Right Tab

Setting Tabs in a Text Box

Inside a text box, you may want to align text in columns using tabs. A text box, by default, contains left alignment tabs that display as light gray marks along the bottom of the horizontal ruler. You can change these default left alignment tabs to center, right, or decimal. To change to a different tab alignment, click the Alignment button located at the left side of the horizontal ruler. Display the desired tab alignment symbol and then click at the desired position on the horizontal ruler. When you set a tab on the horizontal ruler, any default tabs to the left of the new tab are deleted. You can move tabs on the horizontal ruler by using the mouse to drag the tab to the desired position. To delete a tab, use the mouse to drag the tab off of the ruler.

You can also set tabs with options at the Tabs dialog box. To display this dialog box, click the Paragraph group dialog box launcher. At the Paragraph dialog box, click the Tabs button that displays in the lower left corner. At the Tabs dialog box, type a tab position in the *Tab stop position* text box, choose a tab alignment with options in the *Alignment* section, and then click the Set button. Clear a specific tab by typing the tab stop position in the *Tab stop position* text box and then clicking the Clear button. Clear all tabs from the horizontal ruler by clicking the Clear All button. When all desired changes are made, click OK to close the Tabs dialog box and then click OK to close the Paragraph dialog box.

Project 1b Creating a Text Box and Setting Tabs

1. With **PP_C4_P1.pptx** open, make Slide 1 active and then click the Home tab.
2. Click the New Slide button arrow and then click the *Title Only* layout.
3. Click in the placeholder text *Click to add title* and then type **Executive Officers**.
4. Draw a text box by completing the following steps:
   a. Click the Insert tab.
   b. Click the Text Box button in the Text group.
   c. Draw a text box in the slide that is approximately 8 inches wide and 0.5 inch tall.
5. Change tabs in the text box by completing the following steps:

   a. With the insertion point inside the text box, make sure the horizontal ruler displays. (If not, click the View tab and then click the *Ruler* check box in the Show/Hide group.)
   b. Check the alignment button at the left side of the horizontal ruler and make sure the left tab symbol displays.
   c. Position the tip of the mouse pointer on the horizontal ruler below the 0.5-inch mark and then click the left mouse button.
   d. Click once on the Alignment button to display the Center alignment symbol.
   e. Click on the horizontal ruler immediately below the 4-inch mark on the horizontal ruler.
   f. Click once on the Alignment button to display the Right alignment symbol.
   g. Click on the horizontal ruler immediately below the 7.5-inch

   mark. (You may need to expand the size of the text box to set the tab at the 7.5-inch mark.)
6. Type the text in the text box as shown in the slide in Figure 4.3. Make sure you press the Tab key before typing text in the first column (this moves the insertion point to the first tab, which is a left alignment tab). Bold the three column headings—*Name*, *Title*, and *Number*.
7. When you are finished typing the text in the text box, press Ctrl + A to select all of the text in the text box and then change the line spacing to 1.5.
8. With the text still selected, drag the left alignment marker on the horizontal ruler from the 0.5-inch mark to the 0.25-inch mark and then drag the right alignment marker on the horizontal ruler from the 7.5-inch mark on the ruler to the 7-inch mark.
9. Save **PP_C4_P1.pptx**.

Figure 4.3 Project 1b, Slide 2

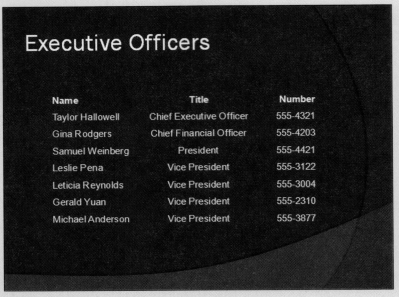

Inserting and Formatting Shapes

QUICK STEPS

Insert a Shape
1. Click Shapes button.
2. Click desired shape at drop-down list.
3. Drag in slide to create shape.

HINT

Many shapes have an adjustment handle you can use to change the most prominent feature of the shape.

Shapes

You can draw shapes in a slide using the Shapes button in the Drawing group or with the Shapes button in the Illustrations group in the Insert tab. With the Shapes button drop-down list, you can choose to draw shapes including lines, basic shapes, block arrows, flow chart symbols, callouts, stars, and banners. Click a shape and the mouse pointer displays as crosshairs (plus sign). Click in the slide to insert the shape or position the crosshairs in the slide and then drag to create the shape. Apply formatting to a shape in a manner similar to formatting a text box. Use buttons in the Drawing group in the Home tab and/or buttons in the Drawing Tools Format tab (shown in Figure 4.1).

If you choose a shape in the *Lines* section of the drop-down list, the shape you draw is considered a **line drawing**. If you choose an option in the other sections of the drop-down list, the shape you draw is considered an **enclosed object**. When drawing an enclosed object, you can maintain the proportions of the shape by holding down the Shift key while dragging with the mouse to create the shape.

Project 1c Drawing and Formatting Lines and Shapes

1. With **PP_C4_P1.pptx** open, make Slide 3 active.
2. Click the New Slide button arrow and then click the *Blank* layout at the drop-down list.
3. Insert and format the square shown in the lower left corner of the slide in Figure 4.4 by completing the following steps:
   a. Make sure the Home tab is selected.

b. Click the Shapes button in the Drawing group.

c. Click the Rectangle shape in the *Rectangles* section of the drop-down list.

d. Hold down the Shift key and then draw a square the approximate size of the square shown in Figure 4.4.

e. With the square selected, click the Quick Styles button in the Drawing group and then click *Moderate Effect - Accent 1* (second option from the left in the fifth row).

f. Click the Drawing Tools Format tab.

g. Change the *Shape Height* and *Shape Width* to *1.6"*.

h. If necessary, drag the square so it is positioned as shown in Figure 4.4.

4. Insert the word *Safety* in the square by completing the following steps:

a. With the Drawing Tools Format tab selected, click the Text Box button in the Insert Shapes group.

b. Click inside the square.

c. Click the Home tab.

d. Change the font to Copperplate Gothic Bold, change the font size to 24, and change the font color to Brown, Accent 2, Darker 50%.

e. Type Safety.

5. Draw and format the line shown in Figure 4.4 by completing the following steps:

a. Click the Insert tab.

b. Click the Shapes button in the Illustrations group and then click *Arrow* in the *Lines* section.

c. Position the mouse pointer (cross hairs) in the upper right corner of the square and then drag up to the approximate location shown in Figure 4.4.

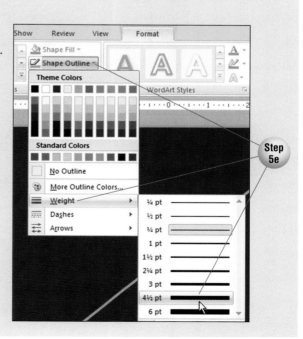

d. With the arrow line selected, click the Drawing Tools Format tab.

e. Click the Shape Outline button arrow in the Shape Styles group, point to *Weight*, and then click *4½ pt* at the side menu.

f. Click the Shape Effects button in the Shape Styles group, point to *Bevel*, and then click *Circle* at the side menu (first option from the left in the top row in the *Bevel* section).

6. Draw a text box and type the text shown in the upper left corner of the slide by completing the following steps:
   a. Click the Text Box button in the Insert Shapes group in the Drawing Tools Format tab.
   b. Click in the upper left side of the slide.
   c. Click the Home tab, change the font size to 28, and then click the Bold button.
   d. Click the Align Text Right button in the Paragraph group.
   e. Type 2009, press the Enter key, and then type Safety Training.
   f. If necessary, drag the text box so it is positioned as shown in Figure 4.4.

7. Draw and format the text box shown near the arrow line by completing the following steps:
   a. Click the Insert tab.
   b. Click the Text Box button in the Text group.
   c. Click in the slide (you determine the position).
   d. Change the font size to 24, click the Bold button, and then change the font color to Orange.
   e. Type 1,000 ASA-trained employees.
   f. Position the mouse pointer on the green rotation handle, hold down the left mouse button, and then rotate the text box so it is angled as shown in Figure 4.4.
   g. Drag the text box so it is positioned next to the arrow line.

8. Save **PP_C4_P1.pptx**.

Figure 4.4 Project 1c, Slide 4

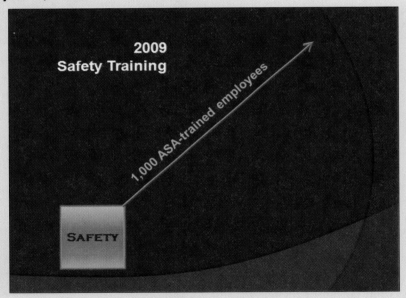

Copying Shapes

To copy a shape, select the shape and then click the Copy button in the Clipboard group in the Home tab. Position the insertion point at the location where you want the copied image and then click the Paste button. You can also copy a selected shape by holding down the Ctrl key while dragging the shape to the desired location.

Displaying Rulers, Gridlines, and Guides

To help position objects such as placeholders, text boxes, and shapes, consider displaying horizontal and vertical rulers, gridlines, and/or drawing guides as shown in Figure 4.5. You can turn the horizontal and vertical ruler on and off with the Ruler check box in the Show/Hide group in the View tab. The Show/Hide group also contains a Gridlines check box. Insert a check mark in this check box and gridlines display in the active slide. Gridlines are intersecting lines that create a grid on the slide and are useful for aligning objects. You can also turn the display of gridlines on and off with the keyboard shortcut, Shift + F9.

QUICK STEPS

Copy a Shape
1. Select desired shape.
2. Click Copy button.
3. Position insertion point at desired location.
4. Click Paste button.
OR
1. Select desired shape.
2. Hold down Ctrl key.
3. Drag shape to desired location.

Figure 4.5 Rulers, Gridlines, and Drawing Guides

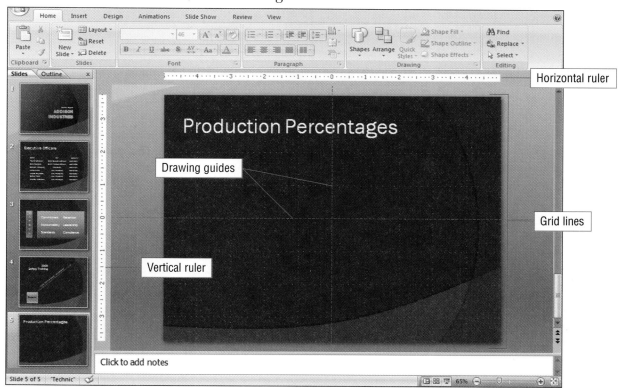

Turn on drawing guides to help position objects on a slide. Drawing guides are horizontal and vertical dashed lines that display on the slide in the Slide pane as shown in Figure 4.5. To turn on the drawing guides, display the Grid and Guides dialog box shown in Figure 4.6. Display this dialog box by selecting an object in the slide, clicking the Drawing Tools Format tab, clicking the Align button in the Arrange group, and then clicking *Grid Settings* at the drop-down list. At the dialog box, insert a check mark in the *Display drawing guides on screen* check box. By default, the horizontal and vertical drawing guides intersect in the middle of the slide. You can move these guides by dragging the guide with the mouse. As you drag the guide, a measurement displays next to the mouse pointer. Drawing guides and gridlines display on the slide but do not print.

You can turn on gridlines with the Gridlines check box in the View tab and you can also turn them on by inserting a check mark in the *Display grid on screen* check box. The horizontal and vertical spacing between the gridlines is 0.083 inch by default. You can change this measurement with the *Spacing* option at the Grid and Guides dialog box.

Figure 4.6 Grid and Guides Dialog Box

With this option active, objects will snap into alignment with the grid lines.

Make this option active if you want a dragged object to snap into alignment with another object.

Insert a check mark in this option to display grid lines.

Insert a check mark in this option to display drawing guides.

As you drag or draw an object on the slide, it is pulled into alignment with the nearest intersection of gridlines. This is because the *Snap objects to grid* option at the Grid and Guides dialog box is active by default. If you want to position an object precisely, you can remove the check mark from the *Snap objects to grid* to turn the feature off or you can hold down the Alt key while dragging an object. If you want an object to be pulled into alignment with another object, insert a check mark in the *Snap objects to other objects* check box.

Project 1d Drawing and Formatting Shapes and Text Boxes

1. With **PP_C4_P1.pptx** open, make sure Slide 4 is active and then insert a new slide by clicking the New Slide button arrow and then clicking *Title Only* at the drop-down list.
2. Turn on the display of gridlines by clicking the View tab and then clicking *Gridlines* to insert a check mark in the check box.

Step 2

3. Click in the title placeholder and then type Production Percentages.

4. With the placeholder selected, turn on drawing guides and turn off the snap-to-grid feature by completing the following steps:

a. Click the Drawing Tools Format tab.

b. Click the Align button in the Arrange group.

c. Click the *Grid Settings* option at the drop-down list.

d. At the Grid and Guides dialog box, click the *Snap objects to grid* check box to remove the check mark.

e. Click the *Display drawing guides on screen* to insert a check mark in the check box.

f. Click OK.

5. Draw the arrow at the left in the slide in Figure 4.7 by completing the following steps:

a. Click outside the title placeholder to deselect it.

b. Click the Insert tab.

c. Click the Shapes button and then click the *Up Arrow* shape (third shape from the left in the top row of the *Block Arrows* section).

d. Position the crosshairs on the intersection of the horizontal drawing guide and the first vertical gridline from the left.

e. Hold down the left mouse button, drag down and to the right until the crosshairs are positioned on the intersection of the third vertical line from the left and the first horizontal line from the bottom, and then release the mouse button. (Your arrow should be the approximate size shown in Figure 4.7.)

f. With the arrow selected, click the Drawing Tools Format tab.

g. Click the Shape Fill button arrow and then click *Light Blue* at the drop-down gallery (seventh color option from the left in the *Standard Colors* section).

h. Click the Shape Fill button arrow, point to *Gradient*, and then click the *Linear Up* option in the *Dark Variations* section (second option from the left in the bottom row of the *Dark Variations* section).

i. Click the Shape Effects button, point to *Bevel*, and then click the *Soft round* option (second option from the left in the second row in the *Bevel* section).

6. Insert a text box in the arrow by completing the following steps:
   a. Click the Insert tab.
   b. Click the Text Box button in the Text group.
   c. Drag to create a text box toward the top of the arrow the approximate size shown at the right.
   d. With the Home tab selected, change the font size to 20, turn on Bold, and then change the font color to Dark Blue.
   e. Click the Center button in the Paragraph group.
   f. Type **Plant 3**, press the Enter key, and then type 48%.
   g. Move and/or size the text box so the text is positioned in the arrow as shown in Figure 4.7.
7. Copy the arrow and text box by completing the following steps:
   a. With the text box selected, hold down the Shift key and then click the arrow. (This selects the arrow and the text box.)
   b. Position the mouse pointer on the border of the selected arrow or text box until the mouse pointer displays with a four-headed arrow attached.
   c. Hold down the Ctrl key, drag the arrow and text box to the right so the tip of the arrow is positioned at the intersection of the horizontal and vertical drawing guides.

Step 7c

8. Move the vertical drawing guide and then copy the arrow and text box by completing the following steps:
   a. Click outside the arrow to deselect the arrow and the text box.
   b. Position the mouse pointer on the vertical drawing guide, hold down the left mouse button, drag right until the mouse pointer displays with *3.00* and a right-pointing arrow in a box, and then release the mouse button.

Step 8b

   c. Click the arrow at the right, hold down the Shift key, and then click the text box inside the arrow.
   d. Hold down the Ctrl, drag the arrow and text box to the right so the tip of the arrow is positioned at the intersection of the horizontal and vertical drawing guides.

9. Increase the height of the middle arrow by completing the following steps:
   a. Click the middle arrow to select it.
   b. Using the mouse, drag the top middle sizing handle up to the next horizontal gridline.
   c. Click the text box in the middle arrow and then drag the text box up to the position shown in Figure 4.7.
   d. Complete similar steps to increase the height of the arrow at the right to the second horizontal gridline. Drag the text box to the position shown in Figure 4.7.
   e. Change the text in the text box in the middle arrow to *Plant 1 72%* and change the text in the text box in the arrow at the right to *Plant 2 91%* (see Figure 4.7).
10. Turn off gridlines, drawing guides, and turn on the snap-to-grid feature by completing the following steps:
    a. Click the text in the title placeholder.
    b. Click the Drawing Tools Format tab.
    c. Click the Align button in the Arrange group.
    d. Click the *Grid Settings* option at the drop-down list.
    e. At the Grid and Guides dialog box, click the *Snap objects to grid* check box to insert a check mark.
    f. Click the *Display grid on screen* option to remove the check mark.
    g. Click the *Display drawing guides on screen* to remove the mark in the check box.
    h. Click OK.
11. Save **PP_C4_P1.pptx**.

Figure 4.7 Project 1d, Slide 5

Grouping/Ungrouping Objects

Group Objects
1. Select desired objects.
2. Click Drawing Tools Format tab.
3. Click Group button.
4. Click *Group* at drop-down list.

If you want to apply the same formatting or make the same adjustments to the size or rotation of objects, group the objects. If you group objects and then apply a formatting such as a shape fill, effect, or shape style, the formatting is applied to each object within the group. With objects grouped, you can apply formatting more quickly to objects in the slide. To group objects, select the objects you want included in the group. You can do this by clicking each object while holding down the Shift key or you can draw a border around the objects you want included. With the objects selected, click the Drawing Tools Format tab, click the Group button in the Arrange group, and then click *Group* at the drop-down list.

You can format an individual object within a group. To do this, click any object in the group and the group border displays around the objects. Click the individual object and then apply the desired formatting. If you no longer want objects grouped, click the group to select it, click the Drawing Tools Format tab, click the Group button in the Arrange group, and then click *Ungroup* at the drop-down list.

HINT

Group objects so you can move, size, flip, or rotate objects at one time.

Project 1e   Grouping and Formatting Objects

1. With **PP_C4_P1.pptx** open, make Slide 3 active.
2. Group the objects and apply formatting by completing the following steps:
   a. Using the mouse, draw a border around the two text boxes in the slide.
   b. Click the Drawing Tools Format tab.
   c. Click the Group button in the Arrange group and then click *Group* at the drop-down list.

Step 2c

   d. Click the More button at the right side of the shape style thumbnails and then click *Intense Effect - Accent 2* at the drop-down gallery (third option from the left in the bottom row).
   e. Click the Shape Outline button arrow and then click *Brown, Accent 3, Darker 50%*.
   f. Click the Shape Outline button arrow, point to *Weight*, and then click *4½ pt*.
3. Make Slide 4 active and then group and format objects by completing the following steps:
   a. Using the mouse, draw a border around all objects in the slide.
   b. Click the Drawing Tools Format tab.
   c. Click the Group button in the Arrange group and then click *Group* at the drop-down list.
   d. Click the Home tab.
   e. Click the Font Color button arrow and then click the *Orange, Accent 1, Lighter 60%* option.
4. Make Slide 1 active and then run the presentation.
5. After running the presentation you decide that you want to change the color of the square shape and the arrow in Slide 4. Do this by completing the following steps:
   a. Make Slide 4 active.
   b. Click any object in the slide. (This selects the border around all of the objects.)
   c. Click the gold square located in the lower left corner of the slide.
   d. Click the Drawing Tools Format tab.

e. Click the More button at the right side of the shape style thumbnails and then click *Intense Effect - Accent 2* at the drop-down gallery (third option from the left in the bottom row).

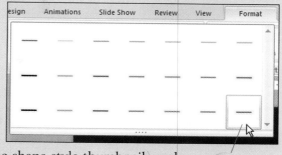

6. Ungroup the objects by completing the following steps:
   a. With the group and square selected, click the Group button in the Arrange group and then click *Ungroup* at the drop-down list.
   b. Click outside any object to deselect the objects.
   c. Click the arrow line.
   d. Click the More button at the right side of the shape style thumbnails and then click the *Intense Line - Accent 6* option (last option in the bottom row).

Step 6d

7. You also decide that you do not like the light yellow border (outline) around the three arrows in Slide 5. Remove the outlines by completing the following steps:
   a. Make Slide 5 active.
   b. Using the mouse, draw a border around the three arrows in the slide.
   c. Click the Drawing Tools Format tab.
   d. Click the Group button in the Arrange group and then click *Group* at the drop-down list.
   e. Click the Shape Outline button in the Shape Styles group and then click *No Outline* at the drop-down gallery.

Step 7e

8. Save **PP_C4_P1.pptx**.

Inserting an Image

You can insert an image such as a picture or clip art in a slide with buttons in the Illustrations group in the Insert tab. Click the Picture button to display the Insert Picture dialog box where you can specify the desired picture file or click the Clip Art button and then choose from a variety of images available at the Clip Art task pane.

Customizing and Formatting an Image

When you insert an image in a slide, the image is selected and the Picture Tools Format tab is active as shown in Figure 4.8. Use buttons in this tab to apply formatting to the image. With options in the Adjust group in the Picture Tools Format tab you can recolor the picture or clip art image and change the brightness and contrast of the image. You can also reset the picture or clip art back to its original color or change to a different image. Use the Compress Pictures button to compress the size of the image file. Compressing a picture makes the color take up fewer bits per pixel without any loss of quality.

PowerPoint provides predesigned styles you can apply to your image. These styles are available in the Picture Styles group along with buttons for changing the image border and applying effects to the image. Use options in the Arrange group to position the image on the page, specify text wrapping in relation to the image, align the image with other objects in the document, and rotate the image. Use the Crop button in the Size group to remove any unnecessary parts of the image and specify the image size with the *Shape Height* and *Shape Width* measurement boxes.

Figure 4.8 Picture Tools Format Tab

Sizing, Cropping, and Moving an Image

You can change the size of an image with the *Shape Height* and *Shape Width* measurement boxes in the Size group in the Picture Tools Format tab or with the sizing handles that display around the selected image. To change size with a sizing handle, position the mouse pointer on a sizing handle until the pointer turns into a double-headed arrow and then hold down the left mouse button. Drag the sizing handle in or out to decrease or increase the size of the image and then release the mouse button. Use the middle sizing handles at the left or right side of the image to make the image wider or thinner. Use the middle sizing handles at the top or bottom of the image to make the image taller or shorter. Use the sizing handles at the corners of the image to change both the width and height at the same time.

The Size group in the Picture Tools Format tab contains a Crop button. Use this button to remove portions of an image. Click the Crop button and the mouse pointer displays with the crop tool attached, which is a black square with overlapping lines, and the image displays with cropping handles around the border. Drag a cropping handle to remove a portion of the image.

Move a selected image by dragging it to the desired location. Move the image by positioning the mouse pointer on the image border until the arrow pointer turns into a four-headed arrow. Hold down the left mouse button, drag the image to the desired position, and then release the mouse button. You can use the arrow keys on the keyboard to move the image in the desired direction. If you want to move the image in small increments (called ***nudging***), hold down the Ctrl key while pressing an arrow key.

Use the rotation handle to rotate an image by positioning the mouse pointer on the green, round rotation handle until the pointer displays as a circular arrow. Hold down the left mouse button, drag in the desired direction, and then release the mouse button.

Arranging Objects

If you want to layer one object on top of another, use the Bring to Front or Send to Back buttons in the Arrange group in the Drawing Tools Format tab or Picture Tools Format tab. For example, if you want an image to display behind a text box, select the image and then click the Send to Back button. If you want a selected object to display on top of other objects in the slide, click the Bring to Front button.

Inserting a Picture

To insert a picture in a document, click the Insert tab and then click the Picture button in the Illustrations group. At the Insert Picture dialog box, navigate to the folder containing the desired picture and then double-click the picture. Use buttons in the Picture Tools Format tab to format and customize the picture.

Project 🔟 **Inserting and Formatting a Picture**

1. With **PP_C4_P1.pptx** open, make Slide 5 active and then click the Home tab.
2. Insert a new slide by clicking the New Slide button arrow and then clicking *Blank* at the drop-down list.
3. Insert a text box by completing the following steps:
   a. Click the Insert tab.
   b. Click the Text Box button in the Text group.
   c. Click in the middle of the slide.
   d. Change the font to Arial Black and the font size to 36.
   e. Click the Center button in the Paragraph group.
   f. Type *Alternative*, press the Enter key, and then type *Energy Resources*.

Step 3h

   g. With the text box selected, click the Drawing Tools Format tab.
   h. Click the Align button and then click *Distribute Horizontally* at the drop-down list.
   i. Click the Align button and then click *Distribute Vertically* at the drop-down list.
4. Insert a picture by completing the following steps:
   a. Click the Insert tab.
   b. Click the Picture button in the Illustrations group.
   c. At the Insert Picture dialog box, navigate to the PowerPoint2007C4 folder on your storage medium and then double-click *Ocean.jpg*.
5. Crop the picture by completing the following steps:
   a. With the picture selected, click the Crop button in the Size group in the Picture Tools Format tab.
   b. Position the mouse pointer (displays with the crop tool attached) on the cropping handle in the middle of the right side of the picture.
   c. Hold down the left mouse button and then drag to the left approximately 0.25 inch. (Use the guideline that displays on the horizontal ruler to crop the picture 0.25 inch.)

Step 5c

d. Complete steps similar to those in Steps 5b and 5c to crop approximately 0.25 inch from the top of the picture. (Use the guideline that displays on the vertical ruler to crop the picture 0.25 inch.)

e. Click the Crop button to turn off cropping.

6. Click in the *Shape Height* measurement box in the Size group, type 5, and then press Enter.

7. Click the Send to Back button in the Arrange group. (This moves the picture behind the text in the text box.)

8. Align the picture by completing the following steps:

a. With the picture selected, click the Home tab.

b. Click the Arrange button in the Drawing group, point to *Align* at the drop-down list, and then click *Distribute Horizontally*.

c. Click the Arrange button, point to *Align*, and then click *Distribute Vertically*.

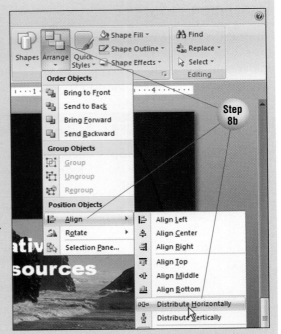

9. Format the picture by completing the following steps:

a. With the picture selected, click the Picture Tools Format tab, click the Recolor button in the Adjust group, and then click the *Accent color 6 Dark* option (last option in the *Dark Variations* row).

b. Click the More button that displays at the right side of the picture style thumbnails and then click *Soft Edge Oval* at the drop-down gallery (second option from the left in the fourth row).

c. Click the Brightness button in the Adjust group and then click *+10%* at the drop-down list.

d. Click the Contrast button in the Adjust group and then click *+20%* at the drop-down list.

e. Click the Compress Pictures button in the Adjust group. At the Compress Pictures dialog box, click OK.

10. Save **PP_C4_P1.pptx**.

Inserting a Picture as a Slide Background

You can insert a picture as the background in an entire slide. To do this, click the Design tab, click the Background Styles button in the Background group, and then click *Format Background* at the drop-down list. At the Format Background dialog box, click the *Picture or texture fill* option in the *Fill* section and then click the File button. At the Insert Picture dialog box, navigate to the desired folder, and then double-click the picture. Click the Close button to close the Format Background dialog box. If you want the picture background to display on all slides, click the Apply to All button at the Format Background dialog box.

QUICK STEPS

Insert Picture as Slide Background
1. Click Design tab.
2. Click Background Styles button, *Format Background*.
3. Click *Picture or texture fill* option.
4. Click File button.
5. Navigate to desired folder.
6. Double-click desired picture.
7. Click Close button.

Project 1g Inserting a Picture as a Slide Background

1. With **PP_C4_P1.pptx** open, make sure Slide 6 is active, and then click the Home tab.
2. Click the New Slide button arrow and then click the *Blank* layout at the drop-down list.
3. Insert a picture background on Slide 7 by completing the following steps:
   a. Click the Design tab.
   b. Click the Background Styles button in the Background group and then click *Format Background* at the drop-down gallery.
   c. At the Format Background dialog box, click the *Picture or texture fill* option in the *Fill* section.
   d. Click the File button that displays near the middle of the dialog box.
   e. At the Insert Picture dialog box, navigate to the PowerPoint2007C4 folder on your storage medium and then double-click *EiffelTower.jpg*.
   f. Click the Close button to close the Format Background dialog box.
   g. Remove the background graphic by clicking the *Hide Background Graphics* check box in the Background group in the Design tab to insert a check mark.
4. Insert a text box by completing the following steps:
   a. Click the Insert tab.
   b. Click the Text Box button in the Text group.
   c. Click in the upper left corner of the slide.
   d. Change the font size to 40.
   e. Type European and then press Enter.
   f. Type Division 2010.
   g. Drag the text box so it is positioned attractively on the slide in the upper left corner.
5. Change the formatting of slides and slide objects by completing the following steps:
   a. Make Slide 3 active.
   b. Click the Design tab.
   c. Click the Colors button in the Themes group and then click *Office* at the drop-down gallery.
   d. Click in the lower right corner of the text box containing the text in columns (this selects the group).

Step 3c

Step 3d

e. Click the Drawing Tools Format tab.

f. Click the More button at the right side of the shape style thumbnails and then click the *Moderate Effect - Accent 1* option (second option from the left in the fifth row).

g. Make Slide 4 active, select the square and the line arrow, click the Drawing Tools Format tab, and then apply the *Moderate Effect - Accent 1* option (second option from the left in the fifth row).

h. Using the mouse, draw a border around all of the objects in the slide, click the Home tab, and then change the font color to Orange.

i. Make Slide 6 active and then click the picture to select it.

j. Click the Picture Tools Format tab.

k. Click the Recolor button in the Adjust group and then click the *No Recolor* option.

6. Save **PP_C4_P1.pptx**.

Step
5k

Inserting a Clip Art Image

Microsoft Office includes a gallery of media images you can insert in a slide such as clip art, photographs, and movie images, as well as sound clips. To insert a clip art image in a slide, click the Insert tab and then click the Clip Art button in the Illustrations group. This displays the Clip Art task pane at the right side of the screen as shown in Figure 4.9. You can also choose a slide layout that contains a content placeholder with a Clip Art button.

Figure 4.9 Clip Art Task Pane

Search for specific images by typing the desired category in this text box and then clicking the Go button.

To view all picture, sound, and motion files, make sure the *Search for* text box in the Clip Art task pane does not contain any text and then click the Go button. When the desired image is visible, click the image to insert it in the document. Use buttons in the Picture Tools Format tab shown in Figure 4.8 to format and customize the clip art image.

If you are searching for specific images, click in the *Search for* text box, type the desired topic, and then click the Go button. For example, if you want to find images related to business, click in the *Search for* text box, type business, and then click the Go button. Clip art images related to *business* display in the viewing area of the task pane. If you are connected to the Internet, Word will search for images at the Office Online Web site matching the topic.

By default (unless it has been customized), the Clip Art task pane displays all media images and sound clips found in all locations. You can narrow the search to specific locations and to specific images. The *Search in* option at the Clip Art task pane has a default setting of *All collections*. This can be changed to *My Collections*, *Office Collections*, and *Web Collections*. The *Results should be* option has a default setting of *Selected media file types*. Click the down-pointing arrow at the right side of this option to display media types. To search for a specific media type, remove the check mark before all options at the drop-down list except the desired type. For example, if you are searching only for photograph images, remove the check mark before Clip Art, Movies, and Sound.

Project 1h — Inserting and Formatting a Clip Art Image

1. With **PP_C4_P1.pptx** open, make Slide 1 active.
2. Insert a clip art image by completing the following steps:
   a. Click the Insert tab.
   b. Click the Clip Art button in the Illustrations group.
   c. At the Clip Art task pane, click the down-pointing arrow at the right side of the *Results should be* option box and then click in the *Photographs*, *Movies*, and *Sounds* check boxes to remove the check marks. (The *Clip Art* check box should be the only one with a check mark.)
   d. Select any text that displays in the *Search for* text box, type industry, and then press Enter.
   e. Click the clip art image in the list box as shown at the right.
   f. Click the down-pointing arrow at the right side of the *Results should be* option box and then click in the *All media types* check box to insert a check mark.
   g. Close the Clip Art task pane by clicking the Close button (contains an X) located in the upper right corner of the task pane.
3. Arrange, size, and position the clip art image by completing the following steps:
   a. With the clip art image selected, click the Rotate button in the Arrange group and then click *Flip Horizontal*.

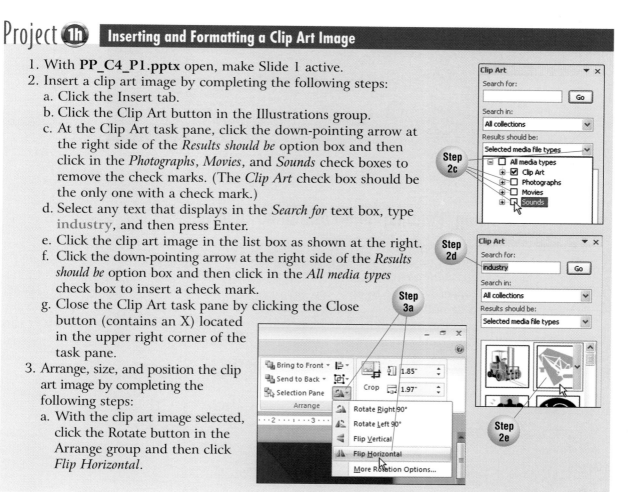

b. Click in the *Shape Height* measurement box, type 4.5, and then press Enter.

c. Click the Recolor button in the Adjust group and then click the *Accent color 5 Light* option at the drop-down gallery (second option from the right in the *Light Variations* section).

d. Click the Contrast button in the Adjust group and then click *+30%* at the drop-down gallery.

e. Click the Send to Back button in the Arrange group.

f. Drag the clip art image so it is positioned as shown in Figure 4.10.

4. Save **PP_C4_P1.pptx**.

Figure 4.10 Project 1h, Slide 1

Sizing, Rotating, and Positioning Objects

As you have learned in this chapter, you can use the sizing handles that display around an object to increase and decrease the size, and use the *Shape Height* and *Shape Width* measurement boxes. You also learned to position objects by dragging the object with the mouse. You can also size and position objects with options at the Size and Position dialog box shown in Figure 4.11. Display this dialog box by clicking the Size group dialog box launcher in the Picture Tools Format tab or the Drawing Tools Format tab.

Figure 4.11 Size and Position Dialog Box

Use options in this dialog box to change the object size, rotation, scaling percentage, and cropping measurements.

Use options at the Size and Position dialog box with the Size tab selected to specify the object size, rotation degree, scaling percentage, and cropping measurements. The Size and Position dialog box with the Position tab selected contains options for specifying the horizontal and vertical position of the object in the slide.

Project 1i · Inserting and Formatting a Clip Art Image

1. With **PP_C4_P1.pptx** open, make Slide 7 active.
2. Click the New Slide button arrow and then click the *Two Content* layout at the drop-down list.
3. Click the placeholder text *Click to add title* and then type Technology.
4. Click the placeholder text *Click to add text* located in the right side of the slide.
5. Click the Bullets button in the Paragraph group to turn off bullets.
6. Change the font size to 36, turn on bold, and change the font color to Orange.
7. Press the Enter key.
8. Type Equipment and then press the Enter key twice.
9. Type Software and then press the Enter key twice.
10. Type Personnel.
11. Insert a clip art image by completing the following steps:
    a. Click the Clip Art button that displays in the middle of the placeholder at the left side of the slide.

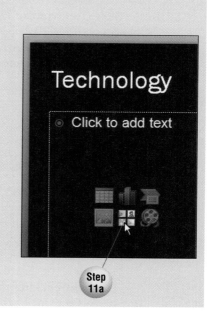

Step 11a

b. At the Clip Art task pane, select any text that displays in the *Search for* text box, type technology, and then press Enter.

c. Click the clip art image in the list box as shown at the right.

d. Close the Clip Art task pane by clicking the Close button (contains an X) located in the upper right corner of the task pane.

Step 11b

Step 11c

12. Scale, rotate, and position the clip art image by completing the following steps:

a. With the clip art image selected, click the Size group dialog box launcher.

b. Click the down-pointing arrow at the right of the *Rotation* option until *–20%* displays in the option box.

c. Select the current percentage in the *Height* option box in the *Scale* section and then type 225.

Step 12b

Step 12c

d. Click the Position tab.

e. Click the down-pointing arrow at the right side of the *Horizontal* option until *0.7"* displays in the option box.

f. Click the down-pointing arrow at the right side of the *Vertical* option until *1.9"* displays in the option box.

g. Click the Close button to close the dialog box.

13. Bring the text in front of the clip art image by completing the following steps:

a. Click in the text to select the text placeholder.

b. Click the Drawing Tools Format tab.

c. Click the Bring to Front button in the Arrange group.

14. Save **PP_C4_P1.pptx**.

Copying Objects within and between Presentations

Earlier in this chapter you learned how to copy shapes within a slide. You can also copy shapes as well as other objects to other slides within the same presentation or to slides in another presentation. To copy an object, select the object and then click the Copy button in the Clipboard group in the Home tab. Make the desired slide active or open another presentation and display the desired slide and then click the Paste button in the Clipboard group. You can also copy an object by right-clicking the object and then clicking *Copy* at the shortcut menu. To paste the object, make the desired slide active, click the right mouse button, and then click *Paste* at the shortcut menu.

1. With **PP_C4_P1.pptx** open, make Slide 1 active.
2. Click the clip art image to select it and then press the Delete key.
3. Open **Addison.pptx**.
4. Click the clip art image located in Slide 1 and then click the Copy button in the Clipboard group.
5. Click the button on the Taskbar representing the **PP_C4_P1.pptx** and then click the Paste button. (This inserts the clip art image in Slide 1.)
6. Make the **Addison.pptx** presentation active and then close the presentation.
7. With the **PP_C4_P1.pptx** open and the clip art image selected, make Slide 2 active and then click the Paste button.
8. Decrease the size and position the clip art by completing the following steps:
   a. Click the Picture Tools Format tab.
   b. Click in the *Shape Height* measurement text box, type 0.8, and then press Enter.
   c. Drag the clip art image so it is positioned in the upper right corner of the slide.
9. Copy the clip art image to other slides by completing the following steps:
   a. With the clip art image selected in Slide 2, click the Copy button in the Clipboard group in the Home tab.
   b. Make Slide 3 active and then click the Paste button in the Clipboard group.
   c. Make each of the following slides active and then paste the clip art image: Slide 4, 5, 6, and 8.
10. Save **PP_C4_P1.pptx**.

Step 8c

Title | Number
Executive Officer | 555-4321

Creating WordArt Text

Use the WordArt feature to insert preformatted, decorative text in a slide. You can also use WordArt to modify text to conform to a variety of shapes. Consider using WordArt to create a company logo, letterhead, flier title, or heading. Insert WordArt in a slide by clicking the Insert tab and then clicking the WordArt button in the Text group. This displays the WordArt drop-down list as shown in Figure 4.12. Click the desired WordArt style at this drop-down list and a text box is inserted in the slide containing the text *Your Text Here*. Type the desired WordArt text and then use the options in the Drawing Tools Format tab to customize the WordArt.

QUICK STEPS

Create WordArt Text
1. Click Insert tab.
2. Click WordArt button.
3. Click desired WordArt style.
4. Type WordArt text.

HINT
Use WordArt to create interesting text effects in slides.

WordArt

Figure 4.12 WordArt Drop-down List

Click the WordArt button to display this drop-down list of predesigned WordArt text options.

HINT

Edit WordArt by double-clicking the WordArt text.

Text Fill

Text Outline

Text Effect

Formatting WordArt Text

When you insert WordArt text in a document, the Drawing Tools Format tab is active. Use options and buttons in this tab to format the WordArt text. Use the WordArt styles to apply predesigned formatting to the WordArt text. Customize the text with the Text Fill, Text Outline, and Text Effects buttons in the WordArt Styles group. Use the Text Fill button to change the fill color, the Text Outline button to change the text outline color, and use the Text Effects button to apply a variety of text effects and shapes.

Click the Text Effects button and then point to *Transform* and a side menu displays with shaping and warping options as shown in Figure 4.13. Use these options to conform the WordArt text to a specific shape.

Figure 4.13 Text Effects Transform Side Menu

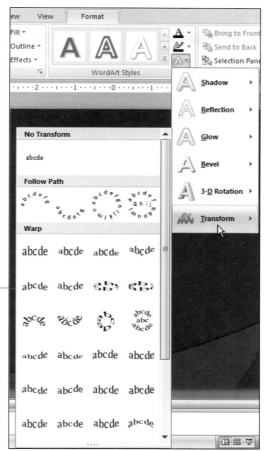

Click an option at this side menu to conform the WordArt text to a specific shape.

Project 1k Inserting and Formatting WordArt

1. With **PP_C4_P1.pptx** open, make sure Slide 8 is active and then click the Home tab.
2. Click the New Slide button arrow and then click the *Blank* layout.
3. Click the Insert tab.
4. Click the WordArt button in the Text group and then click the *Gradient Fill - Accent 6, Inner Shadow* option (second option from the left in the fourth row).
5. Type Addison Industries, press the Enter key, and then type 2010.
6. Click the WordArt text border to change the border from a dashed line to a solid line. (This selects the text box.)

Step 4

7. Click the Text Outline button arrow in the WordArt Styles group and then click the *Dark Blue* color in the *Standard Colors* section.
8. Click the Text Effects button, point to *Glow*, and then click *Accent color 1, 11 pt glow* at the side menu (first option from the left in the third row in the *Glow Variations* section).
9. Click the Text Effects button, point to *Transform*, and then click the *Triangle Up* option (third option from the left in the top row of the *Warp* section).
10. Click in the *Shape Height* measurement box, type 3, and then press Enter.
11. Click in the *Shape Width* measurement box, type 8, and then press Enter.
12. Click the Align button and then click *Distribute Horizontally*.
13. Click the Align button and then click *Distribute Vertically*.
14. Make Slide 6 active.
15. Apply WordArt formatting to the text in the text box by completing the following steps:
    a. Click in the text to select the text box.
    b. Click the text box border to change the border line from a dashed line to a solid line.
    c. With the Drawing Tools Format tab selected, click the More button at the right side of the WordArt style thumbnails, and then click *Fill - Accent 6, Warm Matte Bevel* option (second option from the left in the bottom row).
16. Save **PP_C4_P1.pptx**.

Inserting Text Objects

In Chapter 2 you learned how to insert headers, footers, the date and time, and slide numbers using the Options button in Print Preview. You can also insert these objects in a presentation with buttons in the Text group in the Insert table. Click the Header & Footer button and the Header and Footer dialog box displays with the Slide tab selected. Click the Date & Time or Slide Number button and the same dialog box displays. Use options at this dialog box to insert a header, footer, date, time, and slide number in the active slide or all slides in the presentation. Click the Notes and Handouts tab if you want the objects inserted in handouts, notes pages, and outline pages.

The Text group in the Insert tab also includes a Symbol button. Click this button and the Symbol dialog box displays. Choose a symbol font with the *Font* option in the dialog box, click the desired symbol in the list box, click the Insert button, and then click the Close button. This closes the dialog box and inserts the symbol in the slide at the location of the insertion point.

Project ⑪ Inserting Text Objects in a Presentation

1. With **PP_C4_P1.pptx** open, make Slide 1 active.
2. Insert slide numbers on each slide by completing the following steps:
   a. Click the Insert tab.
   b. Click the Slide Number button in the Text group.
   c. At the Header and Footer dialog box with the Slide tab selected, click the *Slide Number* check box to insert a check mark.
   d. Click the Apply to All button.
3. Insert your name as a footer that prints on handout pages by completing the following steps:
   a. Click the Header & Footer button in the Text group.
   b. At the Header and Footer dialog box, click the Notes and Handouts tab.
   c. Click the *Footer* check box to insert a check mark and then type your first and last names.
   d. Click the Apply to All button.
4. Insert the current date as a header that prints on handout pages by completing the following steps:
   a. Click the Date & Time button in the Text group.
   b. At the Header and Footer dialog box, click the Notes and Handouts tab.
   c. Click the *Date and Time* check box to insert a check mark.
   d. Click the Apply to All button.
5. Insert a symbol by completing the following steps:
   a. Make Slide 2 active.
   b. Click in the text containing the names, titles, and telephone numbers. (This selects the text box.)
   c. Delete the *n* in *Pena* (the fourth last name).
   d. Click the Insert tab and then click the Symbol button.
   e. At the Symbol dialog box, click the down-pointing arrow at the right side of the *Font* option box and then click *(normal text)* at the drop-down list (first option in the list).
   f. Scroll down the symbol list box and then click the ñ symbol (first symbol from the left in the twelfth row).
   g. Click the Insert button and then click the Close button.

6. Insert a text box and a symbol by completing the following steps:
   a. With Slide 2 active, click the Text Box button in the Text group in the Insert tab.
   b. Click in the lower right corner of the slide below the telephone number column.
   c. Change the font size to 24 and the font color to black.
   d. Click the Insert tab.
   e. Click Symbol button.
   f. At the Symbol dialog box, click the down-pointing arrow at the right side of the *Font* option, scroll to the end of the list box, and then click *Wingdings*.
   g. Click the telephone symbol ☎ located in the top row.
   h. Click the Insert button and then click the Close button.
7. Apply a transition and sound of your choosing to all slides.
8. Run the presentation.
9. Print Slide 2.
10. Print the presentation as handouts with six slides per page.
11. Save and then close **PP_C4_P1.pptx**.

CHAPTER summary

- Insert a text box in a slide using the Text Box button in the Text group in the Insert tab.

- Format a text box with options in the Drawing group in the Home tab or with options in the Drawing Tools Format tab.

- Select all objects in a slide by clicking the Select button in the Editing group in the Home tab and then clicking *Select All* or with the keyboard shortcut, Ctrl + A.

- Align selected objects with options from the Align button in the Arrange group in the Drawing Tools Format tab.

- Set tabs in a text box by clicking the Alignment button at the left side of the horizontal ruler until the desired symbol displays and then clicking on a specific location on the ruler. You can set a left, center, right, or decimal tab.

- Insert a shape in a slide with options at the Shapes button in the Drawing group in the Home tab or the Shapes button in the Illustrations group in the Insert tab.

- With options in the Shapes button drop-down list, you can draw a line, basic shapes, block arrows, flow chart symbols, callouts, stars, and banners.

- Copy a shape by selecting the shape, clicking the Copy button in the Clipboard group, positioning the insertion point in the desired position, and then clicking the Paste button in the Clipboard group. You can also copy a shape by holding down the Ctrl key and then dragging the shape to the desired location.

- Turn the horizontal and vertical rulers on and off with the *Ruler* check box in the Show/Hide group in the View tab and turn gridlines on and off with the *Gridlines* check box. You can also turn gridlines as well as drawing guides and the snap-to-grid feature on and off with options at the Grid and Guides dialog box. Display this dialog box by clicking the Align button in the Drawing Tools Format tab and then clicking *Grid Settings* at the drop-down list.

- You can group objects and then apply the same formatting to objects in the group. To group objects, select the objects, click the Group button in the Arrange group in the Drawing Tools Format tab, and then click *Group* at the drop-down list.

- Size images with the *Shape Height* and *Shape Width* measurement boxes in the Picture Tools Format tab or with the sizing handles that display around a selected image.

- Use the Crop button in the Size group in the Picture Tools Format tab to remove portions of an image.

- Move an image by dragging it to the new location. Move an imagine in small increments, called nudging, by holding down the Ctrl key while pressing an arrow key.

- Click the Bring to Front button in the Arrange group in the Drawing Tools Format tab or Picture Tools Format tab to move the selected object on top of other objects in the slide. Click the Send to Back button to move the selected image behind other objects in the slide.

- Insert a picture in a slide with the Picture button in the Illustrations group in the Insert tab.

- Insert a picture as a slide background with options at the Format Background dialog box. Display this dialog box by clicking the Background Styles button in the Background group in the Design tab and then clicking *Format Background*.

- Insert a clip art image with options in the Clip Art task pane. Display this task pane by clicking the Clip Art button in the Illustrations group in the Insert tab or clicking the Clip Art button in a layout content placeholder.

- Size, scale, rotate, and position an object with options in the Size and Position dialog box. Display this dialog box by clicking the Size group dialog box launcher in the Picture Tools Format tab or Drawing Tools Format tab.

- Use the WordArt feature to distort or modify text to conform to a variety of shapes. Insert WordArt by clicking the WordArt button in the Illustrations group in the Insert tab and then clicking the desired option at the drop-down list. Format WordArt text with options in the Drawing Tools Format tab.

- Click the Header & Footer button, Date & Time button, or Slide Number button in the Text group in the Insert tab to display the Header and Footer dialog box with the Slide tab selected.

- Insert a symbol in a slide with options at the Symbol dialog box. Display this dialog box by clicking the Symbol button in the Text group in the Insert tab.

COMMANDS review

FEATURE	TAB, GROUP	BUTTON, OPTION	KEYBOARD SHORTCUT
Text box	Insert, Text		
Shape	Insert, Illustrations or Home, Drawing		
Gridlines	View, Show/Hide	☑ Gridlines	Shift + F9
Rulers	View, Show/Hide	☑ Ruler	
Grid and Guides dialog box	Drawing Tools Format, Arrange	Align ▾ , Grid Settings	
Picture	Insert, Illustrations		
Format Background dialog box	Design, Background	Background Styles ▾ , Format Background	
Clip Art task pane	Insert, Illustrations		
Size and Position dialog box	Drawing Tools Format, Size or Picture Tools Format, Size		
WordArt	Insert, Text		
Header and Footer	Insert, Text		
Date and Time	Insert, Text		
Slide number	Insert, Text		
Symbol dialog box	Insert, Text	Ω	

CONCEPTS check

Completion: In the space provided at the right, indicate the correct term, symbol, or command.

1. The Text Box button is located in the Text group in this tab.   _____

2. Use the sizing handles or these measurement boxes to change the size of a text box.   _____

3. This is the keyboard shortcut to select all objects in a slide.   _____

4. A text box, by default, contains tabs with this alignment.   _____

5. The Drawing group in the Home tab and the Illustrations group in this tab each contain a Shapes button.   _____

6. When dragging a shape to change the size, hold down this key to maintain the proportions of the shape.   _____

7. Copy a shape by holding down this key while dragging the shape to the desired location.   _____

8. Turn drawing guides on and off with options in this dialog box.   _____

9. The Group button is located in this group in the Drawing Tools Format tab.   _____

10. Click the Clip Art button and this displays at the right side of the screen.   _____

11. Use this button in the Size group in the Picture Tools Format tab to remove any unnecessary parts of an image.   _____

12. Use this feature to distort or modify text to conform to a variety of shapes.   _____

SKILLS check
Demonstrate Your Proficiency

1 FORMAT AND ADD ENHANCEMENTS TO A TRAVEL PRESENTATION

1. Open **TravelEngland.pptx** and then save the presentation and name it **PP_C4_A1**.
2. Apply the Solstice design theme.
3. Insert the slide shown in Figure 4.14 with the following specifications:
   a. Make Slide 6 active and then insert a new slide with the *Title Only* layout.
   b. Type the title *Travel England* as shown in the slide.
   c. Draw a text box in the slide and then type the text shown in Figure 4.14. Select and then change the text font size to 40 and change the font color to Brown, Accent 5, Darker 50%.
   d. Apply *Gold, Accent 2, Lighter 80%* shape fill to the text box.
   e. Apply the *Accent color 1, 18 pt glow* shape effect (from the *Glow* side menu).
   f. Size and position the text box so it displays as shown in Figure 4.14.
4. Insert the slide shown in Figure 4.15 with the following specifications:
   a. Make Slide 1 active and then insert a new slide with the *Title Only* layout.
   b. Type the title *Upcoming Tours* as shown in the slide.
   c. Draw a text box in the slide and then set a left tab at the *0.5"* mark on the horizontal ruler, a center tab at the *4.0"* mark, and a right tab at the *7"* mark.
   d. Type the text in columns as shown in Figure 4.15. Bold the heading text *Dates*, *Duration*, and *Price*.
   e. After typing the text, select the text, change the font size to 20, the font color to Brown, Accent 5, Darker 50%, and change the line spacing to 1.5.
   f. Size and position the text box so it displays as shown in Figure 4.15.
5. Insert a picture in Slide 6 as shown in Figure 4.16 with the following specifications:
   a. Insert the picture named **WhiteHorse.jpg**.
   b. Size and move the picture so it displays as shown in Figure 4.16.
6. Insert a picture in Slide 4 as shown in Figure 4.17 with the following specifications:
   a. Insert the picture named **Stonehenge.jpg**.
   b. Crop the picture so it displays as shown in Figure 4.17.
   c. Send the picture behind the text.
   d. Size and move the bulleted text placeholder so it displays as shown in Figure 4.17.
   e. Size and move the picture so it displays as shown in Figure 4.17.
7. Insert a clip art image in Slide 7 as shown in Figure 4.18 with the following specification:
   a. In the Clip Art task pane, search only for clip art images that match the topic *Spring*.
   b. Click the image shown in the Clip Art task pane as shown in Figure 4.18 to insert it in the slide. (The original image contains pink blossoms in the tree instead of green.) If this image is not available, choose another clip art image related to "spring."
   c. Recolor the picture to Accent color 4 Light in the *Light Variations* section.
   d. Size and move the clip art image so it displays as shown in Figure 4.18.

8. Insert a picture as background in Slide 1 as shown in Figure 4.19 with the following specifications:
   a. Click the Design tab, click the Background Styles button, and then click *Format Background* at the drop-down list.
   b. At the Format Background dialog box, insert a check mark in the *Hide background graphics*.
   c. Click the File button, navigate to the PowerPoint2007L1C4 folder on your storage medium and then double-click ***BigBen.jpg***.
   d. At the Format Background dialog box, click the down-pointing arrow at the right side of the *Bottom* option box in the *Stretch Options* section until *-100%* displays in the box.
   e. Close the dialog box.
   f. Size and move the title placeholder so the title displays as shown in Figure 4.19.
   g. Size and move the subtitle placeholder so the subtitle displays as shown in Figure 4.19.
9. Insert the slide shown in Figure 4.20 with the following specifications:
   a. Make Slide 8 active and then insert a new slide with the *Title Only* layout.
   b. Type the title *Travel Discounts!* as shown in Figure 4.20.
   c. Draw the shape shown in the slide in Figure 4.20 using the *Up Ribbon* shape.
   d. Apply the *Subtle Effect - Accent 1* shape style to the shape.
   e. Apply the *Accent color 2, 8 pt glow* shape effect (from the *Glow* side menu).
   f. Create a text box in the shape and then type the text shown in Figure 4.20. Change the font size for the text to 28 and change the font color to Brown, Accent 5, Darker 50%.
   g. Size and position the shape and text box so they display as shown in Figure 4.20.
10. Insert a new slide at the beginning of the presentation with the *Blank* layout. ***Hint: Click above the Slide 1 miniature in the Slides/Outline pane and then click the New Slide button arrow.*** Insert a logo from another presentation by completing the following steps:
    a. Open **FCTCruise.pptx** and then copy the First Choice Travel logo from Slide 1 to Slide 1 in the **PP_C4_A1.pptx** presentation.
    b. Close **FCTCruise.pptx**.
    c. With Slide 1 of **PP_C4_A1.pptx** active and the logo selected, recolor the logo (picture) to Accent color 1 Light.
    d. Position the logo attractively on the slide.
11. Apply a transition and sound of your choosing to each slide.
12. Insert slide numbers on each slide.
13. Insert a footer for notes and handouts pages that prints your first and last names.
14. Run the presentation.
15. Print the presentation as a handout with six slides per page.
16. Save and then close **PP_C4_A1.pptx**.

Figure 4.14 Assessment 1 Step 3

Travel England

"With 6000 years of history, there is so much to see and enjoy that you will want to return time and again."

Figure 4.15 Assessment 1 Step 4

Upcoming Tours

Dates	Duration	Price
April 17 – 24	8 days, 7 nights	$2499 pp
May 15 – 22	8 days, 7 nights	$2499 pp
June 12 – 19	8 days, 7 nights	$2999 pp
July 8 – 18	11 days, 10 nights	$3599 pp
July 24 – 31	8 days, 7 nights	$3099 pp

Figure 4.16 Assessment 1 Step 5

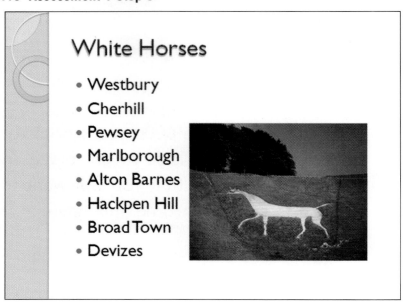

Figure 4.17 Assessment 1 Step 6

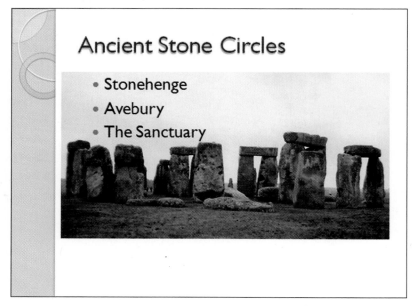

Figure 4.18 Assessment 1 Step 7

Figure 4.19 Assessment 1 Step 8

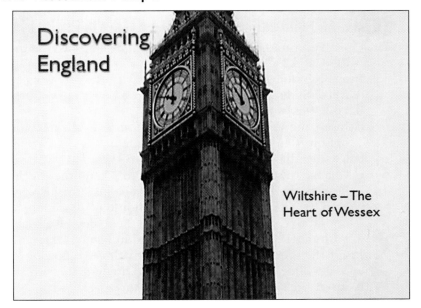

Figure 4.20 Assessment 1 Step 9

Assessment

2 FORMAT AND ADD ENHANCEMENTS TO A GARDENING PRESENTATION

1. Open **PerennialsPresentation.pptx** and then save the presentation and name it **PP_C4_A2**.
2. Insert the slide shown in Figure 4.21 with the following specifications:
   a. Make Slide 2 active and then insert a new slide with the *Blank* layout.
   b. Hide the background graphics.
   c. Insert the WordArt text using *Gradient Fill - Accent 6, Inner Shadow* (second option from the left in the fourth row).
   d. Change the shape of the WordArt to *Wave 1*.
   e. Change the height of the WordArt to *3″* and the width to *9″*.
   f. Display the Format Background dialog box (for help, see Assessment 1, Step 8), click the *Gradient fill* option in the *Fill* section, change the *Preset colors* option to *Daybreak*, and then close the dialog box.
   g. Position the WordArt text as shown in Figure 4.21.
3. Insert the slide shown in Figure 4.22 with the following specifications:
   a. Make Slide 8 active and then insert a new slide with the *Title Only* layout.
   b. Insert the title *English/French Translations* as shown.
   c. Insert a text box, change the font size to 28, change the font color to Light Blue, Accent 5, Darker 25%, set left tabs at the 0.5″ and the 4″ mark on the horizontal ruler, and then type the text in columns. Bold the headings *English Name* and *French Name* and use the Symbol dialog box to insert the special symbols in the French names.
   d. If necessary, move the text box so it is positioned as shown in Figure 4.22.

4. Make Slide 4 active and then make the following changes:
   a. Select the bulleted text and then change the line spacing to 2.0.
   b. With the bulleted text selected, set the bulleted text in two columns. *Hint: Refer to Project 1c in Chapter 3.*
   c. Make sure four bulleted items display in each column.
5. Make Slide 5 active and then insert a clip art image related to *garden* or *gardening*. Size and position the clip art attractively in the slide.
6. Select and then delete Slide 10.
7. Insert the slide shown in Figure 4.23 with the following specifications:
   a. Make Slide 9 active and then insert a new slide with the *Title Only* layout.
   b. Insert the title *Gardening Magazines*.
   c. Create the top shape using the *Bevel* shape.
   d. Draw a text box inside the shape, change the font size to 32, turn on bold, turn on italic, change the alignment to Center, and then type the text in the top shape.
   e. Select the shape and the text box and then copy them two times.
   f. Change the text in the second and third shapes to match what you see in Figure 4.23.
   g. Size and position the shapes and text boxes as shown in Figure 4.23
8. Make Slide 7 active and then insert a clip art image of your choosing.
9. Run the presentation.
10. Print the presentation as a handout with six slides per page.
11. Save **PP_C4_A2.pptx**.

Figure 4.21 Assessment 2 Step 2

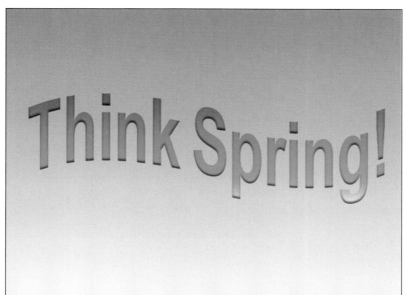

Figure 4.22 Assessment 2 Step 3

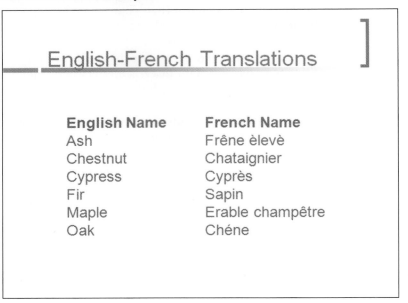

English-French Translations

English Name	French Name
Ash	Frêne èlevè
Chestnut	Chataignier
Cypress	Cyprès
Fir	Sapin
Maple	Erable champêtre
Oak	Chéne

Figure 4.23 Assessment 2 Step 7

Gardening Magazines

Better Homes and Gardens®

Home and Garden

Organic Gardening®

3 COPY A PICTURE FROM A WEB SITE TO A PRESENTATION

1. With **PP_C4_A2.pptx** open, make Slide 6 active.
2. Use the Help feature to find information on copying a picture from a Web page. (Begin by entering "insert a picture or clip art" in the PowerPoint Help window and then press Enter. Click the <u>Insert a picture or clip art</u> hyperlink and then click the "<u>Copy a picture from a Web page</u>" hyperlink.)
3. Using the information you learned about copying a Web page, open your Web browser and then use a search engine of your choosing to search for a picture of at least one flower mentioned in the slide.
4. Copy the picture to the slide and then size and move the picture so it is positioned attractively in the slide. (Consider inserting at least one more picture of one of the flowers mentioned.)
5. Print only Slide 6.
6. Run the presentation.
7. Save and then close **PP_C4_A2.pptx**.

CASE study
Apply Your Skills

Part 1

You work for Honoré Financial Services and the Office Manager, Jason Monroe, has asked you to prepare a presentation for a community workshop he will be conducting next week. Open the Word document named **HonoreFinancialServices.docx** and then use the information in the document to create a presentation with the following specifications:

• Slide 1: Include the company name Honoré Financial Services (use the Symbol feature to create the é in Honoré) and the subtitle *Managing Your Money*.
• Slide 2: Insert the word *Budgeting* as WordArt.
• Slides 3, 4, and 5: Use the bulleted and numbered information to create these slides.
• Slide 6: Create a text box, set tabs, and then type the information in the *Managing Records* section that is set in columns.
• Slide 7: Create a shape and then insert a text box inside the shape with the following slogan *"Retirement Planning Made Easy"*.
• Include at least one picture and one clip art in the presentation.

Apply a design theme of your choosing and add any additional features to improve the visual appeal of the presentation. Insert a transition and sound to each slide and then run the presentation. Save the presentation and name it **PP_C4_CS_P1.pptx**. Print the presentation as a handout with four slides per page.

Mr. Monroe will be conducting a free workshop titled *Financial Planning for the College Student*. Create a slide in the **PP_C4_CS_P1.pptx** presentation (make it the last slide in the presentation) that includes a shape with a text box inside and include information about the workshop inside the text box. You determine the day, the time, and the location for the workshop. Print the slide.

Mr. Monroe would like to post the information about the workshop in various locations in the community and wants to print a number of copies. You decide to copy the shape and the text box and then insert them in a blank Word document. In Word, change the orientation of the page to landscape, increase the size of the shape and text box, and then drag the shape and text box to the middle of the page. Save the Word document and name it **PP_C4_CS_P3**. Print and then close **PP_C4_CS_P3.docx**.

Mr. Monroe has asked you to locate online finance and/or budgeting resources such as newsletters and magazines. He would like you to locate resources and then create a slide with hyperlinks to the resources. Locate at least two online resources and then insert this information with the hyperlinks in a new slide at the end of the **PP_C4_CS_P1.pptx** presentation. Print the slide and then save and close the presentation.

Creating and Formatting PowerPoint Presentations

ASSESSING proficiency

In this unit, you have learned to create, print, save, close, open, view, run, edit, and format a PowerPoint presentation. You also learned how to add transitions and sound to presentations; rearrange slides; customize presentations by changing the design theme; and add visual appeal to slides by inserting text boxes, shapes, pictures, clip art, and symbols.

Note: Before beginning computer assessments, copy to your storage medium the PowerPoint2007U1 folder from the PowerPoint2007 folder on the CD that accompanies this textbook and then make PowerPoint2007U1 the active folder.

Assessment 1 Prepare, Format, and Enhance a Conference Presentation

1. Create a presentation with the text shown in Figure U1.1 using a design theme of your choosing. Use the appropriate slide layout for each slide. After creating the slides, complete a spelling check on the text in slides.
2. Add a transition and sound of your choosing to all slides.
3. Save the presentation and name it **PP_U1_A1**.
4. Run the presentation.
5. Make Slide 1 active and then find all occurrences of *Area* and replace it with *Market*.
6. Make the following changes to Slide 2:
   a. Type Net Income per Common Share over *Net Income*.
   b. Delete *Return on Average Equity*.
7. Make the following changes to Slide 4:
   a. Delete *Shopping*.
   b. Type Business Finance between *Personal Finance* and *E-mail*.
8. Rearrange the slides in the presentation so they are in the following order (only the slide titles are shown below):
   Slide 1 = CORNERSTONE SYSTEMS
   Slide 2 = Corporate Vision
   Slide 3 = Future Goals
   Slide 4 = Industrial Market
   Slide 5 = Consumer Market
   Slide 6 = Financial Review
9. Increase spacing to 1.5 for the bulleted text in Slides 2, 3, 5, and 6.
10. Make Slide 4 active, increase the spacing to 2.0 for the bulleted text, and then format the bulleted text into two columns with three entries in each column.

11. Apply a different theme color to the presentation.
12. Save and then run the presentation.
13. Print the presentation as a handout with six slides per page.
14. Display the Reuse Slides task pane, browse to the PowerPoint2007U1 folder on your storage medium, and then double-click *MarketingPresentation.pptx*.
15. Insert the *Department Reports* slide below Slide 4.
16. Insert the *Services* slide below Slide 2.
17. Close the Reuse Slides task pane.
18. Make Slide 8 active, select the bulleted text, and then create and apply a custom bullet using a money symbol in a complementary color. (You can find a money symbol in the normal font in the Symbol dialog box.)
19. With Slide 8 active, insert a clip art image related to *money* or *finances*. Size and position the clip art attractively in the slide.
20. Move Slide 4 (*Future Goals*) to the end of the presentation.
21. Insert a new slide with the *Title and Content* layout at the end of the presentation with the following specifications:
    a. Insert *Future Goals* as the title.
    b. Type International Market as the first bulleted item and then press Enter.
    c. Copy *Acquisitions*, *Production*, *Technology*, and *Marketing* from Slide 8 and paste them in the content area of the new slide below the first bulleted text. (When copied, the items should be preceded by a bullet. If a bullet displays on a blank line below the last text item, press the Backspace key twice.)
    d. Select the bulleted text and then change the line spacing to 1.5.
22. Make Slide 8 active, select the bulleted items, and then apply numbering.
23. Make Slide 9 active, select the bulleted items, and then apply numbering and change the beginning number to *6*.
24. With Slide 9 active, create a new slide with the *Blank* layout with the following specifications:
    a. Insert the picture named ***Nightscape.jpg*** as a background picture and hide the background graphics. ***Hint: Do this with the Background Styles button in the Design tab.***
    b. Create a text box toward the top of the slide, change the font color to white, increase the font size to 36, and then change the alignment to center.
    c. Type National Sales Meeting, press Enter, type New York City, press Enter, and then type March 3 - 6, 2010.
    d. Move and/or size the text box so the text is positioned centered above the buildings in the picture.
25. Insert slide numbers on each slide.
26. Insert a footer for notes and handouts pages that prints your first and last names.
27. Save and then run the presentation.
28. Print the presentation as a handout with six slides per page.
29. Close **PP_U1_A1.pptx**.

Figure U1.1 Assessment 1

Slide 1	Title	=	CORNERSTONE SYSTEMS
	Subtitle	=	Executive Conference

Slide 2   Title = Financial Review
          Bullets =
- Net Revenues
- Operating Income
- Net Income
- Return on Average Equity
- Return on Average Asset

Slide 3   Title = Corporate Vision
          Bullets =
- Expansion
- Increased Productivity
- Consumer Satisfaction
- Employee Satisfaction
- Area Visibility

Slide 4   Title = Consumer Area
          Bullets =
- Travel
- Shopping
- Entertainment
- Personal Finance
- E-mail

Slide 5   Title = Industrial Area
          Bullets =
- Finance
- Education
- Government
- Production
- Manufacturing
- Utilities

Slide 6   Title = Future Goals
          Bullets =
- Domestic Area
- Acquisitions
- Production
- Technology
- Marketing

Assessment 2 Format and Enhance a Kraft Artworks Presentation

1. Open **ArtworksPresentation.pptx** and then save the presentation and name it **PP_U1_A2**.
2. With Slide 1 active, insert the text *Kraft Artworks* as WordArt and apply at least the following formatting:
   a. Change the shape of the WordArt.
   b. Change the size so the WordArt better fills the slide.
   c. Change the fill to a purple color.
   d. Apply any other formatting to improve the visual appeal of the WordArt.
3. Duplicate Slides 2 and 3.
4. Change the goal number in Slide 4 from *1* to *3* and change the goal text to *Conduct six art workshops at the Community Center.*
5. Change the goal number in Slide 5 from *2* to *4* and change the goal text to *Provide recycled material to public schools for art classes.*
6. With Slide 5 active, insert a new slide with the *Title Only* layout with the following specifications:
   a. Insert the title *Clients* and then format, size, and position the title in the same manner as the title in Slide 5.
   b. Insert a text box, change the font to Comic Sans MS, the font size to 20, the font color to purple, and then type the following text in columns (you determine the tab settings):

School	Contact	Number
Logan Elementary School	Maya Jones	555-0882
Cedar Elementary School	George Ferraro	555-3211
Sunrise Elementary School	Avery Burns	555-3444
Hillside Middle School	Joanna Myers	555-2211
Douglas Middle School	Ray Murphy	555-8100

   c. Select all of the text in the text box and then change the line spacing to 1.5.
7. With Slide 6 active, insert a new slide with the *Blank* layout, hide the background graphic, and then create the slide shown in Figure U1.2 with the following specifications:
   a. Use the *Explosion 1* shape to create the first shape.
   b. Change the fill color of the shape to Gold, Accent 2, Lighter 40% and apply the *Accent color 3, 18 pt glow* effect.
   c. Insert a text box inside the shape, change the font to 40-point Comic Sans MS bold in purple color, change the alignment to center, and then type the text shown in Figure U1.2.
   d. Copy the shape and the text box twice.
   e. Type the appropriate text in each text box as shown in Figure U1.2.
8. With Slide 7 active, insert a new slide with the *Blank* layout, hide the background graphic, and then create the slide shown in Figure U1.3 with the following specifications:
   a. Set the text in the two text boxes at the left and right side of the slide in 54-point Comic Sans MS bold and in purple color. Rotate, size, and position the two text boxes as shown in Figure U1.3.
   b. Use the *Explosion 1* shape to create the shape in the middle of the slide.
   c. Change the fill color of the shape to Gold, Accent 2, Lighter 40%, apply the *Perspective Diagonal Upper Left* shadow effect, and change the shape outline color to purple and the weight to *2¼ pt.*

d. Insert a text box in the middle of the shape, change the font to 28-point Comic Sans MS bold in purple color, change the alignment to center, and then type the text inside the shape as shown in Figure U1.3.

9. Create a footer that prints your first and last names and the current date on handout pages.

10. Print the presentation as a handout with four slides per page.

11. Save and then close **PP_U1_A2.pptx**

Figure U1.2 Assessment 2, Slide 7

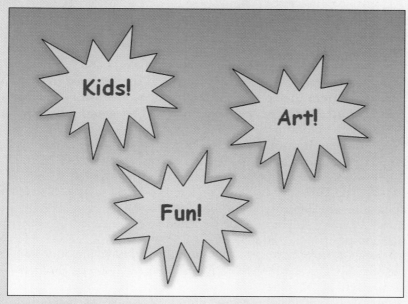

Figure U1.3 Assessment 2, Slide 8

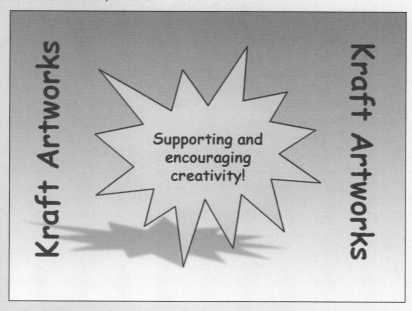

Assessment 3 Create and Apply a Custom Theme to a Job Search Presentation

1. At a blank presentation, apply the *Civic* design.
2. Create custom theme colors named with your first and last names that change the following colors:
   a. Change the Text/Background - Dark 1 color to Dark Yellow, Followed Hyperlink, Lighter 80%.
   b. Change the Text/Background - Dark 2 color to White, Text 1.
   c. Change the Text/Background - Light 2 color to Turquoise, Hyperlink, Darker 25%.
   d. Change the Accent 1 color to Dark Red.
   e. Change the Accent 2 and the Accent 3 color to Red, Accent 1, Darker 50%.
3. Create custom theme fonts named with your first and last names that changes the *Heading font* to Constantia and the *Body font* to Cambria.
4. Save the current theme as a custom theme named with your first and last names. ***Hint: Do this at the Save Current Theme dialog box.***
5. Close the presentation without saving it.
6. Open **JobSearch.pptx** and then save the presentation and name it **PP_U1_A3**.
7. Apply the custom theme named with your first and last names.
8. Insert a clip art image in Slide 5 related to *telephone*, *people*, or *Internet*. You determine the size and position of the image.
9. Insert a clip art image in Slide 6 related to *clock* or *time*. You determine the size and position of the image.
10. Improve the visual display of text in Slides 2, 3, 7, 8, and 9 by increasing the spacing between items and positioning the text placeholders attractively in the slides.
11. Insert the current date and slide number on all slides in the presentation. (The slide numbers will appear in the round circle that is part of the design theme.)
12. Create the header *Job Search Seminar*, the footer *Employment Strategies*, and insert the date and page number for notes and handouts.
13. Add the speaker note *Hand out list of Internet employment sites.* to Slide 5.
14. Apply a transition and sound of your choosing to all slides in the presentation.
15. Save and then run the presentation.
16. Print the presentation as a handout with six slides per page.
17. Print Slide 5 as notes pages.
18. Save and then close **PP_U1_A3.pptx**.
19. Display a blank presentation and then delete the custom theme colors, custom theme fonts, and custom theme you created for this assessment.
20. Close the presentation without saving it.

Assessment 4 Format and Enhance a Medical Plans Presentation

1. Open **MedicalPlans.pptx** and then save the presentation and name it **PP_U1_A4**.
2. Apply a design theme of your choosing.
3. Create a new Slide between Slides 1 and 2 that contains a shape with the text *Medical Plans 2009 - 2010* in a text box inside the shape. You determine the format, position, and size of the shape and text box.

4. Change the bullets to custom bullets (you determine the picture or symbol) for the bullets in Slides 3, 4, and 5.

5. Insert a clip art image related to *medicine* in Slide 4. You determine the color, size, and position of the image.

6. Make Slide 5 active, and then apply the following formatting:
   a. Move the insertion point to the beginning of *Eugene* and then press the Enter key.
   b. Select all of the bulleted text and then change the line spacing to 2.0.
   c. With the bulleted text selected, format the text into two columns. (Make sure each column contains four entries.)
   d. Size and/or move the placeholder so the bulleted text displays attractively in the slide.

7. Apply any additional formatting or elements to improve the visual appeal of the slides.

8. Add a transition and sound of your choosing to the presentation.

9. Run the presentation.

10. Print the presentation as a handout with three slides per page.

11. Save and then close **PP_U1_A4.pptx**.

WRITING activities

The following activities provide you with the opportunity to practice your writing skills along with demonstrating an understanding of some of the important PowerPoint features you have mastered in this unit. Use correct spelling, grammar, and appropriate word choices.

Activity 1 Prepare and Format a Health Plan Presentation

Open Word and then open, print, and close **KeyLifeHealthPlan.docx**. Looking at the printing of this document, create a presentation in PowerPoint that presents the main points of the plan. (Use bullets in the presentation.) Add a transition and sound to the slides. Apply formatting and/or insert images to enhance the visual appeal of the presentation. Save the presentation and name it **PP_U1_Act01**. Run the presentation. Print the presentation as a handout with six slides per page. Save and then close **PP_U1_Act01.pptx**.

Activity 2 Prepare and Format a Clip Art Presentation

At a blank presentation, use the Help feature to find information on inserting a picture or clip art image. ***Hint: Display the PowerPoint Help window, type*** insert picture or clip art***, press Enter, and then click the*** <u>***Insert a picture or clip art***</u> ***hyperlink that displays in the window.*** Print and then read the information and then use the information to create a presentation that includes at least four slides. Format and add visual appeal to the presentation. With the presentation still open, display the Clip Art task pane and then click the <u>Clip art on Office Online</u> hyperlink that displays at the bottom of the task pane. (Your computer needs to be connected to the Internet to complete this activity.) Look over the information that displays at the Microsoft Office Online Clip Art Web site and then create at least three additional slides that contain information on the site. For example, you might create a slide that summarizes the options at the left side of the page, create a slide that includes a clip art from the featured collection, and a slide that lists some interesting clip art categories. Save the completed presentation and name it **PP_U1_Act02**. Add a transition and sound of your choosing to each slide and then run the presentation. Print the presentation as a handout with four slides per page. Close the **PP_U1_Act02.pptx** presentation.

Analyze a Magazine Web Site

Make sure you are connected to the Internet and then explore the Time® magazine Web site at www.time.com. Discover the following information for the site:

- Magazine sections
- The type of information presented in each section
- Services available
- Information on how to subscribe

Use the information you discovered about the Time magazine Web site and create a PowerPoint presentation that presents the information in a clear, concise, and logical manner. Add formatting and enhancements to the presentation to make it more interesting. When the presentation is completed, save it and name it **PP_U1_TimeMag**. Run, print, and then close the presentation.

Microsoft®

PowerPoint®

Unit 2: Customizing and Enhancing PowerPoint Presentations

➤ Creating Tables, Charts, and SmartArt Graphics

➤ Using Slide Masters and Action Buttons

➤ Applying Custom Animation and Setting Up Shows

➤ Integrating, Reviewing, Protecting, and Saving Presentations

PowerPoint

Benchmark Microsoft® PowerPoint 2007

Microsoft Certified Application Specialist Skills—Unit 2

Reference No.	Skill	Pages
1	**Creating and Formatting Presentations**	
1.1	Create new presentations	
1.1.2	Create presentations from templates	235-237
1.1.4	Create presentations from Microsoft Office Word outlines	298-299
1.2	Customize slide masters	
1.2.1	Apply themes to slide masters	222-224
1.2.2	Format slide master backgrounds	223-226
1.3	Add elements to slide masters	221-235
2	**Creating and Formatting Slide Content**	
2.2	Manipulate text	
2.2.1	Cut, copy, and paste text (paste special)	305-307
2.3	Add and link existing content to presentations	
2.3.1	Reuse slides from an existing presentation (apply slide masters)	226-227
2.3.3	Insert hyperlinks	247-249
2.3.4	Insert media clips	285-288
2.4	Apply, customize, modify, and remove animations	
2.4.1	Apply built-in animations	260-261
2.4.2	Modify animations	261, 265-268
2.4.3	Create custom animations	262-272
3	**Working with Visual Content**	
3.1	Create SmartArt diagrams	
3.1.1	Create a SmartArt diagram	184-187, 189-192
3.1.2	Create SmartArt diagrams from bullet points	189-191
3.2	Modify SmartArt diagrams	
3.2.1	Add text to SmartArt diagrams	185, 187, 191-192
3.2.2	Change theme colors	187-188, 190, 192
3.2.3	Add effects using SmartArt Styles	187-188, 192
3.2.4	Change the layout of diagrams	186
3.2.5	Change the orientation of charts	188, 190
3.2.6	Add or remove shapes within SmartArt	185, 190
3.2.7	Change diagram types	186
3.6	Insert and modify charts	
3.6.1	Insert charts	192-202
3.6.2	Change chart types	196-197
3.6.3	Format fill and other effects	199-201
3.6.4	Add chart elements	197-199
3.7	Insert and modify tables	
3.7.1	Insert tables in a slide	176-178
3.7.2	Apply Table Styles to tables	178-180
3.7.3	Change alignment and orientation of table text	180-183
3.7.4	Add images to tables	182
4	**Collaborating on and Delivering Presentations**	
4.1	Review presentations	
4.1.1	Insert, delete, and modify comments	309-312
4.1.2	Show and hide markup	310-312
4.2	Protect presentations	
4.2.1	Add digital signatures to presentations	316-319
4.3	Secure and share presentations	
4.3.1	Identify presentation features not supported by previous versions	319-321
4.3.2	Remove inappropriate information using Document Inspector	314-316
4.3.3	Restrict permissions to a document using Information Rights Management (IRM)	320-321
4.3.4	Mark presentations as final	319, 321
4.3.6	Save presentations as appropriate file types	322-323, 325-330
4.4	Prepare printed materials	
4.4.1	Customize handout masters	237-239
4.5	Prepare for and rehearse presentation delivery	
4.5.1	Show only specific slides in presentations	280-284
4.5.2	Rehearse and time the delivery of a presentation	277-278
4.5.4	Package presentations for a CD	331-332
4.5.5	Set slide show options	276-282

Creating Tables, Charts, and SmartArt Graphics

PERFORMANCE OBJECTIVES

Upon successful completion of Chapter 5, you will be able to:

- Create and format a table
- Modify the design and layout of a table
- Insert an image in a table
- Create SmartArt diagrams
- Modify the design and layout of SmartArt
- Create a SmartArt graphic with bulleted text
- Create and format charts
- Modify the design and layout of charts
- Select and format chart elements
- Create, edit, and format a photo album

powerpoint Chapter 5

Tutorial 5.1
Graphically Representing and
Arranging Data

If you want to present numbers and lists in a slide, consider inserting the information in a table. Use the Tables feature to create data in columns and rows in a manner similar to a spreadsheet. Display data in a slide in a more visual way by creating a SmartArt diagram. The SmartArt feature provides a number of predesigned diagrams and organizational charts. You can create a SmartArt diagram and then modify the design and layout of the diagram.

While a table does an adequate job of representing data, you can create a chart from data to provide a more visual representation of the data. A chart is sometimes referred to as a *graph* and is a picture of numeric data. If you have Microsoft Excel installed on your computer, you can create a chart in a PowerPoint slide. If you do not have Excel installed on your computer, PowerPoint uses the Microsoft Graph feature to create your chart. Projects and assessments in this chapter assume that you have Excel installed on your computer.

You can create a photo album presentation to attractively display personal or business photographs. With the Photo Album feature you can insert pictures and then format the appearance of the pictures in the presentation.

Note: Before beginning computer projects, copy to your storage medium the PowerPoint2007C5 folder from the PowerPoint2007 folder on the CD that accompanies this textbook and then make PowerPoint2007C5 the active folder.

Insert a Table
1. Click Insert Table button in content placeholder.
2. Type number of columns.
3. Press Tab.
4. Type number of rows.
5. Click OK.
OR
1. Click Insert tab.
2. Click Table button.
3. Drag in grid to desired number of columns and rows.

HINT
Add a row to the bottom of a table by positioning the insertion point in the last cell and then pressing the Tab key.

Table

HINT
You can move text to a different cell by selecting the text and then dragging the selected text to a different cell.

Creating a Table

Use the Tables feature to create boxes of information called *cells*. A cell is the intersection between a row and a column. A cell can contain text, characters, numbers, data, graphics, or formulas. If you want to arrange the content of a slide in columns and rows, insert a new slide with the slide layout that includes a content placeholder. Click the Insert Table button in the content placeholder and the Insert Table dialog box displays. At the Insert Table dialog box, type the number of columns, press the Tab key, type the number of rows, and then press Enter. You can also insert a table using the Table button in the Tables group in the Insert tab. Click the Table button, drag the mouse down and to the right to select the desired number of columns and rows, and then click the left mouse button.

When you create a table, the insertion point is located in the cell in the upper left corner of the table. Cells in a table contain a cell designation. Columns in a table are lettered from left to right, beginning with *A*. Rows in a table are numbered from top to bottom beginning with *1*. The cell in the upper left corner of the table is cell A1. The cell to the right of A1 is B1, the cell to the right of B1 is C1, and so on.

Entering Text in Cells

With the insertion point positioned in a cell, type or edit text. Move the insertion point to other cells with the mouse by clicking in the desired cell. If you are using the keyboard, press the Tab key to move the insertion point to the next cell or press Shift + Tab to move the insertion point to the previous cell.

If the text you type does not fit on one line, it wraps to the next line within the same cell. Or, if you press Enter within a cell, the insertion point is moved to the next line within the same cell. The cell vertically lengthens to accommodate the text, and all cells in that row also lengthen. Pressing the Tab key in a table causes the insertion point to move to the next cell in the table. If you want to move the insertion point to a tab stop within a cell, press Ctrl + Tab. If the insertion point is located in the last cell of the table and you press the Tab key, PowerPoint adds another row to the table.

Selecting Cells

You can apply formatting to an entire table or to specific cells, rows, or columns in a table. To identify cells for formatting, select the specific cells using the mouse or the keyboard. Press the Tab key to select the next cell or press Shift + Tab to select the previous cell. Refer to Table 5.1 for additional methods for selecting in a table.

Table 5.1 Selecting in a Table

To select this	Do this
A cell	Position the mouse pointer at left side of cell until pointer turns into a small, black arrow, and then click the left mouse button.
A row	Position the mouse pointer outside the table at the left edge of the row until the pointer turns into a small, black arrow pointing right, and then click the left mouse button. Drag to select multiple rows.
A column	Position the mouse pointer outside the table at the top of the column until the pointer turns into a small, black arrow pointing down, and then click the left mouse button. Drag to select multiple columns.
All cells in a table	Drag to select all cells or press Ctrl + A.
Text within a cell	Position the mouse pointer at the beginning of the text and then hold down the left mouse button as you drag the mouse across the text. (When a cell is selected, the cell background color changes to blue. When text within cells is selected, only those lines containing text are selected.)

Project 1a Creating a Table

1. Open **Conference.pptx** and then save the presentation and name it **PP_C5_P1**.
2. Make Slide 4 active.
3. Insert a table in the slide and enter text into the cells by completing the following steps:
   a. Click the Insert Table button located in the middle of the slide in the content placeholder.
   b. At the Insert Table dialog box, type 2 in the *Number of columns* text box.
   c. Press the Tab key.
   d. Type 5 in the *Number of rows* text box.
   e. Click OK or press Enter.

f. Type the text as displayed in the table below. Press the Tab key to move the insertion point to the next cell or press Shift + Tab to move the insertion point to the previous cell. Do not press Tab after typing the last cell entry.

2010 Sales Projections

Region	Sales
North	$1,683,000
South	$1,552,000
East	$1,778,000
West	$1,299,000

Step 3f

4. Apply formatting to text in specific cells by completing the following steps:
   a. With the insertion point positioned in the table, press Ctrl + A to select all of the text in the table.
   b. Click the Home tab and then change the font size to 32.
   c. Looking at the text set in 32 point size, you decide that you want the text below the headings set in a smaller point size. To do this, position the mouse pointer at the left edge of the second row (to the left of the cell containing *North*) until the pointer turns into a small, black, right-pointing arrow. Hold down the left mouse button, drag down so the remaining rows are selected, and then change the font size to 28.
   d. Click outside the table to deselect it.
5. Save **PP_C5_P1.pptx**.

HINT

Draw a freeform table by clicking the Insert tab, clicking the Table button, and then clicking the *Draw Table* option. Drag in the document to create the table.

Draw Table

Eraser

Shading

Borders

Effects

Changing Table Design

When you create a table, the Table Tools Design tab is selected that contains a number of options for enhancing the appearance of the table as shown in Figure 5.1. With options in the Table Styles group, apply a predesigned style that applies color and border lines to a table. Maintain further control over the predesigned style formatting applied to columns and rows with options in the Table Style Options group. For example, if you want your first column to be formatted differently than the other columns in the table, insert a check mark in the *First Column* check box. Apply additional design formatting to cells in a table with the Shading, Borders, and Effects buttons in the Table Styles group. Draw a table or draw additional rows and/or columns in a table by clicking the Draw Table button in the Draw Borders group. Click this button and the mouse pointer turns into a pencil. Drag in the table to create the desired columns and rows. Click the Eraser button and the mouse pointer turns into an eraser. Drag through the column and/or row lines you want to erase in the table.

Figure 5.1 Table Tools Design Tab

Project 1b Modifying the Table Design

1. With **PP_C5_P1.pptx** open, make sure Slide 4 is active, the table is selected, and the Table Tools Design tab is selected.
2. Click the *First Column* check box in the Table Style Options group to insert a check mark. (This applies bold formatting to the text in the first column.)
3. Click the More button that displays at the right side of the Table Styles thumbnails and then click the *Themed Style 1 - Accent 6* option (last option in the top row).

4. Select the first row of the table.
5. Click the Quick Styles button in the WordArt Styles group and then click *Fill - Accent 3, Outline - Text 2* option (last option in the top row).
6. Click the Text Fill button arrow in the WordArt Styles group and then click *Light Yellow, Text 2, Darker 10%*.

7. Click the Text Outline button arrow in the WordArt Styles group and then click *Green, Accent 6, Lighter 40%*.
8. Click the Pen Weight button arrow in the Draw Borders group and then click *2¼ pt*. (This activates the Draw Table button.)
9. Click the Pen Color button in the Draw Borders group and then click *Green, Accent 6, Darker 25%*.

10. Draw along the border that separates the two columns from the top of the first row to the bottom of the last row.
11. Draw along the border that separates the first row from the second row.
12. Click the Draw Table button to deactivate it.
13. Save **PP_C5_P1.pptx**.

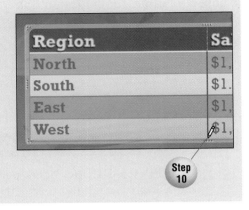

Step 10

Changing Table Layout

To further customize a table consider changing the table layout by inserting or deleting columns and rows and specifying cell alignments. Change table layout with options at the Table Tools Layout tab shown in Figure 5.2. Use options and buttons in the tab to select specific cells, delete and insert rows and columns, merge and split cells, specify cell and table height and width and text alignment in cells, and arrange elements in a slide.

Figure 5.2 Table Tools Layout Tab

Project 1c   Modifying Table Layout

1. With **PP_C5_P1.pptx** open, make sure Slide 4 is active.
2. Click in any cell in the table and then click the Table Tools Layout tab.
3. Click in the cell containing the word *East*.
4. Click the Insert Above button in the Rows & Columns group.
5. Type Central in the new cell at the left, press the Tab key, and then type $1,024,000 in the new cell at the right.
6. Click in the cell containing the word *Region*.
7. Click the Insert Left button in the Rows & Columns group.
8. Click the Merge Cells button in the Merge group.
9. Type Sales Projections in the new cell.

Step 4

10. Click the Text Direction button in the Alignment group and then click *Rotate all text 270°* at the drop-down list.

11. Click the Center button in the Alignment group and then click the Center Vertically button in the Alignment group.
12. Click in the *Table Column Width* measurement box in the Cell Size group, type 1.2, and then press Enter.
13. Click the Table Tools Design tab.
14. Click the Borders button arrow in the Table Styles group (the name of the button changes depending on the last action performed) and then click *Bottom Border* at the drop-down list.

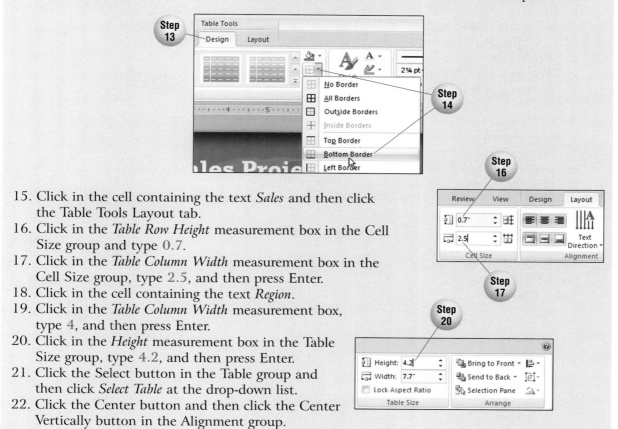

15. Click in the cell containing the text *Sales* and then click the Table Tools Layout tab.
16. Click in the *Table Row Height* measurement box in the Cell Size group and type 0.7.
17. Click in the *Table Column Width* measurement box in the Cell Size group, type 2.5, and then press Enter.
18. Click in the cell containing the text *Region*.
19. Click in the *Table Column Width* measurement box, type 4, and then press Enter.
20. Click in the *Height* measurement box in the Table Size group, type 4.2, and then press Enter.
21. Click the Select button in the Table group and then click *Select Table* at the drop-down list.
22. Click the Center button and then click the Center Vertically button in the Alignment group.

23. After looking at the text in cells, you decide that you want the text in the second column left-aligned. To do this, complete the following steps:
   a. Click in the cell containing the text *Region*.
   b. Click the Select button in the Table group and then click *Select Column* at the drop-down list.
   c. Click the Align Text Left button in the Alignment group.
   d. Click in any cell in the table.

24. Align the table by completing the following steps:
   a. Click the Home tab.
   b. Click the Arrange button in the Drawing group, point to *Align*, and then click *Distribute Horizontally*.
   c. Click the Arrange button, point to *Align*, and then click *Distribute Vertically*.
   d. Looking at the table, you decide that it should be moved down in the slide. To do this, position the mouse pointer on the table border until the pointer displays with a four-headed arrow attached. Hold down the left mouse button, drag down approximately one-half inch, and then release the mouse button.

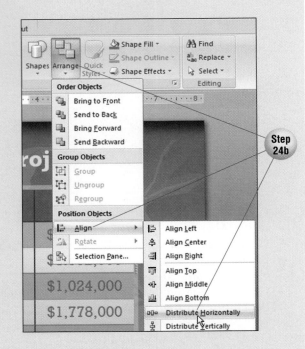

Step 24b

25. Insert a clip art image in the table by completing the following steps:
   a. Click the Insert tab.
   b. Click the Clip Art button in the Illustrations group.
   c. Select any text that displays in the *Search for* text box in the Clip Art task pane, type sales, and then press Enter.
   d. Scroll down the list of clip art images and then click the image shown in Figure 5.3. (If this image is not available, choose a similar clip art image related to sales.)
   e. Close the Clip Art task pane.
   f. With the image selected, click in the Shape Height measurement box in the Size group in the Picture Tools Format tab, type 2.8, and then press Enter.
   g. Drag the clip art image so it is positioned in the table as shown in Figure 5.3.
   h. Click outside the clip art image to deselect it.

26. Save **PP_C5_P1.pptx**.
27. Print Slide 4.

Step 25c

Step 25d

Figure 5.3 Slide 4

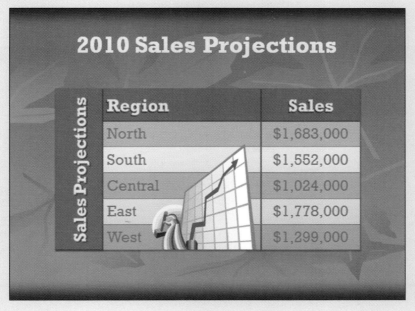

Creating SmartArt

With the SmartArt feature you can insert diagrams and organizational charts in a slide. SmartArt offers a variety of predesigned diagrams and organizational charts that are available at the Choose a SmartArt Graphic dialog box shown in Figure 5.4. Display the Choose a SmartArt Graphic dialog box by clicking the Insert SmartArt Graphic button that displays in a content placeholder or by clicking the Insert tab and then clicking the SmartArt button in the Illustrations group. At the dialog box, *All* is selected in the left panel and all available predesigned diagrams display in the middle panel.

Modifying SmartArt Design

Predesigned diagrams display in the middle panel of the Choose a SmartArt Graphic dialog box. Use the scroll bar at the right side of the middle panel to scroll down the list of diagram choices. Click a diagram in the middle panel and the name of the diagram displays in the right panel along with a description of the diagram type. SmartArt includes diagrams for presenting a list of data; showing data processes, cycles, and relationships; and presenting data in a matrix or pyramid. Double-click a diagram in the middle panel of the dialog box and the diagram is inserted in the slide.

Insert a SmartArt Diagram
1. Click Insert SmartArt Graphic button in content placeholder.
2. Double-click desired diagram.
OR
1. Click Insert tab.
2. Click SmartArt button.
3. Double-click desired diagram.

HINT
Use SmartArt to communicate your message and ideas in a visual manner.

SmartArt

Figure 5.4 Choose a SmartArt Graphic Dialog Box

Double-click the desired SmartArt graphic in this panel.

Choose the SmartArt graphic category from options in this panel.

Click a SmartArt graphic in the middle panel and then read a description of the graphic in this panel.

HINT

Limit the number of shapes and the amount of text to key points.

When you double-click a diagram at the dialog box, the diagram is inserted in the slide and a text pane may display at the left side of the diagram. You can type text in the text pane or directly in the diagram. Apply design formatting to a diagram with options at the SmartArt Tools Design tab shown in Figure 5.5. This tab is active when the diagram is inserted in the slide. With options and buttons in this tab you add objects, change the diagram layout, apply a style to the diagram, and reset the diagram back to the original formatting.

Figure 5.5 SmartArt Tools Design Tab

Project 1d **Inserting and Modifying a SmartArt Diagram**

1. With **PP_C5_P1.pptx** open, make sure Slide 4 is active and then insert a new slide with the *Title and Content* layout.
2. Click in the title placeholder and then type Division Reorganization.
3. Click the Insert SmartArt Graphic button located in the middle of the slide in the content placeholder.

4. At the Choose a SmartArt Graphic dialog box, click *Hierarchy* in the left panel of the dialog box.
5. Double-click the *Horizontal Hierarchy* option (first option from the left in the second row).

6. If a *Type your text here* window displays at the left side of the organizational chart, close the pane by clicking the Text Pane button in the Create Graphic group.
7. Delete one of the boxes in the organizational chart by clicking the border of the top box at the right side of the slide (the top box of the three stacked boxes) and then pressing the Delete key. (Make sure that the selection border that surrounds the box is a solid line and not a dashed line. If a dashed line displays, click the box border again. This should change it to a solid line.)
8. Click *[Text]* in the first box at the left, type Andrew Singh, press the Enter key, and then type Director. Click in each of the remaining boxes and type the text as shown below.

9. Click the More button located at the right side of the styles in the SmartArt Styles group and then click the *Polished* style in the *3-D* section (first option from the left in the top row of the *3-D* section).

10. Click the Change Colors button in the SmartArt Styles group and then click *Gradient Range - Accent 2* (third option from the left in the *Accent 2* section).
11. Change the layout of the organizational chart by clicking the *Table Hierarchy* layout in the Layouts group. Your slide should now look like the slide shown in Figure 5.6.

12. Save **PP_C5_P1.pptx**
13. Print Slide 5.

Figure 5.6 Slide 5

Formatting SmartArt

Apply formatting to a SmartArt diagram with options at the SmartArt Tools Format tab shown in Figure 5.7. With options and buttons in this tab you can change the size and shape of objects in the diagram; apply shapes styles and WordArt styles; change the shape fill, outline, and effects; and arrange and size the diagram. Move the diagram by positioning the arrow pointer on the diagram border until the pointer turns into a four-headed arrow, holding down the left mouse button, and then dragging the diagram to the desired location.

HINT

Nudge selected shape(s) with the up, down, left, or right arrow keys on the keyboard.

Figure 5.7 SmartArt Tools Format Tab

Project 1e Inserting and Formatting a Diagram

1. With **PP_C5_P1.pptx** open, make Slide 1 active.
2. Click the Insert tab and then click the SmartArt button in the Illustrations group.
3. At the Choose a SmartArt Graphic dialog box, click *Relationship* in the left panel of the dialog box.
4. Double-click the *Basic Venn* option shown below.

5. Click in the top shape and type Health.
6. Click in the shape at the left and type Happiness.
7. Click in the shape at the right and type Harmony.
8. Click inside the SmartArt border but outside of any shape.
9. Click the Change Colors button and then click *Colored Fill - Accent 2* (second option from the left in the *Accent 2* section).

10. Click the More button at the right side of the SmartArt Styles group and then click *Polished* at the drop-down gallery (first option from the left in the top row of the *3-D* section).
11. Click the SmartArt Tools Format tab.
12. Click the More button at the right side of the WordArt Styles thumbnails and then click *Fill - Accent 3, Powder Bevel* at the drop-down gallery (fourth option from the left in the *Applies to All Text in the Shape* section).
13. Click the Text Outline button arrow and then click *Light Yellow, Text 2, Darker 25%*.
14. Click the Size button, click in the *Height* measurement box, and then type 3.6.
15. Click in the *Width* measurement box, type 5.5, and then press Enter.
16. Click the Arrange button and then click the Send to Back button that displays in the drop-down list.
17. Drag the SmartArt so it is positioned as shown in Figure 5.8.
18. Drag the title and subtitle placeholders so they are positioned as shown in Figure 5.8.

19. You decide to experiment with rotating and changing the orientation of text in a shape. To do this, complete the following steps:
    a. Click the shape containing the word *Happiness*.
    b. Click the Arrange button in the SmartArt Tools Format tab, click *Rotate* at the drop-down list, and then click *Rotate Left 90°*.
    c. Click the shape containing the word *Harmony*.
    d. Click the Arrange button, click *Rotate* at the drop-down list, and then click *Rotate Left 90°*.
    e. You decide you do not like the text rotated. Return the text to normal orientation by clicking twice on the Undo button on the Quick Access toolbar.
20. Save **PP_C5_P1.pptx**.
21. Print Slide 1.

Figure 5.8 Slide 1

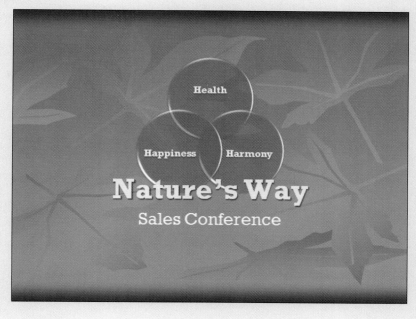

Creating a SmartArt Graphic with Bulleted Text

To improve the visual display of text and to create a professionally-designed image, consider converting bulleted text to a SmartArt graphic. To do this, select the placeholder containing the text you want to convert and then click the Convert to SmartArt Graphic button that displays in the Paragraph group in the Home tab. Click the desired SmartArt graphic at the drop-down gallery or click the *More SmartArt Graphics* option that displays at the bottom of the drop-down gallery. This displays the Choose a SmartArt Graphic dialog box where you can choose a SmartArt graphic.

Project **1f** **Creating a SmartArt Graphic with Bulleted Text**

1. With **PP_C5_P1.pptx** open, make Slide 6 active.
2. Click on any character in the bulleted text.
3. If necessary, click the Home tab.

4. Click the Convert to SmartArt Graphic button that displays in the Paragraph group.
5. At the drop-down gallery that displays, click the *More SmartArt Graphics* option that displays at the bottom of the gallery.

Step 4

Step 5

6. At the Choose a SmartArt Graphic dialog box, click *Cycle* in the left panel, and then double-click *Diverging Radial* in the middle panel.

Step 6

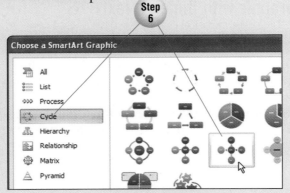

7. Click the Add Shape button in the Create Graphic group in the SmartArt Tools Design tab and then type **Supplies** in the new shape.
8. Change the order of the text in the shapes at the left and right sides of the graphic by clicking the Right to Left button in the Create Graphic group.
9. Click the Change Colors button in the SmartArt Styles group and then click *Colorful Range - Accent Colors 2 to 3* (second option from the left in the *Colorful* section).

Step 9

10. Click the More button at the right of the SmartArt Styles thumbnails and then click *Inset* (second option from the left in the *3-D* section).

11. Click the SmartArt Tools Format tab.
12. Click the middle circle (contains the text *Central Division*).
13. Click three times on the Larger button in the Shapes group.
14. Click inside the SmartArt border but outside of any shape.
15. Click the Size button, click in the *Height* measurement box, and then type 6.6.
16. Click in the *Width* measurement box, type 8.2, and then press Enter.
17. Click the Home tab.
18. With the SmartArt graphic selected, click the Arrange button in the Drawing group, point to *Align*, and then click *Distribute Horizontally*.
19. Click the Arrange button in the Drawing group, point to *Align*, and then click *Distribute Vertically*.
20. Click the Bold button in the Font group.
21. Save **PP_C5_P1.pptx**.
22. Print Slide 6.

Inserting Text in the Text Pane

You can enter text in a SmartArt shape by clicking in the shape and then typing the text. You can also insert text in a SmartArt shape by typing text in the Text pane. Display the Text pane by clicking the Text Pane button in the Create Graphic group in the SmartArt Tools Design tab.

Project 1g Creating a SmartArt Graphic and Inserting Text in the Text Pane

1. With **PP_C5_P1.pptx** open, make sure Slide 6 is active and then insert a new slide with the *Title and Content* layout.
2. Click the title placeholder and type Division Planning.
3. Click the Insert SmartArt Graphic button in the content placeholder.
4. At the Choose a SmartArt Graphic dialog box, click *Process* in the left panel, and then double-click *Alternating Flow* (last option in the top row).
5. If necessary, click the Text Pane button in the Create Graphic group in the SmartArt Tools Design tab to display the *Type your text here* text pane.
6. With the insertion point positioned after the top bullet in the *Type your text here* text pane, type Facility.
7. Click *[Text]* that displays below *Facility* and then type Research market.
8. Continue clicking occurrences of *[Text]* and typing text so the text pane displays as shown at the right.
9. Close the text pane by clicking the Close button (contains an X) that displays up in the upper right corner of the pane. (You can also click the Text Pane button in the Create Graphic group.)

10. Click inside the diagram border but outside any shape. (This deselects any shapes but keeps the diagram selected.)
11. If necessary, click the SmartArt Tools Design tab.
12. Click the Change Colors button in the SmartArt Styles group and then click *Dark 2 Fill*, the last option in the *Primary Theme Colors* section.
13. Click the *Intense Effect* thumbnail that displays in the SmartArt Styles group (if this style is not visible, click the More button at the right side of the SmartArt Styles group and then click the last option in the *Best Match for Document* section).

14. Save **PP_C5_P1.pptx**.
15. Print Slide 7.

Creating a Chart

You can create a variety of charts including bar and column charts, pie charts, area charts, and much more. Table 5.2 describes the eleven basic chart types you can create in PowerPoint. To create a chart, click the Insert Chart button in a content placeholder or click the Insert tab and then click the Chart button in the Illustrations group. This displays the Insert Chart dialog box shown in Figure 5.9. At this dialog box, choose the desired chart type in the list at the left side, click the chart style, and then click OK.

Figure 5.9 Insert Chart Dialog Box

Table 5.2 Types of Charts

Area	An area chart emphasizes the magnitude of change, rather than time and the rate of change. It also shows the relationship of parts to a whole by displaying the sum of the plotted values.
Bar	A bar chart shows individual figures at a specific time, or shows variations between components but not in relationship to the whole.
Bubble	A bubble chart compares sets of three values in a manner similar to a scatter chart, with the third value displayed as the size of the bubble marker.
Column	A column chart compares separate (noncontinuous) items as they vary over time.
Doughnut	A doughnut chart shows the relationship of parts of the whole.
Line	A line chart shows trends and change over time at even intervals. It emphasizes the rate of change over time rather than the magnitude of change.
Pie	A pie chart shows proportions and relationships of parts to the whole.
Radar	A radar chart emphasizes differences and amounts of change over time and variations and trends. Each category has its own value axis radiating from the center point. Lines connect all values in the same series.
Stock	A stock chart shows four values for a stock—open, high, low, and close.
Surface	A surface chart shows trends in values across two dimensions in a continuous curve.
XY (Scatter)	A scatter chart either shows the relationships among numeric values in several data series or plots the interception points between x and y values. It shows uneven intervals of data and is commonly used in scientific data.

When you click OK at the Insert Chart dialog box, a sample chart is inserted in your slide and Excel opens with sample data as shown in Figure 5.10. Type the desired data in the Excel worksheet cells over the existing data. As you type data, the chart in the slide reflects the typed data. To type data in the Excel worksheet, click in the desired cell, type the data, and then press the Tab key to make the next cell active, press Shift + Tab to make the previous cell active, or press Enter to make the cell below active.

Cells used by Excel to create the chart are surrounded by a blue border and the message "To resize chart data range, drag lower right corner of range." displays below the border. If you need to change the data range, position the mouse pointer on the bottom right corner of the border until the mouse pointer displays as a double-headed arrow pointing diagonally. Hold down the left mouse button and then drag up, down, left, and/or right until the border is in the desired location. You can also click in a cell immediately outside the border and, when you insert data, the border will expand. When all data is entered in the worksheet, click the Close button that displays in the upper right corner of the screen. This closes the Excel window and displays the chart in the slide.

QUICK STEPS

Insert a Chart
1. Click Insert Chart button in content placeholder.
2. Click desired chart style and type.
3. Enter data in Excel spreadsheet.
4. Close Excel.
OR
1. Click Insert tab.
2. Click Chart button.
3. Click desired chart style and type.
4. Enter data in Excel spreadsheet.
5. Close Excel.

Figure 5.10 Sample Chart

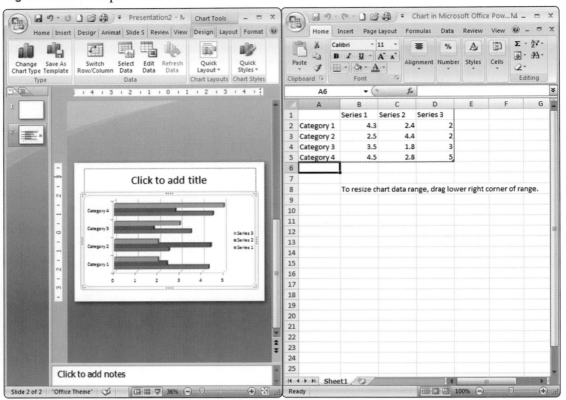

Enter data in cells in the Excel worksheet. The data entered is reflected in the PowerPoint presentation chart.

Project 1h Creating a Chart

1. With **PP_C5_P1.pptx** open, make Slide 3 active.
2. Click the Insert Chart button in the content placeholder.
3. At the Insert Chart dialog box, click *Bar* in the left panel.
4. Click the *Clustered Bar in 3-D* option that displays in the *Bar* section (fourth option from the left) in the middle panel and then click OK.

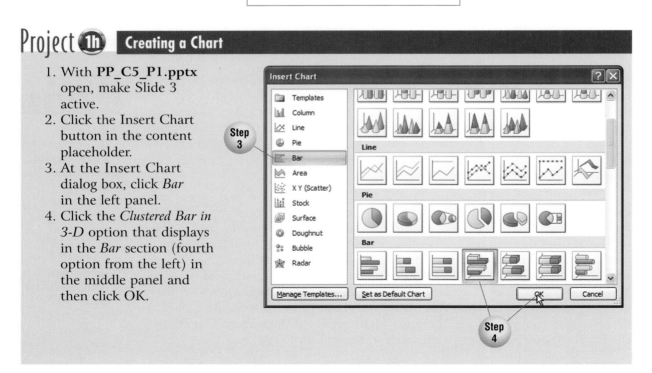

5. In the Excel worksheet, position the mouse pointer on the bottom right corner of the blue border until the mouse pointer displays as a double-headed arrow pointing diagonally. Hold down the left mouse button, drag to the left until the border displays at the right side of column C, and then release the mouse button.

6. Position the mouse pointer on the bottom right corner of the blue border until the pointer displays as a double-headed arrow and then drag down until the border displays at the bottom of row 6.

7. Type the text in cells as shown at the right by completing the following steps:

   a. Click in cell B1 in the Excel worksheet, type **1st Half**, and then press the Tab key.

   b. With cell C1 active, type **2nd Half** and then press the Tab key.

   c. In cell A2, type **North** and then press the Tab key.

   d. Type **$853,000** and then press the Tab key.

   e. Type **$970,000** and then press the Tab key.

   f. Continue typing the remaining data in cells as indicated above.

8. Click the Close button that displays in the upper right corner of the Excel window.

9. Save **PP_C5_P1.pptx**.

Changing Chart Design

When the chart is inserted in the slide, the Chart Tools Design tab is active as shown in Figure 5.11. Use options in this tab to change the chart type, edit chart data, change the chart layout, and apply a chart style.

Figure 5.11 Chart Tools Design Tab

QUICK STEPS

Change Chart Type and Style

1. Make the chart active.
2. Click Chart Tools Design tab.
3. Click Change Chart Type button.
4. Click desired chart type.
5. Click desired chart style.
6. Click OK.

HINT

Click the Save As Template button in the Chart group in the Chart Tools Design tab to save the current chart as a template.

Change Chart Type

Edit Data

After you create a chart, you can change the chart type by clicking the Change Chart Type button in the Type group in the Chart Tools Design tab. This displays the Change Chart Type dialog box. This dialog box contains the same options as the Insert Chart dialog box shown in Figure 5.9. At the Change Chart Type dialog box, click the desired chart type in the left panel and click the desired chart style at the right.

Use options in the Data group in the Chart Tools Design tab to change the order of the data in the chart, select specific data, edit data, and refresh the data. When you create a chart, the cells in the Excel worksheet are linked to the chart in the slide. If you need to edit data in the chart, click the Edit Data button and the Excel worksheet opens. Make the desired changes to cells in the Excel worksheet and then click the Close button.

The chart feature provides a number of predesigned chart layouts and styles you can apply to a chart. Click one of the chart layouts that displays in the Chart Layouts group or click the More button and then click the desired layout at the drop-down list. Apply a chart style to a chart by clicking one of these styles in the Chart Styles group or by clicking the More button and then clicking the desired style at the drop-down list.

Project ⑪ Changing the Chart Type and Editing Data

1. With **PP_C5_P1.pptx** open, make sure Slide 3 is active.
2. Delete the title placeholder by completing the following steps:
   a. Click on any character in the title *2009 Sales by Region*.
   b. Position the mouse pointer on the placeholder border until the pointer displays with a four-headed arrow attached and then click the left mouse button. (This changes the placeholder border from a dashed line to a solid line.)
   c. Press the Delete key. (This removes the title *2009 Sales by Region* and displays the placeholder text *Click to add title*.)
   d. Position the mouse pointer on the placeholder border until the pointer displays with a four-headed arrow attached and then click the left mouse button. (This changes the placeholder border from a dashed line to a solid line.)
   e. Press the Delete key.
3. Click near the chart (but outside any chart elements) to select the chart. (A light turquoise border displays around the chart.)
4. Click the Chart Tools Design tab.
5. Looking at the chart, you decide that the bar chart was not the best choice for the data and decide to change to a column chart. To do this, click the Change Chart Type button in the Type group.

6. At the Change Chart Type dialog box, click the *Column* option in the left panel.
7. Click the *3-D Clustered Column* option (fourth option from the left in the top row in the *Column* section of the dialog box).

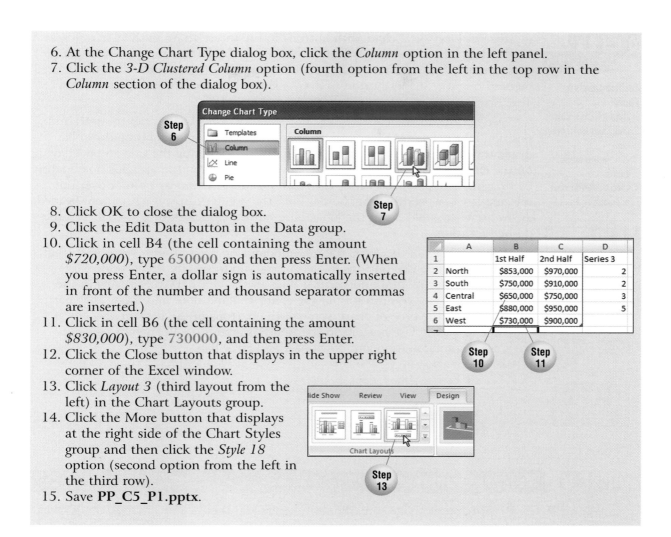

8. Click OK to close the dialog box.
9. Click the Edit Data button in the Data group.
10. Click in cell B4 (the cell containing the amount *$720,000*), type 650000 and then press Enter. (When you press Enter, a dollar sign is automatically inserted in front of the number and thousand separator commas are inserted.)
11. Click in cell B6 (the cell containing the amount *$830,000*), type 730000, and then press Enter.
12. Click the Close button that displays in the upper right corner of the Excel window.
13. Click *Layout 3* (third layout from the left) in the Chart Layouts group.
14. Click the More button that displays at the right side of the Chart Styles group and then click the *Style 18* option (second option from the left in the third row).
15. Save **PP_C5_P1.pptx**.

Formatting Chart Layout

Click the Chart Tools Layout tab and options display for changing and customizing chart elements as shown in Figure 5.12. With options in this tab you can specify chart elements, insert objects, add labels to the chart, customize the chart background, and add analysis items to the chart.

To format or modify a specific element in a chart, select the element. Do this by clicking the element or by clicking the Chart Elements button in the Current Selection group in the Chart Tools Layout tab. With the element selected, apply the desired formatting. Click the Format Selection button in the Current Selection group and a dialog box displays with options for formatting the selected element.

Figure 5.12 Chart Tools Layout Tab

Position Labels in Chart
1. Make the chart active.
2. Click Chart Tools Layout tab.
3. Click desired labels button.
4. Choose desired option at drop-down list.

HINT

Right-click text in a chart element to display the Mini toolbar.

Insert objects in a chart with buttons in the Insert group in the Chart Tools Layout tab. Click the Picture button and the Insert Picture dialog box displays. At this dialog box, navigate to the desired folder and then double-click the desired picture. Use the Shapes button to draw a shape in the chart and use the Draw Text Box button to insert a text box in the chart.

Use options in the Labels group in the Chart Tools Layout tab to insert and position labels. For example, click the Chart Title button and a drop-down list displays with options for removing the chart title, centering the title and overlaying on the chart, and displaying the title above the chart. You can also position a label by dragging it. To do this, select the label, position the mouse pointer over the selected label or over the label border until the pointer displays with a four-headed arrow attached, hold down the left mouse button, and then drag the label to the desired location.

With buttons in the Axes, Background, and Analysis groups, you can further customize a chart. Use buttons in the Axes group to specify if you want major and/or minor horizontal and vertical lines in the chart. With buttons in the Background group, you can format the chart wall and floor and rotate the chart. Depending on the type of chart, some of the buttons in the Background group may not be active. Use buttons in the Analysis group to add analysis elements such as trendlines and up and down bars and error bars.

Project 1j   Modifying Chart Layout

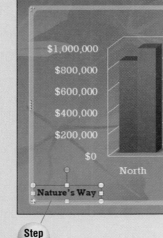

1. With **PP_C5_P1.pptx** open, make sure Slide 3 is active and the chart is selected.
2. Click the Chart Tools Layout tab.
3. Click the Text Box button in the Insert group.
4. Click in the lower left corner of the chart (outside any chart elements).
5. Change the font size to 16, turn on bold, change the font color to Green, Accent 6, Darker 50%, and then type Nature's Way.
6. Click the Drawing Tools Format tab.
7. Click in the *Shape Height* measurement box and then type 0.4.
8. Click in the *Shape Width* measurement box, type 1.7, and then press Enter.
9. Drag the text box down to the lower left corner of the chart.

10. Click inside the chart border but outside any chart elements and then click the Chart Tools Layout tab.
11. Click the Chart Elements button arrow and then click *Chart Title* at the drop-down list.
12. Type 2009 Regional Sales.

13. Click the Data Table button in the Labels group and then click the *Show Data Table with Legend Keys* option at the drop-down list.
14. After looking at the data table, you decide to remove it by clicking the Data Table button in the Labels group and then clicking *None* at the drop-down list.
15. Click the Gridlines button in the Axes group, point to *Primary Vertical Gridlines*, and then click *Major & Minor Gridlines* at the side menu.

16. Increase the height of the chart by positioning the mouse pointer on the four dots that display in the middle of the top border until the pointer displays as a two-headed arrow pointing up and down. Hold down the left mouse button, drag up approximately one inch, and then release the mouse button.
17. Click on any character in the chart title *2009 Regional Sales*.
18. Click the Home tab, change the font size to 32, and change the font color to Light Yellow, Text 2, Darker 10%.
19. Save **PP_C5_P1.pptx**.

Changing Chart Formatting

Customize the format of the chart and chart elements with options in the Chart Tools Format tab as shown in Figure 5.13. The tab contains the same Current Selection group as the Chart Tools Layout tab. With the other options in the tab you can apply a predesigned style to a shape, a predesigned WordArt style to text, and arrange and size the chart.

Figure 5.13 Chart Tools Format Tab

The Shape Styles group in the Chart Tools Format tab contains predesigned styles you can apply to shapes in the chart. Click the More button at the right side of the style in the group and a drop-down gallery displays of shape styles. Use the buttons that display at the right side of the Shape Styles group to apply fill, an outline, and an effect to a selected shape. The WordArt Styles group contains predesigned styles you can apply to text in a chart. Use the buttons that display at the right side of the WordArt Styles group to apply fill, an outline, or an effect to text in a chart.

Project 1k Changing Chart Formatting

1. With **PP_C5_P1.pptx** open, make sure Slide 3 is the active slide and the chart is selected.
2. Click the Chart Tools Format tab.
3. Click the Chart Elements button arrow in the Current Selection group and then click *Series "2nd Half"* at the drop-down list. (This selects the green bars in the chart representing second half sales.)
4. Click the More button at the right side of the Shapes Style thumbnails and then click the *Colored Fill - Dark 1* option (first option from the left in the second row).

5. With the second half bars still selected, click the Shape Fill button arrow in the Shape Styles group, point to *Gradient*, and then click *Linear Down* (second option from the left in the top row in the *Dark Variations* section).

6. With the second half bars still selected, click the Shape Effects button in the Shape Styles group, point to *Bevel*, and then click the *Circle* option (first option from the left in the *Bevel* section of the side menu).

7. Click one of the teal bars that represent the first half sales amounts. (This selects all teal bars in the chart.)

8. Click the Shape Fill button arrow in the Shape Styles group and then click *Light Yellow, Text 2, Darker 10%*.

9. With the first half bars still selected, click the Shape Effects button in the Shape Styles group, point to *Bevel*, and then click the *Circle* option at the side menu.

10. Save **PP_C5_P1.pptx**.

11. Print Slide 3.

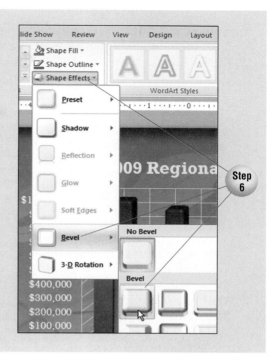

Use buttons in the Arrange group to send the chart behind other objects, move it to the front of other objects, specify the alignment, and rotate the chart. You can size a chart by selecting the chart and then dragging a border. You can also size a chart to specific measurements with the Shape Height and Shape Width measurement boxes in the Size group in the Chart Tools Format tab. Change the height or width by clicking the up- or down-pointing arrows that display at the right side of the measurement box or click the current measurement in the measurement box and then type a specific measurement.

QUICK STEPS

Change Chart Height and/or Width
1. Make the chart active.
2. Click Chart Tools Format tab.
3. Insert desired height and/or width in *Shape Height* and/or *Shape Width* measurement boxes.

Shape Height

Shape Width

Project 11 Creating and Formatting a Pie Chart

1. With **PP_C5_P1.pptx** open, make Slide 6 active and then insert a new slide with the *Title and Content* layout.
2. Click the title placeholder text and then type Division Budget.
3. Click the Insert tab and then click the Chart button in the Illustrations group.
4. At the Insert Chart dialog box, click *Pie* in the left panel.
5. Click the *Pie in 3-D* option (second option from the left in the *Pie* section) and then click OK.

6. In the Excel worksheet, position the mouse pointer on the bottom right corner of the border until the mouse pointer displays as a double-headed arrow pointing diagonally. Hold down the left mouse button and then drag down until the border displays at the bottom of row 7.

Step 6

7. Type the text in cells as shown at the right.
8. When all data is entered, click the Close button that displays in the upper right corner of the Excel window.
9. With the Chart Tools Design tab selected, click the More button at the right side of the Chart Styles group and then click the *Style 26* option (second option from the left in the fourth row).
10. Click the Chart Tools Layout tab.
11. Click the Chart Title button in the Labels group and then click *None* at the drop-down list.
12. Click the Data Labels button in the Labels group and then click *Inside End* at the drop-down list.
13. Click the Chart Tools Format tab.
14. Click the piece of pie containing *10%*. (Make sure only the one piece of pie is selected.)
15. Click the Shape Fill button arrow in the Shape Styles group and then click *Light Yellow, Text 2, Darker 75%*.
16. Click the piece of pie containing *9%*. (Make sure only the one piece of pie is selected.)
17. Click the Shape Fill button arrow in the Shape Styles group and then click *Light Green, Accent 5, Darker 50%*.
18. Click the piece of pie containing *12%*. (Make sure only the one piece of pie is selected.)
19. Click the Shape Fill button arrow in the Shape Styles group and then click *Dark Teal, Accent 1, Lighter 40%*.
20. Click the Chart Elements button in the Current Selection group and then click *Chart Area* at the drop-down list.
21. Click in the *Shape Height* measurement box in the Size group, type 6, and then press Enter.
22. Click the Align button in the Arrange group and then click *Distribute Vertically*.
23. Drag the chart down approximately one-half inch.
24. Apply a transition and sound of your choosing to all slides in the presentation.
25. Save **PP_C5_P1.pptx**.
26. Run the presentation.
27. Print Slide 7 and then close **PP_C5_P1.pptx**.

Step 7

Step 12

Project 2   Create and Format a Travel Photo Album

You will use the photo album feature to create a presentation containing travel photographs. You will also apply formatting and insert elements in the presentation.

Creating a Photo Album

With PowerPoint's photo album feature, you can create a presentation containing personal or business pictures. You can customize and format the appearance of pictures by applying interesting layouts, frame shapes, and themes and you can also insert elements such as captions and text boxes. To create a photo album, click the Insert tab, click the Photo Album button arrow, and then click *New Photo Album* at the drop-down list. This displays the Photo Album dialog box as shown in Figure 5.14.

To insert pictures in the photo album, click the File/Disk button and the Insert New Pictures dialog box displays. At this dialog box, navigate to the desired folder and then double-click the picture you want inserted in the album. This inserts the picture name in the *Pictures in album* list box in the dialog box and also previews the picture in the *Preview* section. As you insert pictures in the photo album, the picture names display in the *Pictures in album* list box in the order in which they will appear in the presentation. When you have inserted the desired pictures in the photo album, click the Create button. This creates the photo album as a presentation and displays the first slide. The photo album feature creates the first slide with the title *Photo Album* and inserts the user's name.

QUICK STEPS

Create Photo Album
1. Click Insert tab.
2. Click Photo Album button arrow.
3. Click *New Photo Album*.
4. Click File/Disk button.
5. Double-click desired pictures.
6. Make desired changes at Photo Album dialog box.
7. Click Create button.

Photo Album ▾

Figure 5.14 Photo Album Dialog Box

Insert a picture by clicking this button and then double-clicking the picture at the Insert New Pictures dialog box.

Choose a picture and then preview it in this Preview box.

Photo Album

Album Content

Insert picture from:
File/Disk...

Insert text:
New Text Box

Picture Options:
☐ Captions below ALL pictures
☐ ALL pictures black and white

Pictures in album:

Preview:

No preview is available for this selection

↑ ↓   Remove

Album Layout

Picture layout: Fit to slide
Frame shape: Rectangle
Theme: Browse...

Create   Cancel

1. At a blank screen, click the Insert tab, click the Photo Album button arrow, and then click *New Photo Album* at the drop-down list.
2. At the Photo Album dialog box, click the File/Disk button.
3. At the Insert New Pictures dialog box, navigate to the PowerPoint2007C5 folder on your storage medium and then double-click *Cityscape.jpg*.
4. At the Photo Album dialog box, click the File/Disk button, and then double-click *Nightscape.jpg* at the Insert New Pictures dialog box.
5. Insert the following images: *Stonehenge.jpg*, *BigBen.jpg*, *WhiteHorse.jpg*, and *VictoriaBC.jpg*.
6. Click the Create button. (This opens a presentation with each image in a slide and the first slide containing the default text *Photo Album* followed by your name (or the user name for the computer).

7. Save the presentation and name it **PP_C5_P2.pptx**.
8. Run the presentation.

Editing and Formatting a Photo Album

Edit Photo Album
1. Click Insert tab.
2. Click Photo Album button arrow.
3. Click *Edit Photo Album*.
4. Make desired changes at Edit Photo Album dialog box.
5. Click Update button.

If you want to make changes to a photo album presentation, open the presentation, click the Insert tab, click the Photo Album button arrow, and then click *Edit Photo Album* at the drop-down list. This displays the Edit Photo Album dialog box, which contains the same options as the Photo Album dialog box.

Rearrange the order of slides in the photo album presentation by clicking the desired slide in the *Pictures in album* list box and then clicking the button containing the up-pointing arrow to move the slide up in the order or clicking the button containing the down-pointing arrow to move the slide down in the order. Remove a slide by clicking the desired slide in the list box and then clicking the Remove button. With the buttons below the *Preview* box in the Edit Photo Album dialog box, you can rotate the picture in the slide, increase or decrease the contrast, and increase or decrease the brightness of the picture.

The *Picture layout* option in the *Album Layout* group has a default setting of *Fit to slide*. At this setting the picture in each slide will fill most of the slide. You can change this setting by clicking the down-pointing arrow at the right side of the option. With options at the drop-down list, you can specify that you want one picture inserted in the slide, two pictures, or four pictures. You can also specify that you want the one, two, or four pictures inserted in slides with titles.

If you change the *Picture layout* option to something other than the default of *Fit to slide*, the *Frame shape* option becomes available. Click the down-pointing arrow at the right side of the option and a drop-down list displays with framing options. You can choose a rounded frame, single frame, double frame, or a soft or shadow effect frame.

You can apply a theme to the photo album presentation by clicking the Browse button located at the right side of the *Theme* option box and then double-clicking the desired theme in the Choose Theme dialog box. This dialog box contains the predesigned themes provided by PowerPoint.

If you want to include a caption with the pictures, change the *Picture layout* to one, two, or four slides, and then click the *Captions below ALL pictures* check box located in the *Picture Options* section of the dialog box. PowerPoint will insert a caption below each picture that contains the name of the picture. You can edit the caption in the slide in the presentation. If you want to display all of the pictures in your photo album in black and white, click the *ALL pictures black and white* check box in the *Picture Options* section.

Click the New Text Box button in the Edit Photo Album dialog box and a new slide containing a text box is inserted in the presentation. In the presentation, you can edit the information in the text box. When all changes are made to the photo album, click the Update button located toward the bottom right side of the dialog box.

Project 2b   Editing and Formatting a Photo Album

1. With **PP_C5_P2.pptx** open, click the Insert tab, click the Photo Album button arrow, and then click *Edit Photo Album* at the drop-down list.
2. At the Edit Photo Album dialog box, make the following changes:
   a. Click *VictoriaBC* in the *Pictures in album* list box and then click three times on the up-pointing arrow that displays below the list box. (This moves *VictoriaBC* so it is positioned between *Nightscape* and *Stonehenge*).

b. Click the down-pointing arrow at the right side
   of the *Picture layout* option and then click *1 picture*
   at the drop-down list.

c. Click the down-pointing arrow at the right side of
   the *Frame shape* option and then click *Center Shadow
   Rectangle* at the drop-down list.

d. Click the Browse button located at the right side
   of the *Theme* option box. At the Choose Theme
   dialog box, scroll down the list box and then
   double-click *Trek.thmx*.

e. Click the *Captions below ALL pictures* check box to
   insert a check mark.

f. Click *WhiteHorse* in the *Pictures in album* list box and then click the New Text Box button
   that displays at the left side of the list box. (This inserts a new slide containing a text box
   at the end of the presentation.)

g. Click the Update button located in the lower right corner of the dialog box.

3. At the presentation, make the following formatting changes:

   a. Click the Design tab.

   b. Click the Colors button in the Themes group and then click *Metro* at the drop-down
      gallery.

   c. Click the Background Styles button in the
      Background group and then click *Style 2* at
      the drop-down list.

4. Make Slide 1 active and then make the
   following changes:

   a. Select the text *PHOTO ALBUM* and then
      type travel album. (The text will display in
      all caps.)

   b. Select any text that displays after the word *by*
      and then type your first and last names.

   c. Click the Insert tab and then click the
      Picture button.

   d. At the Insert Picture dialog box, navigate to
      the PowerPoint2007C5 folder on your storage
      medium and then double-click **FCTLogo.jpg**.

   e. Click the Recolor button in the Adjust group
      in the Picture Tools Format tab and then click
      Set Transparent Color at the drop-down list.

    f. Move the mouse pointer (pointer displays with a tool attached) to any white portion of the logo and then click the left mouse button. (This changes the white fill to transparent fill and allows the blue background to show through.)

    g. Change the height of the logo to *3.5"* and then position the logo attractively in the slide.

5. Make Slide 2 active and then edit the caption by completing the following steps:

    a. Click on any character in the caption *Cityscape*.

    b. Select *Cityscape* and then type New York City Skyline.

6. Complete steps similar to those in Step 5 to change the following captions:

    a. Slide 3: Change *Nightscape* to *New York City at Night*.

    b. Slide 4: Change *VictoriaBC* to *Victoria, British Columbia*.

    c. Slide 5: Change *Stonehenge* to *Stonehenge, Wiltshire County*.

    d. Slide 6: Change *BigBen* to *Big Ben, London*.

    e. Slide 7: Change *WhiteHorse* to *White Horse, Wiltshire County*.

7. Make Slide 8 active and then make the following changes:

    a. Select the text *Text Box* and then type Call First Choice Travel at 555-4500 to book your next travel tour.

    b. Select the text, change the font size to 48, change the font color to Blue, and change the alignment to Center.

8. Apply a transition and sound of your choosing to each slide.

9. Run the presentation.

10. Save **PP_C5_P2.pptx**.

Formatting Pictures

If you format slides in the presentation instead of the Edit Photo Album dialog box, you may lose some of those changes if you subsequently display the Edit Photo Album dialog box, make changes, and then click the Update button. Consider making your initial editing and formatting changes at the Edit Photo Album dialog box and then make final editing and formatting changes in the presentation.

    Since a picture in a slide in a photo album is an object, you can format it with options at the Drawing Tools Format tab and the Picture Tools Format tab. With options at the Drawing Tools Format tab, you can insert shapes, apply a shape style to the picture and caption (if one is displayed), apply a WordArt style to caption text, and arrange and size the picture. Use options in the Picture Tools Format tab to adjust the color of the picture, apply a picture style, and arrange and size the picture.

Project **2c**   **Formatting Pictures in a Presentation**

1. With **PP_C5_P2.pptx** open, make Slide 2 active.

2. Format the picture in Slide 2 by completing the following steps:

    a. Click the picture to select it.

    b. Click the Drawing Tools Format tab.

c. Click the More button at the right side of the shape styles and then click *Subtle Effect - Accent 1* (second option from the left in the fourth row).

Step 2c

3. Apply the same style to the pictures in Slides 3 through 7 by making each slide active, clicking the picture, and then pressing F4. (Pressing F4 repeats the style formatting.)
4. Make Slide 2 active and then apply a WordArt style to the caption text by completing the following steps:
   a. With Slide 2 active, click the picture to select it.
   b. Click the Drawing Tools Format tab.
   c. Click the More button at the right side of the WordArt styles and then click *Gradient Fill - Accent 4, Reflection* (last option in the fourth row).
5. Apply the same WordStyle style to caption text in Slides 3 through 7 by making each slide active, clicking the picture, and then pressing F4.
6. Run the presentation
7. Print the presentation as a handout with four slides per page.
8. Save and then close **PP_C5_P2.pptx**.

CHAPTER summary

- Use the Tables feature to create columns and rows of information. Create a table with the Insert Table button in a content placeholder or with the Table button in the Tables group in the Insert tab.

- A cell is the intersection between a row and a column. Columns in a table are lettered from left to right beginning with *A*. Rows are numbered from top to bottom beginning with *1*.

- Change the table design with options and buttons in the Table Tools Design tab.

- Change the table layout with options and buttons in the Table Tools Layout tab.

- Use the SmartArt feature to insert predesigned diagrams and organizational charts in a slide. Click the Insert SmartArt Graphic button in a content placeholder or click the SmartArt button in the Illustrations group in the Insert tab to display the Choose a SmartArt Graphic dialog box.

- When you insert a SmartArt diagram in a slide, the SmartArt Tools Design tab is active. Use options and buttons in this tab to change the diagram layout, apply a style to the diagram, and reset the diagram back to the original formatting.

- Use buttons in the SmartArt Tools Format tab to change the size and shapes of objects in the diagram; apply shape styles; change the shape fill, outline, and effects; and arrange and size the diagram.

- Create a SmartArt graphic with bulleted text by clicking in the bulleted text placeholder, clicking the Convert to SmartArt Graphic button in the Paragraph group in the Home tab, and then clicking the desired SmartArt diagram at the drop-down gallery.

- You can insert text directly into a SmartArt diagram shape or at the Text pane. Display this pane by clicking the Text Pane button in the Create Graphic group in the SmartArt Tools Design tab.

- A chart is a visual presentation of data and you can create a variety of charts as described in Table 5.2.

- To create a chart, display the Insert Chart dialog box by clicking the Insert Chart button in a content placeholder or clicking the Chart button in the Illustrations group in the Home tab.

- Enter chart data in an Excel worksheet. When entering data, press Tab to make the next cell active, press Shift + Tab to make the previous cell active, and press Enter to make the cell below active.

- Modify a chart design with options and buttons in the Chart Tools Design tab. Change the chart type with the Change Chart Type button, change the order of data in a chart with options in the Data group, apply a chart layout with options in the Chart Layouts group, and apply styles to a chart with options in the Chart Styles group.

- Cells in the Excel worksheet used to create a chart are linked to the chart in the slide. To edit chart data, click the Edit Data button in the Chart Tools Design tab and then make changes to text in the Excel worksheet.

- The Chart Tools Layout tab contains options and buttons for inserting objects in a chart such as a picture, shape, or text box and inserting and removing labels, axes, gridlines, and backgrounds.
- Customize the format of a chart and chart elements with options and buttons in the Chart Tools Format tab. You can select the chart or a specific element, apply a style to a shape, apply a WordArt style to text, and arrange and size the chart.
- Use the Photo Album feature to create a presentation containing pictures and then edit and format the pictures. Create a Photo Album by clicking the Insert tab, clicking the Photo Album button arrow, and then clicking *New Photo Album* at the drop-down list.
- At the Photo Album dialog box (or the Edit Photo Album dialog box), insert pictures and then use options to customize the photo album.
- Edit a photo album presentation by opening the presentation, clicking the Insert tab, clicking the Photo Album button arrow, and then clicking *Edit Photo Album* at the drop-down list.
- Use options in the Drawing Tools Format tab and the Picture Tools Format tab to format pictures in a photo album presentation.

COMMANDS review

FEATURE	RIBBON TAB, GROUP	BUTTON, OPTION	PLACEHOLDER BUTTON
Insert Table dialog box	Insert, Tables	, Insert Table	
Choose a SmartArt Graphic dialog box	Insert, Illustrations		
Convert bulleted text to SmartArt	Home, Paragraph		
Text pane	SmartArt Tools Design, Create Graphic	Text Pane	
Insert Chart dialog box	Insert, Illustrations		
Create photo album	Insert, Illustrations	, New Photo Album	
Edit photo album	Insert, Illustrations	, Edit Photo Album	

CONCEPTS check

Completion: In the space provided at the right, indicate the correct term, symbol, or command.

1. Display the Insert Table dialog box by clicking this button in a content placeholder.

   _____

2. This term refers to the intersection between a row and a column.

   _____

3. Use this keyboard shortcut to move the insertion point to the next cell.

   _____

4. This is the keyboard shortcut to select all cells in a table.

   _____

5. The Table Styles group is located in this tab.

   _____

6. Use options and buttons in this tab to delete and insert rows and columns and merge and split cells.

   _____

7. Click this button in a content placeholder to display the Choose a SmartArt Graphic dialog box.

   _____

8. When you insert a SmartArt diagram in a slide, this tab is active.

   _____

9. Create a SmartArt diagram with bulleted text by clicking in the text placeholder, clicking this button, and then clicking the desired SmartArt graphic at the drop-down list.

   _____

10. Click the Chart button in this group in the Insert tab to display the Insert Chart dialog box.

    _____

11. Insert a chart in a slide and this tab is active.

    _____

12. To edit data in a chart, click the Edit Data button in this group in the Chart Tools Design tab.

    _____

13. This group in the Chart Tools Format tab contains predesigned styles you can apply to shapes in a chart.

    _____

14. This group in the Chart Tools Format tab contains predesigned styles you can apply to chart text.

    _____

15. To create a photo album, click the Insert tab, click the Photo Album button arrow, and then click this at the drop-down list.

_____

16. To insert captions below pictures in a photo album, insert a check mark in this check box in the Edit Photo Album dialog box.

_____

17. Click the down-pointing arrow at the right of this option in the Edit Photo Album dialog box to display a list of framing choices.

_____

SKILLS check
Demonstrate Your Proficiency

Assessment

1 CREATE AND FORMAT TABLES AND SMARTART IN A RESTAURANT PRESENTATION

1. Open **Dockside.pptx** and save the presentation and name it **PP_C5_A1**.
2. Make Slide 6 active and then create the table shown in the slide in Figure 5.15 with the following specifications:
   a. Create a table with three columns and six rows.
   b. Type the text in cells as shown in Figure 5.15.
   c. Apply the *Medium Style 4 - Accent 3* style to the table.
   d. Select all of the text in the table, center the text vertically, change the font size to 20 points, and change the font color to Turquoise, Accent 2, Darker 50%.
   e. Change the height of the table to 3.7 inches. (The width should be set at 9 inches.)
   f. Center the text in the first row.
   g. Center the text in the third column.
   h. Position the table as shown in Figure 5.15.
3. Make Slide 4 active and then create the table shown in the slide in Figure 5.16 with the following specifications:
   a. Create a table with four columns and three rows.
   b. Select the entire table, change the vertical alignment to center, and then change the font size to 28.
   c. Merge the cells in the first column, change the text direction to *Rotate all text 270°*, change the alignment to center, change the font size to 40, and then type Lunch.
   d. Merge the cells in the third column, change the text direction to *Rotate all text 270°*, change the alignment to center, change the font size to 40, and then type Dinner.
   e. Type the remaining text in cells as shown in Figure 5.16.
   f. Change the height of the table to 3 inches.
   g. Change the width of the first and third columns to 1.2 inches.
   h. Change the width of the second and fourth columns to 2.5 inches.

i. Insert a check mark in the *Banded Columns* check box in the Table Style Options group in the Table Tools Design tab and remove the check marks from the other check boxes in the group.
j. Apply the *Medium Style 4 - Accent 3* style to the table.
k. Select all of the text in the table and then change the font color to Turquoise, Accent 2, Darker 50%.
l. Position the table on the slide as shown in Figure 5.16.
4. Make Slide 5 active and then create the SmartArt organizational chart shown in the slide in Figure 5.17 with the following specifications:
a. Choose the *Organization Chart* diagram at the Choose a SmartArt Graphic dialog box.
b. Delete the second box so your chart appears with the same number of boxes and in the same order as the organizational chart in Figure 5.17.
c. Type the text in the boxes as shown in Figure 5.17.
d. Change the color to Colorful Range – Accent Colors 3 to 4.
e. Apply the *Cartoon* SmartArt style.
f. Apply the *Fill - White, Drop Shadow* WordArt style to text.
g. Change the height of the organizational chart to 5 inches and change the width to 8.5 inches.
h. Position the organizational chart in the slide as shown in Figure 5.17.
5. Make Slide 1 active and then format the title and create the SmartArt diagram shown in the slide in Figure 5.18 with the following specifications:
a. Select the title *The Dockside Café* and then change the font to Lucida Calligraphy.
b. Create the SmartArt diagram with the *Linear Venn* option located in the *Relationship* group. Type the text in the shapes as shown in Figure 5.18.
c. Change the colors to *Colorful - Accent Colors*.
d. Apply the *Intense Effect* SmartArt style.
e. Apply the *Fill - White, Drop Shadow* WordArt style to text.
f. Change the height of the diagram to 4.2 inches and the width to 6.8 inches.
g. Position the SmartArt diagram on the slide as shown in Figure 5.18.
6. Make Slide 2 active, select the bulleted text placeholder, and then convert the bulleted text to a *Basic Matrix* diagram as shown in the slide in Figure 5.19 with the following specifications:
a. Change the colors to *Colorful - Accent Colors*.
b. Apply the *Cartoon* SmartArt style.
c. Apply the *Fill - White, Drop Shadow* WordArt style to text.
d. Change the height of the diagram to 4.8 inches and the width to 5.5 inches.
e. Position the SmartArt diagram on the slide as shown in Figure 5.19.
7. Make Slide 3 active and then insert a clip art image related to "menu." Size and position the image attractively on the slide.
8. Apply a transition and sound of your choosing to all slides in the presentation.
9. Run the presentation.
10. Print the presentation as a handout with six slides per page.
11. Save and then close **PP_C5_A1.pptx**.

Figure 5.15 Assessment 1, Slide 6

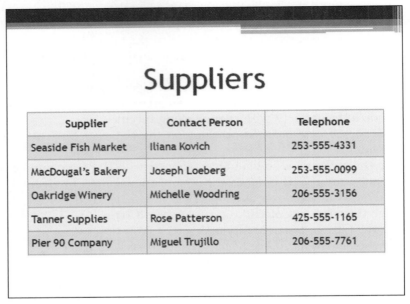

Figure 5.16 Assessment 1, Slide 4

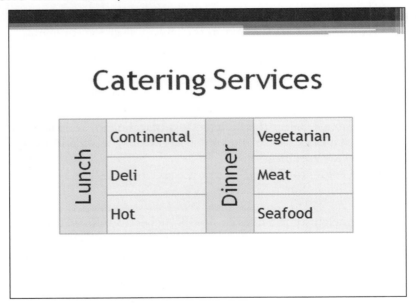

Figure 5.17 Assessment 1, Slide 5

Figure 5.18 Assessment 1, Slide 1

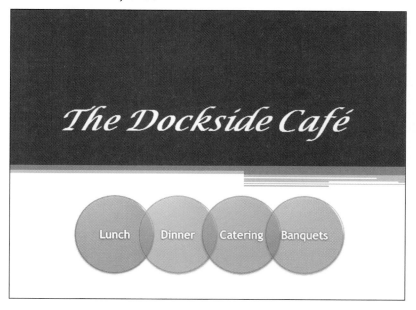

Figure 5.19 Assessment 1, Slide 2

Assessment

2 CREATE AND FORMAT CHARTS IN A MARKETING PRESENTATION

1. Open **MarketingPresentation.pptx** and save the presentation and name it **PP_C5_A2**.
2. Make Slide 2 active, insert a new slide with the *Title and Content* layout, and then create the chart shown in the slide in Figure 5.20 with the following specifications:
   a. Type the slide title as shown in Figure 5.20.
   b. Use the pie chart option *Pie in 3-D* to create the chart.
   c. Type the following information in the Excel worksheet:

	Amount
Salaries	47%
Equipment	18%
Supplies	4%
Production	21%
Distribution	10%

   d. Change the chart layout to *Layout 3*.
   e. Insert data labels on the outside end.
   f. Change the shape fill of the piece of pie containing *10%* to *White, Accent 3, Darker 35%*.
3. Print Slide 3.
4. After looking at the slide, you realize that two of the percentages are incorrect. Edit the Excel data and change *47%* to *42%* and change *10%* to *15%*.
5. With Slide 3 active, insert a new slide with the *Title and Content* layout and then create the chart shown in the slide in Figure 5.21 with the following specifications:
   a. Type the slide title as shown in Figure 5.21.
   b. Use the line chart option *Line with Markers* to create the chart.

c. Type the following information in the Excel worksheet:

	Revenues	Expenses
1st Qtr	$789,560	$670,500
2nd Qtr	$990,450	$765,000
3rd Qtr	$750,340	$780,000
4th Qtr	$980,400	$875,200

d. Apply the *Style 42* chart style.
e. Click the Data Table button in the Chart Tools Layout tab and then click the *Show Data Table with Legend Keys* option.
f. Select and then delete the legend.
g. Insert major and minor vertical gridlines.
h. Select the plot area and then change the shape fill color to Light Green, Accent 1, Lighter 80%. (The Shape Fill button is located in the Chart Tools Format tab.)
i. Select the chart area and then change the shape fill color to Green, Accent 2, Darker 50%.
j. Select the expenses line (*Series "Expenses"*) and then change the shape fill to Red and the shape outline to Red.
k. Select the revenues line (*Series "Revenues"*) and then change the shape fill and the shape outline to Light Green, Accent 1, Darker 50%.

6. Apply a transition and sound of your choosing to each slide in the presentation.
7. Run the presentation.
8. Print the presentation as a handout with three slides per page.
9. Save and then close **PP_C5_A2.pptx**.

Figure 5.20 Assessment 2, Slide 3

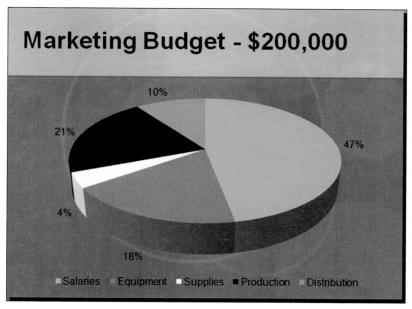

Figure 5.21 Assessment 2, Slide 4

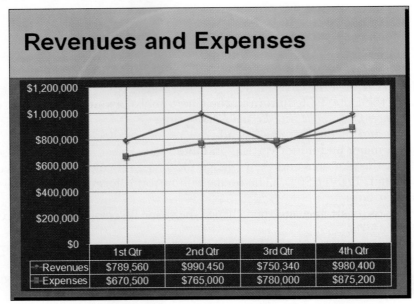

Assessment

3 CREATE A SCENERY PHOTO ALBUM

1. At a blank screen, create a new photo album.
2. At the Photo Album dialog box, insert the following images:
   AlderSprings.jpg
   CrookedRiver.jpg
   Mountain.jpg
   Ocean.jpg
   Olympics.jpg
   River.jpg
3. Change the *Picture layout* option to *1 picture with title*.
4. Change the *Frame shape* option to *Simple Frame, White*.
5. Apply the *Paper* theme.
6. Click the Create button.
7. At the presentation, change the theme colors to *Solstice* and the background style to *Style 8*. **Hint: Do this with buttons in the Design tab.**
8. Insert the following titles in the specified slides:
   Slide 2 = Alder Springs, Oregon
   Slide 3 = Crooked River, Oregon
   Slide 4 = Mt. Rainier, Washington
   Slide 5 = Pacific Ocean, Washington
   Slide 6 = Olympic Mountains, Washington
   Slide 7 = Salmon River, Idaho
9. Make Slide 1 active, select any name that follows *by*, and then type your first and last names.
10. Save the presentation and name it **PP_C5_A3**.
11. Print the presentation as a handout with four slides per page.
12. Close **PP_C5_A3.pptx**.

4   CREATE A SALES AREA CHART

1. Open **PP_C5_A2.pptx** and then save the presentation and name it **PP_C5_A4**.
2. Make Slide 4 active and then insert a new slide with the *Title and Content* layout.
3. Use Excel's Help feature to learn more about chart types and then create an area chart (use the *Area* chart type) with the data shown below. Apply design, layout, and/or formatting to improve the visual appeal of the chart. Type **Sales by Region** as the slide title.

	Region 1	Region 2	Region 3
Sales 2007	$650,300	$478,100	$225,500
Sales 2008	$623,100	$533,600	$210,000
Sales 2009	$725,600	$478,400	$296,500

4. Print Slide 5.
5. Save and then close **PP_C5_A4.pptx**.

CASE study

Apply Your Skills

Part 1

You are an administrator for Terra Energy Corporation and you are responsible for preparing a presentation for a quarterly meeting. Open the Word document named **TerraEnergy.docx** and then use the information to prepare a presentation with the following specifications:

- Create the first slide with the company name and the subtitle of *Quarterly Meeting*.
- Create a slide that presents the Executive Team information in a table.
- Create a slide that presents the phases information in a table (the three columns of text in the *Research and Development* section). Insert a column at the left side of the table that includes the text *New Product* rotated.
- Create a slide that presents the development team information in a SmartArt organizational chart.
- Create a slide that presents the revenues information in a chart (you determine the type of chart).
- Create a slide that presents the United States sales information in a chart (you determine the type of chart).

Apply a design theme of your choosing and add any additional features to improve the visual appeal of the presentation. Insert a transition and sound to each slide and then run the presentation. Save the presentation and name it **PP_C5_CS_P1.pptx**. Print the presentation as a handout with four slides per page.

Part 2

Last year, a production project was completed and you want to display a graphic that illustrates the primary focus of the project. Create a slide and insert a *Funnel* SmartArt graphic (in the *Relationship* group) with the following information in the shapes inside the funnel (turn on the Text pane to type the information in the shapes):

> Updated Systems
> Safety Programs
> Market Expansion

Insert the information *Higher Profits* below the funnel. Apply formatting to the SmartArt graphic to improve the visual appeal. Print the slide and then save **PP_C5_CS_P1.pptx**.

Part 3

The presentation should include information on the corporation's stock. Use the Help feature to learn about stock charts and then create a high-low-close stock chart with the following information:

Date	High	Low	Close
01/01/2010	23	20.25	21.875
02/01/2010	28.625	25.25	26.375
03/01/2010	32.375	28	30.125
04/01/2010	27.125	24.5	26.375
05/01/2010	25.125	22.875	24.25

Apply formatting to the chart to improve the readability and appeal of the chart. Print the slide and then save **PP_C5_CS_P1.pptx**.

Part 4

You have created an Excel chart containing information on department costs. You decide to improve the visual appeal of the chart and then create a link from the presentation to the chart. Open Excel and then open **DepartmentCosts.xlsx**. Apply additional formatting to the pie chart to make it easy to read and understand the data. Save and then close the workbook and exit Excel. Create a new slide in the **PP_C5_CS_P1.pptx** presentation that includes a hyperlink to the **DepartmentCosts.xlsx** workbook. Run the presentation and when the slide displays containing the hyperlinked text, click the hyperlink, view the chart in Excel, and then exit Excel. Print the presentation as a handout with four slides per page. Save and then close **PP_C5_CS_P1.pptx**.

Using Slide Masters and Action Buttons

PERFORMANCE OBJECTIVES

Upon successful completion of Chapter 6, you will be able to:

- **Format slides in Slide Master view**
- **Apply themes and backgrounds in Slide Master view**
- **Delete placeholders and slide master layouts**
- **Insert elements in Slide Master view**
- **Create and rename a custom slide layout**
- **Insert a new slide master**
- **Save a presentation as a template**
- **Customize a handout in Handout Master view**
- **Customize notes pages in Notes Master view**
- **Insert action buttons**
- **Create hyperlinks**

powerpoint Chapter 6

SNAP

Tutorial 6.1
Working with Masters
Tutorial 6.2
Creating and Customizing a
Presentation

If you make design or formatting changes and you want the changes to affect all slides in the presentation, consider making the changes in a slide master in the Slide Master view. Along with the Slide Master view, you can make changes to all pages in a handout with options in the Handout Master view and all notes pages in the Notes Master view. You can insert action buttons in a presentation to connect to slides within the same presentation, connect to another presentation, connect to a Web site, or connect to another program. You can also connect to a Web site by inserting a hyperlink to the site.

Note: Before beginning computer projects, copy to your storage medium the PowerPoint2007C6 folder from the PowerPoint2007 folder on the CD that accompanies this textbook and then make PowerPoint2007C6 the active folder.

P roject **1** **Create a Travel Presentation and Apply Formatting in Slide Master View**

You will apply formatting to a blank presentation in Slide Master view, insert slides in the presentation, insert elements in Slide Master view, insert a custom slide layout, and insert a new slide master.

QUICK STEPS

Display Slide Master View
1. Click View tab.
2. Click Slide Master button.

HINT

Create a consistent look to your slides by customizing slides in Slide Master view.

Slide Master

Close Master View

Customizing Slide Masters

When creating a presentation, you can apply a design theme to the presentation to provide colors and formatting. If you make changes to a slide and want the changes to affect all slides in the presentation, make the change in a slide master. You can customize a slide master by changing the theme, theme colors, and/or theme fonts; changing the location of and inserting placeholders; applying a background style; and changing the page setup and slide orientation. If you know you want to customize slides, consider making the changes in Slide Master view before you create each slide. If you apply a slide master to an existing presentation, some items on slides may not conform to the new formatting.

To display the Slide Master view, click the View tab and then click the Slide Master button in the Presentation Views group. This displays the Slide Master tab, a blank slide master in the Slide pane, and inserts slide master thumbnails in the slide thumbnail pane. The largest thumbnail in the pane is the slide master and the other thumbnails represent associated layouts. Position the mouse pointer on a slide thumbnail and the name of the thumbnail displays in a box by the thumbnail. Figure 6.1 displays a blank presentation in Slide Master view. To specify the slide master or layout you want to customize, click the desired thumbnail in the slide thumbnail pane. With the slide master layout displayed in the Slide pane, make the desired changes and then click the Close Master View button.

Applying Themes to Slide Masters

You can apply themes, theme colors, theme fonts, and theme effects with buttons in the Edit Theme group in the Slide Master tab. Click the Themes button and a drop-down list displays with available predesigned themes and also any custom themes you have created. Click the desired theme and the theme formatting is applied to the slide master. Complete similar steps to apply theme colors, theme fonts, and theme effects.

Aa
Themes

Figure 6.1 Slide Master View

Click the desired slide master in the slide thumbnail pane and then make desired changes to the layout.

Click to edit Master title style

Click to edit Master subtitle style

Project 1a **Formatting a Slide Master**

1. Display a blank presentation.
2. Click the View tab and then click the Slide Master button in the Presentation Views group.

Step 2

Step 4

Step 5

3. Click the top (and largest) slide master thumbnail in the slide thumbnail pane (*Office Theme Slide Master*). (This displays the slide master layout in the Slide pane.)
4. Click the Themes button in the Edit Theme group in the Slide Master tab.
5. Click *Solstice* at the drop-down gallery.
6. Click the Colors button in the Edit Theme group and then click *Metro* at the drop-down gallery.
7. Click the Fonts button in the Edit Theme group and then click the *Foundry* option at the drop-down gallery.
8. Change the font color and alignment for the title style by completing the following steps:
   a. Select the text *Click to edit Master title style* that displays in the slide master in the Slide pane.

b. Click the Home tab.
c. Click the Font Color button arrow and then click the *Turquoise, Accent 4, Darker 25%* option.

d. Click the Center button in the Paragraph group.
9. Change the font color by completing the following steps:
a. Select all of the bulleted text in the slide master.
b. Make sure the Home tab is selected.
c. Click the Font Color button arrow and then click the *Periwinkle, Accent 5, Darker 50%* option.
10. Change the color of the first two bullets by completing the following steps:
a. Select the text following the first two bullets.
b. Click the Bullets button arrow in the Paragraph group in the Home tab and then click *Bullets and Numbering* at the drop-down gallery.
c. At the Bullets and Numbering dialog box with the Bulleted tab selected, click the Color button and then click the *Turquoise, Accent 4, Darker 25%* color option.
d. Click OK to close the dialog box.
11. Click the Slide Master tab.
12. Click the Close Master View button.
13. Save the presentation and name it **TravelMaster.pptx**.

HINT

Background styles are derived from the theme colors and background intensities in the theme. If you change the theme, background styles are updated.

Applying and Formatting Backgrounds

Like the Background group in the Design tab, the Background group in the Slide Master tab contains the Background Styles button and the *Hide Background Graphics* check box. If you want to change the background graphic for all slides, make the change at the slide master. To do this, display the presentation in Slide Master view and then click the desired slide master layout in the slide thumbnail pane. Click the Background Styles button and then click a background at the drop-down gallery. Or, click the *Format Background* option and choose the desired options at the Format Background dialog box. If you want to remove the background graphic for slides, click the *Hide Background Graphics* check box to insert a check mark.

Deleting Placeholders

If you want to remove a placeholder for all slides in a presentation, consider deleting the placeholder in the Slide Master view. To do this, display the presentation in Slide Master view, click the desired slide master layout in the slide thumbnail pane, click the placeholder border (make sure the border displays as a solid line), and then press the Delete key. You can also remove a title placeholder from a slide master by clicking the *Title* check box in the Master Layout group to remove the check mark. Remove footer placeholders by clicking the *Footer* check box to remove the check mark.

Deleting Slide Master Layouts

In Slide Master view, a slide master displays for each available layout. If you know that you will not be using a particular layout in the presentation, you can delete the layout slide master. To do this, display the presentation in Slide Master view, click the desired slide layout thumbnail in the slide thumbnail pane, and then click the Delete button in the Edit Master group.

QUICK STEPS

Delete Slide Master Layouts
1. Display presentation in Slide Master view.
2. Click desired slide layout thumbnail.
3. Click Delete button.

HINT
You can also delete a slide layout by right-clicking the layout in the slide thumbnail pane and then clicking *Delete Layout* at the shortcut menu.

Project 1b   Applying and Formatting Background Graphics

1. With **TravelMaster.pptx** open, click the View tab and then click the Slide Master button in the Presentation Views group.
2. Click the top slide layout thumbnail (*Solstice Slide Master*) in the slide thumbnail pane.
3. Format the background by completing the following steps:
   a. Click the Background Styles button in the Background group and then click *Format Background* at the drop-down gallery.
   b. At the Format Background dialog box, click the *Gradient fill* option.
   c. Click the *Preset colors* button and then click the *Fog* option at the drop-down list (last option in the second row).
   d. Click the down-pointing arrow at the right side of the *Type* option and then click *Path* at the drop-down list.
   e. Click the Close button.
4. Apply a picture to the background of the title slide layout (the picture will appear only on this layout) by completing the following steps:
   a. Click the second slide layout thumbnail (*Title Slide Layout*) in the slide thumbnail pane.
   b. Click the *Hide Background Graphics* check box to insert a check mark.
   c. Click the Background Styles button in the Background group and then click *Format Background* at the drop-down list.
   d. At the Format Background dialog box, click the *Picture or texture fill* option.

e. Click the File button (located below the *Insert from* option).
f. At the Insert Picture dialog box, navigate to the PowerPoint2007C6 folder on your storage medium and then double-click ***Stonehenge.jpg***.
g. Click the Close button to close the Format Background dialog box.
h. Remove the two small green circles that appear in the slide master in the Slide pane by clicking each circle and then pressing the Delete key.
i. Click on any character in the text *Click to edit Master title style* and then press Ctrl + E. (This is the keyboard shortcut for centering.)
j. Drag the placeholder so it is positioned above the stones and centered horizontally. (Make sure the bottom border of the placeholder is positioned above the stones.)
5. Delete the Master subtitle style placeholder by clicking the placeholder border (make sure the border displays as a solid line) and then pressing the Delete key.
6. Remove the footer placeholders from the layout by clicking the *Footers* check box in the Master Layout group to remove the check mark.

Step 6

7. Delete slide layouts that you will not be using in the presentation by completing the following steps:
   a. Click the fourth slide layout thumbnail in the slide thumbnail pane.
   b. Scroll down the pane until the last slide layout thumbnail is visible.
   c. Hold down the Shift key and then click the last slide layout thumbnail.
   d. Click the Delete button in the Edit Master group. (The slide thumbnail pane should contain the slide master and two associated layouts.)
8. Click the Close Master View button.
9. Delete the slide that currently displays in the Slide pane. (This displays a blue background with the text *Click to add first slide*. The presentation does not contain any slides, just formatting.)
10. Save ***TravelMaster.pptx***.

Step 7d

Inserting Slides in a Customized Presentation

If you customize slides in a presentation in Slide Master view, you can use the presentation formatting in other presentations. You can save the formatted presentation as a template or you can save the presentation in the normal manner and then open the presentation, save it with a new name, and then type text in slides. You can also insert slides into the current presentation using the Reuse Slides task pane. (You learned about this task pane in Chapter 2.) To use this task pane, click the Home tab, click the New Slide button arrow, and then click *Reuse Slides* at the drop-down list. This displays the Reuse Slides task pane at the right side of the screen. Click the Browse button and then click the *Browse File* option at the drop-down list. At the Browse dialog box, navigate to the desired folder and then double-click the desired presentation. Insert slides into the current presentation by clicking the desired slide in the task pane.

1. With **TravelMaster.pptx** open, save the presentation with Save As and name it **PP_C6_P1**.
2. Make sure the Home tab is active, click the New Slide button arrow, and then click *Title Slide* at the drop-down list.
3. Click the *Click to add title* text in the current slide and then type Wiltshire, England.
4. Insert slides into the current presentation from an existing presentation by completing the following steps:

Step 2

   a. Click the New Slide button arrow and then click *Reuse Slides* at the drop-down list.
   b. Click the Browse button in the Reuse Slides task pane and then click *Browse File* at the drop-down list.
   c. At the Browse dialog box, navigate to the PowerPoint2007C6 folder on your storage medium and then double-click ***TravelEngland.pptx***.
   d. Click the *Wiltshire* slide in the Reuse Slides task pane. (This inserts the slide in the presentation and applies the custom formatting to the slide.)
   e. Click the *Ancient Stone Circles* slide in the Reuse Slides task pane.
   f. Click the *Ancient Wiltshire* slide in the Reuse Slides task pane.
   g. Click the *White Horses* slide in the Reuse Slides task pane.
   h. Click the Close button located in the upper right corner of the Reuse Slides task pane to close the task pane.

Step 4b

Step 4d

5. With Slide 5 active, format the bulleted text into two columns by completing the following steps:
   a. Click in any character in the bulleted text.
   b. Move the insertion point so it is positioned immediately following *Marlborough*.
   c. Press the Enter key (to insert a blank line) and then click the Bullets button in the Paragraph group in the Home tab to remove the bullet.
   d. Press Ctrl + A to select all of the bulleted text.
   e. Click the Line Spacing button in the Paragraph group and then click *2.0* at the drop-down list.
   f. Click the Columns button in the Paragraph group and then click *Two Columns* at the drop-down list.
6. With Slide 5 active, insert a new slide by completing the following steps:
   a. Click the New Slide button arrow and then click the *Title Slide* layout at the drop-down list.
   b. Click in the text *Click to add title* and then type Call Lucy at 555-4500.
7. Save **PP_C6_P1.pptx**.
8. Print the presentation as a handout with six slides per page. (The picture backgrounds will not print.)

Inserting Elements in a Slide Master

As you learned in Chapter 2, you can display a presentation in Print Preview and then insert a header, footer, or the date and time that print on every slide in the presentation. You can also insert these elements in a slide master. For example, to insert a header or footer in slides, display the presentation in Slide Master view, click the Insert tab, and then click the Header & Footer button in the Text group. At the Header and Footer dialog box with the Slide tab selected, make the desired changes, click the Notes and Handouts tab, make the desired changes, and then click the Apply to All button. You can also insert additional elements in the Slide Master view such as a picture, clip art image, shape, SmartArt graphic, or chart. Insert any of these elements in the normal manner in a slide in Slide Master view.

Project 1d Inserting Elements in Slide Master View

1. With **PP_C6_P1.pptx** open, insert a header, a footer, and the date and time by completing the following steps:
   a. Click the View tab.
   b. Click the Slide Master button in the Presentation Views group.
   c. Click the slide master thumbnail (the top slide thumbnail in the slide thumbnail pane).
   d. Click the Insert tab.
   e. Click the Header & Footer button in the Text group.
   f. At the Header and Footer dialog box with the Slide tab selected, click the *Date and time* check box to insert a check mark.
   g. Make sure the *Update automatically* option is selected. (With this option selected, the date and/or time will automatically update each time you open the presentation.)
   h. Click the *Slide number* check box to insert a check mark.
   i. Click the *Footer* check box to insert a check mark and then type your first and last names in the *Footer* text box.

j. Click the Notes and Handouts tab.

k. Click the *Date and time* check box to insert a check mark.

l. Make sure the *Update automatically* option is selected.

m. Click the *Header* check box and then type the name of your school.

n. Click the *Footer* check box and then type your first and last names.

o. Click the Apply to All button.

2. Insert the First Choice Travel logo in the lower left corner of the slide master by completing the following steps:

a. Click the Picture button in the Illustrations group.

b. At the Insert Picture dialog box, navigate to the PowerPoint2007C6 folder on your storage medium and then double-click **FCTLogo.jpg**.

c. Click in the *Shape Height* measurement box in the Size group in the Picture Tools Format tab, type 0.55, and then press Enter.

d. Drag the logo so it is positioned in the lower left corner of the slide as shown at the right.

e. Click the Send to Back button in the Arrange group.

f. Click outside the logo to deselect it.

3. With the Slide Master tab selected, click the Close Master View button.

4. Run the presentation and notice the logo and other elements in the slides.

5. Print the presentation as a handout with six slides per page.

6. Save **PP_C6_P1.pptx**.

Creating and Renaming a Custom Slide Layout

You can create your own custom slide layout in Slide Master view and then customize the layout by inserting or deleting elements and applying formatting to placeholders and text. To create a new slide layout, click the Insert Layout button in the Edit Master group in the Slide Master tab. This inserts in the Slide pane a new slide containing a Master title style placeholder and footer placeholders. Customize the layout by inserting or deleting placeholders and applying formatting to placeholders.

PowerPoint will automatically assign the name *Custom Layout* to a slide layout you create. If you create another slide layout, PowerPoint will name it *1_Custom Layout*, and so on. Consider renaming your custom layout to a name that describes the layout. To rename a layout, make sure the desired slide layout is active, and then click the Rename button in the Edit Master group. At the Rename Layout dialog box, type the desired name, and then click the Rename button.

Inserting Placeholders

You can insert placeholders in a predesigned slide layout or you can insert a custom slide layout and then insert placeholders. Insert a placeholder by clicking the Insert Placeholder button arrow in the Master Layout group and then clicking the desired placeholder option at the drop-down list. If you click the slide master, the Insert Placeholder button is dimmed. If you delete a placeholder from the slide master, you can reinsert the placeholder with options at the Master Layout dialog box. Display this dialog box by clicking the Master Layout button and any placeholder that has been removed from the slide master displays in the dialog box as an active option with an empty check box. Reinsert the placeholder by inserting a check mark in the desired placeholder check box and then clicking OK to close the dialog box.

Creating Custom Prompts

Some placeholders in a custom layout may contain generic text such as *Click to add Master title style* or *Click to edit Master text styles*. In Slide Master view, you can select this generic text and replace it with custom text. You might want to insert text that describes what you want entered into the placeholder.

Project 1e Inserting a Layout and Placeholder

1. With **PP_C6_P1.pptx** open, click the View tab and then click the Slide Master button in the Presentation Views group.
2. Click the bottom slide layout thumbnail in the slide thumbnail pane.
3. Click the Insert Layout button in the Edit Master group. (This inserts in the Slide pane a new slide with a Master title style placeholder, the logo, and the footer information.)
4. Format and move the placeholder by completing the following steps:
   a. Select the text *Click to edit Master title style*.
   b. Click the Home tab, click the Text Shadow button (to turn off shadowing), turn on bold, change the font to Tahoma, change the font size to 28 points, and change the font color to Light Blue.

c. Move the placeholder so it is positioned along the bottom of the slide just above the footer placeholder.

Step 4c

Click to edit Master title style

First Choice TRAVEL

3/27/2010   Student Name

5. Click the Slide Master tab.
6. Insert a Picture placeholder by completing the following steps:
   a. Click the Insert Placeholder button arrow.
   b. Click *Picture* at the drop-down list.
   c. Drag in the slide in the Slide pane to create a placeholder that is approximately 7.5 inches wide and 3.5 inches high.
   d. Click the Drawing Tools Format tab.
   e. Click in the *Shape Height* measurement box and then type 3.5.
   f. Click in the *Shape Width* measurement box, type 7.5, and then press Enter.
   g. Drag the placeholder so it is balanced in the slide.
   h. Click outside the placeholder to deselect it.
   i. Position the mouse pointer immediately left of the word *Picture* in the placeholder until the pointer turns into an I-beam and then click the left mouse button. (This removes the word *Picture* and inserts the insertion point in the placeholder.)
   j. Type Insert company logo.

Step 6a

Step 6b

Step 6e

Step 6f

7. Remove the footer and slide number placeholders by completing the following steps:
   a. Click the footer placeholder (located along the bottom of the slide in the Slide pane).
   b. Click the border of the placeholder to select it (the border turns into a solid line) and then press the Delete key.
   c. Click the slide number placeholder, click the placeholder border, and then press the Delete key.
   d. Drag the date placeholder so it is positioned at the right side of the slide.
8. If necessary, click the Slide Master tab.
9. Rename the custom slide layout by completing the following steps:
   a. Click the Rename button in the Edit Master group.
   b. At the Custom Layout dialog box, type Logo Layout.
   c. Click the Rename button.

Rename Layout

Layout name:
Logo Layout

Rename
Cancel

Step 9b

Step 9c

10. Click the Close Master View button.
11. Insert a slide using the new slide layout by completing the following steps:
    a. Make Slide 6 active.

b. Click the New Slide button arrow.
c. Click the *Logo Layout* option at the drop-down list.
d. Click the Insert Picture from File button in the slide.
e. At the Insert Picture dialog box, navigate to the PowerPoint2007C6 folder on your storage medium and then double-click **FCTLogo.jpg**.
f. Click in the text *Click to add title* and then type Monthly special – 20% discount on Wiltshire tour.
12. Save **PP_C6_P1.pptx**.

Step 11b

Step 11c

Inserting a New Slide Master

A PowerPoint presentation can contain more than one slide master (and associated layouts). To insert a new slide master, display the presentation in Slide Master view and then click the Insert Slide Master button in the Edit Master group. This inserts the slide master and all associated layouts below the existing slide master and layouts in the slide thumbnail pane. You can also insert a slide master and all associated layouts with a design theme applied. To do this, click below the existing slide master and associated layouts, click the Themes button in the Edit Theme group, and then click the desired theme at the drop-down gallery. A slide master containing the chosen design theme is inserted below the existing thumbnails.

Preserving Slide Masters

Preserve Slide Master
1. Display presentation in Slide Master view.
2. Click desired slide master thumbnail.
3. Click Preserve button.

If you delete all slide layouts that follow a slide master, PowerPoint will automatically delete the slide master. You can protect a slide master from being deleted by "preserving" the master. To do this, click the desired slide master thumbnail and then click the Preserve button in the Edit Master group. If you insert a slide master using the Insert Slide Master button, the Preserve button is automatically active. When a slide master is preserved, a preservation icon displays below the slide number in the slide thumbnail pane.

Changing Page Setup

The Page Setup group in the Slide Master tab contains two buttons. By default, slides display in the landscape orientation (wider than tall). You can change this to portrait orientation (taller than wide) by clicking the Slide Orientation button in the Page Setup group and then clicking *Portrait* at the drop-down list. Click the Page Setup button and the Page Setup dialog box displays with options for changing slide width and height; slide numbering; and applying slide orientation to slides or notes, handouts, and outline pages.

1. With **PP_C6_P1.pptx** open, insert a second slide master by completing the following steps:
   a. Click the View tab and then click the Slide Master button in the Presentation Views group.
   b. Click below the bottom slide layout in the slide thumbnail pane. (You want the slide master and associated layouts to display below the original slide master and not take the place of the original.)
   c. Click the Themes button in the Edit Theme group and then click *Flow* at the drop-down gallery. (Notice the slide master and associated layouts that display in the slide thumbnail pane below the original slide master and associated layouts and notice the preservation icon that displays below the slide master number 2.)
   d. Click the Colors button in the Edit Theme group and then click *Apex* at the drop-down gallery.
   e. Click the Fonts button and then click *Foundry* at the drop-down gallery.

Step 1b

2. Insert a footer, the date and time, and slide numbers in the slide master by completing the following steps:
   a. Click the Insert tab.
   b. Click the Header & Footer button in the Text group.
   c. At the Header and Footer dialog box with the Slide tab selected, click the *Date and time* check box to insert a check mark.
   d. Make sure the *Update automatically* option is selected. (With this option selected, the date and/or time will automatically update each time you open the presentation.)
   e. Click the *Slide number* check box to insert a check mark.
   f. Click the *Footer* check box to insert a check mark and then type your first and last names in the *Footer* text box.
   g. Click the Apply to All button.
3. Click the Slide Master tab.
4. Click the third layout below the new slide master (*Section Header Layout*), scroll down to the bottom of the slide thumbnail pane, hold down the Shift key, click the bottom thumbnail, and then click the Delete button in the Edit Master group. (This deletes all but two of the associated layouts with the new slide master.)
5. Format the slide layout below the new slide master by completing the following steps:
   a. Click the layout (Title Slide Layout) below the new slide master.
   b. Click the Background Styles button in the Background group and then click *Format Background*.
   c. At the Format Background dialog box, click the *Picture or texture fill* option.
   d. Click the File button (located below the *Insert from* option).
   e. At the Insert Picture dialog box, navigate to the PowerPoint2007C6 folder on your storage medium and then double-click **Nightscape.jpg**.
   f. Click the *Hide background graphics* check box to insert a check mark.
   g. Click the Close button.
   h. Click in the text *Click to edit Master title style* and then press Ctrl + E. (This centers the text.)
   i. Drag the placeholder up so the text displays above the buildings.
   j. Select and then delete the subtitle placeholder.
   k. Click the *Footers* check box in the Master Layout group to remove footer placeholders.
6. Click the Close Master View button.

7. Insert a new slide by completing the following steps:
   a. Make Slide 7 active.
   b. Click the New Slide button arrow and then click the Flow Title Slide (the slide with the image of the New York City night skyline).
   c. Click in the text *Click to add title* and then type New York City Tour.

8. Insert a new slide by completing the following steps:
   a. With Slide 8 active, click the New Slide button. (This inserts the Flow Title and Content layout.)
   b. Click the text *Click to add title* and then type Manhattan Tour.
   c. Click the text *Click to add text* and then type the following bulleted text:
      - Times Square
      - Madison Square Garden
      - Greenwich Village
      - Soho
      - Little Italy
      - Battery Park

9. Insert the following text in slides using the Flow Title and Content layout:

   Slide 10   Dinner Cruise
      - Three-hour cruise
      - Manhattan skyline
      - Five-course gourmet dinner
      - Entertainment
      - Dancing
   Slide 11   City Pass
      - Empire State Building
      - Statue of Liberty
      - Ellis Island
      - Rockefeller Center
      - United Nations Building
      - Bronx Zoo
   Slide 12   Museum Passes
      - Museum of Modern Art
      - Guggenheim Museum
      - American Museum of Natural History
      - Metropolitan Museum of Art
      - Ellis Island Museum
      - Brooklyn Museum of Art

10. Insert a new slide by completing the following steps:
    a. With Slide 12 active, click the New Slide button arrow and then click the Flow Title Slide (the slide with the image of the New York City night skyline).
    b. Click in the text *Click to add text* and then type Call Beth at 555-4500.

11. Insert a new slide with the Logo Layout by completing the following steps:
   a. With Slide 13 active, click the New Slide button arrow and then click the Solstice Logo Layout.
   b. Click the Insert Picture from File button in the slide.
   c. At the Insert Picture dialog box, navigate to the PowerPoint2007C6 folder on your storage medium and then double-click *FCTLogo.jpg*.
   d. Click in the text *Click to add title* and then type Complimentary airport shuttle when you book your New York tour.
12. Assume that the presentation is going to be inserted into a larger presentation and that the starting slide number will be 12 (instead of 1). Change the beginning slide number by completing the following steps:
   a. Click the View tab and then click the Slide Master button.
   b. Click the top slide master in the slide thumbnail pane.
   c. Click the Page Setup button in the Page Setup group.
   d. At the Page Setup dialog box, select the current number in the *Number slides from* text box and then type 12.
   e. Click OK to close the dialog box.
   f. Click the Close Master View button.
13. Print the presentation as a handout with six slides per page.
14. Save and then close **PP_C6_P1.pptx**.

Step 12e

Step 12d

Project 2 — Save a Template and Create a Travel Presentation with the Template

You will save a travel presentation as a template and then use the template to create and format a travel presentation. You will insert elements in the presentation in Handout Master view and Notes Master view, change the presentation zoom, and view the presentation in grayscale and black and white.

Saving a Presentation as a Template

If you create custom formatting that you will use for future presentations, consider saving the presentation as a template. The advantage to saving your presentation as a template is that you cannot accidentally overwrite the presentation. When you open a template and then click the Save button on the Quick Access toolbar, the Save As dialog box automatically displays.

To save a presentation as a template, click the Office button and then click *Save As*. At the Save As dialog box, click the down-pointing arrow at the right side of the *Save as type* option and then click *PowerPoint Template (*.potx)* at the drop-down list. Type a name for the template in the *File name* text box and then click the Save button. The template is automatically saved in the C:\Program Files\Microsoft Office\Templates\ folder. If you want to save the template to another location, navigate to the desired folder in the Save As dialog box and then save the template.

To create a presentation based on a template, click the Office button and then click *New*. Recently used templates display in the *Recently Used Templates* section of the dialog box. If the desired template displays in this section, double-click the template (or click the template and then click the Create button). If the desired template does not display in the *Recently Used Templates* section, click the *My Templates* option in the *Templates* section. At the New Presentation dialog box with the My Templates tab selected, double-click the desired template.

If you created a template in a location other than the default, open a presentation based on the template by clicking the Office button and then clicking *New*. At the New Presentation dialog box, double-click the desired template in the *Recently Used Templates* section. If the template does not display in the section, click the *New from existing* option in the *Templates* section. At the New from Existing Presentation dialog box, navigate to the desired folder and then double-click the desired template.

After opening a presentation template, insert the desired slides and make any other formatting or design changes and then click the Save button on the Quick Access toolbar. At the Save As dialog box, type a name for the presentation and then click the Save button.

If you no longer need a template, delete the template at the New Presentation dialog box with the My Templates tab selected. To do this, click the Office button and then click *New*. At the New Presentation dialog box, click *My Templates* in the *Templates* section. At the New Presentation dialog box with the My Templates tab selected, right-click the template you want to delete and then click *Delete* at the shortcut menu. At the message asking if you want to delete the template, click the Yes button. If you saved a template to a location other than the default, delete the template in the same manner as you delete a presentation. To do this, display the Open dialog box, navigate to the desired folder, click the template you want to delete, click the Delete button on the dialog box toolbar, and then click Yes at the message that displays.

Project **2a** | **Saving a Presentation as a Template**

1. Open **TravelMaster.pptx**.
2. Click the Office button and then click *Save As* at the drop-down list.
3. At the Save As dialog box, click the down-pointing arrow at the right side of the *Save as type* option and then click *PowerPoint Template (*.potx)* at the drop-down list.

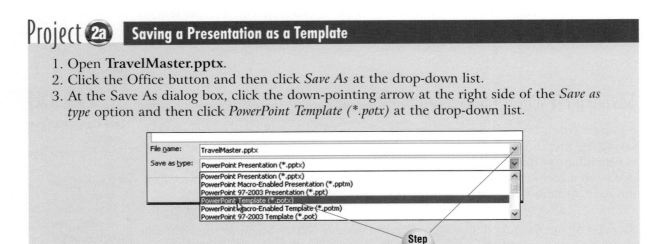

4. Navigate to the PowerPoint2007C6 folder on your storage medium.
5. Select the name that currently displays in the *File name* text box and then type
   XXXTravelTemplate (type your initials rather than the *XXX*).
6. Click the Save button.

7. Close the **XXXTravelTemplate.potx** template.
8. Open the template and save it as a presentation by completing the following steps:
   a. Click the Office button and then click *New* at the drop-down list.
   b. At the New Presentation dialog box, click the *New from existing* option in the *Templates* section.
   c. At the New from Existing Presentation dialog box, navigate to the PowerPoint2007C6 folder on your storage medium and then double-click *XXXTravelTemplate.potx*.
9. Save the presentation and name it **PP_C6_P2**.

Customizing the Handout Master

As you learned in Chapter 2, you can choose to print a presentation as individual slides, handouts, notes pages, or an outline. If you print a presentation as handouts or an outline, PowerPoint will automatically print the current date in the upper right corner of the page and the page number in the lower right corner. You can customize the handout with options in the Print Preview tab and you can also customize a handout in the Handout Master view. Display a presentation in Handout Master view by clicking the View tab and then clicking the Handout Master button in the Presentation Views group. With options in the Handout Master tab, you can move, resize, and format header and footer placeholders, change page orientation, and specify the number of slides you want printed on each page.

With buttons in the Page Setup group, you can display the Page Setup dialog box with options for changing the size and orientation of the handout page, changing the handout and/or slide orientation, and specifying the number of slides you want printed on the handout page. By default, a handout will contain a header, footer, date, and page number placeholder. You can remove any of these placeholders by removing the check mark before the placeholder option in the Placeholders group. For example, to remove the page number placeholder, click the *Page Number* check box in the Placeholders group to remove the check mark.

The Edit Theme group contains buttons for changing the theme color, font, and effects. Click the Themes button and the options in the drop-down gallery are dimmed, indicating that the themes are not available for the handout. If you apply a background style to the handout master, you can change theme colors by clicking the Colors button and then clicking the desired color theme at the drop-down gallery. Apply theme fonts by clicking the Fonts button and then clicking the desired fonts theme at the drop-down gallery.

Apply a background style to the handout page by clicking the Background Styles button in the Background group and then clicking one of the predesigned styles. You can also click the *Format Background* option and then make changes at the Format Background dialog box. Remove any background graphics by clicking the *Hide background graphics* check box to insert a check mark.

Project 2b Customizing the Handout Master

1. With **PP_C6_P2.pptx** open, click the New Slide button arrow and then click *Reuse Slides* at the drop-down list.
2. In the Reuse Slides task pane, click the Browse button, and then click the *Browse File* option at the drop-down list.
3. Navigate to the PowerPoint2007C6 folder on your storage medium and then double-click **ParisTour.pptx**.
4. Insert the second, third, fourth, and fifth slides from the Reuse Slides task pane into the current presentation.
5. Close the Reuse Slides task pane.
6. Edit the Title Slide Layout in Slide Master view by completing the following steps:
   a. Click the View tab and then click the Slide Master button.
   b. Click the second thumbnail in the slide thumbnail pane (*Title Slide Layout*).
   c. Click the Background Styles button in the Background group and then click *Format Background* at the drop-down list.
   d. At the Format Background dialog box, click the File button (displays below the *Insert from* text).
   e. At the Insert Picture dialog box, navigate to the PowerPoint2007C6 folder on your storage medium and then double-click **EiffelTower.jpg**.
   f. Click the Close button to close the Format Background dialog box.
   g. Select the text *Click to edit Master title style*, click the Home tab, click the Font Color button arrow, and then click *Turquoise, Accent 4, Lighter 60%* at the drop-down gallery.
   h. Click the Slide Master tab.
   i. Click the Close Master View button.
7. Make Slide 1 active, click in the text *Click to add title*, and then type Paris Tour.
8. Size and move the text placeholder so *Paris Tour* displays in a blue area on the slide (not over the tower).
9. Display each slide and then make adjustments to the position of clip art images and/or placeholders.
10. Make Slide 5 active and then create a new slide with the *Title Slide* layout. Type Call Greg at 555-4500.
11. Save **PP_C6_P2.pptx**.
12. Click the View tab and then click the Handout Master button in the Presentation Views group.

Step 12

13. Click the Handout Orientation button in the Page Setup group and then click *Landscape* at the drop-down list.
14. Click in the Header placeholder on the page and then type your first and last names.
15. Click in the Footer placeholder and then type Paris Tour.
16. Click the Background Styles button and then click *Style 10* at the drop-down list (second option from the left in the third row).
17. Click the Colors button in the Edit Theme group and then click *Metro* at the drop-down list.
18. Click the Fonts button in the Edit Theme group and then click *Foundry* at the drop-down list.
19. Edit the header text by completing the following steps:
    a. Click in the header placeholder and then click on any character in your name.
    b. Move the insertion point so it is positioned immediately right of the last character in your last name.
    c. Type a comma, press the spacebar, and then type your course number and title.
    d. Click in the handout page outside of any placeholder.
20. Click the Close Master View button.
21. Print the presentation as a handout with four slides per page. (The handout background style and the pictures will not print.)
22. Save **PP_C6_P2.pptx**

Step 14

Step 15

Customizing the Notes Master

You can insert notes in a presentation and then print the presentation as notes pages and the notes will print below the slide. If you want to insert or format text or other elements as notes on all slides in a presentation, consider making the changes in the Notes Master view. Display this view by clicking the View tab and then clicking the Notes Master button in the Presentation Views group. This displays a notes page along with the Notes Master tab. Many of the buttons and options in this tab are the same as the ones in the Handout Master tab.

Notes Master

Project 2c   Customizing the Notes Master

1. With **PP_C6_P2.pptx** open, click the View tab and then click the Notes Master button in the Presentation Views group.
2. Click the *Body* check box in the Placeholders group to remove the check mark.
3. Click the Fonts button in the Edit Theme group and then click *Foundry* at the drop-down list.
4. Click the Insert tab.

Step 2

5. Click the Text Box button in the Text group.
6. Click in the notes page below the slide.
7. Type Visit www.first-choice.emcp.net for a listing of all upcoming tours.
8. Size and position the text box below the slide.

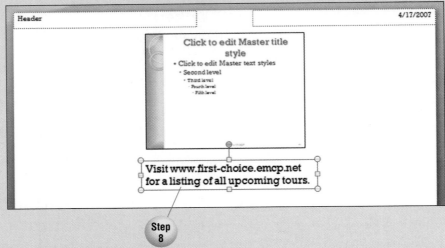

Step 8

9. Click the Insert tab and then click the Picture button in the Illustrations group.
10. At the Insert Picture dialog box, navigate to the PowerPoint2007C6 folder on your storage medium and then double-click *FCTLogo.jpg*.
11. Change the height of the logo to *0.5"*. (This changes the width to *1"*.)
12. Drag the logo so it is positioned below the text.

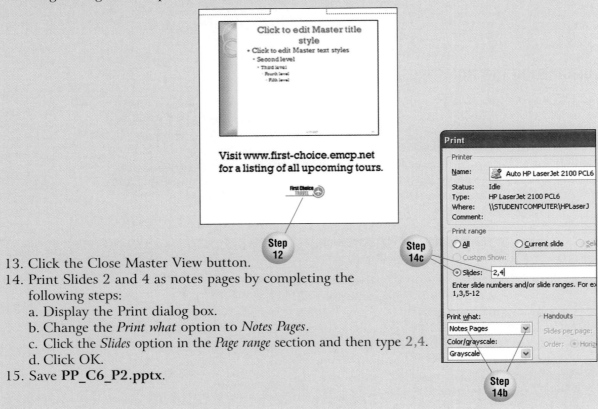

Step 12

Step 14c

Step 14b

13. Click the Close Master View button.
14. Print Slides 2 and 4 as notes pages by completing the following steps:
   a. Display the Print dialog box.
   b. Change the *Print what* option to *Notes Pages*.
   c. Click the *Slides* option in the *Page range* section and then type *2,4*.
   d. Click OK.
15. Save **PP_C6_P2.pptx**.

Using View Tab Options

You have used buttons in the Presentation Views group in the View tab to display your presentation in various views such as Normal, Slide Sorter, Slide Master, Handout Master, and Notes Master. In addition to viewing buttons, the View tab includes options for showing or hiding the ruler and gridlines; zooming in or out in the slide; viewing the slide in color, grayscale, or black and white; and working with windows including arranging, splitting, and switching windows.

Changing the Zoom

You can change the display size of the slide in the Slide pane or slides in the Slides/Outline pane with the Zoom button in the View tab and also with the Zoom slider bar located at the right side of the Status bar. Click the Zoom button in the View tab and the Zoom dialog box displays. Use options in this dialog box to increase or decrease the display size of slides in the Slides/Outline pane or the slide in the Slide pane. To change the zoom with the Zoom slider bar, use the mouse to drag the slider bar button to the left to decrease the display size or to the right to increase the display size. Click the button with the minus symbol that displays at the left side of the Zoom slider bar to decrease the display percentage or click the button with the plus symbol that displays at the right side of the Zoom slider bar to increase the display percentage. Click the percentage number that displays at the left side of the slider bar and the Zoom dialog box displays.

Project 2d Viewing a Presentation

1. With **PP_C6_P2.pptx** open, make Slide 1 active and then click the slide in the Slide pane.
2. Click the View tab.
3. Increase and decrease the zoom by completing the following steps:
   a. Click the Zoom button. (This displays the Zoom dialog box.)
   b. At the Zoom dialog box, click the *33%* option and then click OK.
   c. Click the Zoom button, click the *66%* option in the Zoom dialog box, and then click OK.
   d. Click the Slide 2 thumbnail in the Slides/Outline pane.
   e. Click the Zoom button, click the *66%* option in the Zoom dialog box, and then click OK. (Because the slide in the Slides/Outline pane was active, the percentage display changed for the thumbnails in the pane.)

Step 3b

   f. Position the mouse pointer on the Zoom slider bar button (located at the right side of the Status bar), drag the button to the right to increase the size of the slide in the Slide pane, and then drag the slider bar to the left to decrease the size of the slide.
   g. Click the percentage number that displays at the left side of the Zoom slider bar (this displays the Zoom dialog box).
   h. Click the *66%* option in the Zoom dialog box and then click OK.
   i. Click the Slide 3 thumbnail in the Slide/Outline pane.
   j. Click the Zoom button in the View tab.
   k. Type *45* in the *Percentage* text box and then click OK.

4. View the slides in grayscale by completing the following steps:
   a. Click the slide in the Slides pane to make it active and then click the Grayscale button in the Color/Grayscale group in the View tab.
   b. Click some of the buttons in the Grayscale tab to display the slides in varying grayscale options.
   c. Click the Back To Color View button.

Step 4a

5. View the slides in black and white by completing the following steps:
   a. Click the View tab and then click the Pure Black and White button in the Color/Grayscale group in the View tab.
   b. Click some of the buttons in the Black And White tab to display the slides in varying black and white options.
   c. Click the Back To Color View button.
6. Open a new window and arrange the windows by completing the following steps:
   a. Click the View tab and then click the New Window button in the Window group in the View tab. (This opens the same presentation in another window. Notice that the name on the title bar displays followed by a colon and the number 2.)

Step 6a

   b. Click the Arrange All button to arrange the two presentation windows. (This arranges the presentations as tiles with the title bar of each presentation visible as well as a portion of each presentation.)
   c. Click the Cascade button. (This arranges the two presentations with the presentations overlapping with the title bar for each presentation visible as well as a portion of the top presentation.)

Step 6d

   d. Click the Switch Windows button and then click the *PP_C6_P2.pptx:1* option at the drop-down list. (Notice the presentation name in the title bar now displays followed by a colon and the number 1.)
   e. Click the Close button that displays in the upper right corner of the currently active presentation. (The Close button contains an X.)
   f. Click the Maximize button that displays in the upper right corner of the presentation window. (The Maximize button displays immediately left of the Close button.)

7. With the View tab active, click the Grayscale button in the Color/Grayscale group and then click the Inverse Grayscale button in the Change Selected Object group.
8. Print the presentation as a handout with six slides per page.
9. Click the Back To Color View button.

Step 6f

10. Save and then close **PP_C6_P2.pptx**.

Project ③ Insert Action Buttons and Hyperlinks in a Job Search Presentation

You will open a job search presentation and then insert action buttons that display the next slide, the first slide, and another presentation. You will also create a hyperlink from text in a slide to a site on the Internet.

Inserting Action Buttons

Action buttons are drawn objects on a slide that have a routine attached to them which is activated when the viewer or the speaker clicks the button. For example, you could include an action button that displays the next slide in the presentation, a file in another program, or a specific Web page. Creating an action button is a two-step process. You draw the button using an Action Button shape in the Shapes button drop-down list and then you define the action that will take place with options in the Action Settings dialog box. You can customize an action button in the same manner as customizing a drawn object. When the viewer or speaker moves the mouse over an action button during a presentation, the pointer changes to a hand with a finger pointing upward to indicate clicking will result in an action.

To display the available action buttons, click the Insert tab and then click the Shapes button in the Illustrations group. Action buttons display at the bottom of the drop-down list. Hover the mouse pointer over a button and the name as well as the action it performs displays in a box above the button. The action attached to an action button occurs when you run the presentation and then click the button.

QUICK STEPS

Create Action Button
1. Make desired slide active.
2. Click Insert tab.
3. Click Shapes button.
4. Click desired action button.
5. Drag in slide to create button.
6. Make desired changes at Action Settings dialog box.

HINT
Apply formatting to an action button with options in the Drawing Tools Format tab.

Project ③a Inserting Action Buttons

1. Open **JobSearch.pptx** and then save the presentation with the name **PP_C6_P3**.
2. Make the following changes to the presentation:
   a. Display the presentation in Slide Master view.
   b. Click the top slide master in the slide thumbnail pane.
   c. Change the theme to *Verve*.
   d. Change the theme colors to *Metro*.
   e. Change the theme fonts to *Concourse*.
   f. Click the Insert tab and then click the Header & Footer button.
   g. At the Header and Footer dialog box with the Slide tab selected, click the *Date and time* check box and make sure *Update automatically* is selected.
   h. Click the *Slide number* check box to insert a check mark.
   i. Click the Notes and Handouts tab.
   j. Click the *Date and time* check box.
   k. Click the *Header* check box and then type the name of your school.
   l. Click the *Footer* check box and then type your first and last names.
   m. Click the Apply to All button.
   n. Click the Slide Master tab and then close Slide Master view.

3. Insert an action button in Slide 1 that will display the next slide by completing the following steps:
   a. Make Slide 1 active.
   b. Click the Insert tab and then click the Shapes button.
   c. At the drop-down list, click *Action Button: Forward or Next* (second option from the left) that displays at the bottom of the drop-down list.
   d. Move the crosshair pointer to the lower right corner of the slide and then drag to create a button as shown below.

Step 3d

Step 3b

Step 3c

   e. At the Action Settings dialog box, click OK. (The default setting is *Hyperlink to Next Slide*.)
   f. With the button selected, click the Home tab.
   g. Click the Quick Styles button in the Drawing group in the Drawing Tools Format tab and then click the *Colored Outline - Accent 1* option (second option from the left in the top row).

Step 3g

4. Insert an action button in Slide Master view that will display the next slide by completing the following steps:
   a. Display the presentation in Slide Master view.
   b. Click the top slide master thumbnail.

c. Click the Insert tab and then click the Shapes button.

d. At the drop-down list, click *Action Button: Forward or Next* (second option from the left).

e. Move the crosshair pointer to the lower right corner of the slide master and then drag to create a button as shown at the right.

Step
4e

f. At the Action Settings dialog box, click OK. (The default setting is *Hyperlink to Next Slide*.)

g. Click the Slide Master tab and then click the Close Master View button.

5. Make Slide 1 active and then run the presentation, clicking the action button to advance slides. When you click the action button on the last slide (Slide 9) nothing happens because it is the last slide. Press the Esc key to end the presentation.

6. Change the action button on Slide 9 by completing the following steps:

a. Make Slide 9 active.

b. Click the Insert tab and then click the Shapes button.

c. At the drop-down list, click *Action Button: Home* (fifth button from the left).

d. Drag to create a button on top of the previous action button.

e. At the Action Settings dialog box with the *Hyperlink to: First Slide* option selected, click OK.

f. Deselect the button.

7. Display Slide 1 in the Slide pane and then run the presentation. Navigate through the slide show by clicking the action button. When you click the action button on the last slide, the first slide displays. End the slide show by pressing the Esc key.

8. Print the presentation as a handout with six slides per page.

9. Save **PP_C6_P3.pptx**.

Step
6b

Step
6c

Linking to a Web Site

You can specify that an action button links to a Web site during a presentation. To do this, draw an Action button. At the Action Settings dialog box, click the *Hyperlink to* option, click the down-pointing arrow at the right side of the *Hyperlink to* option box, and then click *URL* at the drop-down list. At the Hyperlink To URL dialog box, type the Web address in the URL text box, and then click OK. Click OK to close the Action Settings dialog box. Other actions you can link to using the *Hyperlink to* drop-down list include: Next Slide, Previous Slide, First Slide, Last Slide, Last Slide Viewed, End Show, Custom Show, Slide, Other PowerPoint Presentation, and Other File.

Project **3b**   **Linking to a Web Site and Another Presentation**

1. With **PP_C6_P3.pptx** open, add an action button that will link to another presentation by completing the following steps:
   a. Make Slide 4 active.
   b. Click the Insert tab and then click the Shapes button.
   c. At the drop-down list, click *Action Button: Help* (second button from the right).
   d. Draw the action button to the left of the existing button located in the lower right corner of the slide.
   e. At the Action Settings dialog box, click the *Hyperlink to* option.
   f. Click the down-pointing arrow at the right side of the *Hyperlink to* option box and then click *Other PowerPoint Presentation* at the drop-down list. (You will need to scroll down the list to display this option.)

   g. At the Hyperlink to Other PowerPoint Presentation dialog box, navigate to the PowerPoint2007C6 folder on your storage medium and then double-click **Contacts.pptx**.
   h. At the Hyperlink to Slide dialog box, click OK.
   i. Click OK to close the Action Settings dialog box.
2. Add an action button that will link to a Web site address by completing the following steps:
   a. Make Slide 5 active.
   b. Click the Insert tab and then click the Shapes button.
   c. At the drop-down list, click *Action Button: Information* (sixth from the left).

d. Draw the action button to the left of the existing button located in the lower right corner of the slide.

e. At the Action Settings dialog box, click the *Hyperlink to* option.

f. Click the down-pointing arrow at the right of the *Hyperlink to* option box, and then click *URL* at the drop-down list.

g. At the Hyperlink To URL dialog box, type www.usajobs.gov and then click OK.

h. Click OK to close the Action Settings dialog box.

i. Click outside the button to deselect it.

3. Run the presentation by completing the following steps:

a. Make sure you are connected to the Internet.

b. Make Slide 1 active.

c. Click the Slide Show button in the view area on the Status bar.

d. Navigate through the slide show to Slide 4.

e. Click the action button in Slide 4 containing the question mark. (This displays Slide 1 of **Contacts.pptx**.)

f. Navigate through the three slides in **Contacts.pptx**. Continue clicking the mouse button until you return to Slide 4 of **PP_C6_P3.pptx**.

g. Display Slide 5 and then click the action button containing the lowercase *i*. (If you are connected to the Internet, the job site of the United States Federal Government displays.)

h. Click a few links at the Web site.

i. When you are finished viewing the Web site, close your Web browser.

j. Continue viewing the remainder of the presentation.

k. When Slide 1 displays, press the Esc key to end the presentation.

4. Print the presentation as a handout with nine slides per page.

5. Save **PP_C6_P3.pptx**.

Creating Hyperlinks

In Project 3b, you created hyperlinks using action buttons. You can also create hyperlinks with options at the Insert Hyperlink dialog box shown in Figure 6.2. To display this dialog box, select a key word or phrase in a slide, click the Insert tab, and then click the Hyperlink button in the Links group. You can also display the Insert Hyperlink dialog box with the keyboard shortcut Ctrl + K. At the Insert Hyperlink dialog box, type the Web address in the *Address* text box and then click OK.

QUICK STEPS

Create Hyperlink
1. Make desired slide active.
2. Select text.
3. Click Insert tab.
4. Click Hyperlink button.
5. Type Web address or file name in *Address* text box.

HINT

Hyperlinks are active when running the presentation, not when creating it.

Hyperlink

Figure 6.2 Insert Hyperlink Dialog Box

Type the Web address in this text box.

Project 3c Inserting Hyperlinks

1. With **PP_C6_P3.pptx** open, insert a new slide by completing the following steps:
   a. Make Slide 5 active.
   b. Click the Home tab.
   c. Click the New Slide button arrow and then click the *Title Slide* layout.
   d. Click the text *Click to add title* and then type Internet Job Resources.
   e. Click the text *Click to add subtitle* and then type Employment Resources, press Enter, and then type America's Job Bank.
2. Add a hyperlink to the Employment Resources site by completing the following steps:
   a. Select *Employment Resources* in Slide 6.
   b. Click the Insert tab and then click the Hyperlink button in the Links group.
   c. At the Insert Hyperlink dialog box, type www.employment-resources.com in the *Address* text box. (PowerPoint automatically inserts *http://* at the beginning of the address.)

Step 2c

   d. Click OK to close the Insert Hyperlink dialog box.

3. Add a hyperlink to the America's Job Bank site by completing the following steps:
   a. Select *America's Job Bank* in Slide 6.
   b. Click the Hyperlink button in the Links group in the Insert tab.
   c. At the Insert Hyperlink dialog box, type www.ajb.dni.us in the *Address* text box.
   d. Click OK to close the Insert Hyperlink dialog box.
4. Copy the action button in Slide 1 to Slide 6 by completing the following steps:
   a. Make Slide 1 active.
   b. Click the action button to select it.
   c. Press Ctrl + C to copy the button.
   d. Make Slide 6 active.
   e. Press Ctrl + V to paste the button.
5. Run the presentation by completing the following steps:
   a. Make sure you are connected to the Internet.
   b. Make Slide 1 active.
   c. Click the Slide Show button in the view area on the Status bar.
   d. Navigate through the slides. When you reach Slide 6, click the <u>Employment Resources</u> hyperlink.
   e. Scroll through the employment site and then close the Web browser.
   f. Click the <u>America's Job Bank</u> hyperlink.
   g. Scroll through the America's Job Bank site and then close the Web browser.
   h. Continue viewing the remainder of the presentation. (When Slide 1 displays, press the Esc key to end the presentation.)
6. Print only Slide 6 of the presentation.
7. Save and then close **PP_C6_P3.pptx**.

CHAPTER summary

- Display a presentation in Slide Master view by clicking the View tab and then clicking the Slide Master button in the Presentation Views group.
- Close Slide Master view by clicking the Close Master View button.
- In Slide Master view, slide master thumbnails display in the slide thumbnail pane.
- Use buttons in the Edit Theme group in the Slide Master tab to apply a design theme, theme colors, and theme fonts.
- Use buttons in the Background group in the Slide Master tab to apply a predesigned background style, display the Format Background dialog box with options for applying background styles, and hide background graphics.
- Delete a placeholder by clicking in the placeholder, clicking the placeholder border, and then pressing the Delete key.
- Delete a slide master in Slide Master view by clicking the desired slide master thumbnail in the slide thumbnail pane and then clicking the Delete button in the Edit Master group.
- In Slide Master view, you can display the Header and Footer dialog box with the Slide tab selected and then insert the date and time, slide number, and/or a footer. At the Header and Footer dialog box with the Notes and Handouts tab selected, you can insert the date and time, a header, page numbers, and/or a footer.
- Create a custom slide layout by clicking the Insert Layout button in the Edit Master group in the Slide Master tab. Rename the custom slide layout by clicking the Rename button in the Edit Master group, typing the desired name at the Rename Layout dialog box, and then clicking the Rename button.
- Insert placeholders in a slide layout or custom slide layout by clicking the Insert Placeholder button arrow in the Master Layout group and then clicking the desired placeholder at the drop-down list. To reinsert a deleted placeholder, click the Master Layout button, click the check box of the desired placeholder in the drop-down list, and then click OK to close the dialog box.
- In Slide Master view, create custom prompts by selecting generic text in a placeholder and then typing the desired text.
- Click the Insert Slide Master button in Slide Master view to insert a new slide master and associated slide layouts. You can also insert a new slide master by applying a design theme in Slide Master view.
- Save a presentation as a template by changing the *Save as type* option at the Save As dialog box to *PowerPoint Template (*.potx)*.
- To open a presentation based on a template, click the Office button and then click *New*. At the New Presentation dialog box, double-click the desired template in the *Recently Used Templates* section. If the desired template is not visible, click the *My Templates* option and, at the New Presentation dialog box with the My Templates tab selected, double-click the desired template.

- To open a presentation based on a template saved in a location other than the default location, double-click the desired template in the *Recently Used Templates* section of the New Presentation dialog box or click the *New from existing* option. At the New from Existing Presentation dialog box, navigate to the desired folder and then double-click the desired template.

- Delete a template by displaying the New Presentation dialog box with the My Templates tab selected, right-clicking the theme, and then clicking *Delete* at the shortcut menu. Delete a template saved in a location other than the default in the same manner as deleting a presentation.

- You can customize a handout with options in the Handout Master view. Display this view by clicking the View tab and then clicking the Handout Master button in the Presentation Views group.

- You can customize notes pages with options in the Notes Master view. Display this view by clicking the View tab and then clicking the Notes Master button in the Presentation Views group.

- In addition to changing the view, you can use buttons in the View tab to show/hide the ruler and/or gridlines; change the zoom display; view slides in color, grayscale, or black and white; and arrange, split, and switch windows.

- Action buttons are drawn objects in a slide that have a routine attached, such as displaying the next slide, the first slide, a Web site, or another PowerPoint presentation.

- Create an action button by clicking the Insert tab, clicking the Shapes button, clicking the desired button at the drop-down list, and then dragging in the slide to create the button.

- Create a hyperlink in a slide by selecting text in the slide, clicking the Insert tab, and then clicking the Hyperlink button in the Links group. At the Insert Hyperlink dialog box, type the Web site address or file location and then click OK.

COMMANDS review

FEATURE	RIBBON TAB, GROUP	BUTTON, OPTION	KEYBOARD SHORTCUT
Slide Master view	View, Presentation Views		
New Presentation dialog box		, New	
New Presentation dialog box with My Templates tab selected		, New, My Templates	
Handout Master view	View, Presentation Views		
Notes Master view	View, Presentation Views		
Action buttons	Insert, Illustrations		
Insert Hyperlink dialog box	Insert, Links		Ctrl + K

CONCEPTS check

Test Your Knowledge

Completion: In the space provided at the right, indicate the correct term, symbol, or command.

1. To display a presentation in Slide Master view, click this tab and then click the Slide Master button.

   _____

2. Click this button to close Slide Master view.

   _____

3. This group in the Slide Master tab contains buttons for applying a theme, theme colors, and theme fonts.

   _____

4. This dialog box with the Slide tab selected contains options for inserting the date and time, a slide number, and a footer.

   _____

5. To create a new slide layout in Slide Master view, click this button in the Edit Master group.

   _____

6. To save a presentation as a template, choose this option at the *Save as type* drop-down list at the Save As dialog box.

   _____

7. Delete a template at the New Presentation dialog box with this tab selected.

   _____

8. Change to this view to customize handouts.

   _____

9. Change to this view to customize notes pages.

   _____

10. The Zoom slider bar is located at the right side of this bar.

    _____

11. Click this button to display a drop-down list that includes action buttons.

    _____

12. Insert this action button in a slide to display the next slide in the presentation.

    _____

13. Insert this action button in a slide to display the first slide in the presentation.

    _____

14. This is the keyboard shortcut to display the Insert Hyperlink dialog box.

    _____

SKILLS check

Demonstrate Your Proficiency

1 FORMAT A PRESENTATION IN SLIDE MASTER VIEW AND THEN SAVE THE PRESENTATION AS A TEMPLATE

1. Display a blank presentation, click the View tab, and then click the Slide Master button.
2. Click the top slide master thumbnail in the slide thumbnail pane.
3. Apply the *Urban* theme, change the theme colors to *Paper*, and change the theme fonts to *Flow*.
4. Apply the *Style 2* background style.
5. Select the text *Click to edit Master title style*, click the Home tab, change the font color to Olive Green, Accent 1, Darker 50%, and then turn on bold.
6. Select the text *Second level* in the slide master, click the Home tab, and then change the font color to Orange, Accent 2, Darker 50%.
7. Insert the **WELogo.jpg** in the master slide, change the height of the logo to 0.5″, and drag the logo to the lower left corner of the slide master. (With the logo selected, change the background of the logo to transparent by clicking the Recolor button in the Picture Tools Format tab, clicking the *Set Transparent Color* option, and then clicking on a white portion of the logo. This removes the white background so the yellow slide background displays.)
8. Select the date placeholder and then move the placeholder to the lower right corner of the slide.
9. Select the footer placeholder and then drag it down to the lower right corner of the slide immediately left of the date placeholder.
10. Click the Slide Master tab.
11. Click the first slide layout below the slide master.
12. Click the *Footers* check box in the Master Layout group to remove the footer and date placeholders.
13. Select and then delete the slide layouts from the third layout below the slide master (the *Section Header Layout*) to the last layout.
14. Preserve the slide masters by clicking the top slide master in the slide thumbnail pane, clicking the Slide Master tab, and then clicking the Preserve button in the Edit Master group.
15. Click the Close Master View button.
16. Save the presentation as a template to the PowerPoint2007C6 folder on your storage medium and name the template **XXXPublicationTemplate** (use your initials in place of the *XXX*).
17. Close **XXXPublicationTemplate.potx**.

Assessment

2 USE A TEMPLATE TO CREATE A PUBLICATIONS PRESENTATION

1. Open **XXXPublicationTemplate.potx**. (To do this, display the New Presentation dialog box and then click *New from existing*. At the New from Existing Presentation dialog box, navigate to the PowerPoint2007C6 folder on your storage medium, and then double-click ***XXXPublicationTemplate.potx***.)
2. Save the presentation and name it **PP_C6_A2**.
3. Click the *Click to add title* text in the current slide and then type Worldwide Enterprises.
4. Click the *Click to add subtitle* text and then type Company Publications.
5. Display the Reuse Slides task pane, browse to PowerPoint2007C6 folder on your storage medium, and then double-click **Publications.pptx**.
6. Insert the second, third, fourth, and fifth slides from the Reuse Slides task pane into the current presentation and then close the task pane.
7. Insert a second slide master with the following specifications:
   a. Display the presentation in Slide Master view.
   b. Click in the slide thumbnail pane below the bottom slide layout.
   c. Change the theme to *Foundry*, the colors to *Paper*, and the fonts to *Flow*.
   d. Apply the *Style 2* background style.
   e. Select the *Click to edit Master title style* text, click the Home tab, turn off text shadow, turn on bold, and change to left alignment.
   f. Select the text *Second level* and then change the font color to Orange, Accent 2, Darker 50%.
   g. Click the Slide Master tab.
8. Select and then delete slide layouts from the third layout (*Section Header Layout*) below the new slide master to the last layout.
9. Insert headers, footers, slide numbers, and dates with the following specifications:
   a. Click the Insert tab, display the Header and Footer dialog box with the Slide tab selected, insert the date and time to update automatically (choose a format that inserts the date and time in figures), and insert slide numbers.
   b. Click the Notes and Handouts tab, insert the date and time to update automatically (choose a format that inserts the date and time in figures), insert a header that prints your first and last names, insert a footer that prints *Worldwide Enterprises*, and then click the Apply to All button.
   c. Click the top slide master in the slide thumbnail pane and then increase the width of the date and time placeholder so the date and time display on one line.
10. Close Slide Master view.
11. Make Slide 5 active and then insert a new slide using the new Foundry Title Slide layout and then type *Worldwide Enterprises* as the title and *Preparing the Company Newsletter* as the subtitle.
12. Insert the following text in slides using the Foundry Title and Content layout:
    Slide 7   Preparing the Newsletter

    - Maintain consistent elements from issue to issue
    - Consider the following when designing the newsletter
      - Focus
      - Balance
      - White space
      - Directional flow

Slide 8   Preparing the Newsletter
- Choose paper size and weight
- Determine margins
- Specify column layout
- Choose nameplate layout and format
- Specify heading format
- Determine newsletter colors

13. Select the bulleted text in Slide 8 and then change the line spacing to *1.5*.
14. Make Slide 7 active and then insert a clip art image related to newsletters.
15. Insert a transition and sound of your choosing to the presentation.
16. Run the presentation.
17. Print the presentation as a handout with four slides per page.
18. Save and then close **PP_C6_A2.pptx**.

Assessment

3 INSERT ACTION BUTTONS IN A GARDENING PRESENTATION

1. Open **PerennialsPresentation.pptx** and then save the presentation with the name **PP_C6_A3**.
2. Make Slide 1 active and then insert an action button in the lower right corner of the slide that displays the next slide.
3. Display the presentation in Slide Master view, click the top slide master in the slide thumbnail pane, create an action button in the lower right corner of the slide that displays the next slide, and then close Slide Master view.
4. Make Slide 8 active and then create an action button that displays the first slide in the presentation.
5. Make Slide 2 active and then insert a second action button in the lower right corner that will link to the presentation **MaintenancePresentation.pptx** (located in the PowerPoint2007C6 folder on your storage medium).
6. Display Slide 8 and then make the following changes:
   a. Delete text *Better Homes and Gardens*® and then type Organic Gardening®.
   b. Select *Organic Gardening*® and then create a hyperlink with the text to the Web site www.organicgardening.com.
7. Make sure you are connected to the Internet and then run the presentation beginning with Slide 1. Navigate through the slide show by clicking the next action button and display the connected presentation by clicking the information action button. At Slide 8, click the *Organic Gardening*® hyperlink (if you are connected to the Internet). Scroll through the site and click a couple different hyperlinks that interest you. After viewing a few Web pages in the magazine, close your Web browser. When you click the action button on the last slide, the first slide displays. End the slide show by pressing the Esc key.
8. Print the presentation as a handout with four slides per page.
9. Save and then close **PP_C6_A3.pptx**.

4 CREATE AN ACTION BUTTONS PRESENTATION

1. In this chapter, you learned to insert a number of action buttons in a slide. Experiment with the other action buttons (click the Insert tab, click the Shapes button, and then point to Action Buttons) and then prepare a PowerPoint presentation with the following specifications:

   a. The first slide should contain the title of your presentation.

   b. Include one slide for each of the eleven action buttons that includes the specific name as well as an explanation of the button.

   c. Apply a design theme of your choosing to the presentation.

2. Save the presentation and name it **PP_C6_A4**.

3. Print the presentation as a handout with six slides per page.

4. Close **PP_C6_A4.pptx**.

CASE study

Apply Your Skills

Part 1

You are the training manager for Anchor Corporation and one of your job responsibilities is conducting new employee orientations. You decide that a PowerPoint presentation will help you deliver information to new employees during the orientation. You know that you will be creating other PowerPoint presentations so you decide to create a template. Create a presentation template with attractive formatting that includes a design theme, theme colors, theme fonts, and include an anchor clip art image in the lower left corner of most of the slides. Apply any other formatting or design elements to increase the appeal of the presentation. Save the presentation as a template on your storage medium with the name **AnchorTemplate** and make sure it contains the file extensions *.potx*. Close the template.

Part 2

You have a document with notes about information on types of employment appointments, employee performance, and compensation. Open the Word document named **AnchorNewEmployees.docx** and then use the information to prepare a presentation using the **AnchorTemplate.potx** template. Save the completed presentation with the name **PP_C6_CS_P2** and make sure it has the file extension *.pptx*. Apply a transition and sound to each slide in the presentation, print the presentation as a handout, and then close the presentation.

Part 3

Open the Word document named **AnchorGuidelines.docx** and then use the information in the document to prepare a presentation using the **AnchorTemplate.potx** template. Save the completed presentation with the name **PP_C6_CS_P3** and make sure it contains the file extension *.pptx*. Apply a transition and sound to each slide in the presentation, print the presentation as a handout, and then close the presentation.

During the new employee presentation you want to refer to a chart of employee classifications, so you decide to create a link to an Excel spreadsheet. Open the **PP_C6_CS_P2.pptx** presentation and then create a new slide that contains a hyperlink to the Excel workbook named **ACClassifications.xlsx**. Run the presentation, link to the Excel chart, and then continue running the remaining slides in the presentation. Print only the new slide and then save and close **PP_C6_CS_P2.pptx**.

The information you used to create the **PP_C6_CS_P3.pptx** presentation was taken from a document that is part of a new employee handbook. You decide that you want to create a link in your presentation to the Word document to show employees the additional information in the document. Create a new slide in the **PP_C6_CS_P3.pptx** presentation that includes an action button that links to the Word document named **ComputerGuidelines.docx**. Include other action buttons for navigating in the presentation. Run the presentation, link to the Word document, and then continue running the remaining slides in the presentation. Print only the new slide and then save and close **PP_C6_CS_P3.pptx**.

Applying Custom Animation and Setting Up Shows

PERFORMANCE OBJECTIVES

Upon successful completion of Chapter 7, you will be able to:

- Apply built-in animations
- Modify and remove animations
- Create custom animations
- Apply custom animation effects
- Modify and remove animation effects
- Animate shapes, images, SmartArt, and chart elements
- Apply a build
- Draw motion paths
- Set up a slide show
- Set rehearse timings for slides
- Hide slides
- Create, run, edit, and print a custom show
- Insert and customize sounds and movie clips

Tutorial 7.1
Enhancing Presentations
Tutorial 7.2
Using Special Features
Tutorial 7.3
Maintaining Presentations and
Creating Custom Shows

Animation or movement will add visual appeal and interest to your presentation when used appropriately. PowerPoint provides a number of built-in animation effects as well as custom animation effects you can apply to elements in a slide. You can apply animation effects with options in the Animations tab and with options in the Custom Animation task pane. In this chapter, you will learn how to apply built-in and custom animation effects as well as how to insert sound and media clips to create dynamic presentations.

In some situations, you may want to prepare a self-running presentation where the presentation runs on a continuous loop. You can customize a presentation to run continuously and also rehearse the time you want each slide to remain on the screen. You can also create a custom slide show to present only specific slides in a presentation. In this chapter, you will learn how to prepare self-running presentations and how to create and edit custom slide shows.

Note: Before beginning computer projects, copy to your storage medium the PowerPoint2007C7 folder from the PowerPoint2007 folder on the CD that accompanies this textbook and then make PowerPoint2007C7 the active folder.

Project 1 Apply Animation Effects to Elements in Marketing Presentation

You will open a marketing presentation and then apply built-in animation effects to the title slide and apply animation effects in Slide Master view to the remaining slides. You will remove some of the animation effects and then apply custom animation effects to elements in slides such as entrance and emphasis effects.

QUICK STEPS

Apply Built-in Animation
1. Click desired item.
2. Click Animations tab.
3. Click *Animate* option.
4. Click desired animation at drop-down list.

HINT

You can animate text, objects, graphics, SmartArt diagrams, charts, hyperlinks, and sound.

HINT

When you apply an animation effect to an object in a slide, an animation icon displays below the slide number in the Slides/Outline pane.

Preview

Applying Built-in Animation Effects

You can animate items such as text or objects in a slide to add visual interest to your presentation. Displaying items one at a time helps your audience focus on a single topic or point as you present it. PowerPoint includes a number of built-in animations you can apply to items in a slide. These built-in animations can be modified to fit your specific needs. You may want items to appear one right after the other or in groups. You can control the direction that the item comes from and the rate of speed. Try not to overwhelm your audience with too much animation. In general, you want them to remember the content of your presentation and not the visual effects.

To animate an item, click the desired item, click the Animations tab, and then click the *Animate* option in the Animations group. At the drop-down list that displays, click the desired animation. Built-in animations are grouped into three categories—*Fade*, *Wipe*, and *Fly In*. Depending on the item selected, each group may contain a list of specific items. For example, if you select a placeholder containing bulleted text, each group contains the choices *All At Once* and *By 1st Level Paragraphs*. If you select an object such as a chart, each group contains choices for animating specific chart items. If you want to apply animation effects to slides created with the same layout, apply the effect in Slide Master view.

If you want to see the animation effects in your slide without running the presentation, click the Preview button in the Animations tab. Click this button and the animation effect you applied to the active slide displays on the slide in the Slide pane. When you apply animation effects to items in a slide, an animation icon displays below the slide number in the Slides/Outline pane.

Project 1a Applying Built-in Animations

1. Open **MarketingPresentation.pptx** and save the presentation with the name **PP_C7_P1**.
2. Make sure Slide 1 is active and then apply built-in animations to the title and subtitle by completing the following steps:
   a. Click in the title *CORNERSTONE SYSTEMS*.
   b. Click the Animations tab.
   c. Click the down-pointing arrow at the right of the *Animate* option in the Animations group and then click *Fade* at the drop-down list. (If you hover the mouse pointer over the option, the slide in the Slide pane will preview the animation.)

   d. Click in the subtitle *Marketing Report*.
   e. Click the down-pointing arrow at the right side of the *Animate* option and then click *All At Once* in the *Fade* group at the drop-down list.
   f. Click the Preview button in the Animations tab to see the animation effect in the slide in the Slide pane.

3. Apply animations to Slides 2 through 4 in Slide Master view by completing the following steps:
   a. Click the View tab and then click the Slide Master button in the Presentation Views group.
   b. Click the third slide master layout in the slide thumbnail pane (*Title and Content Layout*).
   c. Click in the text *Click to edit Master title style*.
   d. Click the Animations tab, click the down-pointing arrow at the right side of the *Animate* option, and then click *Fly In* at the drop-down list.
   e. Click in the bulleted text.
   f. Click the down-pointing arrow at the right side of the *Animate* option and then click *By 1st Level Paragraphs* in the *Fly In* group in the drop-down list.
   g. Click the Slide Master tab and then click the Close Master View button.

4. Make Slide 1 active and then run the presentation. Click the mouse button to advance items in slides and to advance slides. Notice how the bulleted text in Slides 2 through 4 displays one item at a time.
5. Save **PP_C7_P1.pptx**.

Removing Built-in Animations

Remove Animation
1. Click desired item.
2. Click Animations tab.
3. Click *Animate* option.
4. Click *No Animation.*

Remove the built-in animation effect from an item by clicking the item, clicking the down-pointing arrow at the right side of the *Animate* option, and then clicking *No animation* at the drop-down list. If you applied animation in Slide Master view, display the presentation in Slide Master view, click the slide master layout containing the animation, click the desired item, and then remove the animation.

Project 1b Removing Animations

1. With **PP_C7_P1.pptx** open, make Slide 1 active and then remove the animation from the title and subtitle by completing the following steps:
   a. Click the title *CORNERSTONE SYSTEMS*.
   b. Click the Animations tab.
   c. Click the down-pointing arrow at the right of the *Animate* option in the Animations group and then click *No Animation*.
   d. Click the subtitle *Marketing Report*, click the down-pointing arrow at the right side of the *Animate* option, and then click *No Animation*.
2. Remove the animation effect for Slides 2 through 4 by completing the following steps:
   a. Click the View tab and then click the Slide Master button.
   b. Click the third slide master layout in the slide thumbnail pane (*Title and Content Layout*).
   c. Click in the text *Click to edit Master title style*.
   d. Click the Animations tab, click the down-pointing arrow at the right side of the *Animate* option drop-down list, and then click *No Animation* at the drop-down list.
   e. Click the Slide Master tab and then click the Close Master View button.
3. Make Slide 1 active and then run the presentation.
4. Save **PP_C7_P1.pptx**.

Step 1c

[Screen illustration: Home, Insert, Design, Animations tabs; Animate: Fade; drop-down list showing No Animation, Fade, Wipe, Fly In, Custom Animation...; Preview, Custom A..., Slides, Outline]

Applying Custom Animations

Display Custom Animation Task Pane
1. Click Animations tab.
2. Click Custom Animation button.

If you want to customize animation effects and have more control over the order of animations in a slide, use options at the Custom Animation task pane shown in Figure 7.1. Display this task pane by clicking the Custom Animation button in the Animations group in the Animations tab. You can also display the Custom Animation task pane by clicking the down-pointing arrow at the right side of the *Animate* option in the Animations tab and then clicking *Custom Animation*.

Figure 7.1 Custom Animation Task Pane

Click the Add Effect button to apply entrance, emphasis, exit and motion paths animation effects to selected item.

Use options in the Modify section to customize animation effects. The options vary depending on the animation effect applied to the selected item.

When an animation effect is applied to an item, the item displays in this list box.

Click the Play button to preview the animation effects applied to the current slide.

Applying Effects

The Add Effect button in the Custom Animation task pane provides four types of effects you can apply to custom animation settings for items. You can apply an effect as an item *enters* the slide and also as an item *exits* the slide. You can apply *emphasis* to an item that is already visible, and you can also apply a *motion path* to an item that will cause it to move in a specific pattern or even off the slide.

To apply an entrance effect to an item, click the Add Effect button in the Custom Animation task pane, point to *Entrance*, and then click one of the options that displays in the side menu. The list of options in the side menu varies and displays the most recently used options. An animation icon displays at the left side of the option in the side menu and provides a visual representation of the animation effect. Click the *More Effects* option at the bottom of the side menu and the Add Entrance Effect dialog box displays containing additional entrance effects.

Click the Add Effect button, point to *Exit*, and a side menu displays with the same options as the side menu for *Entrance* effects. Click the *More Effects* option at the bottom of the side menu and the Add Exit Effect dialog box displays containing additional exit effects.

Click the Add Effect button, point to *Emphasis* and a side menu displays with options to emphasize the text or item. The options in the side menu vary depending on the most recently used options. If a text item is selected, options display for changing the font, font style, or font size and growing, shrinking, or spinning the text. If an object item is selected, options such as grow, shrink, or spin display.

QUICK STEPS

Apply Entrance Effect
1. Click desired item.
2. Click Add Effect button in Custom Animation task pane.
3. Point to *Entrance*.
4. Click desired option at side menu.

Apply Exit Effect
1. Click desired item.
2. Click Add Effect button in Custom Animation task pane.
3. Point to *Exit*.
4. Click desired option at side menu.

Apply Emphasis Effect
1. Click desired item.
2. Click Add Effect button in Custom Animation task pane.
3. Point to *Emphasis*.
4. Click desired option at side menu.

HINT

You can apply both an entrance and an exit animation effect to an object in a slide.

Apply Motion Path
1. Click desired item.
2. Click Add Effect button in Custom Animation task pane.
3. Point to *Motion Paths*.
4. Click desired option at side menu.

Click the *More Effects* option at the bottom of the side menu and the Add Emphasis Effect dialog box displays containing additional emphasis effects.

With options from the *Motion Paths* side menu, you can specify a path you want an item to follow as it is appearing on the slide. Click the Add Effect button, point to *Motion Paths*, and a side menu displays with options for drawing a motion path in a specific direction. For example, if you want an item to move left when running the presentation, click the Add Effect button, point to *Motion Paths*, and then click *Left* at the side menu. Choose the *Freeform* option if you want to draw your own path in the slide. Click the *More Motion Paths* option at the bottom of the side menu and the Add Motion Path dialog box displays with additional motion options.

When you apply an animation effect or effects to a slide, you can play the animations by clicking the Play button located toward the bottom of the task pane. The animation effect displays in the slide in the Slide pane and a time indicator displays along the bottom of the task pane with a vertical line indicating the progression of time (in seconds). You can begin a presentation from the task pane by clicking the Slide Show button located toward the bottom of the task pane.

Project 1c   Applying Animation Effects

1. With **PP_C7_P1.pptx** open, apply an animation effect to the title and subtitle in Slide 1 by completing the following steps:
   a. Make Slide 1 active.
   b. Click the Animations tab and then click the Custom Animation button in the Animations group. (This displays the Custom Animation task pane at the right side of the screen. The task pane list box should be empty.)
   c. Click the title *CORNERSTONE SYSTEMS*.
   d. Click the Add Effect button, point to *Entrance*, and then click an option in the side menu (you choose the option). (The list of options varies and displays the most recently used options.)
   e. Click the subtitle *Marketing Report*.
   f. Click the Add Effect button, point to *Exit*, and then click an option in the side menu.

Step 1b

2. Apply an animation effect to the title of Slides 2 through 4 by completing the following steps:
   a. Click the View tab and then click the Slide Master button.
   b. Click the third slide master layout in the slide thumbnail pane (*Title and Content Layout*).
   c. Click in the bulleted text.
   d. Click the Animations tab, click the down-pointing arrow at the right side of the *Animate* option, and then click *No Animation* at the drop-down list.
   e. Click in the text *Click to edit Master title style*.
   f. Click the Add Effect button in the Custom Animation task pane, point to *Emphasis*, and then click *Spin*. (The location of the *Spin* option may vary.)

Step 2f

g. Click in the bulleted text, click the Add Effect button, point to *Entrance*, and then click an option in the side menu.

h. Click the Slide Master tab and then click the Close Master View button.

3. Click the Play button located toward the bottom of the Custom Animation task pane to view the animation effects. (Notice the time indicator along the bottom of the task pane and the vertical line indicating the progression of time.)

Step 3

4. Make Slide 1 active and then run the presentation by clicking the Slide Show button located toward the bottom of the task pane. Click the mouse button to begin animation effects and to advance slides.

5. Close the Custom Animation task pane.

6. Save **PP_C7_P1.pptx**.

Modifying Animation Effects

When you apply an effect to an item, modification options display in the task pane below the Add Effect button. The options that display vary depending on the effect applied. For example, if you apply an entrance effect, the Modify section of the task pane displays with options for customizing when the item starts animating, the direction of the animation, and the speed of the animation. Change a modification option by clicking the down-pointing arrow at the right side of the option and then clicking the desired option at the drop-down list.

When you apply an animation effect to an item, the item name or description displays in the task pane list box. Hover the mouse pointer over an item and a description of the animation effect applied to the item displays in a box above the item. If you click the down-pointing arrow at the right side of an item in the list box, a drop-down list displays with options for modifying or customizing the animation effect. For example, you can use options at the drop-down list to specify when you want the item inserted in the slide. Generally, items display in a slide when you click the mouse button. You can change this to *With Previous* or *With Next* and the item will appear on the slide with the previous item or the next item.

Changing Animation Effects

When you apply an effect to an item using the Add Effect button in the Custom Animation task pane, the item name or description displays in the task pane list box. If you want to change the animation effect applied to an item, click the item in the list box, click the Change button (previously the Add Effect button), and then apply the desired entrance, emphasis, exit, or motion path effect.

Removing an Animation Effect

If you want to remove an animation effect from an item, click the item in the task pane list box and then click the Remove button that displays toward the top of the task pane. You can also remove animation from an item by clicking the down-pointing arrow at the right side of the item in the list box and then clicking *Remove* at the drop-down list.

QUICK STEPS

Change Animation Effect
1. Click item in Custom Animation task pane list box.
2. Click Change button.
3. Apply animation.

Remove Animation Effect
1. Click item in Custom Animation task pane list box.
2. Click Remove button.

QUICK STEPS

Reorder Animation Items
1. Click item in Custom Animation task pane list box.
2. Click Up Re-Order arrow or Down Re-Order arrow.

Reordering Items

When you apply an effect to an item using the Add Effect button in the Custom Animation task pane, the item name or description displays in the task pane list box preceded by a number. This number indicates the order in which items will appear in the slide. When more than one item displays in the list box, you can change the order of an item by clicking the item in the list box and then clicking the Up Re-Order arrow or the Down Re-Order arrow located below the task pane list box.

Project 1d Removing, Modifying, and Reordering Animation Effects

1. With **PP_C7_P1.pptx** open, make Slide 1 active.
2. Modify the start setting for the slide title animation effect by completing the following steps:
   a. Display the Custom Animation task pane by clicking the Animations tab and then clicking the Custom Animation button.
   b. Click the Title 1 item that displays in the task pane list box.
   c. Click the down-pointing arrow at the right side of the *Start* option in the *Modify* section of the task pane and then click *With Previous*. (At this setting the title animation effect will begin as soon as the slide displays without you having to click the mouse button. Notice that the number 1 preceding the item in the list box changed to a zero.)

3. Change the animation effect to the subtitle and modify the animation effect by completing the following steps:
   a. Click the Marketing Report item in the task pane list box.
   b. Click the Change button in the task pane, point to *Emphasis*, and then click *Grow/Shrink* at the side menu. (The location of the *Grow/Shrink* may vary.)
   c. Click the down-pointing arrow at the right side of the *Start* option in the *Modify* section of the task pane and then click *With Previous*.
   d. Click the down-pointing arrow at the right side of the *Speed* option and then click *Fast*.

4. Remove animations from slides in Slide Master view by completing the following steps:
   a. Click the View tab and then click the Slide Master button.
   b. Click the third slide master layout in the slide thumbnail pane (*Title and Content Layout*).

c. Click the Title 1 item in the task pane list box and then click the Remove button.

d. Click the content placeholder item in the task pane list box and then click the Remove button.

e. Click the Slide Master tab and then click the Close Master View button.

5. Make Slide 2 active and then apply and customize animation effects by completing the following steps:

a. Click the title *Department Reports*.

b. Click the Add Effect button in the Custom Animation task pane, point to *Entrance* and then click *More Effects*.

c. At the Add Entrance Effect dialog box, scroll down the list box and then click *Spiral In* in the *Exciting* section.

d. Click OK to close the dialog box.

e. Click in the bulleted text.

f. Click the Add Effect button, point to *Entrance*, and then click an option in the side menu.

g. Click the clip art image.

h. Click the Add Effect button, point to *Entrance*, and then click an option in the side menu.

6. Click the Play button to view the animation effects.

7. After viewing the animation effects, you decide that you want the clip art to animate before the bulleted text and you want the animation effects to begin with the previous animation (instead of a mouse click). With Slide 2 active, complete the following steps:

a. Click the Picture 3 item in the task pane list box.

b. Click the Up Re-Order button located toward the bottom of the task pane. (This moves the *Picture 3* item between the Title 1 and the content placeholder items.)

c. Click the down-pointing arrow at the right side of the *Start* option in the *Modify* section of the task pane and then click *With Previous*.

d. Click the Title 1 item in the task pane list box, click the down-pointing arrow at the right side of the item, and then click *Start With Previous* at the drop-down list.

8. Apply to Slides 3 and 4 animation effects similar to those you applied to Slide 2.

9. Make Slide 1 active and then run the presentation. After running the presentation, make any changes or modifications to animation effects.

10. Close the Custom Animation task pane.

11. Save and then close **PP_C7_P1.pptx**.

Step 7d

Project ② Apply Custom Animation Effects to Elements in Slides in an Online Learning Presentation

You will open an online learning presentation and then apply animation effects to shapes, a clip art image, elements in SmartArt graphics, and elements in a chart. You will also apply a build to bulleted text that dims a previous point and draw a motion path in a slide.

Animating Shapes and Images

You can animate individual shapes or images such as clip art images in a slide in the same manner as animating a title or text content placeholder. You can select more than one shape and then apply the same animation effect to the shapes. To select more than one shape, click the first shape, hold down the Shift key, and then click any additional shapes.

Project ②a   Animating Shapes and a Clip Art Image

1. Open **OnlineLearning.pptx** and then save the presentation and name it **PP_C7_P2**.

2. Make Slide 8 active (this slide contains one large object with three smaller objects hidden behind it) and then animate objects and apply exit effects by completing the following steps:

   a. Display the Custom Animation task pane by clicking the Animations tab and then clicking the Custom Animation button.

   b. Click the large object in the slide.

   c. Click the Add Effect button, point to *Exit*, and then click the *More Effects* option.

   d. At the Add Exit Effect dialog box, click the *Spiral Out* option in the *Exciting* section, watch the animation effect in the slide, and then click OK.

   e. With the large object selected, drag it down the slide to display a portion of the three objects behind.

f. Click the small object at the left, click the Add Effect button, point to *Entrance*, and then click *More Effects*.

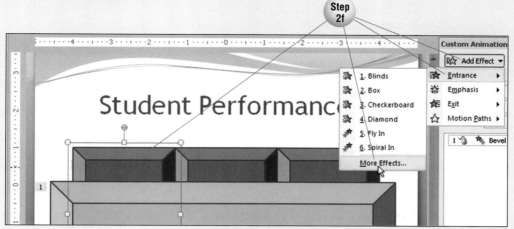

g. At the Add Entrance Effect dialog box, click *Spinner* in the *Moderate* section, and then click OK.
h. Select the middle object, hold down the Shift key, and then click the object at the right. (This selects both objects.)
i. Click the Add Effect button, point to *Entrance*, and then click *Spinner* at the side menu. (Notice that the two objects are numbered *3* in the task pane list box and are set to enter the slide at the same time. You will change this in the next step.)
j. Click the bottom item in the task pane list box, click the down-pointing arrow at the right side of the item, and then click *Start On Click* at the drop-down list.
k. Apply emphasis to the middle object by clicking the middle object, clicking the Add Effect button, pointing to *Emphasis*, and then clicking *Grow/Shrink* at the side menu. (The bottom two items in the task pane list box are the two effects applied to the middle object. Notice that the animation icons are different, indicating different effects. Hover the mouse pointer over an item to view a description of the animation effect.)

l. Reposition the large object over the three smaller objects.
m. Click the Play button to play the animation effects in the slide.

3. Make Slide 9 active and apply and modify animation effects and change animation order by completing the following steps:

a. Apply an entrance animation effect of your choosing to the text box containing the text *Online learning continues to evolve!*

b. Apply an entrance animation effect of your choosing to the text box containing the text *Stay tuned!*

c. Click the clip art image to select it.

d. Apply the *Spin* emphasis animation effect.

e. Click the down-pointing arrow at the right side of the *Amount* option in the *Modify* section of the task pane and then click *Two Spins* at the drop-down list.

f. Click the down-pointing arrow at the right side of the *Speed* option and then click *Fast*.

g. Click once on the Up Re-Order Arrow (located toward the bottom of the task pane). This moves the clip art image item in the list box above the *Stay tuned!* text box item.

h. Click the Play button to play the animation effects in the slide.

4. Save **PP_C7_P2.pptx**.

Step 3e

QUICK STEPS

Animating a SmartArt Graphic

Animate SmartArt Graphic
1. Click SmartArt graphic.
2. Apply desired animation effect.
3. Click SmartArt graphic item in Custom Animation task pane list box.
4. Click down-pointing arrow at right of item.
5. Click *Effect Options*.
6. Click down-pointing arrow at right of *Group graphic*.
7. Click desired grouping option.

You can apply animation effects to a SmartArt graphic and animate the graphic or individual elements in the graphic. To animate a specific element in a graphic, select the element and then apply an animation effect. Click the item in the task pane list box, click the down-pointing arrow at the right side of the item, and then click *Effect Options* at the drop-down list. This displays the effect options dialog box with a SmartArt Animation tab. Click this tab and then use the *Group graphic* option to specify whether you want the elements grouped as one object, all at once, one by one, from the center at once, or from the center one by one. The name of the effect options dialog box varies depending on the animation effect applied. For example, when you apply the *Ease In* entrance animation effect to the SmartArt graphic in Project 2b, the Effect Options dialog box displays with the name Ease In.

Project 2b   Animating SmartArt

1. With **PP_C7_P2.pptx** open, make Slide 4 active and then animate objects in the SmartArt graphic by completing the following steps:

a. Click the shape in the SmartArt graphic containing the word *Convenient*. (Make sure the white sizing handles display only around the shape.)

b. Click the Add Effect button in the task pane, point to *Entrance*, and then click the *More Effects* option.

c. At the Add Entrance Effect dialog box, click *Ease In* in the *Moderate* section of the dialog box.

d. Click OK to close the dialog box.

e. Click the down-pointing arrow at the right side of the content placeholder item in the task pane list box and then click *Effect Options*.

f. At the Ease In effect options dialog box, click the SmartArt Animation tab.

g. Click the down-pointing arrow at the right side of the *Group graphic* option and then click *One by one* at the drop-down list. (This will allow you to apply different effects to the four objects in the SmartArt graphic.)

h. Click OK to close the dialog box. (Watch the animation effect play in the slide in the Slide pane.)

i. Expand the list of SmartArt graphic objects in the list box by clicking the small double arrows that display in a blue shaded box below the content placeholder item. (This expands the list to display four items.)

j. Click in the second item in the list box, click the Change button, point to *Entrance*, and then click the *More Effects* option.

k. At the Add Entrance Effect dialog box, click the *Sling* option in the *Exciting* section and then click OK.

l. Click the third item in the list box, click the Change button, point to *Entrance*, and then click *Sling* at the side menu. (The *Sling* option was added to the side menu.)

m. Click the fourth item in the list box, click the Change button, point to *Entrance*, and then click *Sling* at the side menu.

2. Make Slide 6 active and then apply and modify animation effects by completing the following steps:

a. Click the shape containing the text *Multi-Media*.

b. Apply the *Circle* entrance animation effect to the shape. (This effect is located in the *Basic* section of the Add Entrance Effect dialog box.)

c. Click the content placeholder item in the list box, click the down-pointing arrow at the right side of the option, and then click *Effect Options* at the drop-down list.

d. At the Circle dialog box, click the SmartArt Animation tab.

e. Click the down-pointing arrow at the right side of the *Group graphic* option and then click *One by one* at the drop-down list.

f. Click OK to close the dialog box.

g. Click the down-pointing arrow at the right side of the *Speed* option in the *Modify* section of the task pane and then click *Fast* at the drop-down list.

3. Save **PP_C7_P2.pptx**.

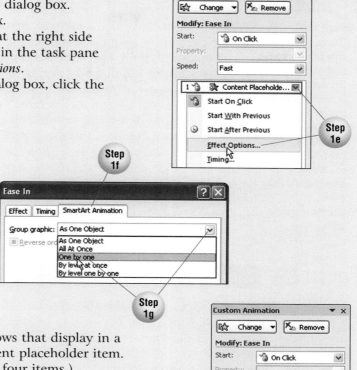

Animating a Chart

Animate Chart
1. Click chart.
2. Apply desired animation effect.
3. Click chart item in Custom Animation task pane list box.
4. Click down-pointing arrow at right of item.
5. Click *Effect Options.*
6. Click down-pointing arrow at right of *Group graphic.*
7. Click desired grouping option.

Like a SmartArt graphic, you can animate a chart or elements in a chart. Displaying data in a chart may have a more dramatic effect if the chart is animated. Bringing in one element at a time also allows you to discuss each piece of the data as it displays. Specify how you want the chart animated in the slide with options in the effect options dialog box. Apply an animation effect to a chart, click the down-pointing arrow at the right of the chart item in the Custom Animation task pane list box, and then click *Effect Options.* At the effect options dialog box (the name varies depending on the animation effect applied to the chart), click the Chart Animation tab and then specify how you want chart elements grouped. For example, you can group chart elements on one object or by series or category. Click the Effect tab and the dialog box displays with options for applying enhancements to the animation such as sound. Click the Timing tab to display options for controlling the timing of the animation effects such as the start time, amount of delay, and speed.

Project 2c   Animating Elements in a Chart

1. With **PP_C7_P2.pptx** open, make Slide 3 active and then animate chart elements by completing the following steps:
   a. Click in the chart placeholder to select the chart. (Make sure you do not have a chart element selected.)
   b. Add the *Dissolve In* entrance animation effect (located in the *Basic* section of the Add Entrance Effect dialog box).
   c. Click the down-pointing arrow at the right side of the content placeholder item in the list box and then click *Effect Options.*
   d. At the Dissolve In dialog box with the Effect tab selected, click the down-pointing arrow at the right side of the *Sound* option, scroll down the drop-down list, and then click the *Click* option.

Step 1d

   e. Click the Timing tab.
   f. Click the down-pointing arrow at the right side of the *Speed* option and then click *1 seconds (Fast)* at the drop-down list.
   g. Click the Chart Animation tab.
   h. Click the down-pointing arrow at the right side of the *Group chart* option and then click *By Category* at the drop-down list.
   i. Click OK to close the dialog box.
2. Save **PP_C7_P2.pptx**.

Applying a Build

In Project 1a, you applied a *build* to bulleted text in a slide. A build displays important points on a slide one point at a time keeping the audience's attention focused on the current point. You can further customize a build by causing a previous point to dim when the next point displays. To customize a build, choose a color option with the *After animation* option in the effect options dialog box with the Effect tab selected.

HINT

You can group text (in a bulleted text placeholder) at the effect options dialog box by first, second, third, fourth, or fifth levels.

Project 2d Applying a Build Animation

1. With **PP_C7_P2.pptx** open, make Slide 7 active and then apply an animation effect and modify the effect by completing the following steps:
   a. Click in the bulleted text.
   b. Apply the *Fly In* entrance animation effect.
   c. Click the down-pointing arrow at the right side of the *Direction* option in the *Modify* section of the task pane and then click *From Left* at the drop-down menu.
   d. Click the down-pointing arrow at the right side of the content placeholder item in the task pane list box and then click *Effect Options* at the drop-down list.
   e. At the Fly In dialog box, make sure the Effect tab is selected, click the down-pointing arrow at the right side of the *After animation* option and then click the yellow color (second color from the right).
   f. Click OK to close the dialog box.
2. Make Slide 2 active and then complete steps similar to those in Step 1 to apply a build animations effects to the bulleted text in the slide.
3. Save **PP_C7_P2.pptx**.

Step 1c

Step 1e

Drawing Motion Paths

One of the options at the Add Effect button drop-down list is *Motion Paths*. Point to this option and a side menu displays with an option for specifying an animation motion for an object in the slide. You can choose one of the predesigned motion paths or you can choose to draw your own path. To draw your own motion path, point to *Draw Custom Path* and then click *Freeform*. Using the mouse, drag in the slide to create the path. When the path is completed, double-click the mouse button.

QUICK STEPS

Draw Motion Path
1. Click Add Effect button in Custom Animation task pane.
2. Point to *Motion Paths*.
3. Point to *Draw Custom Path*.
4. Click *Freeform*.
5. Drag in slide to create path.
6. Double-click mouse.

Project 2e — Drawing a Motion Path

1. With **PP_C7_P2.pptx** open, make Slide 5 active and then animate the star on the map by completing the following steps:
   a. Click the star object in the slide (located below the heading *North America*).
   b. Click the Add Effect button, point to *Motion Paths*, point to *Draw Custom Path*, and then click *Freeform*.

Step 1a

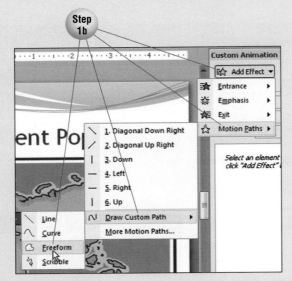

Step 1b

c. Position the mouse pointer (displays as crosshairs) on the star, hold down the left mouse button, draw a path through each of the five locations on the map ending back in the original location, and then double-click the left mouse button. (If a Custom Path dialog box displays, click the Cancel button.)
   d. Click the Play button to play the animation effect in the slide.
2. Save **PP_C7_P2.pptx**.
3. Run the presentation and click the mouse button to advance slides and elements on slides as needed.
4. Print the presentation as a handout with six slides per page.
5. Close the Custom Animation task pane.

Setting Up a Slide Show

Control how the presentation displays with options at the Set Up Show dialog box shown in Figure 7.2. With options at this dialog box, you can set slide presentation options, specify how you want slides to advance, and set screen resolution.

Figure 7.2 Set Up Show Dialog Box

Click this option to set up the presentation on a continuous loop.

Click this option to show the presentation without narration.

Click this option to show the presentation without animation effects.

Run Presentation without Animation
1. Click Slide Show tab.
2. Click Set Up Slide Show button.
3. Click *Show without animation.*
4. Click OK.

Set Up Slide Show

Running a Presentation without Animation

If a presentation contains numerous animation effects, you can choose to run the presentation without the animations. To do this, click the Slide Show tab and then click the Set Up Slide Show button in the Set Up group. At the Set Up Show dialog box, click the *Show without animation* check box to insert a check mark, and then click OK. Changes you make to the Set Up Show dialog box are saved with the presentation.

Project 2f ⬛ **Running a Presentation without Animation**

1. With **PP_C7_P2.pptx** open, specify that you want to run the presentation without animation by completing the following steps:
   a. Click the Slide Show tab.
   b. Click the Set Up Slide Show button in the Set Up group.
   c. At the Set Up Show dialog box, click the *Show without animation* check box to insert a check mark.
   d. Click OK to close the dialog box.
2. Run the presentation and notice that the animation effects do not play.
3. Specify that you want the presentation to run with animations by completing the following steps:
   a. Click the Slide Show tab and then click the Set Up Slide Show button.
   b. At the Set Up Show dialog box, click the *Show without animation* check box to remove the check mark and then click OK.
4. Save and then close **PP_C7_P2.pptx**.

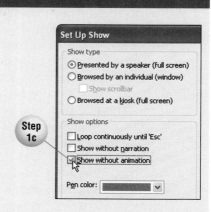

Step 1c

Project 3 — Prepare a Self-Running Adventure Presentation and Create Custom Shows

You will open a travel tour presentation and then customize it to be a self-running presentation set on a continuous loop. You will also hide slides and create and edit custom shows.

Setting Up a Presentation to Loop Continuously

In Chapter 1, you learned how to set automatic times for advancing slides. Insert a check mark in the *Automatically After* check box in the Advance Slide section in the Animations tab and then insert the desired number of seconds in the time box. If you want to have the ability to advance a slide more quickly than the time applied, leave the check mark in the *On Mouse Click* option. With this option active, you can let the slide advance the specified number of seconds or you can click the left mouse button to advance the slide sooner. Remove the check mark from the *On Mouse Click* button if you do not want to advance slides with the mouse.

In some situations, such as at a trade show or convention, you may want to prepare a self-running presentation. A self-running presentation is set up on a continuous loop and does not require someone to run the presentation. To design a self-running presentation, display the Set Up Show dialog box and then insert a check mark in the *Loop continuously until 'Esc'* option. With this option active, the presentation will continue running until you press the Esc key.

Project 3a — Preparing a Self-Running Presentation

1. Open **AdventureTours.pptx** and then save the presentation with the name **PP_C7_P3**.
2. Insert slides by completing the following steps:
   a. Click below the last slide miniature in the Slides/Outline pane.
   b. Make sure the Home tab is selected, click the New Slide button arrow, and then click *Reuse Slides* at the drop-down list.
   c. At the Reuse Slides task pane, click the Browse button and then click *Browse File*.
   d. At the Browse dialog box, navigate to the PowerPoint2007C7 folder on your storage medium and then double-click *PeruTour.pptx*.
   e. Click each slide in the Reuse Slides task pane in the order in which they display beginning with the top slide.
   f. Close the Reuse Slides task pane.
3. Add transition and sound effects and specify a time for automatically advancing slides by completing the following steps:
   a. Click the Animations tab.
   b. Click in the *Automatically After* check box to insert a check mark.
   c. Click the up-pointing arrow at the right side of the time box until *00:05* displays.

Step 3b

Step 3c

d. Click the *On Mouse Click* check box to remove the check mark.

e. Click the *Fade Smoothly* slide transition (second slide transition option from the left) in the Transition to This Slide group.

f. Click the down-pointing arrow at the right side of the *Transition Sound* option and then click *Breeze* at the drop-down list.

g. Click the Apply To All button in the Transition to This Slide group.

4. Set up the presentation to run continuously by completing the following steps:

a. Click the Slide Show tab.

b. Click the Set Up Slide Show button in the Set Up group.

c. At the Set Up Show dialog box, click in the *Loop continuously until 'Esc'* check box to insert a check mark. (Make sure *All* is selected in the *Show slides* section and *Using timings, if present* is selected in the *Advance slides* section.)

d. Click OK to close the dialog box.

5. Click Slide 1 to select it and then run the presentation. (The slides will advance automatically after five seconds.)

6. After viewing the presentation at least twice, press the Esc key on the keyboard.

7. Save **PP_C7_P3.pptx**.

Setting Automatic Times for Slides

Applying the same time to all slides is not very practical unless the same amount of text occurs on every slide. In most cases, some slides should be left on the screen longer than others. Apply specific times to a slide with buttons on the Rehearsal toolbar. Display this toolbar by clicking the Slide Show tab and then clicking the Rehearse Timings button in the Set Up group. This displays the first slide in the presentation in Slide Show view with the Rehearsal toolbar located in the upper left corner of the slide. The buttons on the Rehearsal toolbar are identified in Figure 7.3.

Figure 7.3 Rehearsal Toolbar

Set Automatic Times for Slides
1. Click Slide Show tab.
2. Click Rehearse Timings button.
3. Using Rehearsal toolbar, specify time for each slide.
4. Click Yes.

Next   Pause

Repeat

When the slide displays on the screen, the timer on the Rehearsal toolbar begins. Click the Next button on the Rehearsal toolbar when the slide has displayed for the appropriate amount of time. If you want to stop the timer, click the Pause button. Click the Pause button again to resume the timer. Use the Repeat button on the Rehearsal toolbar if you get off track and want to reset the time for the current slide. Continue through the presentation until the slide show is complete. After the last slide, a message displays showing the total time for the presentation and asks if you want to record the new slide timings. At this message, click Yes to set the times for each slide recorded during the rehearsal. If you do not want to use the rehearsed timings when running a presentation, click the Slide Show tab and then click in the Use Rehearsed Timings check box to remove the check mark.

Project 3b Setting Rehearse Timings for Slides

1. With **PP_C7_P3.pptx** open, remove the automatic times for slides by completing the following steps:
   a. Click the Slide Show tab.
   b. Click the Set Up Slide Show button.
   c. At the Set Up Show dialog box, click the *Loop continuously until 'Esc'* check box to remove the check mark.
   d. Click OK to close the dialog box.
2. Set times for the slides to display during a slide show by completing the following steps:
   a. Make Slide 1 active.
   b. With the Slide Show tab active, click the Rehearse Timings button in the Set Up group.
   c. The first slide displays in Slide Show view and the Rehearsal toolbar displays. Wait until the time displayed for the current slide reaches four seconds and then click Next. (If you miss the time, click the Repeat button to reset the clock back to zero for the current slide.)

Step 2c

   d. Set the times for remaining slides as follows:
      Slide 2 = 5 seconds
      Slide 3 = 6 seconds
      Slide 4 = 5 seconds
      Slide 5 = 6 seconds
      Slide 6 = 3 seconds
      Slide 7 = 6 seconds
      Slide 8 = 7 seconds
      Slide 9 = 7 seconds

e. After the last slide displays, click Yes at the message asking if you want to record the new slide timings.

f. Click the Normal button in the view area on the Status bar.

3. Click the Set Up Slide Show button to display the Set Up Show dialog box, click the *Loop continuously until 'Esc'* check box to insert a check mark, and then click OK to close the dialog box.

4. Run the presentation. (The slide show will start and run continuously.) Watch the presentation until it has started for the second time and then end the show by pressing the Esc key.

5. Save **PP_C7_P3.pptx**.

Recording Narration

Record Narration
1. Click Slide Show tab.
2. Click Record Narration button.
3. Click OK.
4. Narrate slides.
5. Click Save.

▶ Record Narration

You can record narration with your presentation that will play when the presentation is running. To record narration you must have a microphone connected to your computer. To begin the narration, click the Record Narration button in the Set Up group in the Slide Show tab. At the Record Narration dialog box, click the Set Microphone Level button. At the Microphone Check dialog box, dictate the text in quotes so the microphone setup wizard can make sure your microphone is working properly and to adjust the volume levels. Click OK to close the Microphone Check dialog box and then click OK to close the Record Narration dialog box. Your presentation begins and the first slide fills the screen. Begin your narration, clicking the mouse button to advance to each slide. When you have narrated all of the slides in the presentation, a message displays telling you that the narrations have been saved with each slide and asking if you want to save the slide timings. At this message, click the Save button.

The narration in a presentation plays by default when you run the presentation. You can run the presentation without the narration by displaying the Set Up Show dialog box and then inserting a check mark in the *Show without narration* check box in the *Show options* section.

Project 3c Recording Narration

This is an optional project. Before beginning the project, check with your instructor to determine if you have a microphone available for recording.

1. With **PP_C7_P3.pptx** open, save the presentation and name it **PP_C7_C3Narration**.
2. Remove the continuous loop option and remove timings by completing the following:
   a. Click the Slide Show tab.
   b. Click the Set Up Slide Show button.
   c. At the Set Up Show dialog box, click the *Loop continuously until 'Esc'* check box to remove the check mark.
   d. Click OK to close the dialog box.
   e. Click the Animations tab.
   f. Click the down-pointing arrow at the right side of the time box until *00:00* displays.
   g. Click the *Automatically After* check box to remove the check mark.
   h. Click the *On Mouse Click* option to insert a check mark.
   i. Click the Apply To All button.
3. Make Slide 1 active and then record narration by completing the following steps:

a. Click the Slide Show tab and then click the Record Narration button in the Set Up group.

Step 3b

b. At the Record Narration dialog box, click the Set Microphone Level button.

c. At the Microphone Check dialog box, dictate the text in quotes, and then click the OK button.

d. At the Record Narration dialog box, click OK.

e. When the first slide displays, either read the information or provide your own narrative of the slide and then click the left mouse button.

f. At the next slide, continue your narration and then click the left mouse button when completed.

g. Continue narrating each slide (either using some of the information in the slides or creating your own narration).

h. After narrating the last slide (the slide about accommodations for the Peru tour), press the Esc key.

i. At the message telling you that the narrations have been saved with each slide and asking if you want to save the slide timings, click the Save button.

4. With Slide 1 active, run the presentation. If your computer has speakers, you will hear your narration as the presentation runs.

5. Run the presentation without narration by completing the following steps:

a. Click the Set Up Slide Show button in the Slide Show tab.

b. At the Set Up Show dialog box, click in the *Show without narration* check box to insert a check mark.

c. Click OK.

d. Run the presentation beginning with Slide 1. (The presentation will run automatically with the timing established when you were recording your narration but without the narration.)

Step 5b

6. Save and then close **PP_C7_P3Narration.pptx**.

Hiding Slides

Hide Slide
1. Make slide active.
2. Click Slide Show tab.
3. Click Hide Slide button.

A presentation you create may be presented to a number of different groups or departments. In some situations, you may want to hide specific slides in a presentation depending on the audience. To hide a slide in a presentation, make the desired slide active, click the Slide Show tab, and then click the Hide Slide button in the Set Up group. When a slide is hidden, a square with a slash through it displays behind the slide number in the Slides/Outline pane. The slide is visible in the Slides/Outline pane in Normal view and also in the Slide Sorter view. To remove the hidden icon and redisplay the slide when running a presentation, click the slide miniature in the Slides/Outline pane, click the Slide Show tab, and then click the Hide Slide button.

Setting Up Monitors

With options in the Monitors group in the Slide Show tab, you can specify screen resolution and show the presentation on two different monitors. The Resolution option in the Slide Show tab displays the current resolution for your monitor. If you hover your mouse over the option, an expanded ScreenTip displays with information telling you that you can choose a screen resolution and that a smaller resolution generally displays faster while a larger resolution generally displays the presentation slower but with more visual detail.

If you have two monitors connected to your computer or are running PowerPoint on a laptop with dual-display capabilities, you can choose the *Presenter View* option in the Monitors group. With this option active, you display your presentation in full-screen view on one monitor and display your presentation in a special speaker view on the other.

Project 3d | Changing Monitor Resolution

Check with your instructor before completing this project to determine if you can change monitor resolution.

1. Open **PP_C7_P3.pptx**.
2. Remove the continuous loop option and remove timings by completing the following:
   a. Click the Slide Show tab.
   b. Click the Set Up Slide Show button.
   c. At the Set Up Show dialog box, click the *Loop continuously until 'Esc'* check box to remove the check mark.
   d. Click OK to close the dialog box.
   e. Click the Animations tab.
   f. Click the down-pointing arrow at the right side of the time box until *00:00* displays.
   g. Click the *Automatically After* check box to remove the check mark.
   h. Click the *On Mouse Click* option to insert a check mark.
   i. Click the Apply To All button.
3. Hide Slide 2 by completing the following steps:
   a. Click the Slide 2 miniature in the Slides/Outline pane.
   b. Click the Slide Show tab and then click the Hide Slide button in the Set Up group.
4. Change the monitor resolution by completing the following steps:
   a. Note the current monitor resolution that displays in the *Resolution* option box in the Monitors group.
   b. Click the down-pointing arrow at the right side of the *Resolution* option and then click *800 × 600* at the drop-down list.

5. Run the presentation and notice the resolution and that Slide 2 does not display (since it is hidden).
6. Unhide Slide 2 by clicking the Slide 2 miniature in the Slides/Outline pane and then clicking the Hide Slide button in the Set Up group in the Slide Show tab.
7. Return the monitor resolution to the original setting by clicking the down-pointing arrow at the right side of the *Resolution* option in the Monitors group in the Slide Show tab and then clicking the original resolution at the drop-down list.
8. Save **PP_C7_P3.pptx**.

HINT

Create custom shows to customize a presentation for a variety of audiences.

Custom
Slide Show ▾

Creating a Custom Show

You can select specific slides within a presentation to create a presentation within a presentation. This might be useful in situations where you want to show only a select number of slides to a particular audience. To create a custom show, click the Slide Show tab, click the Custom Slide Show button in the Start Slide Show group, and then click *Custom Shows* at the drop-down list. At the Custom Shows dialog box, click the New button and the Define Custom Show dialog box displays similar to what you see in Figure 7.4.

Figure 7.4 Define Custom Show Dialog Box

Type a name for the custom show in this text box.

Slides in the presentation display in this list box.

To add a slide to the custom show, click the slide in this list box and then click the Add button.

At the Define Custom Show dialog box, type a name for the custom presentation in the *Slide show name* text box. To insert a slide in the custom show, click the slide in the *Slides in presentation* list box and then click the Add button. This inserts the slide in the *Slides in custom show* list box. Continue in this manner until all desired slides are added to the custom show. If you want to change the order of the slides in the *Slides in custom show* list box, click one of the arrow keys to move the selected slide up or down in the list box. When the desired slides are inserted in the *Slides in custom show* list box and in the desired order, click OK. You can create more than one custom show in a presentation.

Running a Custom Show

To run a custom show within a presentation, click the Custom Slide Show button in the Slide Show tab and then click the desired custom show at the drop-down list. You can also choose a custom show by displaying the Set Up Show dialog box and then clicking the *Custom show* option. If the presentation contains more than one custom show, click the down-pointing arrow at the right of the *Custom show* option and then click the show name at the drop-down list.

Editing a Custom Show

A custom show is saved with the presentation and can be edited. To edit a custom show, open the presentation, click the Custom Slide Show button in the Slide Show tab, and then click *Custom Shows* at the drop-down list. At the Custom Shows dialog box, click the custom show name you want to edit and then click the Edit button. At the Define Custom Show dialog box, make the desired changes to the custom show such as adding or removing slides or changing the order of slides. When all changes have been made, click the OK button.

Printing a Custom Show

You can print a custom show with the *Custom Show* option in the Print dialog box. To do this, display the Print dialog box, click the *Custom Show* option in the *Print range* section, and then click OK. If the presentation includes more than one show, click the down-pointing arrow at the right side of the *Custom Show* option at the Print dialog box, click the desired show, and then click OK.

QUICK STEPS

Create Custom Show
1. Click Slide Show tab.
2. Click Custom Slide Show button.
3. Click *Custom Shows.*
4. Click New button.
5. Make desired changes at Define Custom Show dialog box.
6. Click OK.

Run Custom Show
1. Click Slide Show tab.
2. Click Custom Slide Show button.
3. Click desired custom show.

Edit Custom Show
1. Click Slide Show tab.
2. Click Custom Slide Show button.
3. Click desired custom show.
4. Click Edit button.
5. Make desired changes at Define Custom Show dialog box.
6. Click OK.

Print Custom Show
1. Display Print dialog box.
2. Click *Custom Show.*
3. Click OK.

Project 3e — Creating, Editing, and Running Custom Shows

1. With **PP_C7_P3.pptx** open, save the presentation and name it **PP_C7_P3Custom**.
2. Create two custom shows by completing the following steps:
   a. Click the Slide Show tab, click the Custom Slide Show button, and then click *Custom Shows* at the drop-down list.
   b. At the Custom Shows dialog box, click the New button.

Step 2b

c. At the Define Custom Show dialog box, type **PeruTourCustom** in the *Slide show name* text box.

d. Click Slide 6 in the *Slides in presentation* list box and then click the Add button. (This adds the slide to the *Slides in custom show* list box.)

e. Click each of the remaining slides in the list box (Slides 7, 8, and 9) and click the Add button.

f. Click OK to close the Define Custom Show dialog box.

g. At the Custom Shows dialog box, click the New button.

h. At the Define Custom Show dialog box, type **FijiTourCustom** in the *Slide show name* text box.

i. Add Slides 1 through 5 to the *Slides in custom show* list box.

j. Click OK to close the dialog box.

k. Click the Close button to close the Custom Shows dialog box.

3. Run the *PeruTourCustom* custom show by completing the following steps:

a. Click the Custom Slide Show button in the Slide Show tab and then click *PeruTourCustom* at the drop-down list.

b. Click the left mouse button to advance slides.

c. Click the Custom Slide Show button, click *FijiTourCustom* at the drop-down list, and then view the presentation. (Click the left mouse button to advance slides.)

4. Edit the FijiTourCustom custom slide show by completing the following steps:

a. Click the Custom Slide Show button in the Slide Show tab and then click *Custom Shows* at the drop-down list.

b. At the Custom Shows dialog box, click *FijiTourCustom* in the *Custom shows* list box and then click the Edit button.

c. At the Define Custom Show dialog box, click Slide 2 in the *Slides in custom show* list box and then click three times on the down-pointing arrow at the right side of the list box. (This moves the slide to the bottom of the list.)

d. Click OK to close the dialog box.

e. Click the Close button to close the Custom Shows dialog box.

5. Run the FijiTourCustom custom show.

6. Save and then close **PP_C7_P3Custom.pptx**.

Step 2c

Step 2d

Step 3a

Step 4b

Step 4c

roject **4** Insert a Sound and a Movie Clip in a Presentation

You will open a presentation and then insert a sound clip, movie clip, and clip art image with motion. You will also customize the sound and movie clips to play automatically when running the presentation.

Inserting Sounds and Movie Clips

Adding sound and/or movie clips to a presentation will turn a slide show into a true multimedia experience for your audience. Including a variety of elements in a presentation will stimulate interest in your presentation and keep the audience motivated.

To add a sound to your presentation, click the Insert tab and then click the Sound button in the Media Clips group. At the Insert Sound dialog box, navigate to the desired folder and then double-click the sound file. You can also insert a sound by clicking the Sound button arrow and then clicking an option at the drop-down list. With the list options you can choose to insert a sound from a file or clipboard, play an audio track, or record a sound.

When you insert a sound from the Insert Sound dialog box, a message displays asking how you want the sound to start when the slide displays in the slide show. Click the Automatically button if you want the sound to begin when the slide displays or click the When Clicked button if you want the sound to begin when you click the sound icon.

A sound file in a slide can be embedded or linked. PowerPoint will embed only sound files with the file extension *.wav* (waveform audio data) and all other sound file types are linked to the slide. If you move a linked sound file, PowerPoint may not be able to locate the file. If possible, save the sound file in the same folder as the presentation so PowerPoint can find the sound file when you run the presentation.

Adding a movie clip is a similar process to adding sound. Click the Movie button in the Media Clips group in the Insert tab to display the Insert Movie dialog box. At this dialog box, navigate to the folder containing the movie clip file and then double-click the file. You can also click the Movie button arrow and then click *Movie from File* to display the Insert Movie dialog box or click the *Movie from Clip Organizer* to display the Clip Art task pane with images containing motion.

Insert Sound Clip
1. Click Insert tab.
2. Click Sound button.
3. Double-click desired sound file.

Insert Movie Clip
1. Click Insert tab.
2. Click Movie button.
3. Double-click desired movie file.

1. Open **PotentialPresentation.pptx** and then save the presentation with the name **PP_C7_P4**.
2. Insert a movie clip and sound in a new slide by completing the following steps:
   a. Make Slide 6 active.
   b. Click the New Slide button arrow and then click the *Blank* layout.
   c. Click the Insert tab.
   d. Click the Movie button in the Media Clips group.
   e. At the Insert Movie dialog box, navigate to the SoundandVideo folder on the CD that accompanies this textbook, and then double-click the file named *TakeOff.mpeg*.
   f. At the message asking how you want the movie to start, click the Automatically button.
   g. Resize the image so it fills the entire slide.
3. Add a sound clip to the new slide (Slide 7) that will automatically play by completing the following steps:
   a. Click the Sound button in the Media Clips group.
   b. At the Insert Sound dialog box, navigate to the SoundandVideo folder on the CD that accompanies this textbook, and then double-click the file named *Greatfire.mid*.
   c. At the message asking how you want the sound to start, click the Automatically button.
4. Insert a clip art image with motion (the motion will display when you run the presentation) by completing the following steps:
   a. Make Slide 2 active.
   b. Click the Movie button arrow and then click *Movie from Clip Organizer* at the drop-down list.
   c. Click the clip art image shown at the right. (If this image is not available, choose another.)
   d. Close the Clip Art task pane.
   e. With the image selected in the slide, click the Recolor button and then click *Accent color 2 Dark* (third from the left in the *Dark Variations* section).
   f. Click in the *Shape Height* measurement box in the Size group, type 1.8, and then press Enter.
   g. Move the image so it is positioned below and to the right of the bulleted text.
5. Display Slide 1 in the Slide pane and then run the presentation. When the last slide (Slide 7) displays, watch the movie clip, listen to the sound (the sound plays after the movie clip plays), and then press the Esc key to end the slide show.
6. Save **PP_C7_P4.pptx**.

Step 4b

Step 4c

Customizing Sounds and Movie Clips

When you insert a sound clip in a slide, you can customize the sound with options in the Sound Tools Options tab. With options in this tab, you can change the sound volume, specify sound options, and arrange and size the sound icon. When you insert a movie clip, the Movie Tools Options tab is available. This tab contains many of the same options as the Sound Tools Options tab.

Project 4b Customizing a Sound and Movie Clip

1. With **PP_C7_P4.pptx** open, assume that you want the sound and movie clips to play continuously. To do this, complete the following steps:
   a. Make Slide 7 active.
   b. Click the movie clip in the slide.
   c. Click the Movie Tools Options tab.
   d. Click the *Loop Until Stopped* check box in the Movie Options group.

Step 1c

Step 1d

   e. Click the sound icon and then click the Sound Tools Options tab.
   f. Click the *Loop Until Stopped* check box in the Sound Options group.
   g. Click the *Hide During Show* check box in the Sound Options group.
2. You want the sound and movie clip to play when Slide 7 displays during the presentation. To do this, you will need to customize the start options in the Custom Animation task pane by completing the following steps:
   a. Click the Animations tab.
   b. Click the Custom Animation button.
   c. Click the Greatfire.mid item in the task pane list box.
   d. Click the down-pointing arrow at the right side of the Greatfire.mid item and then click the *Start With Previous* option.
   e. Close the Custom Animation tab.

Step 2c

Step 2d

3. Make Slide 1 active and then run the presentation. When you reach Slide 7, watch the movie clip and listen to the sound and then end the slide show.
4. Print the slides as handouts with four slides per page.
5. Save and then close the presentation.

Project 5 Play a Sound throughout a Presentation

You will open a job search presentation, set it up as a self-running presentation, and then insert a sound that plays throughout the presentation.

Playing a Sound throughout a Presentation

In Project 4a, you inserted a sound object that played when a specific slide displayed. You can also insert a sound file in a presentation and have the sound continue through all slides in a presentation. Generally, you would add a sound for the entire presentation when setting up a self-running presentation. To include a sound clip in a self-running presentation, insert the sound, click the down-pointing arrow at the right side of the *Play Sound* option in the Sound Tools Options tab, and then click *Play across slides* at the drop-down list.

Project ⑤ Inserting Sound and Playing throughout Presentation

1. Open **JobSearch.pptx** and then save the presentation with the name **PP_C7_P5**.
2. Apply the *Module* design theme.
3. Suppose you are going to display this presentation at a trade show and you want to set it up as a self-running presentation. To do this, complete the following steps:
   a. Click the Animations tab.
   b. Click in the *On Mouse Click* check box to remove the check mark.
   c. Click in the *Automatically After* check box to insert a check mark.
   d. Click the up-pointing arrow at the right side of the time box until *00:05* displays.
   e. Click the *Fade Through Black* transition (third from left) in the Transition to This Slide group.
   f. Click the Apply To All button in the Transition to This Slide group.
   g. Click the Slide Show tab and then click the Set Up Slide Show button in the Set Up group.
   h. At the Set Up Show dialog box, click in the *Loop continuously until 'Esc'* option check box to insert a check mark. (Make sure *All* is selected in the *Show slides* section and *Using timings, if present* is selected in the *Advance slides* section.)
   i. Click OK to close the dialog box.

4. To add more interest to the presentation, you decide to add a sound that plays throughout the presentation. To do this, complete the following steps:
   a. Make Slide 1 the active slide.
   b. Click the Insert tab and then click the Sound button in the Media Clips group.
   c. At the Insert Sound dialog box, navigate to the SoundandVideo folder on the CD that accompanies this textbook, and then double-click the file named ***Greenspace.mid***.
   d. At the message asking how you want the sound to start, click the Automatically button.
   e. Click the down-pointing arrow at the right side of the *Play Sound* option in the Sound Tools Option tab and then click *Play across slides* at the drop-down list.

   f. Move the sound icon down to the bottom right corner of the slide.
5. With Slide 1 the active slide, run the presentation.
6. After viewing the presentation at least twice, press the Esc key on the keyboard.
7. Print the presentation as a handout with nine slides per page.
8. Save and then close **PP_C7_P5.pptx**.

CHAPTER summary

- Apply a built-in animation to an item in a slide by clicking the Animations tab, clicking the down-pointing arrow at the right side of the *Animate* option in the Animations group, and then clicking the desired animation at the drop-down list.

- Click the Preview button in the Animations tab to view animation effects in a slide without running the presentation.

- Remove a built-in animation effect from an item by clicking the item, clicking the down-pointing arrow at the right side of the *Animate* option in the Animations tab, and then clicking *No animation*.

- Apply custom animation effects with options at the Custom Animation task pane. Display this task pane by clicking the Animations tab and then clicking the Custom Animation button.

- With the Add Effect button in the Custom Animation task pane you can apply entrance, emphasis, exit, and motion path effects to an item in a slide.

- Click the Play button located toward the bottom of the Custom Animation task pane to play any animation effects in the current slide.

- Modify animation effects with options in the *Modify* section in the Custom Animation task pane. The options in the *Modify* section vary depending on the effect applied.

- Change animation effects by clicking the item in the Custom Animation task pane and then clicking the Change button, remove an animation effect by clicking the Remove button, and reorder items by clicking the Up Re-Order arrow or Down Re-Order arrow.

- Animate a shape or image by clicking the object and then applying the desired animation effects.

- Animate specific elements in a SmartArt graphic with options in the effect options dialog box with the SmartArt tab selected. To display this dialog box, apply an animation effect to the SmartArt element, click the item in the task pane representing the element, click the down-pointing arrow at the right side of the item, and then click *Effect Options*.

- Animate specific elements in a chart with options in the effect options dialog box with the Chart Animation tab selected.

- Apply a build that dims the previous item in a slide with the *After animation* option at the effect options dialog box with the Effect tab selected.

- Draw a custom motion path in a slide by clicking the Add Effect button in the Custom Animation task pane, pointing to *Motion Paths*, pointing to *Draw Custom Path*, and then clicking *Freeform*. Using the mouse, drag in the slide to create the path.

- Customize a slide show with options in the Set Up Show dialog box. Display this dialog box by clicking the Set Up Slide Show button in the Set Up group in the Slide Show tab.

- To prepare a self-running presentation, display the Set Up Show dialog box and insert a check mark in the *Loop continuously until 'Esc'* option.

- To apply specific times to slides, click the Rehearse Timings button in the Set Up group in the Slide Show. This displays the first slide in the presentation with a rehearsal toolbar in the upper left corner. Use buttons on this toolbar to set, pause, or repeat timings.

- To record a narration for a presentation, click the Slide Show tab, click the Record Narration button, make any desired changes at the Record Narration dialog box, and then click OK.

- Hide or unhide a slide in a presentation by clicking the Hide Slide button in the Set Up group in the Slide Show tab.

- Specify screen resolutions with the *Resolution* option in the Monitors group in the Slide Show tab.

- Create a custom slide show, which is a presentation within a presentation, with options in the Define Custom Shows dialog box. Display this dialog box by clicking the Slide Show tab, clicking the Custom Slide Show button, and then clicking *Custom Shows*. At the Custom Shows dialog box, click the New button.

- To run a custom slide show, click the Custom Slide Show button in the Slide Show tab and then click the desired custom show at the drop-down list. You can also run a custom slide show by choosing the desired show with the *Custom show* option in the Set Up Show dialog box.

- Edit a custom show by clicking the custom show name in the Custom Shows dialog box, clicking the Edit button, and then making desired changes at the Define Custom Show dialog box.

- Print a custom show with the *Custom Show* option in the Print dialog box.

- To insert a sound file in a slide, click the Insert tab, click the Sound button, and then double-click the desired sound file at the Insert Sound dialog box.

- To insert a movie clip in a slide, click the Insert tab, click the Movie button, and then double-click the desired movie clip file at the Insert Movie dialog box.

- Customize sound with options in the Sound Tools Options tab and customize a movie clip with options in the Movie Tools Options tab.

- To play a sound throughout a self-running presentation, insert the sound, click the down-pointing arrow at the right side of the *Play Sound* option in the Sound Tools Options tab, and then click *Play across slides* at the drop-down list.

COMMANDS review

FEATURE	RIBBON TAB, GROUP	BUTTON, OPTION
Built-in animations	Animations, Animations	Animate: No Animation ▾
Custom Animation task pane	Animations, Animations	Custom Animation
Set Up Show dialog box	Slide Show, Set Up	
Rehearsal toolbar	Slide Show, Set Up	Rehearse Timings
Record Narration dialog box	Slide Show, Set Up	Record Narration
Hide/unhide slide	Slide Show, Set Up	
Define Custom Show dialog box	Slide Show, Start Slide Show	, Custom Shows
Insert Sound dialog box	Insert, Media Clips	
Insert Movie dialog box	Insert, Media Clips	

CONCEPTS check

Test Your Knowledge

Completion: In the space provided at the right, indicate the correct term, symbol, or command.

1. To display built-in animations, click the down-pointing arrow at the right side of this option in the Animations tab.

   _____

2. Click this button in the Animations tab to view the animation effects applied to elements in the current slide.

   _____

3. Click the Add Effect button in the Custom Animation task pane and four options display—*Entrance*, *Exit*, *Motion Paths*, and this.

   _____

4. Use this option in the Effect Options dialog box with the SmartArt Animation tab selected to specify a grouping.

   _____

5. When animating chart elements, click this tab at the Effect Options dialog box to apply enhancements to the animation such as sound.

   _____

6. This term refers to displaying important points one at a time in a slide when running a presentation.

   _____

7. To display a presentation without animation effects, insert a check mark in the *Show without animation* check box in this dialog box.

   _____

8. Click this button in the Slide Show tab to display the first slide in the presentation in Slide Show view with the Rehearsal toolbar visible.

   _____

9. The Hide Slide button is located in this tab.

   _____

10. Specify the slides you want included in a custom show with options at this dialog box.

   _____

11. Print a custom slide show by clicking the *Custom Show* option in this section of the Print dialog box.

   _____

12. The Sound button and Movie button are located in this group in the Insert tab.

   _____

13. Customize a sound file with options in this tab.

   _____

14. To play a sound throughout a presentation, insert the sound, click the down-pointing arrow at the right side of the *Play Sound* option in the Sound Tools Options tab, and then click this option.

   _____

SKILLS check
Demonstrate Your Proficiency

1 APPLY BUILT-IN ANIMATION EFFECTS TO A TRAVEL PRESENTATION

1. Open **FCTCruise.pptx** and then save the presentation with the name **PP_C7_A1**.
2. Make Slide 1 active, click the company logo, and then apply the *Fade* built-in animation.
3. Display the presentation in Slide Master view, click the top slide master layout in the slide thumbnail pane, and then apply the following animations:
   a. Apply the *Fade* built-in animation to the title style.
   b. Apply the *By 1st Level Paragraphs* in the *Wipe* section to the bulleted text.
   c. Close the Slide Master view.
4. Run the presentation.
5. Save and then close **PP_C7_A1.pptx**.

2 APPLY CUSTOM ANIMATION EFFECTS TO AN EMPLOYEE ORIENTATION PRESENTATION

1. Open **GlobalEmployeeOrientation.pptx** and then save the presentation with the name **PP_C7_A2**.
2. Make Slide 2 active and then apply the following custom animations to the SmartArt graphic:
   a. Apply the *Blinds* entrance animation effect.
   b. Change the SmartArt animation so the graphic is grouped *One by one*.
      Hint: Do this at the Blinds dialog box. Display this dialog box by clicking the content placeholder item in the Custom Animation task pane list box, clicking the down-pointing arrow at the right side of the item, and then clicking Effect Options at the drop-down list.
   c. Change the direction to *Vertical* and the speed to *Fast*.
3. Make Slide 3 active and then apply the following custom animations to the organizational chart:
   a. Apply the *Blinds* entrance animation effect.
   b. Change the SmartArt animation so the graphic is grouped *By branch one by one*.
   c. Change the speed to *Fast*.
4. Make Slide 4 active and then apply the following custom animations to the bulleted text (click on any character in the bulleted text):
   a. Apply the *Color Typewriter* entrance animation effect.
   b. Set the text to dim after animation to a light blue color.
5. Apply the following custom animations to the clip art image in Slide 4:
   a. Apply the *Spin* emphasis animation effect.
   b. Set the amount of spin for the clip art image to *Two Spins* and the speed to *Very Fast*.
   c. Change the *Start* option to *With Previous*.
   d. Reorder the items in the task pane list box so the clip art displays first when running the presentation.

6. Make Slide 5 active, select the SmartArt graphic, and apply a custom animation effect so the elements in the SmartArt graphic fade in one by one.
7. Make Slide 6 active and then apply the following custom animation effects to the images with the following specifications:
   a. Apply the *Fly Out* exit animation effect to the *Free Education* gift package, change the direction to *To Right*, and change the speed to *Fast*.
   b. Apply the *Box* entrance animation effect to the diploma/books clip art image.
   c. Move the *Free Education* gift package so the bulleted text underneath displays, apply the *Descend* entrance animation effect to the bulleted text, and then move the gift package back to the original location.
   d. Apply the *Fly Out* exit animation effect to the *Free Toys and Fitness* gift package, change the direction to *To Left*, and change the speed to *Fast*.
   e. Apply the *Box* entrance animation effect to the notebook computer clip art image.
   f. Move the *Free Toys and Fitness* gift package so the bulleted text underneath displays, apply the *Descend* entrance animation effect to the bulleted text, and then move the gift package back to the original location.
8. Make Slide 1 active and then run the presentation.
9. Save **PP_C7_A2.pptx**.
10. Display the presentation in Slide Master view, click the top slide master layout in the slide thumbnail pane, apply an entrance animation effect of your choosing to the title, and then close Slide Master view.
11. Make Slide 1 active and then apply the following custom animation effects:
    a. Click the globe clip art image and then draw a freeform motion path so the image will circle around the slide and return back to the original location.
    b. Apply the *Spiral In* entrance animation effect to the *New Employee Orientation* placeholder.
12. Run the presentation.
13. Print the presentation as a handout with all slides on one page.
14. Save and then close **PP_C7_A2.pptx**.

Assessment

3 APPLY ANIMATION EFFECTS AND SOUND TO A JOB SEARCH PRESENTATION

1. Open **JobSearch.pptx** and then save the presentation with the name **PP_C7_A3**.
2. Apply a design theme of your choosing to the presentation.
3. Add appropriate clip art to one or two slides.
4. Apply animation effects to slides in the presentation.
5. Insert the **Greenspace.mid** sound clip (located in the SoundandVideo folder on the CD that accompanies this textbook) in Slide 9 so it plays when you click the sound icon.
6. Create a custom show named *Interview* that contains Slides 1, 3, 6, 7, and 9.
7. Run the Interview custom show. (After you have displayed all elements on Slide 9, click the sound icon to play the music. After listening to the music for a period of time, end the presentation.)
8. Print the Interview custom show as a handout with all slides on one page.
9. Edit the Interview custom show by removing Slide 2.
10. Print the Interview custom show again as a handout with all slides on one page.
11. Save and then close **PP_C7_A3.pptx**.

4 INSERT A SOUND FROM THE CLIP ORGANIZER INTO A TRAVEL PRESENTATION

1. Experiment with inserting sounds from the clip organizer and then open **HawaiiTour.pptx** and save the presentation with the name **PP_C7_A4**.
2. Insert a song from the sound clip organizer (such as *Hawaii Farewell, Hawaii Song, Light Piano*, or any other song of your choosing) into the first slide in the presentation.
3. Set up the presentation to run on an endless loop and the sound to play across all slides and continuously as long as the presentation is running. (Display the Custom Animation task pane and make sure the song item displays at the beginning of the list and is set to *Start With Previous*.)
4. Run the presentation.
5. Print the presentation as a handout with all slides on one page.
6. Save and then close **PP_C7_A4**.

CASE study
Apply Your Skills

Part 1

You are a trainer in the Training Department at Riverside Services. You are responsible for coordinating and conducting software training in the company. Your company hires contract employees and some of those employees work at home and need to have a computer available. You will be conducting a short training for contract employees on how to purchase a personal computer. Open the Word document named **PCBuyingGuidelines.docx** and then use the information in the document to prepare your presentation. Make sure you keep the slides uncluttered and easy to read. Consider inserting clip art or other images in some of the slides. Insert custom animation effects to each slide in the presentation. Run the presentation and then make any necessary changes to the animation effects. Save the presentation and name it **PP_C7_CS_P1**. Print the presentation as a handout.

Part 2

Some training sessions on purchasing a personal computer are only scheduled for twenty minutes. For these training sessions, you want to cover only the information about selecting computer hardware components. With the **PP_C7_CS_P1.pptx** presentation open, create a custom show (you determine the name) that contains only the slides pertaining to selecting hardware components. Run the custom show and then print the custom show. Save **PP_C7_CS_P1.pptx**.

Part 3

You would like to insert a sound file that plays at the end of the presentation and decide to find free sound files on the Internet. Log on to the Internet and then use a search engine to search for "free sound clips" or "free audio clips." When you find a site, make sure that you can download and use the sound clip without violating copyright laws. Download a sound clip and then insert it in the last slide in your presentation. Set up the sound clip to play after all of the elements display on the slide. Save and then close **PP_C7_CS_P1.pptx**.

Part 4

The training manager has asked you to view the Microsoft training tutorial on adding sound effects to a presentation. She wants you to complete the tutorial and also complete the practice session on inserting sound files into a presentation. (The training will take approximately 45 minutes to an hour.) Display the PowerPoint Help window, type Add sound effects to a presentation, and then press Enter. Click the <u>Add sound effects to a presentation</u> hyperlink in the PowerPoint Help window. Complete the tutorial and then complete the practice on inserting sound files. When you have completed the practice steps, save the presentation to the PowerPoint2007C7 folder on your storage medium and name it **PC_C7_CS_P4**. Run the presentation and then print the presentation as a handout with six slides per page. Save and then close the presentation.

Integrating, Reviewing, Protecting, and Saving Presentations

PERFORMANCE OBJECTIVES

Upon successful completion of Chapter 8, you will be able to:

- Import a Word outline into a presentation
- Export a presentation to Word
- Copy and paste data
- Copy and paste data using the Clipboard task pane
- Link and embed objects
- Download design templates
- Insert, edit, and delete comments
- Modify presentation properties
- Inspect, encrypt, mark as final, and add a digital signature to a presentation
- Run the compatibility checker
- Save presentations in different formats
- Save slides as images
- Save a presentation as a Web page
- Package a presentation for a CD

Tutorial 8.1
Embedding and Linking Objects
Tutorial 8.2
Sharing Data and Comments
Tutorial 8.3
Preparing Presentations for
   Remote Delivery

Share objects between programs in the Microsoft Office suite by importing and exporting data, copying and pasting objects, copying and embedding objects, or copying and linking objects. The method you choose depends on how you use the information and whether the data is static or dynamic. If you use PowerPoint in a workgroup environment, you may want to insert comments in a presentation and then share the presentation with others in your group. In a workgroup environment, you might also want to protect presentations and prepare presentations for distribution. In this chapter, you will learn how to complete these tasks as well as how to download design templates from Microsoft Office Online, save a presentation in various formats, and package a presentation for a CD.

Note: Before beginning computer projects, copy to your storage medium the PowerPoint2007C8 folder from the PowerPoint2007 folder on the CD that accompanies this textbook and then make PowerPoint2007C8 the active folder.

Project ❶ Import a Word Outline and Copy and Paste Items between Programs

You will create a PowerPoint presentation using a Word document and then copy and paste an Excel chart and a Word table into slides in the presentation.

QUICK STEPS

Import a Word Outline
1. Open blank presentation.
2. Click New Slide button arrow.
3. Click *Slide from Outline.*
4. Double-click desired document.

Importing a Word Outline

You can import a Word document containing text formatted with heading styles into a PowerPoint presentation. Text formatted with a Heading 1 style becomes the title of a new slide. Text formatted with a Heading 2 style becomes first level text, paragraphs formatted with a Heading 3 style become second level text, and so on. To import a Word outline, open a blank presentation, click the New Slide button arrow in the Slides group in the Home tab, and then click *Slides from Outline* at the drop-down list. At the Insert Outline dialog box, navigate to the folder containing the Word document and then double-click the document. If text in the Word document does not have heading styles applied, PowerPoint creates an outline based on each paragraph of text in the document.

You can import an outline document from a Word 97-2003 document (.doc), a Word 2007 document (.docx), or a rich text format document (.rtf) into a PowerPoint presentation.

Project ❶a ▸ Importing a Word Outline

1. At a blank presentation, click the New Slide button arrow and then click *Slides from Outline* at the drop-down list.
2. At the Insert Outline dialog box, navigate to the PowerPoint2007C8 folder on your storage medium and then double-click *WordOutline01.docx*.
3. Apply the *Solstice* design theme, apply the *Metro* colors theme, and apply the *Foundry* fonts theme.
4. Delete Slide 1.
5. Format the current Slide 1 by completing the following steps:
   a. Change the slide layout by clicking the Layout button in the Slides group in the Home tab and then clicking the *Title Only* layout at the drop-down list.
   b. Click the text *Adventure Tours* to select the placeholder and then drag the placeholder down toward the bottom of the slide and center the text horizontally (click the Center button in the Paragraph group in the Home tab).

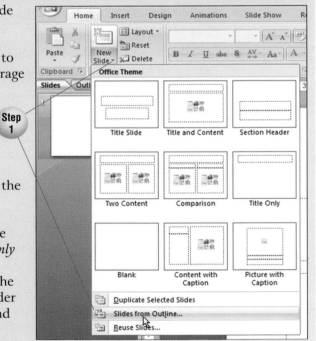

Step 1

   c. Insert the **FCTLogo.jpg** (do this with the Picture button in the Insert tab) and then increase the size of the logo so it fills a good portion of the upper part of the slide.

   d. Recolor the logo (picture) to Accent color 4 Light. *Hint: Do this with the Recolor button in the Adjust group in the Picture Tools Format tab.*

6. Make Slide 2 active and then change the layout to *Title Only*.
7. Make Slide 3 active, change the line spacing to 2.0 for the bulleted text, and then insert a clip art image of your choosing related to *travel* or *spring*.
8. Make Slide 4 active and then change the line spacing to 1.5 for the bulleted text.
9. Save the presentation and name it **PP_C8_P1**.

Exporting a Presentation to Word

You can export a PowerPoint presentation to a Word document and you can edit and format the presentation in Word. You can print slides as handouts in PowerPoint; however, you may prefer to export the presentation to Word to have greater control over the formatting of the handouts. To export the presentation that is currently open, click the Office button, point to *Publish*, and then click *Create Handouts in Microsoft Office Word*. At the Send To Microsoft Office Word dialog box shown in Figure 8.1, select the page layout you want to use in Word and then click OK.

The first four page layout options will export slides as they appear in PowerPoint with lines to the right or below the slides. The last option will export the text only as an outline. If you select the *Paste link* option, the Word document will be automatically updated whenever changes are made to the PowerPoint presentation.

QUICK STEPS

Export a Presentation to Word
1. Click Office button.
2. Point to *Publish*.
3. Click *Create Handouts in Microsoft Office Word*.
4. Select page layout.
5. Click OK.

Figure 8.1 Send To Microsoft Office Word Dialog Box

Click the desired layout for the display of slides in the Word document.

Click the *Paste link* option if you want the slides in the Word document and the PowerPoint presentation to be connected.

1. With **PP_C8_P1.pptx** open, click the Office button, point to *Publish*, and then click *Create Handouts in Microsoft Office Word*.

2. At the Send To Microsoft Office Word dialog box, click the *Blank lines next to slides* option and then click OK.

3. When all of the slides are inserted in the Word document, select the first column (the presentation was inserted in a table in Word) and then turn on bold.
4. Select the third column (contains the lines) and then change the font color to Red.
5. Save the document and name it **PP_C8_P1_Word**.
6. Print and then close **PP_C8_P1_Word.docx**.
7. Exit Word.

Copying and Pasting Data

Use the Copy and Paste buttons in the Clipboard group in the Home tab to copy data such as text or an object from one program and then paste it into another program. For example, in Project 1c, you will copy an Excel chart and then paste it into a PowerPoint slide. You can move and size a copied object, such as a chart, like any other object.

1. With **PP_C8_P1.pptx** open, make Slide 2 active.
2. Open Excel and then open the workbook named **Top5Tours.xlsx** located in the PowerPoint2007C8 folder on your storage medium.
3. Click the chart to select it. (Make sure you select the chart and not an element in the chart.)
4. Click the Copy button in the Clipboard group in the Home tab.

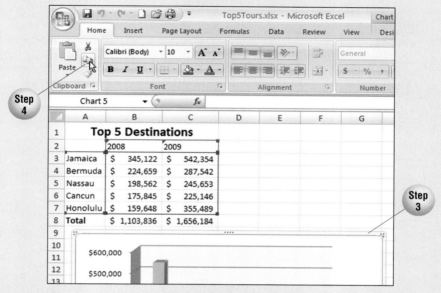

5. Close the **Top5Tours.xlsx** workbook and exit Excel.
6. In PowerPoint, with Slide 2 active, click the Paste button in the Clipboard group in the Home tab.
7. Resize and move the chart so it fills a good portion of the slide below the title and to the right of the slide design background.
8. Modify the chart by completing the following steps:
   a. Make sure the chart is selected and then click the Chart Tools Design tab.
   b. Click the More button at the right side of the chart styles thumbnails and then click *Style 38* at the drop-down gallery (sixth option from the left in the fifth row).
   c. Click the Chart Tools Format tab.
   d. Click the Shape Outline button arrow in the Shape Styles group and then click *No Outline* at the drop-down gallery.

9. Display Slide 1 in the Slide pane and then run the presentation.
10. Print only Slide 2.
11. Save **PP_C8_P1.pptx**.

Using the Clipboard Task Pane

Use the Clipboard task pane to collect and paste multiple items. You can collect up to 24 different items and then paste them in various locations. Turn on the display of the Clipboard task pane by clicking the Clipboard group dialog box launcher. The Clipboard task pane displays at the left side of the screen as shown in Figure 8.2.

Figure 8.2 Clipboard Task Pane

Click this button to paste all items from the Clipboard task pane to the slide.

Click this button to clear all items from the Clipboard task pane.

Copied items display in the Clipboard task pane. Click the item to insert it in the slide.

HINT

Click the Options button at the bottom of the Clipboard task pane to customize the display of the task pane.

Select data or an object you want to copy and then click the Copy button in the Clipboard group. Continue selecting text or items and clicking the Copy button. To insert an item, position the insertion point in the desired location and then click the button in the Clipboard task pane representing the item. If the copied item is text, the first 50 characters display. When all desired items are inserted, click the Clear All button to remove any remaining items from the Clipboard task pane. If you want to paste all items from the Clipboard task pane at once, click the Paste All button.

1. With **PP_C8_P1.pptx** open, make Slide 4 active and then insert a new slide with the *Title and Content* layout.
2. Click the text *Click to add title* and then type Spring Treks. Select *Spring Treks* and then turn on bold.
3. Copy text from Word by completing the following steps:
   a. Open Word and then open **AdventureTreks.docx**.
   b. Click the Clipboard group dialog box launcher to display the Clipboard task pane.
   c. If any data displays in the Clipboard task pane, click the Clear All button located toward the top of the task pane.
   d. Select the text *Yucatan Adventure – 10 days* (including the paragraph mark following the text—consider turning on the display of nonprinting characters) and then click the Copy button in the Clipboard group.

   e. Select the text *Mexico Adventure – 14 days* and then click the Copy button.
   f. Select the text *Caribbean Highlights – 16 days* and then click the Copy button.
   g. Select the text *California Delights – 7 days* and then click the Copy button.
   h. Select the text *Canyon Adventure – 10 days* and then click the Copy button.
   i. Select the text *Canadian Parks – 12 days* and then click the Copy button.
   j. Select the text *Royal Canadian Adventure – 14 days* and then click the Copy button.
4. Click the button on the Taskbar representing **PP_C8_P1.pptx** and then paste items from the Clipboard task pane by completing the following steps:
   a. With Slide 5 active, click the text *Click to add text*.
   b. Click the Clipboard group dialog box launcher to display the Clipboard task pane.
   c. Click the *California Delights* item in the Clipboard task pane.
   d. Click the *Canadian Parks* item in the Clipboard task pane.
   e. Click the *Caribbean Highlights* item in the Clipboard task pane.
   f. Click the *Mexico Adventure* item in the Clipboard task pane.

g. Click the *Yucatan Adventure* item in the Clipboard task pane. (Press the Backspace key twice to remove the bullet below *Yucatan Adventure* and the blank line.)

5. Select the bulleted text, change the line spacing to 1.5, change the font color to Periwinkle, Accent 5, Darker 25%, and turn on bold.

6. Clear the Clipboard task pane by clicking the Clear All button located in the upper right corner of the task pane.

7. Close the Clipboard task pane by clicking the Close button (contains an *X*) located in the upper right corner of the task pane.

8. Make Slide 1 the active slide and then run the presentation.

9. Print the presentation as a handout with all slides on one page.

10. Save and then close **PP_C8_P1.pptx**.

11. Make Word the active program, close **AdventureTreks.docx**, and then exit Word.

Project 2   Embed and Link Excel Charts to a Presentation

You will open a company funds presentation and then copy an Excel pie chart and embed it in a PowerPoint slide. You will also copy and link an Excel column chart to a slide and then update the chart in Excel.

Linking and Embedding Objects

One of the reasons the Microsoft Office suite is used extensively in business is because it allows data from an individual program to seamlessly integrate into another program. For example, a chart depicting the sales projections created in Excel can easily be added to a slide in a presentation to the company board of directors on the new budget forecast.

Integration is the process of completing a file by adding parts to it from other sources. Duplicating data that already exist in another program should be a rare instance. Copy and paste objects from one application to another when the content is not likely to change. If the content is dynamic, the copy and paste method becomes problematic and prone to error. To illustrate this point, assume one of the outcomes from the presentation to the board of directors is a revision to the sales projections. The chart that was originally created in Excel has to be updated to reflect the new projections. The existing chart in PowerPoint needs to be deleted and then the revised chart in Excel copied and pasted to the slide. Both Excel and PowerPoint need to be opened and edited to reflect this change in projection. In this case, copying and pasting the chart was not efficient.

To eliminate the inefficiency of the copy and paste method, you can integrate data between programs using ***object linking and embedding***. Object linking and embedding (OLE) is the sharing of data from one program to another. An object can be text in a presentation, data in a table, a chart, a picture, a slide, or any combination of data that you would like to share between programs. The program that was used to create the object is called the ***source*** and the program the object is linked or embedded to is called the ***destination***.

Embedding and linking are two methods you can use to integrate data in addition to the copy and paste method. When an object is embedded, the content in the object is stored in both the source and the destination programs. When you edit an embedded object in the destination program, the source program in which the program was created opens. If the content in the object is changed in the source program, the change is not reflected in the destination program and vice versa. Linking inserts a code into the destination file connecting the destination to the name and location of the source object. The object itself is not stored within the destination file. If a change is made to the content in the source program, the destination program reflects the change automatically.

Your decision to integrate data by embedding or linking will depend on whether the data is dynamic or static. If the data is dynamic, then linking the object is the most efficient method of integration. You can embed or copy and paste static data from the source to the destination program.

HINT
Static data remains the same while dynamic data changes periodically or continually.

Embedding Objects

An object that is embedded will be stored in both the source *and* the destination programs. The content of the object can be edited in *either* the source or the destination; however, a change made in one will not be reflected in the other. The difference between copying and pasting and embedding is that embedded objects can be edited with the source program's editing tabs and options.

Since embedded objects are edited within the source program, the source program must reside on the computer when the presentation is opened for editing. If you are preparing a presentation that will be edited on another computer, you may want to check before embedding any objects to verify that the other computer has the same programs.

To embed an object, open both programs and both files. In the source program, click the desired object and then click the Copy button in the Clipboard group in the Home tab. Click the button on the Taskbar representing the destination program file and then position the insertion point at the location where you want the object embedded. Click the Paste button arrow in the Clipboard group and then click *Paste Special* at the drop-down list. At the Paste Special dialog box, click the source of the object in the *As* list box and then click OK.

You can edit an embedded object by double-clicking the object. This displays the object with the source program tabs and options. Make any desired changes and then click outside the object to exit the source program tabs and options. You can apply animation effects to an embedded object with the same techniques you learned in Chapter 7.

QUICK STEPS

Embed an Object
1. Open source program.
2. Select desired object.
3. Click Copy button.
4. Open destination program.
5. Click Paste button arrow.
6. Click *Paste Special*.
7. Click source of object.
8. Click OK.

Project **2a**   **Embedding an Excel Chart in a Presentation**

1. Open **FundsPresentation.pptx** and then save the presentation with the name **PP_C8_P2**.
2. Open Excel and then open the workbook named **Funds01.xlsx** located in the PowerPoint2007C8 folder on your storage medium.
3. Click the chart to select it. (Make sure the chart is selected and not an element in the chart.)
4. Click the Copy button in the Clipboard group in the Home tab.
5. Click the button on the Taskbar representing **PP_C8_P2.pptx**.

6. Make Slide 4 active.
7. Click the Paste button arrow and then click *Paste Special* at the drop-down list.
8. At the Paste Special dialog box, make sure *Microsoft Office Graphic Object* is selected in the *As* list box and then click OK.

Step 8

Step 7

9. Double-click the chart.
10. Click the More button at the right side of the Chart Styles thumbnails and then click *Style 4* (fourth option from the left in the top row).
11. Click the Chart Tools Format tab.
12. Click in the *Shape Height* measurement box and then type 6.
13. Click in the *Shape Width* measurement box, type 9.5, and then press Enter.
14. Press Ctrl + B to bold the text in the pie.
15. Center the pie chart in the slide below the title.
16. Save **PP_C8_P2.pptx**.
17. Click the button on the Taskbar representing **Funds01.xlsx**, close the workbook, and then exit Excel.

Step 12

Step 13

Link an Object
1. Open source program.
2. Select desired object.
3. Click Copy button.
4. Open destination program.
5. Click Paste button arrow.
6. Click *Paste Special*.
7. Click *Paste link* option.
8. Click OK.

Linking Objects

If the content of the object that you will integrate between programs is likely to change, then link the object from the source program to the destination program. Linking the object establishes a direct connection between the source and destination program. The object is stored in the source program only. The destination program will have a code inserted into it that indicates the name and location of the source of the object. Whenever the presentation containing the link is opened, a message displays saying that the presentation contains links and the user is prompted to update the links. This process of updating links is referred to as *Dynamic Data Exchange* (DDE).

To link an object, open both programs and open both program files. In the source program file, click the desired object and then click the Copy button in the Clipboard group in the Home tab. Click the button on the Taskbar representing the destination program file and then position the insertion point in the desired location. Click the Paste button arrow in the Clipboard group in the Home tab and then click *Paste Special* at the drop-down list. At the Paste Special dialog box, click the source program for the object in the *As* list box, click the *Paste link* option located at the left side of the *As* list box, and then click OK.

Project 2b | Linking an Excel Chart to a Presentation

1. With **PP_C8_P2.pptx** open, open Excel and then open **Funds02.xlsx** located in the PowerPoint2007C8 folder on your storage medium.
2. Save the workbook with Save As and name it **MoneyMarketFunds**.
3. Copy and link the chart to a slide in the presentation by completing the following steps:
   a. Click the chart to select it.
   b. Click the Copy button in the Clipboard group in the Home tab.
   c. Click the button on the Taskbar representing **PP_C8_P2.pptx**.
   d. Make Slide 5 active.
   e. Click the Paste button arrow and then click *Paste Special* at the drop-down list.
   f. At the Paste Special dialog box, click the *Paste link* option.
   g. Make sure *Microsoft Office Excel Chart Object* is selected in the *As* list box.
   h. Click OK.

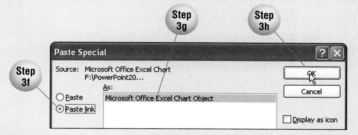

   i. Increase the size of the chart in the slide so it fills a good portion of the slide below the title. Move the chart so it appears balanced below the title.
4. Click the button on the Taskbar representing **MoneyMarketFunds.xlsx**.
5. Close **MoneyMarketFunds.xlsx** and exit Excel.
6. Make Slide 1 active and then run the presentation.
7. Print Slide 5.
8. Save and then close **PP_C8_P2.pptx**.

Editing Linked Objects

Edit linked objects in the source program in which they were created. Open the document, workbook, or presentation containing the object, make the changes as required, and then save and close the file. If both the source and destination programs are open at the same time, the changed content is reflected immediately in both programs.

Project 2c Editing Linked Data

1. Open Excel and then open **MoneyMarketFunds.xlsx**.
2. Make the following changes to data in the following cells:
   a. Change B2 from *13%* to *17%*.
   b. Change B3 from *9%* to *12%*.
   c. Change B6 from *10%* to *14%*.
3. Click the Save button on the Quick Access toolbar to save the edited workbook.
4. Close **MoneyMarketFunds.xlsx** and then exit Excel.
5. In PowerPoint, open **PP_C8_P2.pptx**.
6. At the message telling you that the presentation contains links, click the Update Links button.
7. Print the presentation as a handout with all of the slides on one page.
8. Save and then close **PP_C8_P2.pptx**.

	A	B	C
1		Percentage	
2	2005	17%	
3	2006	12%	
4	2007	18%	
5	2008	4%	
6	2009	14%	

Step 2a
Step 2b
Step 2c

Project 3 Download and Apply a Design Template to a Presentation and Prepare the Presentation for Distribution

You will download a design template from Microsoft Office Online and apply the template to a company presentation. You will insert, edit, and delete comments in the presentation; modify the presentation properties; inspect the presentation; and encrypt the presentation with a password.

QUICK STEPS

Download a Design
1. Click Office button.
2. Click *New*.
3. Click *Design slides* option.
4. Click desired category.
5. Click desired design.
6. Click Download button.

HINT
Microsoft checks the validity of your Microsoft Office software each time you download a template.

Downloading Designs

PowerPoint 2007 provides a number of design templates you can apply to a presentation. The Microsoft Office Online site contains additional design templates you can download and apply to a presentation. To view the available design templates for downloading, click the Office button and then click *New* at the drop-down list. At the New Presentation dialog box, click the *Design slides* option in the *Microsoft Office Online* section in the left panel. This displays categories of design templates in the middle panel. Click a category and design templates in the category display in the middle panel with information about the design in the right panel.

Some design thumbnails in the middle panel may contain a small logo of shoulders and a head indicating that the design template was created by a member of the Microsoft Office Online Community and Microsoft cannot guarantee that the design will work or that the design template is free from viruses or defects.

To download a design template, click the desired template in the middle panel and then click the Download button located in the lower right corner of the dialog box. At the message that displays telling you that templates are only available to customers running genuine Microsoft Office, click the Continue button. When the download is complete, the design template is applied to the open presentation and is also available in the Themes group in the Design tab.

Note: Check with your instructor before downloading a design template. To download a template you must have access to the Internet and access to the hard drive. If the Target the market design template *is already downloaded, skip steps 1 through 10 below. If you do not have access to the design template or cannot download, open ISPresentation.pptx, save it with the name PP_C8_P3, apply a design theme of your choosing, and then continue with step 11.*

1. At a blank presentation, click the Office button and then click *New* at the drop-down list.
2. At the New Presentation dialog box, click the *Design slides* option in the *Microsoft Office Online* section in the left panel.
3. Click the *Business* option in the *Design slides* section in the middle panel.
4. Scroll down the list of design templates and then click the *Target the market design template* (shown at the right).
5. Click the Download button that displays in the lower right corner of the dialog box.
6. At the message telling you that the templates are only available to customers running genuine Microsoft Office, click the Continue button. (This applies the design template to the current presentation.)
7. Close the presentation without saving it.
8. Open **ISPresentation.pptx** and then save the presentation with the name **PP_C8_P3**.

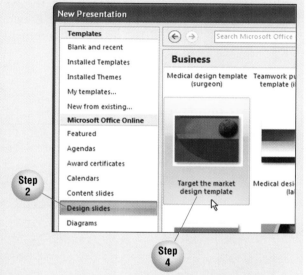

Step 2

Step 4

9. Apply the new design template by clicking the Design tab, clicking the More button at the right side of the theme thumbnails, and then clicking the *Target the market design template* theme that displays in the *Custom* section of the drop-down gallery.
10. Click the Colors button in the Themes group and then click *Office Theme 5* at the drop-down gallery.
11. Make each slide active and then make any formatting changes to elements so they appear attractively in the slide.
12. Save **PP_C8_P3.pptx**.

Inserting Comments

If you are sending out a presentation for review and want to ask reviewers specific questions or provide information about slides in a presentation, insert a comment. To insert a comment, display the desired slide and then position the insertion point where you want the comment to appear. Click the Review tab and then click the New Comment button in the Comments group. At the comment box that displays, similar to the one shown in Figure 8.3, type the desired comment. After typing the desired comment, click outside the comment box and a small yellow box displays with the user's initials and a comment number. Comments by individual users are numbered sequentially beginning with 1.

QUICK STEPS

Insert a Comment
1. Click Review tab.
2. Click New Comment button.
3. Type comment text.

New Comment

Show Markup

Next

Previous

To print comments, display the Print dialog box, choose how you want slides printed with the *Print what* option, and then make sure the *Print comments and ink markup* check box contains a check mark. Comments print on a separate page after the presentation is printed.

By default, the Show Markup button is active (displays with an orange background) in the Comments group in the Review tab. With this button active, comment boxes display in slides. If you want to hide comment boxes, click the Show Markup button to deactivate it. You can use the Next button and the Previous button in the Comments group in the Review tab to display comments in a presentation. Click the Next button to display the next comment in the presentation or click the Previous button to display the previous comment. If you turn off the display of comment boxes, you can use the Next and Previous buttons to display comments.

Figure 8.3 Comment Box

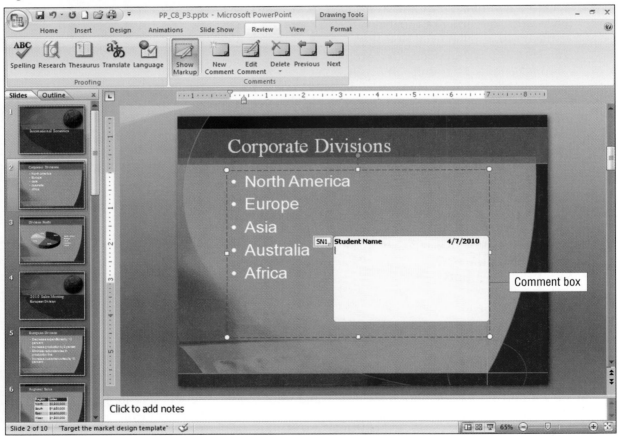

1. With **PP_C8_P3.pptx** open, make Slide 2 active and then insert a comment by completing the following steps:
   a. Position the insertion point immediately right of the word *Australia*.
   b. Click the Review tab.
   c. Click the New Comment button in the Comments group.
   d. Type the following in the comment box: Include information on New Zealand branch.

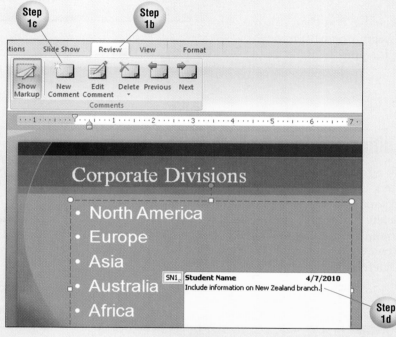

2. Make Slide 3 active and then insert a comment by completing the following steps:
   a. Click in the chart to select it. (Make sure you select the chart and not a chart element.)
   b. Click the New Comment button in the Comments group.
   c. Type the following in the comment box: Include a chart showing profit amounts.
3. Make Slide 5 active, position the insertion point immediately right of the word *line* at the end of the third bulleted item, and then insert the comment Provide detailed information on how this goal will be accomplished.
4. Make Slide 8 active, position the insertion point immediately right of the word *Singapore* in the second bulleted item, and then insert the comment Who will be managing the Singapore office?
5. Click the Previous button in the Comments group to display the comment box in Slide 5.
6. Click the Previous button to display the comment box in Slide 3.

7. Click the Show Markup button in the Comments group in the Review tab to turn off the display of comment boxes.
8. Click Slide 5 and notice that the comment box is not visible.
9. Click the Next button to display the comment box in Slide 2.
10. Click the Show Markup button to turn on the display of comment boxes.

11. Print the presentation and the comments by completing the following steps:
   a. Click the Office button and then click *Print*.
   b. At the Print dialog box, change the *Print what* to *Handouts* with six slides per page.
   c. Make sure the *Print comments and ink markup* check box contains a check mark.
   d. Click OK.
12. Make Slide 1 active and then run the presentation beginning with Slide 1.
13. Save **PP_C8_P3.pptx**.

Step 11b

Step 11c

Step 11d

Editing and Deleting Comments

Edit Comment

Delete

To edit text in a comment box, click the comment box you want to edit and then click the Edit Comment button in the Comments group in the Review tab. This expands the comment box and positions the insertion point inside the box. To delete a comment from a slide, click the small box containing the user's initials and comment number and then click the Delete button in the Comments group in the Review tab. You can also right-click the box containing the initials and then click Delete at the shortcut menu.

Project 3c Editing and Deleting Comments

1. With **PP_C8_P3.pptx** open, make Slide 8 active and then edit the comment by completing the following steps:
   a. Click the comment box containing the user's initials and comment number.
   b. Make sure the Review tab is active and then click the Edit Comment button in the Comments group.
   c. Select and delete the text in the comment box and then type Check with Sandy Cates to determine who will be appointed branch manager.
2. Delete the comment in Slide 3 by completing the following steps:
   a. Click twice on the Previous button to display Slide 3 and the comment in the slide.
   b. Click the Delete button in the Comments group in the Review tab.
3. Print the presentation as a handout with six slides per page and make sure the comments print.
4. Save **PP_C8_P3.pptx**.

Step 2b

Preparing a Presentation for Distribution

If you work with other employees or colleagues, you may want to share and distribute your presentations. You can prepare your presentation for distribution with options at the Office button Prepare side menu, which you can display by clicking the Office button and then pointing to *Prepare*.

Modifying Presentation Properties

Each presentation you create has properties information attached to the presentation such as the type and location of the presentation and when the presentation was created, modified, and accessed. Along with this information, you can add additional properties information such as a presentation title, subject, category, and keywords. Add additional properties information at the document information panel similar to the one shown in Figure 8.4. Display this panel by clicking the Office button, pointing to *Prepare*, and then clicking the *Properties* option at the side menu. You can type specific information in each of the text boxes in the properties panel to describe the presentation and to help you search for the presentation at a later date. To move the insertion point to the next text box, press the Tab key. To move the insertion point to the previous text box, press Shift + Tab.

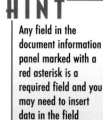

HINT
Any field in the document information panel marked with a red asterisk is a required field and you may need to insert data in the field before saving your presentation.

Figure 8.4 Document Information Panel

Type information about the presentation in the text boxes in the document information panel.

ⓘ Document Properties ▾			Location: F:\PowerPoint2007C8\PP_C8_P3.pptx			✳ Required field ✕
Author:	Title:	Subject:	Keywords:	Category:	Status:	
Comments:						

Along with the document information panel, you can also insert specific information about the presentation with options at the Properties dialog box. To display this dialog box, click the Document Properties button that displays in the upper left corner of the document information panel and then click *Advanced Properties*. At the Properties dialog box, click a specific tab and then insert the desired information or read the information that displays.

QUICK STEPS

Modify Presentation Properties
1. Click Office, *Prepare, Properties.*
2. Type, edit, or delete property information.
3. Click Close button.

1. With **PP_C8_P3.pptx** open, display the document information panel by clicking the Office button, pointing to *Prepare*, and then clicking *Properties* at the side menu.
2. Select the name that appears in the *Author* text box (unless it is your name) and then type your first and last names.
3. Press the Tab key twice (this makes the *Subject* text box active) and then type International Securities Corporate Meeting.
4. Press the Tab key and then type the following words in the *Keywords* text box: International Securities, sales, divisions.
5. Press the Tab key and then type sales meeting in the *Category* text box.
6. Press the Tab key twice and then type the following in the *Comments* text box: This is a presentation prepared for the corporate meeting.

7. Close the document information panel by clicking the Close button located in the upper right corner of the panel.
8. Save **PP_C8_P3.docx**.

Inspecting a Presentation

HINT

Inspect your document for personal and hidden data before distributing it to others.

PowerPoint includes a document inspection feature you can use to inspect your presentation for personal data, hidden data, and metadata. Metadata is data that describes other data such as presentation properties information. You may want to remove some personal or hidden data before you share your presentation with other people. Check your presentation for personal or hidden data by clicking the Office button, pointing to *Prepare*, and then clicking *Inspect Document* at the side menu. This displays the Document Inspector dialog box shown in Figure 8.5.

Figure 8.5 Document Inspector Dialog Box

Remove the check mark from those options that you do not want the document inspector to check.

By default, the document inspector will check all of the items listed in the dialog box. If you do not want the inspector to check a specific item in your presentation, remove the check mark. For example, if you know your presentation contains comments and/or annotations, click the *Comments and Annotations* check box to remove the check mark. Click the Inspect button located toward the bottom of the dialog box and the document inspector scans the presentation identifying information.

When the inspection is complete, the results display in the dialog box. A check mark before an option indicates that the inspector did not find the specific items. If an exclamation point is inserted before an option, the inspector found items and displays a list of the items. If you want to remove the found items, click the Remove All button that displays at the right side of the desired option. Click the Close button to close the Document Inspector dialog box.

Inspect a Presentation
1. Click Office button, *Prepare, Inspect Document.*
2. Remove check marks from items you do not want checked.
3. Click Inspect button.

1. With **PP_C8_P3.pptx** open, click the Office button, point to *Prepare*, and then click *Inspect Document*.
2. At the Document Inspector dialog box, you decide you do not want to check the presentation for XML data, so click the *Custom XML Data* check box to remove the check mark.

3. Click the Inspect button.
4. Read through the inspection results and then remove all comments by clicking the Remove All button that displays at the right side of the *Comments and Annotations* section.

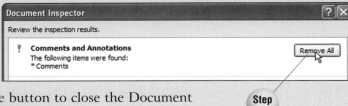

5. Click the Close button to close the Document Inspector dialog box.
6. Save **PP_C8_P3.pptx**.

Encrypting a Presentation

Encrypt a Presentation
1. Click Office button, *Prepare, Encrypt Document.*
2. Type a password.
3. Press Enter.
4. Type same password again.
5. Click OK.

You can insert a password in a presentation to ensure that the presentation is opened only by someone who knows the password. You can protect a presentation with a password with the *Encrypt Document* option at the Office button Prepare side menu. Click the *Encrypt Document* option at the Prepare side menu and the Encrypt Document dialog box displays as shown in Figure 8.6. In the dialog box, type a password and then press the Enter key. At the Confirm Password dialog box, type the password again and then click OK.

You can also insert a password in a presentation by displaying the Save As dialog box, clicking the Tools button located in the lower left corner of the dialog box, and then clicking *General Options*. At the General Options dialog box, type a password in the *Password to open* text box, press the Tab key, type the same password in the *Password to modify* text box, and then click OK.

HINT

A strong password contains a mix of uppercase and lowercase letters as well as numbers and symbols.

Figure 8.6 Encrypt Document Dialog Box

Project 3f Encrypting a Presentation with a Password

1. With **PP_C8_P3.pptx** open, click the Office button, point to *Prepare*, and then click *Encrypt Document*.
2. At the Encrypt Document dialog box, type your initials in all uppercase letters.
3. Press the Enter key.
4. At the Confirm Password dialog box, type your initials again in uppercase letters and then click OK.
5. Save and then close **PP_C8_P3.pptx**.
6. Open **PP_C8_P3.pptx**. At the Password dialog box, type your initials in uppercase letters and then press Enter.
7. Close **PP_C8_P3.pptx**.

Step 2

Project 4 Protect and Check Compatibility of an Online Learning Presentation

You will open an online learning presentation, add a digital signature to the presentation, mark it as final, and run a compatibility check on the presentation.

Adding a Digital Signature to a Presentation

You can apply a digital signature to a presentation to authenticate the presentation and ensure that the content of the presentation has not been changed or tampered with after it was digitally signed. When you apply a digital signature to a presentation, the presentation is locked so that it cannot be edited or changed unless you remove the digital signature. Before applying a digital signature, you must obtain a signature. You can obtain a digital signature from a commercial certification authority or you can create your own digital signature. When you create your digital signature, it is saved on the hard drive or the network. Depending on how your system is set up, you might be prevented from using a certificate.

To add a digital signature, click the Office button, point to *Prepare*, and then click *Add a Digital Signature* at the side menu. At the message displaying information about the digital signature, click OK. At the Signs dialog box, shown in Figure 8.7,

QUICK STEPS

Insert a Digital Signature
1. Click Office button, Prepare, Add a Digital Signature.
2. Type purpose for signing document.
3. Click Sign.
4. Click OK.

Signatures

type text in the *Purpose for signing this document* text box that identifies the reason for the signature and then click the Sign button. At the message telling you that the signature was successfully saved with the presentation, click OK. This opens the Signatures task pane at the right side of the screen and also inserts a Signatures button toward the left side of the Status bar. Turn on or off the Signatures task pane by clicking the Signatures button on the Status bar.

Figure 8.7 Sign Dialog Box

Type in this text box the explanation of why a digital signature is attached to the presentation.

Remove a Digital Signature
1. Click Signatures button at left side of Status bar.
2. Hover mouse pointer over signature in Signatures task pane.
3. Click down-pointing arrow at right of signature.
4. Click *Remove Signature* at drop-down list.

To remove a digital signature from a presentation, click the Signatures button on the Status bar to turn on the display of the Signatures task pane. Move the mouse pointer over the signature in the Signatures task pane list box, click the down-pointing arrow at the right side of the signature, and then click *Remove Signature* at the drop-down list. At the message asking if you are sure you want to remove permanently the digital signature, click Yes. At the message telling you that the signature has been removed, click OK and then close the Signatures task pane.

Project 4a   Adding and Removing a Digital Signature

Check with your instructor before completing this project.

1. Open the presentation named **OnlineLearning.pptx** and then save the presentation and name it **PP_C8_P4**.
2. Click the Office button, point to *Prepare*, and then click *Add a Digital Signature*.
3. At the message displaying information about the digital signature, click OK.
4. At the Sign dialog box, type **Presentation prepared for training seminar by Student Name.** (Type your first and last names in place of *Student Name*.)
5. Click the Sign button.

Step 4

Step 5

6. At the message telling you that the signature was successfully saved, click OK.
7. Close the Signatures task pane by clicking the Close button located in the upper right corner of the task pane.
8. Click each of the tabs in the ribbon and notice that most buttons and options are not active since the digital signature prevents the presentation from being altered.
9. Remove the digital signature by completing the following steps:

Step 9a

a. Click the Signatures button located toward the left side of the Status bar. (This displays the Signatures task pane.)
b. Hover the mouse pointer over the signature in the Signatures task pane, click the down-pointing arrow at the right side of the signature, and then click *Remove Signature* at the drop-down list.

Step 9b

c. At the message asking if you are sure you want to remove permanently the digital signature, click Yes.
d. At the message telling you that the signature has been removed, click OK.
e. Close the Signatures task pane.
10. Save **PP_C8_P4.pptx**.

Marking a Presentation as Final

You can save your presentation as a read-only presentation and mark it as final with the *Mark as Final* option at the Office button Prepare side menu. To use this feature, click the Office button, point to *Prepare*, and then click *Mark as Final*. At the message telling you that the presentation will be marked as final and then saved, click the OK button. A message box displays with information telling you that the presentation is marked as final to indicate that editing is complete and that it is the final version of the presentation. The message further indicates that when a presentation is marked as final, the status property is set to "Final" and typing, editing, commands, and proofing marks are turned off. It also tells you that you can identify a presentation marked as final when the *Mark As Final* icon displays toward the left side of the Status bar. At this message, click OK.

Running the Compatibility Checker

PowerPoint includes a compatibility checker that will check your presentation and identify elements that are not supported or will act differently in previous versions of PowerPoint. Some features not supported by previous versions of PowerPoint include custom slide layouts; heading and body fonts; and some shapes, pictures, objects, and SmartArt. For example, if you save a presentation containing heading and body fonts and a SmartArt graphic as a PowerPoint 2003 presentation, the heading and body are converted to static formatting and the SmartArt graphic is converted to an uneditable picture.

QUICK STEPS

Mark a Presentation as Final
1. Click Office button, Prepare, Mark as Final.
2. Click OK.
3. Click OK.

HINT
Use the compatibility checker to determine the elements in a presentation not supported by previous versions of PowerPoint.

Run the Compatibility Checker
1. Click Office button, *Prepare, Run Compatibility Checker*.
2. At Microsoft Office PowerPoint Compatibility Checker dialog box, click OK.

To determine the compatibility of the features in your presentation, click the Office button, point to *Prepare*, and then click *Run Compatibility Checker*. This displays the Microsoft Office PowerPoint Compatibility Checker dialog box similar to the one shown in Figure 8.8. This dialog box displays a summary of the elements in the presentation that are not compatible with previous versions of PowerPoint and indicates what will occur with the elements when the presentation is saved and then opened in a previous version. By default, PowerPoint will run the compatibility checker when you save a presentation in an earlier version of PowerPoint. If you do not want the compatibility checker to check your presentations, remove the check mark from the *Check compatibility when saving in PowerPoint 97-2003 formats* option at the Microsoft Office PowerPoint Compatibility Checker dialog box.

Figure 8.8 Microsoft Office PowerPoint Compatibility Checker Dialog Box

This dialog box displays information on what will happen to text or elements if the presentation is saved in a previous version of PowerPoint.

Restricting Permissions to a Presentation

In Microsoft Office 2007, Information Rights Management (IRM) is used to restrict permissions to a presentation. Permissions is the term given to the viewing and editing rights that you assign to an individual. You can grant one person the ability to read but not change the presentation and another person the ability to read and edit but not print the presentation. By restricting the presentation you can prevent confidential data from being changed, printed, or copied. You can also add an expiration date on a presentation so that after the specified date, the presentation is no longer available.

To be able to use the Restrict Permission feature, you must have previously installed the Windows Rights Management Software (RMS). The computer that you are using requires the RMS client. You also need the ability to connect to a Windows 2003 or later server running RMS. The server is used to distribute licenses to individuals who want to access a restricted presentation. For example, if you grant permission to a person to edit a presentation, the first time the individual opens the restricted presentation, he or she connects to the server for authentication and downloads a license.

If you have the RMS client software and access to a licensing server, you can restrict permissions to the active presentation by clicking the Office button, pointing to *Prepare*, pointing to *Restrict Permission*, and then clicking *Do Not Distribute*. This opens the Permission dialog box. Click the *Restrict permission to this document* check box and then assign the access rights you want to grant to individual users. Users are identified by e-mail address. The following permission levels are available:

- *Read*. Individual can read the presentation but cannot edit, print, or copy.
- *Change*. Individual can read, edit, and save changes but cannot print.
- *Full Control*. Individual can read, edit, save changes, and print; essentially any task that the author can do is also available to a person granted full control permission.

If you receive a presentation that is restricted, a *Do Not Distribute* message appears in the message bar when the presentation is opened.

Project 4b — Checking the Compatibility of Elements and Marking a Presentation as Final

1. With **PP_C8_P4.pptx** open, you need to send the presentation to a colleague who is using Microsoft PowerPoint 2003 and decide to check the compatibility of the presentation to determine what will happen to elements not supported by the 2003 version. Run the compatibility checker by completing the following steps:
   a. Click the Office button, point to *Prepare,* and then click *Run Compatibility Checker* at the side menu.
   b. At the Microsoft Office PowerPoint Compatibility Checker dialog box, read the information about the elements not supported by 2003 and what will happen to the elements.
   c. Click OK to close the dialog box.

2. Mark the presentation as final by completing the following steps:
   a. Click the Office button, point to *Prepare,* and then click *Mark as Final*.
   b. At the message telling you that the presentation will be marked as final and then saved, click OK.
   c. At the message that displays, click OK.
   d. Click each of the tabs in the ribbon and notice that most of the buttons and options are dimmed and unavailable.

3. Close **PP_C8_P4.pptx**

Step 1a

Prepare the document for distribution

Properties
View and edit presentation properties, such as Title, Author, and Keywords.

Inspect Document
Check the presentation for hidden metadata or personal information.

Encrypt Document
Increase the security of the presentation by adding encryption.

Add a Digital Signature
Ensure the integrity of the presentation by adding an invisible digital signature.

Mark as Final
Let readers know the presentation is final and make it read-only.

Run Compatibility Checker
Check for features not supported by earlier versions of PowerPoint.

PowerPoint Options   Exit PowerPoint

roject 5 Save Presentations in Different Formats and Package a Presentation for CD

You will save presentations in a number of formats including PowerPoint Show, a previous version of PowerPoint, PDF format, and save slides as graphic images. You will also save a presentation as a Web page and then package the presentation for a CD.

Saving Presentations in Different Formats

HINT

PowerPoint 2007 does not support saving to PowerPoint 95 or earlier versions.

With the *Save as type* option at the Save As dialog box, you can choose to save a presentation in a variety of formats such as an earlier version of PowerPoint, as a PowerPoint show, as a PDF file, or as a Web page. You can also save a presentation in other formats using the Office button Save As side menu. Click the Office button, point to *Save As*, and a side menu displays as shown in Figure 8.9. The first option in the side menu, *PowerPoint Presentation*, will save a presentation in the default format (**.pptx*).

Figure 8.9 Save As Side Menu

Point to the Save As option in the Office button drop-down list to display this side menu of save options.

Saving a Presentation as a PowerPoint Show

Choose the *PowerPoint Show* option to save a presentation in the *.ppsx* format, which will open a presentation in Slide Show view without opening PowerPoint. For example, you can save a presentation in PowerPoint Show format, display My Computer in Windows, double-click the presentation, and it automatically opens on the screen in Slide Show view.

Project 5a — Saving a Presentation as a PowerPoint Show

1. Open **OnlineLearning.pptx** and then save the presentation with the name **PP_C8_P5**.
2. Click the Office button, point to *Save As*, and then click *PowerPoint Show*.
3. At the Save As dialog box, type PP_C8_P5_Show and then press Enter.
4. Close **PP_C8_P5_Show.ppsx**.
5. Display the My Computer window by clicking the Start button and then clicking *My Computer*.
6. In the My Computer window, double-click the drive representing your storage medium.
7. Navigate to the PowerPoint2007C8 folder on your storage medium and then double-click *PP_C8_P5_Show.ppsx*. (This starts the presentation in Slide Show view.)
8. Run the presentation.
9. Close the My Computer window.

Saving a Presentation in a Previous Version

If you create presentations that others will open in a previous version of PowerPoint, consider saving the presentation in the PowerPoint 97-2003 format. If you save a presentation in a previous version, the presentation name displays in the title bar followed by the words *[Compatibility Mode]*. In this mode, some PowerPoint 2007 features may not be available.

Project 5b — Saving a Presentation in a Previous Version

1. Open **PP_C8_P5.pptx**.
2. Click the Office button, point to *Save As*, and then click *PowerPoint 97-2003 Presentation* at the side menu.
3. At the Save As dialog box, type PP_C8_P5_2003format and then press Enter.
4. At the Microsoft Office PowerPoint Compatibility Checker dialog box, click the Continue button.
5. Close **PP_C8_P5_2003format.ppt**.

Saving in PDF Format

The portable document format (PDF) was developed by Adobe Systems® and is a format that captures all of the elements of a file as an electronic image. You can view a PDF file on any application on any computer, making this format the most widely used for transferring files to other users. A presentation saved in PDF format is printer-friendly and most, if not all, of the presentation's original appearance is maintained.

Before saving a PowerPoint presentation in PDF format, you must install an add-in download from the Microsoft Web site. To determine whether or not the download is installed, click the Office button and then point to the *Save As* option. If the add-in is installed, you will see the option *PDF or XPS* in the side menu. If the add-in is not downloaded, you will see the option *Find add-ins for other file formats* in the side menu. To download the add-in, click the *Find add-ins for other file formats* option at the side menu. This displays the PowerPoint Help window with information on how to download the add-in.

When you save a presentation in PDF format, the presentation opens in Adobe Reader, which is an application designed to view your presentation. You will be able to navigate in the presentation but you will not be able to make any changes to it.

Project 5c Saving a Presentation in PDF Format

1. Open **PP_C8_P5.pptx**.
2. Click the Office button, point to *Save As*, and then click *PDF or XPS* in the side menu. (If this option does not display, the PDF add-in download has not been installed.)

3. At the Save As dialog box with the *Save as type* option set at *PDF (*.pdf)*, click the Publish button.

Step 3

4. Scroll through the presentation in Adobe Reader.
5. Click the Close button located in the upper right corner of the window to close Adobe Reader.

Saving Slides as Images

You can save a PowerPoint presentation in a variety of formats including saving slides within a presentation as graphic images. Some graphic image formats you can use to save a presentation include GIF (Graphics Interchange Format), JPEG (Joint Photographic Experts Group), and TIF (Tag Image File).

The GIF format is limited to 256 colors and is more effective for scanned images, line drawings, and black and white images rather than color photographs. The JPEG file format supports 16 million colors and is effective for photographs and complex graphics. The TIF file format is best for storing bit-mapped images on personal computers and can be any resolution, black and white, grayscale, and color.

To save a slide or all slides in a presentation in a graphic format, open the presentation, display the Save As dialog box, and then change the *Save as type* option to the desired format. Type a name for the slide or presentation and then press Enter or click Save. At the message that displays, click the Every Slide button if you want every slide in the presentation saved as a graphic image or click the Current Slide Only button if you want only the current slide saved as a graphic image.

If you click the Every Slide button, a message displays telling you that all slides in the presentation were saved as separate files in a folder. The name of the folder is the name that you type in the *File name* text box in the Save As dialog box.

Project 5d   **Saving Slides as Graphic Images**

1. With **PP_C8_P5.pptx** open, display the Save As dialog box.
2. Click the down-pointing arrow at the right side of the *Save as type* option at the Save As dialog box, scroll down the drop-down list, and then click *JPEG File Interchange Format (*.jpg)*.

Step 2

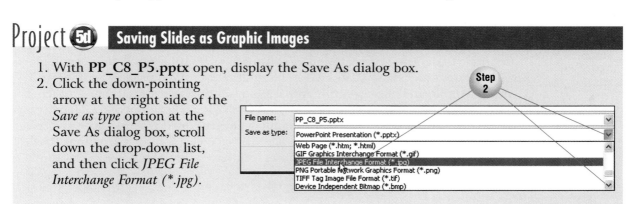

3. Select the current name in the *File name* text box and then type **OnlinePresentationSlides**.
4. Click the Save button.
5. At the message that displays, click the Every Slide button.
6. At the message telling you that each slide has been saved as a separate file in the OnlinePresentationSlides folder, click OK.
7. Open Word.
8. At a blank document, change the font size to 18, turn on bold, change the alignment to center, and then type **Online Learning – It just makes sense!**
9. Press the Enter key twice and then insert one of the slides saved in JPEG format by completing the following steps:
   a. Click the Insert tab and then click the Picture button in the Illustrations group.
   b. At the Insert Picture dialog box, navigate to the OnlinePresentationSlides folder in the PowerPoint2007C8 folder on your storage medium and then double-click *Slide3.JPG*.

10. Format the image in the document by completing the following steps:
    a. Click in the *Shape Height* measurement box in the Size group in the Picture Tools Format tab, type 2.8, and then press Enter.
    b. Click the *Drop Shadow Rectangle* option in the Picture Styles group.
11. Press Ctrl + End to move the insertion point to the end of the document, press the Enter key, and then complete steps similar to those in Steps 9 and 10 to insert the image *Slide4.JPG* in the document.

12. Save the document and name it **PP_C8_P5_Word**.
13. Print and then close **PP_C8_P5_Word.docx**.
14. Exit Word.

HINT

Publish your presentation to the Web to make it available to colleagues for viewing.

Saving a Presentation as a Web Page

The Internet is fast becoming a preferred choice as a presentation medium. Once a presentation has been published to the Internet, anyone around the world with Internet access can view your presentation. If you are traveling to several remote locations to deliver a presentation, you can access the slides from any computer with Internet access. You can save a presentation as a Web page as a folder with an HTML file and all supporting files or you can save a presentation as a Web page as a single file with all supporting files. *HTML* is an acronym for Hypertext Markup Language, which is the programming language used to code pages to display graphically on the World Wide Web. HTML is a collection of instructions that includes *tags* applied to text and graphics to instruct the Web browser software how to properly display the page.

3. At the Save As dialog box with the *Save as type* option set at *PDF (*.pdf)*, click the Publish button.

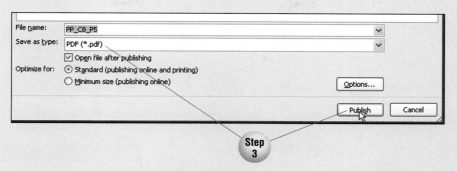

Step 3

4. Scroll through the presentation in Adobe Reader.
5. Click the Close button located in the upper right corner of the window to close Adobe Reader.

Saving Slides as Images

You can save a PowerPoint presentation in a variety of formats including saving slides within a presentation as graphic images. Some graphic image formats you can use to save a presentation include GIF (Graphics Interchange Format), JPEG (Joint Photographic Experts Group), and TIF (Tag Image File).

The GIF format is limited to 256 colors and is more effective for scanned images, line drawings, and black and white images rather than color photographs. The JPEG file format supports 16 million colors and is effective for photographs and complex graphics. The TIF file format is best for storing bit-mapped images on personal computers and can be any resolution, black and white, grayscale, and color.

To save a slide or all slides in a presentation in a graphic format, open the presentation, display the Save As dialog box, and then change the *Save as type* option to the desired format. Type a name for the slide or presentation and then press Enter or click Save. At the message that displays, click the Every Slide button if you want every slide in the presentation saved as a graphic image or click the Current Slide Only button if you want only the current slide saved as a graphic image.

If you click the Every Slide button, a message displays telling you that all slides in the presentation were saved as separate files in a folder. The name of the folder is the name that you type in the *File name* text box in the Save As dialog box.

Project 5d Saving Slides as Graphic Images

1. With **PP_C8_P5.pptx** open, display the Save As dialog box.
2. Click the down-pointing arrow at the right side of the *Save as type* option at the Save As dialog box, scroll down the drop-down list, and then click *JPEG File Interchange Format (*.jpg)*.

Step 2

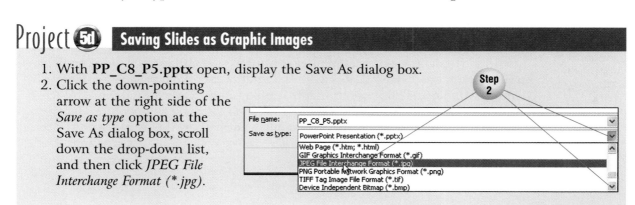

3. Select the current name in the *File name* text box and then type **OnlinePresentationSlides**.
4. Click the Save button.
5. At the message that displays, click the Every Slide button.
6. At the message telling you that each slide has been saved as a separate file in the OnlinePresentationSlides folder, click OK.
7. Open Word.
8. At a blank document, change the font size to 18, turn on bold, change the alignment to center, and then type **Online Learning – It just makes sense!**
9. Press the Enter key twice and then insert one of the slides saved in JPEG format by completing the following steps:
   a. Click the Insert tab and then click the Picture button in the Illustrations group.
   b. At the Insert Picture dialog box, navigate to the OnlinePresentationSlides folder in the PowerPoint2007C8 folder on your storage medium and then double-click *Slide3.JPG*.

Step 9b

10. Format the image in the document by completing the following steps:
    a. Click in the *Shape Height* measurement box in the Size group in the Picture Tools Format tab, type 2.8, and then press Enter.
    b. Click the *Drop Shadow Rectangle* option in the Picture Styles group.

Step 10b

11. Press Ctrl + End to move the insertion point to the end of the document, press the Enter key, and then complete steps similar to those in Steps 9 and 10 to insert the image *Slide4.JPG* in the document.
12. Save the document and name it **PP_C8_P5_Word**.
13. Print and then close **PP_C8_P5_Word.docx**.
14. Exit Word.

HINT

Publish your presentation to the Web to make it available to colleagues for viewing.

Saving a Presentation as a Web Page

The Internet is fast becoming a preferred choice as a presentation medium. Once a presentation has been published to the Internet, anyone around the world with Internet access can view your presentation. If you are traveling to several remote locations to deliver a presentation, you can access the slides from any computer with Internet access. You can save a presentation as a Web page as a folder with an HTML file and all supporting files or you can save a presentation as a Web page as a single file with all supporting files. *HTML* is an acronym for Hypertext Markup Language, which is the programming language used to code pages to display graphically on the World Wide Web. HTML is a collection of instructions that includes *tags* applied to text and graphics to instruct the Web browser software how to properly display the page.

Fortunately, PowerPoint will translate the slides into Web pages for you so you can publish presentations to the Internet without having to learn HTML programming. To do this, open the presentation you want to save as a Web page, display the Save As dialog box, change the *Save as type* option to *Single File Web Page (*.mht; *.mhtml)*, and the Save As dialog box displays as shown in Figure 8.10.

Figure 8.10 Save As Dialog Box

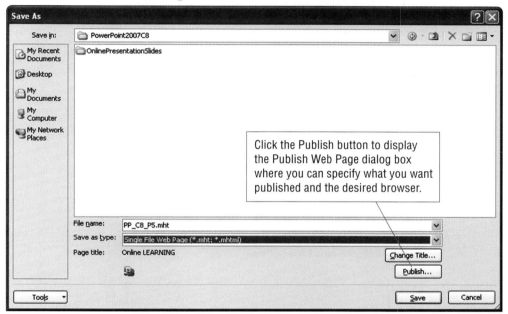

At the Save As dialog box, click the Publish button and the Publish as Web Page dialog box displays as shown in Figure 8.11. If you do not want to convert all of the slides in the presentation, specify the starting slide number in the *Slide number* text box and the ending slide number in the *through* text box in the *Publish what?* section. You can convert to specific versions of Web browser software with the options in the *Browser support* section. Click the Web Options button to display the Web Options dialog box displayed in Figure 8.12.

Figure 8.11 Publish as Web Page Dialog Box

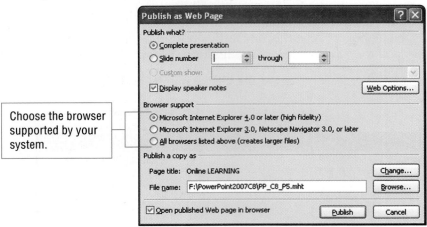

Choose the browser supported by your system.

Figure 8.12 Web Options Dialog Box

When PowerPoint converts the presentation to HTML format, navigation buttons are created for users to navigate through the slides in the Web browser. The default colors for the navigation buttons are *White text on black*. You can select different color schemes with the *Colors* option at the Web Options dialog box with the General tab selected. If the target browser is Microsoft Internet Explorer version 4.0 or later, you can select *Show slide animation while browsing*.

Click the Files tab at the Web Options dialog box and options display for determining how the Web page files will be organized. By default, PowerPoint creates a folder in the conversion process and stores all of the files in the folder. The screen size can be set at the dialog box with the Pictures tab selected. Click the down-pointing arrow to the right of the *Screen size* text box and then click a screen resolution from the drop-down list. Use options at the Web Options dialog box with the Encoding tab selected to specify a different language code for saving the Web page.

When a presentation is converted to HTML with *All browsers listed above* as the Browser support option at the Publish as Web Page dialog box, additional files are created from the original presentation as follows: separate graphic files are created for each slide; separate graphic files are created for the navigation buttons and other navigation assistance tools; separate HTML files are created for each slide; a text-only version is created for each page for browser software that does not support graphics; and finally, an outline page is created that becomes the index frame where the user can select the page titles for each slide. The outline page is the opening page in the left frame that is displayed in the Web browser. A single presentation file can result in several files being created after conversion to Web pages.

If you are directly connected to a company intranet or Web server, contact the system administrator to find out the destination folder you need to specify in the *Publish a copy as File name* text box. Use the Browse button next to the *File name* option box to navigate to the correct folder. If you are not directly connected to an intranet or Web server, specify a folder on your system to copy the files so that you can later send to a Web server by modem or disk.

Click the Publish button in the Publish as Web Page dialog box to begin the conversion once all of the options have been set. If you would like to view the completed Web pages in your Web browser software when the conversion is complete, click the *Open published Web page in browser* check box before clicking the Publish button. Navigate through the presentation using the slide titles in the left frame of the browser window or the navigation buttons located along the bottom of the window.

Project 5e · Saving a Presentation as a Web Page

1. With **PP_C8_P5.pptx** open, display the Save As dialog box and then change the *Save as type* option to *Single File Web Page (*.mht; *.mhtml)*.
2. Click the Publish button.

3. At the Publish as Web Page dialog box, click the Web Options button in the *Publish what?* section.
4. At the Web Options dialog box with the General tab selected, click the down-pointing arrow at the right of the *Colors* text box and then click *Black text on white* at the drop-down list.
5. Click OK to close the Web Options dialog box.
6. At the Publish as Web Page dialog box, choose the target browser in the *Browser support* section that applies to your school. Check with your instructor if you are not sure which target browser you should be using. The default selection is *Microsoft Internet Explorer 4.0 or later*.

7. Click the Browse button next to the *File name* option box, make sure the correct folder is displayed for storing the presentation, and then click OK.

8. If necessary, click the *Open published Web page in browser* check box to insert a check mark.

9. Click the Publish button.

10. In a few moments, the conversion will be complete and the Microsoft Internet Explorer or other default browser window will open with the opening page of the presentation displayed.

11. Navigate through the presentation by clicking the slide titles along the left frame, or using the Next Slide and Previous Slide navigation buttons along the bottom of the window. When you have finished viewing all of the slides, close the Internet Explorer or other browser window.

Step 8

Step 9

12. Close **PP_C8_P5.pptx** without saving the changes.

13. Open **GlobalEmployeeOrientation.pptx**.

14. Display the Save As dialog box and then change the *Save as type* option to *Web Page (*.htm; *.html)*.

15. Click the Publish button.

Step 14

Step 15

16. At the Publish as Web Page dialog box, choose the target browser in the *Browser support* section that applies to your school. Check with your instructor if you are not sure which target browser you should be using. The default selection is *Microsoft Internet Explorer 4.0 or later*.

17. Click the Browse button next to the *File name* option box, make sure the correct folder is displayed for storing the presentation, and then click OK.

18. Make sure the *Open published Web page in browser* check box contains a check mark.

19. Click the Publish button.

20. In a few moments, the conversion will be complete and the Microsoft Internet Explorer or other default browser window will open with the opening page of the presentation displayed.

21. Navigate through the presentation by clicking the slide titles along the left frame, or using the Next Slide and Previous Slide navigation buttons along the bottom of the window. When you have finished viewing all of the slides, close the Internet Explorer or other browser window.

22. Close **GlobalEmployeeOrientation.pptx** without saving the changes.

Packaging a Presentation for a CD

The safest way to transport a PowerPoint presentation to another computer is to use the Package for CD feature. With this feature, you can copy a presentation including all of the linked files, fonts used, and PowerPoint Viewer program in case the destination computer does not have PowerPoint installed on it onto a CD or to a folder or network location. To use the Package for CD feature, click the Office button, point to *Publish*, and then click the *Package for CD* option at the side menu. This displays the Package for CD dialog box shown in Figure 8.13.

Figure 8.13 Package for CD Dialog Box

Click this button to copy the presentation and all related files to a specific folder.

Click this button to copy the presentation and all related files to a CD.

At the Package for CD dialog box, type a name in the *Name the CD* text box and then click the Copy to CD button. If you want to copy the presentation to a specific folder (instead of a CD), click the Copy to Folder button.

Click the Options button at the Package for CD dialog box and the Options dialog box displays as shown in Figure 8.14. Insert a check mark in the check box for those features you want to be included on the CD or in the folder or remove the check mark from those you do not want to include. If the computer you will be using does not contain the PowerPoint program, make sure the *Viewer Package* option is selected. The PowerPoint Viewer allows you to run a presentation on a computer that does not contain PowerPoint. (By default, the PowerPoint Viewer is installed when you install PowerPoint.) If charts or other files are linked to the presentation, insert a check mark in the *Linked files* check box and, if the destination computer does not have the same fonts installed, insert a check mark in the *Embedded TrueType fonts* check box.

HINT
PowerPoint Viewer does not support files that are formatted for Microsoft PowerPoint 97 or earlier versions.

Figure 8.14 Options Dialog Box

Make sure this option is selected if you want the PowerPoint Viewer saved with the presentation.

Insert a check mark in this option to ensure that any linked files are saved with the presentation.

Insert a check mark in this option if the presentation contains TrueType fonts.

Options

Package type
- ⦿ Viewer Package (update file formats to run in PowerPoint Viewer)
  Select how presentations will play in the viewer:
  [Play all presentations automatically in the specified order ▾]
- ○ Archive Package (do not update file formats)

Include these files
(These files will not display in the Files to be copied list)
- ☑ Linked files
- ☐ Embedded TrueType fonts

Enhance security and privacy
Password to open each presentation: [   ]
Password to modify each presentation: [   ]
- ☐ Inspect presentations for inappropriate or private information

[OK]   [Cancel]

Project 5f **Using the Package for CD Feature**

1. Open **GlobalEmployeeOrientation.pptx**.
2. Click the Office button, point to *Publish*, and then click *Package for CD*. (If a dialog box displays with information about the PowerPoint Viewer, click OK.)
3. At the Package for CD dialog box, type **PP_C8_P5_CD** in the *Name the CD* text box.
4. Click the Options button.
5. At the Options dialog box, make sure the *Linked files* option contains a check mark.
6. Insert a check mark in the *Embedded TrueType fonts* check box.
7. Click OK to close the Options dialog box.
8. At the Package for CD dialog box, click the Copy to Folder button.
9. At the Copy to Folder dialog box, click the Browse button.
10. Navigate to your storage medium.
11. Click the Select button.
12. At the Copy to Folder dialog box, click OK.
13. At the message asking if you want to include linked files in the presentation, click the Yes button.
14. After the presentation is saved, close the Package for CD dialog box by clicking the Close button.
15. Close **GlobalEmployeeOrientation.pptx**.

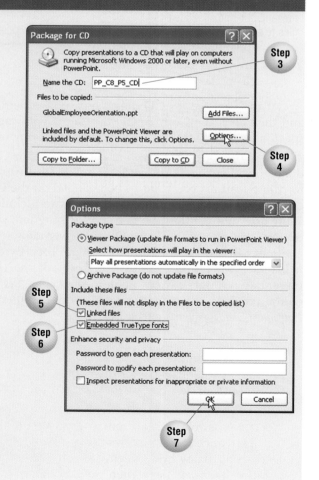

Package for CD

Copy presentations to a CD that will play on computers running Microsoft Windows 2000 or later, even without PowerPoint.

Name the CD: PP_C8_P5_CD

Files to be copied:
GlobalEmployeeOrientation.ppt   [Add Files...]

Linked files and the PowerPoint Viewer are included by default. To change this, click Options.   [Options...]

[Copy to Folder...]   [Copy to CD]   [Close]

Step 3
Step 4

Options

Package type
- ⦿ Viewer Package (update file formats to run in PowerPoint Viewer)
  Select how presentations will play in the viewer:
  [Play all presentations automatically in the specified order ▾]
- ○ Archive Package (do not update file formats)

Include these files
(These files will not display in the Files to be copied list)
- ☑ Linked files
- ☑ Embedded TrueType fonts

Enhance security and privacy
Password to open each presentation: [   ]
Password to modify each presentation: [   ]
- ☐ Inspect presentations for inappropriate or private information

[OK]   [Cancel]

Step 5
Step 6
Step 7

CHAPTER summary

- Import a Word outline document into a presentation by clicking the New Slide button arrow and then clicking *Slides from Outline*. At the Insert Outline dialog box, double-click the desired Word document.

- Export a PowerPoint presentation to a Word document by clicking the Office button, pointing to *Publish*, and then clicking *Create Handouts in Microsoft Office Word*. At the Send To Microsoft Office Word dialog box, select the desired page layout, and then click OK.

- Use the Copy and Paste buttons in the Clipboard group to copy data from one program to another.

- Use the Clipboard task pane to collect and paste up to 24 items. Click the Clipboard group dialog box launcher to turn on the display of the task pane.

- Integration is the process of completing a file by adding parts to it from other sources.

- An object created in one program of the Microsoft Office suite can be copied, linked, or embedded to another program in the suite. The program containing the original object is called the source and the program the object is pasted to is called the destination.

- An embedded object is stored in both the source and the destination programs.

- Link an object if the content is subject to change. Linking will ensure that the content in the destination always reflects the current content in the source. A linked object is stored in the source program only. The destination program contains a code indicating the name and location of the source.

- The content in a link is edited by opening the presentation containing the linked object in the source program, making the required changes, and then saving and closing the file.

- Download design templates at the New Presentation dialog box. To download, click the *Design slides* option in the dialog box, click a category, click the desired template, and then click the Download button.

- Insert, edit, and delete comments with buttons in the Comments group in the Review tab.

- Click the Show Markup button in the Comments group in the Review tab to turn on/off the display of comments.

- Modify document properties at the document information panel. Display this panel by clicking the Office button, pointing to *Prepare*, and then clicking *Properties*.

- Inspect a presentation for personal data, hidden data, and metadata with options at the Document Inspector dialog box. Display this dialog box by clicking the Office button, pointing to *Prepare*, and then clicking *Inspect Document* at the side menu.

- Insert a password in a presentation to ensure that the presentation is opened only by someone who knows the password. Insert a password in the Encrypt Document dialog box, which you can display by clicking the Office button, pointing to *Prepare*, and then clicking *Encrypt Document*.

- Apply a digital signature to a presentation to vouch for the authenticity of the presentation. Once a digital signature is applied to a presentation, the presentation is locked and cannot be edited or changed without first removing the digital signature.

- Run the compatibility checker to check your presentation and identify elements that are not supported or will act differently in previous versions of PowerPoint. Run the checker by clicking the Office button, pointing to *Prepare*, and then clicking *Run Compatibility Checker*.

- Save presentations in different formats with options at the Office button Save As side menu. You can also save presentations in different formats with the *Save as type* option at the Save As dialog box.

- Save a presentation as graphic images by saving the presentation in a format such as GIF, JPEG, or TIF. Use the *Save as type* option at the Save As dialog box to specify the file format. You can choose to save an individual slide within a presentation or all slides in the presentation.

- You can save a presentation as a Web page using either the *Single File Web Page (*.mht; *mhtml)* or *Web Page (*htm; *.html)* file format available from the *Save as type* option in the Save As dialog box.

- Use the Package for CD feature to copy a presentation including all of the linked files, fonts used, and PowerPoint Viewer onto a CD or to a folder or network location. To use the feature, click the Office button, point to *Publish*, and then click *Package for CD*.

COMMANDS review

FEATURE	RIBBON TAB, GROUP	BUTTON, OPTION
Insert Outline dialog box	Home, Slides	, Slides from Outline
Send To Microsoft Office Word dialog box		, Publish, Create Handouts in Microsoft Office Word
Clipboard task pane	Home, Clipboard	
Paste Special dialog box	Home, Clipboard	, Paste Special
New Presentation dialog box		, New
Insert comment	Review, Comments	
Edit comment	Review, Comments	
Delete comment	Review, Comments	
Previous comment	Review, Comments	
Next comment	Review, Comments	
Document information panel		, Prepare, Properties
Document Inspector dialog box		, Prepare, Inspect Document
Encrypt Document dialog box		, Prepare, Encrypt Document
Digital signature		, Prepare, Add a Digital Signature
Microsoft Office PowerPoint Compatibility Checker dialog box		, Prepare, Run Compatibility Checker
Package for CD		, Publish, Package for CD

CONCEPTS check

Test Your Knowledge

Completion: In the space provided at the right, indicate the correct term, symbol, or command.

1. Display the Insert Outline dialog box by clicking the New Slide button arrow and then clicking this option.

   _____

2. Display the Send To Microsoft Office Word dialog box by clicking the Office button, pointing to this option, and then clicking Create Handouts in Microsoft Office Word.

   _____

3. To link or embed an object, open this dialog box in the destination program after copying the source object.

   _____

4. Display this dialog box to display and download design templates from Microsoft Office Online.

   _____

5. The New Comment button is located in the Comments group in this tab.

   _____

6. Click the Office button, point to *Prepare*, and then click *Properties* and this displays.

   _____

7. Display the Document Inspector dialog box by clicking the Office button, pointing to *Prepare*, and then clicking this option.

   _____

8. Apply this to a presentation to vouch for the authenticity of the presentation.

   _____

9. Choose this option at the Office button Save As side menu to save a presentation with the *.ppsx* file extension.

   _____

10. The letters PDF are an acronym for this.

   _____

11. Three graphic image formats include GIF, TIF, and this.

   _____

12. HTML is an acronym for this, which is a programming language used to code pages to display graphically on the World Wide Web.

   _____

13. Use this feature to copy a presentation onto a CD or to a folder or network location.

   _____

SKILLS check

Demonstrate Your Proficiency

1 COPY WORD AND EXCEL DATA INTO A SALES CONFERENCE PRESENTATION

1. Open **HerbalPresentation.pptx** and then save the presentation and name it **PP_C8_A1**.
2. Make Slide 2 active and then complete the following steps:
   a. Open Excel and then open the workbook named **SalesProjections.xlsx** (located in your PowerPoint2007C8 folder on your storage medium).
   b. Copy the chart and paste it into Slide 2.
   c. Resize the chart so it fills most of the slide below the title.
   d. Close the workbook and exit Excel.
3. Make Slide 4 active and then complete the following steps:
   a. Draw a text box in the slide.
   b. Open Word and then open the document named **HerbalRemedies.docx**.
   c. Copy the first three terms and the paragraph below each term in the document to the text box in Slide 4.
   d. Select the text in the placeholder, change the font to Rockwell, and then change the font size to 24. (If necessary, size and move the text box so the text is positioned attractively on the slide.)
   e. Move and/or resize the placeholder so it fills most of the slide below the title.
4. Make Slide 5 active and then complete the following steps:
   a. Draw a text box in the slide.
   b. Make active the **HerbalRemedies.docx** Word document.
   c. Copy the last two terms and the paragraph below each term in the document and paste them into Slide 5.
   d. Select the text in the placeholder, change the font to Rockwell, and then change the font size to 24.
   e. Move and/or resize the placeholder so it fills most of the slide below the title.
5. Make Word active, close **HerbalRemedies.docx,** and then exit Word.
6. Make PowerPoint active and then apply custom animation effects to each slide.
7. Run the presentation.
8. Save **PP_C8_A1.pptx**.
9. Export the presentation to a Word document that prints blank lines next to slides.
10. Save the Word document and name it **PP_C8_A1_Word**.
11. Print and then close **PP_C8_A1_Word.docx**.
12. Save and then close **PP_C8_A1.pptx**.

2 COPY AND LINK WORD AND EXCEL DATA INTO A COMMUNICATIONS PRESENTATION

1. Open **CommunicationPresentation.pptx** and then save the presentation with the name **PP_C8_A2**.
2. Open Word and then open the document named **VerbalSkills.docx** (located in the PowerPoint2007C8 folder on your storage medium).
3. Copy the table and embed it (use the Paste Special dialog box) into Slide 5.
4. Resize the table so it better fills the slide.
5. Make Word active, close the **VerbalSkills.docx** document, and then exit Word.
6. Open Excel and then open the workbook named **NonverbalCues.xlsx** (located in the PowerPoint2007C8 folder on your storage medium).
7. Copy the chart and link it to Slide 6. Resize the chart so it fills a majority of the slide below the title.
8. Save and then close **PP_C8_A2.pptx**.
9. Make the following change to the chart in **NonverbalCues.xlsx**:
   a. Select the chart and then apply the *Style 18* chart style. **Hint: Do this in the Chart Tools Design tab.**
   b. Apply the *Gradient Fill-Accent 4, Reflection* WordArt style. **Hint: Do this in the Chart Tools Format tab.**
   c. Change the shape outline to *No Outline*.
   d. Change the amount in B2 from *35%* to *38%*.
   e. Change the amount in B3 from *25%* to *22%*.
10. Save and then close **NonverbalClue.xlsx** and then exit Excel.
11. In PowerPoint, open **PP_C8_A2.pptx**. (At the message that displays when you open the presentation, click the Update Links button.)
12. Make Slide 2 active and then insert the following comment after the second bulleted item: Ask Lauren to provide a specific communication example.
13. Make Slide 4 active and then insert the following comment after the third bulleted item: Insert a link here to the writing presentation prepared by Sylvia.
14. Make Slide 8 active and then insert the following comment after the third bulleted item: Distribute evaluation forms to audience.
15. Run the presentation.
16. Save the presentation and then print the presentation as a handout with all slides on one page and make sure the comments print.
17. Delete the comments.
18. Run the compatibility checker.
19. Save the presentation in *PowerPoint 2003-2007 Presentation* format and name it **PP_C8_A2_2003format**.
20. Close **PP_C8_A2_2003format.ppt**.

3 SAVE SLIDES IN JPEG FORMAT AND INSERT SLIDES IN A TRAVEL PRESENTATION

1. Open **FCTTours.pptx**, save all slides in the presentation in the JPEG graphic format, and then close **FCTTours.pptx**.
2. Open **FCTQtrMeeting.pptx** and then save the presentation with the name **PP_C8_A3**.
3. Make Slide 4 active and then insert each of the four slides you saved in JPEG format in Step 1 with the following specifications:
   a. Use the Picture button in the Insert tab to insert each JPEG graphic slide.
   b. Change the height of each JPEG slide image to *2.4"*.
   c. Position all four JPEG graphic slides in Slide 4 so they are balanced in the slide and do not overlap the slide background graphic or title.
4. Make Slide 1 active and then run the presentation.
5. Save **PP_C8_A3.pptx**.
6. Save **PP_C8_A3.pptx** with Save As and name it **PP_C8_A3_Animation**.
7. Apply an animation effect of your choosing to the logo and the subtitle in Slide 1.
8. Apply an animation effect of your choosing to the titles in Slides 2, 3, 5, and 6.
9. Apply a custom build animation to the bulleted text in Slides 2, 3, 5, and 6 that causes the previous point to dim when the next point displays.
10. Make Slide 1 active and then run the presentation.
11. Save and then close **PP_C8_A3_Animation.pptx**.
12. Open **PP_C8_A3.pptx** and then save the presentation as a single file Web page.
13. In your browser, navigate through the presentation.
14. After viewing all of the slides, close your browser window and then close **PP_C8_A3.pptx** without saving the changes.

4 DOWNLOAD AND FILL IN A COURSE COMPLETION CERTIFICATE

1. Display the New Presentation dialog box and look for award certificates you can download from the Microsoft Office Online site.
2. Download the award certificate named *Certificate of completion for course*. (If this certificate is not available, download one of your choosing.)
3. Fill in the certificate with the appropriate information. (Use your school's name for the company name.)
4. Save the completed certificate and name it **PP_C8_A4**.
5. Print and then close **PP_C8_A4.pptx**.

CASE study
Apply Your Skills

Part 1

You work for Rocky Mountain Family Medicine and are responsible for preparing education and training materials and publications for the center. You want to be able to insert the center logo in publications so you decide to save the logo as a graphic image. To do this, open the presentation (one slide) named **RMFMLogo.pptx** and then save the slide as a JPEG graphic image.

Part 2

You are responsible for presenting information on childhood diseases at an education class at a local community center. Open the Word document named **ChildhoodDiseases.docx** and then use the information to create a presentation with the following specifications:

- Apply the *Flow* design theme.
- Change the layout for the first slide to *Title Only*, type an appropriate title for the presentation, and then move the title to the bottom of the slide. Insert the **RMFMLogo.jpg** graphic image in the first slide and then size and position the logo attractively on the slide. (Consider setting transparent color to the background of the logo graphic image. Do this with the *Set Transparent Color* option in the Recolor button drop-down list in the Picture Tools Format tab.)
- Create additional slides with the information in the **ChildhoodDiseases.docx** Word document.
- Apply any additional enhancements to improve the presentation.

Run the presentation and then save the presentation with the name **PP_C8_CS_P2**. Print the presentation as a handout with six slides per page and then close the presentation.

Part 3

You need to prepare a presentation for an upcoming education and training meeting. Import the Word outline document named **RMFMOutline.docx** into a PowerPoint presentation and then make the following changes:

- Apply the *Flow* design theme.
- Create the first slide with the *Title Only* layout, insert the **RMFMLogo.jpg** graphic image, and then size and position the logo in the same manner as the first slide in **PP_C8_CS_P2.pptx**. Insert the title *Education and Training* in the title placeholder.
- Change the layout to *Title Only* for the Community Contacts slide and then copy the table from the Word document **RMFMContacts.docx** and paste it into the Community Contacts slide. Increase the size of the table so it better fills the slide.
- Change the layout to *Title Only* for the Current Enrollment slide and then copy the chart from the Excel workbook **RMFMEnrollment.xlsx** and link it to the Current Enrollment slide.
- Apply any additional enhancements to improve the presentation.

Run the presentation and then save the presentation with the name **PP_C8_CS_P3**. Print the presentation as a handout with six slides per page and then close the presentation. You check the enrollments for classes and realize that more people have enrolled so you need to update the numbers in the Excel workbook. Open the **RMFMEnrollment.xlsx** Excel workbook and then change *46* to *52*, *38* to *40*, and *24* to *27*. Save and then close the workbook. Open the **PP_C8_CS_P3.pptx** presentation and then update the links. Print only the Current Enrollment slide and then close the presentation.

Part

4

You decide that you want to include information in the **PP_C8_CS_P2.pptx** presentation on measles. Using the Internet, search for information on measles such as symptoms, complications, transmission, and prevention. Include this information in new slides in the **PP_C8_CS_P2.pptx** presentation. Run the presentation and then print only the new slides. Save and then close the presentation.

Part

5

Rocky Mountain Family Medicine has a Web site that contains information about the center as well as educational information. You decide to save the childhood diseases presentation as a Web page that visitors to the Web site can view. Open **PP_C8_CS_P2.pptx** and then save the presentation as a single file Web page. View the presentation in your default browser and then close the presentation.

ASSESSING proficiency

In this unit, you have learned to add visual elements to presentations such as tables, charts, and SmartArt graphics; create a photo album; apply formatting in Slide Master view; insert action buttons; apply custom animation effects; and set up slide shows. You also learned how to copy, embed, and link data between programs; how to insert comments; and how to protect and prepare a presentation.

powerpoint Unit 2

Note: Before beginning computer assessments, copy to your storage medium the PowerPoint2007U2 folder from the PowerPoint2007 folder on the CD that accompanies this textbook and then make PowerPoint2007U2 the active folder.

Assessment 1 Save a Slide in JPEG Format and Copy and Link Objects in a Presentation

1. Open **GreenSpaceLogo.pptx**, save the only slide in the presentation as a JPEG graphic image, and then close **GreenSpaceLogo.pptx**.
2. Open **GreenSpacePresentation.pptx** and then save the presentation with the name **PP_U2_A1**.
3. Display the presentation in Slide Master view and then make the following changes:
   a. Click the top slide master thumbnail.
   b. Select the text *CLICK TO EDIT MASTER TITLE STYLE* and then change the font color to *Green*.
   c. Select the text *Click to edit Master text styles*, change the font color to Gold, Accent 3, Darker 50%, and then change the bullet color to Green.
   d. Close Slide Master view.
4. Make Slide 1 active and then make the following changes:
   a. Insert the **GreenSpaceLogo.jpg** graphic image.
   b. Set transparent color for the logo background. (Do this with the *Set Transparent Color* option at the Recolor button drop-down list in the Picture Tools Format tab.)
   c. Size and position the logo so it is positioned attractively on the slide. (Consider offsetting the image slightly to the right to balance it with the slide title.)
5. Make Slide 6 active and then insert the following data in a table. You determine the formatting of the table and the formatting of the data in the table:

Project	Contact	Completion Date
Moyer-Sylvan Complex	Barry MacDonald	07/31/2010
Waterfront Headquarters	Jasmine Jefferson	02/15/2011
Linden Square	Marion Van Horn	09/30/2011
Village Green	Parker Alderton	12/31/2011
Cedar Place Market	Gerry Halderman	03/31/2012

6. Make Slide 7 active and then insert the following data in a SmartArt organizational chart. You determine the organization and formatting of the chart:

Avery Trinidad
Lead Designer

Mary Pirone — Structural Engineer
Craig Stafford — Ergonomic Designer
Kenneth Chan — Urban Designer

Diana Warren — Research Assistant
Justin Charone — Draftsperson

7. Make Slide 5 active and then create a column chart with the following data. Delete the chart title and chart legend. You determine the formatting and layout of the chart.

	Revenues
1st Qtr.	$25,250,000
2nd Qtr.	$34,000,000
3rd Qtr.	$22,750,000
4th Qtr.	$20,500,000

8. Make Slide 8 active and then insert a SmartArt diagram with the *Repeating Bending Process* diagram (found in the *Process* group) with the following information. You determine the design and formatting of the SmartArt diagram.

Mission Analysis
Requirements Analysis
Function Allocation
Design
Verification

9. Check each slide and make any changes that improve the visual appeal of the slide.
10. Make Slide 1 active and then run the presentation.
11. Make Slide 3 active, click immediately right of the slide title, and then insert the comment Check with Marilyn about adding River View Mall to this list.
12. Make Slide 4 active, click immediately right of the word *Australia* in the bulleted text, and then insert the comment What happened to the plans to open an office in Sydney?
13. Print the presentation as a handout with four slides per page and make sure the comments print.
14. Save and then close **PP_U2_A1.pptx**.

Assessment 2 Copy and Paste Data between Programs and Insert Action Buttons in a Telecommunications Presentation

1. Open **TelecomPresentation.pptx** and then save the presentation with the name **PP_U2_A2**.
2. Make Slide 6 active and then create a new Slide 7 (with the Title and Content layout) with the following specifications:
   a. Insert the title *APPLICATION* in the slide.
   b. Open Word and then open **WordConcepts.docx**.
   c. Display the Clipboard task pane. (Make sure the task pane is empty. If not, click the Clear All button.)
   d. Select and then copy *RECEIVING* and the paragraph below it.
   e. Select and then copy *STORING* and the paragraph below it.
   f. Select and then copy *TRANSMITTING* and the paragraph below it.
   g. Display the **PP_U2_A2.pptx** presentation.
   h. Click in the bulleted text *Click to add text*.
   i. Turn on the display of the Clipboard task pane.
   j. Paste the *TRANSMITTING* item in the slide.
   k. Paste the *RECEIVING* item in the slide.
   l. Clear and then close the Clipboard.
   m. Select all of the bulleted text and then change the font size to 28. Delete the bullet below the last paragraph.
   n. Make the **WordConcepts.docx** document active, close the Clipboard task pane, close the document, and then exit Word.
3. Make Slide 1 active and then insert an action button with the following specifications:
   a. Use the *Action Button: Forward or Next* option to draw the button.
   b. Draw the button in the lower right corner of the slide and make it approximately one-half inch in size.
   c. Change the shape fill of the button to Blue, Accent 2, Lighter 40%.
4. Display the presentation in Slide Master view and then make the following changes:
   a. Click the top slide master thumbnail.
   b. Insert an action button in the lower right corner of the slide with the same specifications as those in Step 3.
   c. Close Slide Master view.
5. Run the presentation. (Use the action buttons to advance slides. At the last slide, press the Esc key.)
6. Create a footer that prints your first and last names and include the date in the upper right corner on handout pages.
7. Print the presentation as a handout with four slides per page.
8. Save and then close **PP_U2_A2.pptx**

Assessment 3 Save a Template Presentation and Copy, Embed, and Link Objects between Programs

1. Display a blank presentation, click the View tab, and then click the Slide Master button.
2. Click the top slide master thumbnail in the slides thumbnail pane.
3. Apply the *Technic* theme and change the theme colors to *Median*.
4. Apply the *Style 8* background style.
5. Insert **ISLogo.jpg** in the master slide (use the Picture button in the Insert tab), change the height of the logo to one inch, and drag the logo to the

lower left corner of the slide master. Set transparent color for the logo background. (Do this with the *Set Transparent Color* option at the Recolor button drop-down list in the Picture Tools Format tab.)

6. Close Slide Master view.
7. Save the presentation as a template to the PowerPoint2007U2 folder on your storage medium and name the template **XXXISTemplate** (use your initials in place of the *XXX*).
8. Close **XXXISTemplate.potx**.
9. Open **XXXISTemplate.potx**. (To do this, display the New Presentation dialog box and then click *New from existing*. At the New from Existing Presentation dialog box, navigate to the PowerPoint2007U2 folder on your storage medium and then double-click **XXXISTemplate.potx**.)
10. Save the presentation and name it **PP_U2_A3**.
11. Create the first slide with the following specifications:
    a. Choose the *Blank* layout.
    b. Use WordArt to create the text *International Securities*. (You determine the shape and formatting of the WordArt text.)
12. Create the second slide with the following specifications:
    a. Choose the *Title Slide* layout.
    b. Type European Division as the subtitle.
    c. Type 2010 SALES MEETING as the title.
13. Create the third slide with the following specifications:
    a. Choose the *Title Only* layout.
    b. Type REGIONAL SALES as the title.
    c. Open Excel and then open **ISWorkbook01.xlsx**.
    d. Save the workbook with Save As and name it **ISSalesWorkbook**.
    e. Select cells A1 through D5 (the cells containing data) and then copy and embed the cells in Slide 3.
    f. Increase the size of the cells so they better fill the slide.
14. Create the fourth slide with the following specifications:
    a. Choose the *Title and Content* layout.
    b. Type 2011 GOALS as the title.
    c. Type the following as the bulleted items:
       ♦ Increase product sales by 15 percent
       ♦ Open a branch office in Spain
       ♦ Hire one manager and two additional account managers
       ♦ Decrease production costs by 6 percent
15. Create the fifth slide with the following specifications:
    a. Choose the *Title and Content* layout.
    b. Type HIRING TIMELINE as the title.
    c. Create a table with two columns and five rows and then type the following text in the cells in the table. (You determine the formatting of the cells.)

Task	Date
Advertise positions	03/01/2010 to 04/30/2010
Review resumes	05/15/2010 to 06/01/2010
Conduct interviews	06/15/2010 to 07/15/2010
Hire personnel	08/01/2010

16. Create the sixth slide with the following specifications:
    a. Choose the *Title Only* layout.
    b. Type PRODUCTION EXPENSES as the title.
    c. Make Excel the active program and then close **ISSalesWorkbook.xlsx**.
    d. Open **ISWorkbook02.xlsx**.

e. Save the workbook with Save As and name it **ISExpensesWorkbook**.

f. Copy and then link the pie chart in **ISExpensesWorkbook.xlsx** to Slide 6.

g. Increase the size of the pie chart so it better fills the slide.

h. Make Excel active, close **ISExpensesWorkbook.xlsx**, and then exit Excel.

17. Run the presentation.

18. Create a footer that prints your first and last names in the lower left corner and include the current date in the upper right corner on handout pages.

19. Print the presentation as a handout with four slides per page.

20. Save and then close **PP_U2_A3.pptx**.

21. Open Excel and then open **ISExpensesWorkbook.xlsx**.

22. Make the following changes:

a. B2: Change *38% to 41%*

b. B3: Change *35% to 32%*

c. B4: Change *18% to 21%*

d. B5: Change *9% to 6%*

23. Save, print, and close **ISExpensesWorkbook.xlsx** and then exit Excel.

24. With PowerPoint the active program, open **PP_U2_A3.pptx**. (At the message that displays, click the Update Links button.)

25. Display Slide 3, double-click the cells, and then make the following changes to the data in the embedded cells:

a. C2: Change *2,678,450 to 2,857,300*

b. C3: Change *1,753,405 to 1,598,970*

c. C4: Change *1,452,540 to 1,635,400*

26. Run the presentation.

27. Print the slides as a handout with four slides per page.

28. Save **PP_U2_A3.pptx**.

29. Apply a transition and sound of your choosing to all slides in the presentation.

30. Use the Rehearse Timings feature to set the following times for the slides to display during a slide show:

Slide 1 = 3 seconds

Slide 2 = 3 seconds

Slide 3 = 6 seconds

Slide 4 = 5 seconds

Slide 5 = 6 seconds

Slide 6 = 5 seconds

31. Set up the slide show to run continuously.

32. Run the presentation beginning with Slide 1. Watch the slide show until the presentation has started for the second time and then end the show.

33. Save and then close the presentation.

Assessment 4 Apply Custom Animation Effects to a Travel Presentation

1. Open **AustraliaTour.pptx** and then save the presentation with the name **PP_U2_A4**.

2. With Slide 1 active, apply a *Fly In* entrance animation effect to the title *Australia Tour* that has the title fly in from the bottom.

3. Display the presentation in Slide Master view and then make the following changes:

a. Click the third slide master thumbnail.

b. Apply a *Fly In* entrance animation effect to the title that has the title fly in from the top.

c. Apply a *Fly In* entrance animation effect to the bulleted text that has the text fly in from the left and then dim when the next bullet displays.

d. Close Slide Master view.

4. Make Slide 5 active, select the sun shape that displays above *Sydney*, and then draw a freeform motion path from Sydney to Melbourne, Tasmania, Adelaide, Perth, Derby, Darwin, Cairns, and then back to Sydney. Change the speed to *Very Slow*.

5. Make Slide 6 active and then make the following changes:

a. Click the bottom shape to select it. (You may want to move the top two shapes out of the way.)

b. Apply a *Fly In* entrance animation effect that has the shape fly in from the left. Apply a *Fly Out* exit animation effect that has the shape fly out to the right.

c. Click the middle shape to select it and then apply a *Fly In* entrance animation effect that has the shape fly in from the left. Apply a *Fly Out* exit animation effect that has the shape fly out to the right.

d. Click the top shape to select it and then apply a *Fly In* entrance animation effect that has the shape fly in from the left.

e. Position the shapes so they are stacked on top of each other so you do not see a portion of the shapes behind.

6. Save **PP_U2_A4.pptx**.

7. Make Slide 1 active, run the presentation, and make sure the custom animation effects play correctly.

8. Print the presentation as a handout with all slides on one page.

9. Close **PP_U2_A4.pptx**.

Assessment 5 Inspect a Presentation and Save a Presentation in Different Formats

1. Open **PP_U2_A1.pptx** and then save the presentation with the name **PP_U2_A5**.

2. Inspect the presentation using the Document Inspector dialog box and remove comments from the presentation.

3. Run the compatibility checker.

4. Save the presentation in *PowerPoint 97-2003* format and name it **PP_U2_A5_2003format**. (Click the Continue button at the compatibility checker message.)

5. Close **PP_U2_A5_2003format.ppt**.

6. Open **PP_U2_A5.pptx** and then save the presentation as a single file Web page.

7. Run the presentation in your Web browser.

8. After viewing all of the slides, close your browser window.

9. Close **PP_U2_A5.pptx** without saving the changes.

WRITING activities

The following activities give you the opportunity to practice your writing skills along with demonstrating an understanding of some of the important PowerPoint features you have mastered in this unit. Use correct grammar, appropriate word choices, and clear sentence structure.

Activity 1 **Prepare and Format a Travel Presentation**

You work for First Choice Travel and you are responsible for preparing a presentation on travel vacations. Open the Word document named **TravelVacations.docx** and then print the document. Close the document and then exit Word. Using the information in the document, prepare a PowerPoint presentation with the following specifications:

1. Create a presentation that presents the main points of the document.
2. Rehearse and set times for the slides to display during a slide show. You determine the number of seconds for each slide.
3. Insert a song into the first slide from the sound clip organizer (or from any resource available to you).
4. Set up the presentation to run on an endless loop and the sound to play across all slides and continuously as long as the presentation is running.
5. Run the presentation. (The slide show will start and run continuously.) Watch the presentation until it has started for the second time and then end the show by pressing the Esc key.
6. Save the presentation and name it **PP_U2_Act01**.
7. Print the presentation as a handout with six slides per page.
8. Close **PP_U2_Act01.pptx**.

Activity 2 **Prepare and Format a Presentation on Media Files**

Using PowerPoint's Help feature, learn more about types of media files you can add to a PowerPoint presentation and compatible multimedia file formats. (Search specifically for *types of media files you can add* and *compatible multimedia file formats*.) Using the information you find in the Help files, create a presentation with *at least* the following specifications:

- Slide containing the title of the presentation and your name

- Create at least two slides that contain file types you can add to the Microsoft Clip Organizer. (Search for additional information on file types, search for *file formats that are supported in PowerPoint 2007*. Use this additional information to further describe file types.)

- Create at least three slides each containing information on a compatible audio file format including the file format, extension, and a brief description of the format.

- Create at least three slides each containing information on a compatible video file format including the file format, extension, and a brief description of the format.

- If you are connected to the Internet, search for Web sites where you can download free audio clips and then include this information in a slide as well as a hyperlink to the site.

Save the completed presentation and name it **PP_U2_Act02**. Run the presentation and then print the presentation as a handout with six slides per page. Close **PP_U2_Act02.pptx**.

INTERNET research

Presenting Office 2007

Make sure you are connected to the Internet and then explore the Microsoft Web site at www.microsoft.com. Browse the various categories and links on the Web site to familiarize yourself with how information is organized.

Create a PowerPoint presentation that could be delivered to someone who has just purchased Office 2007 and wants to know how to find more information about the software from the Microsoft Web site. Include points or tips on where to find product release information and technical support. Include hyperlinks to important pages at the Microsoft Web site. Add formatting and enhancements to make the presentation as dynamic as possible. Save the presentation and name it **PP_U2_Office2007**. Run the presentation and then print the presentation as a handout with six slides per page. Close **PP_U2_Office2007.pptx**.

JOB study

Creating a Skills Presentation

You are preparing a presentation that you will use when presenting information on jobs at your local job fair. Open the Word document named **JobDescriptions.docx**, print the document, and then close the document and exit Word. Use the information in the document to prepare slides that describe each job (do not include the starting salary). Using the Internet, locate information on two other jobs that interest you and then create a slide for each job that provides information on job responsibilities. Determine the starting salary for the two jobs and then use that information along with the starting salary information for the jobs in the Word document to create a chart that displays the salary amounts. Locate at least two online job search Web sites and then include them in your presentation along with hyperlinks to the sites. Insert action buttons to move to the next page for the first slide through the second from the end. On your final slide, create an action button to return to the first slide.

Save the presentation and name it **PP_U2_JobStudy**. Run the presentation and then print the presentation as a handout with six slides per page. Close **PP_U2_JobStudy.pptx**.

INDEX

Formatting
    background graphics, 225–226
    backgrounds in slide master, 224
    chart layout, 197–198
    charts, changing, 199–201
    clip art images, 141–142, 143–144
    diagrams, 187–189
    with Format Painter, 80–81
    identifying cells for, 176
    images, 135–136
    with Mini toolbar, 78
    objects, 134–135
    paragraphs, 82
    photo album, 204–207
    pictures, 137–138
    pictures, in photo album
        presentation, 210
    pie charts, 201–202
    presentations, 76–81
    presentations, in Word, 299
    shapes, 126–128
    shapes and text boxes, 130–133
    slide master, 223–224
    SmartArt, 187
    text boxes, 120, 121–124, 151
    WordArt text, 146, 147–148
From Beginning button, 10, 21
From Current Slide button, 21
Full control permission level, 321

G

General Options dialog box, 316
GIF. *See* Graphics Interchange
    Format
Go button, 141
Gradient
    applying, 95
    customizing, 99
Graph feature, 175
Graphic images: saving slides as,
    325–326
Graphics Interchange Format:
    saving presentations in, 325,
    334
Graphs, 175
Grayscale: viewing slides in, 241, 251
Grid and Guides dialog box, 130,
    131, 133, 151, 153
Gridlines, 129, 153
    displaying, 129–130
    showing/hiding, 241, 251
    turning on/off, 151
Gridlines check box, 129, 130
Group button, 134, 151
Grouping: objects, 134–135, 151
Guides: displaying, 129–130

H

Handout master: customizing,
    237–239
Handout Master button, 251
Handout Master view, 221, 237,
    251
Handouts
    changing orientation of, 101

customizing, 251
making changes to all pages in,
    221
objects inserted in, 148
printing, 59
printing presentations as, 60
slide orientation applied to, 232
slides printed as, 299
Header & Footer button, 148, 149,
    152
Header and Footer dialog box, 60,
    61, 148, 149, 250
    displaying, 68
    with Notes and Handouts tab
        selected, 61
Header and Footer feature, 153
Header placeholders: formatting,
    237
Headers: inserting in presentations,
    60–61
Heading 1 style: text formatted
    with, 298
Heading 2 style: text formatted
    with, 298
Headings: WordArt used for, 145
Height: of text boxes, 120
Help: getting in a dialog box, 64
Help button, 63, 64, 68
Help feature, 64
    preparing presentations and,
        65–66
    using, 63, 65–66
Hidden data: inspecting
    presentations for, 314
Hide All hyperlink: in Help window,
    64
Hide Background Graphics check
    box, 224
Hide Slide button, 280
Hiding: slides, 280
Home tab, 75, 76
    Font group buttons in, 77
    Paragraph group in, 82
Horizontal lines: major/minor, in
    charts, 198
Horizontal ruler, 129
    turning on/off, 151
HTML. *See* Hypertext Markup
    Language
HTML format: presentations
    converted to, 327–328
Hyperlink button, 247, 251
Hyperlinks
    creating, 247, 251
    inserting, 248–249
Hyperlink to Other PowerPoint
    Presentation dialog box, 246
Hyperlink To URL dialog box, 246
Hypertext Markup Language, 326

I

I-beam pointer: in PowerPoint
    window, 9
Icons
    animation, 260, 263
    preservation, 232

slide, 27, 50
sound, 285, 286
Illustrations group, 137, 141, 151,
    152, 183, 187, 192, 243
Images
    animating, 268–270, 289
    customizing and formatting,
        135–136
    inserting, 135
    moving, 151
    selected, moving, 136
    sizing, 151
    sizing, cropping, and moving,
        136
Importing
    data, 297
    Word outline, 298–299, 333
Increase Font Size button, 77
Increase List Level button, 82, 83,
    91
Indentation: paragraph, 85
Information Rights Management,
    320
Insert button, 149
Insert Chart button, 192, 194, 209
Insert Chart dialog box, 193, 194,
    209, 210
Insert group, 198
Insert Hyperlink dialog box, 247,
    248, 251
Inserting
    action buttons, 221, 243–245
    clip art images, 140, 141–142,
        143–144
    comments, 309–312, 333, 335
    diagrams, 187–189
    document properties, 314
    elements in Slide Master view,
        228–229
    elements in slides, 119–153
    headers and footers, 60–61
    hyperlinks, 248–249
    images, 135
    new slide master, 232
    objects in charts, 198
    pictures, 137–138
    pictures, as slide background,
        139–140
    pictures, in photo album, 203
    pictures, in slides, 151
    placeholders, 230
    shapes, 126, 151
    slides, 54
    slides, in presentations, 227
    sounds and movie clips,
        285–286, 290
    symbols in slides, 152
    text, in slides, 44–45
    text, in text pane, 191–192
    text, into SmartArt diagram
        shapes, 209
    text, into Text pane, 209
    text boxes, 121–124
    text boxes, in slides, 151
    text objects in presentations,
        148–150
    WordArt, 147–148

Using the Student Resources CD

Most of the projects in this textbook require you to open an existing file. The student data files needed for each chapter (or unit performance assessment) are organized in subfolders on the Student Resources CD that accompanies this textbook. On the first page of each chapter, instructions will direct you to copy the necessary folder from the CD to your storage medium. After completing the chapter work, delete the chapter folder before copying the next chapter's folder.

Copying a Folder from the Student Resources CD

Copy a folder from the CD to your storage medium (such as a USB flash drive) by completing the following steps:
1. Insert the CD that accompanies this textbook in the CD drive.
2. Insert your USB flash drive in an available USB port. *Note: When you plug in a USB flash device with content on it, Windows XP opens a window displaying "What do you want Windows to do?" Click the Cancel button to remove the window. You may receive startup messages in Windows XP. Check with your instructor if you need assistance using the storage device.*
3. At the Windows XP desktop, open the My Computer window by clicking the Start button and then clicking My Computer at the Start menu.
4. Double-click the CD drive in the contents pane.
5. Double-click the desired level (or program) and unit folder name in the contents pane.
6. Click once on the desired chapter (or unit performance assessment) subfolder name to select it.
7. Click the Copy this folder hyperlink in the *File and Folder Tasks* section of the task pane.
8. At the Copy Items dialog box, click the drive letter for the storage medium (drive containing your USB flash drive) and then click the Copy button. For example: Removable Disk (F:).
9. After the folder is copied, close the My Computer window by clicking the Close button (white X on red background) that displays in the upper right corner of the window.

Deleting a Folder from Your Storage Medium

Note: Check with your instructor before deleting a folder. Before copying a chapter folder onto your storage medium, delete any previous chapter folders by completing the following steps:
1. Insert your storage medium (such as a USB flash drive) in the USB port.
2. At the Windows XP desktop, open the My Computer window by clicking the Start button and then clicking My Computer at the Start menu.
3. Double-click the drive letter for the storage medium (drive containing your USB flash drive). For example: Removable Disk (F:).
4. Click the chapter folder in the list box.
5. Click the Delete this folder hyperlink in the *File and Folder Tasks* section of the task pane.
6. At the message asking if you want to remove the folder and all its contents, click Yes.
7. If a message display asks if you want to delete a read-only file, click Yes to All.
8. Close the My Computer window by clicking the Close button (white X on red background) that displays in the upper right corner of the window.

Viewing or Printing Chapter Projects Model Answers

The Student Resources CD also contains model answers in PDF format for the projects within each chapter so you can check your work. These model answer PDF files are locked and marked with a watermark. (Model answers are not provided for the end-of-chapter exercises—Skills Check and Case Study.)

To access the PDF files, you will need to have Adobe Reader installed on your computer's hard drive. The free program is available for download by clicking the Get Adobe Reader button at www.adobe.com. Once Adobe Reader is installed, double-click the Student Resources CD icon in the My Computer window, double-click the *ProjectsModelAnswers* folder, double-click the desired level (or program) and unit subfolder name, double-click the desired chapter subfolder name, and then double-click the appropriate file name. You can view and/or print the file to compare it with your work.